CHURCHILL: THE POWER OF WORDS

www.**transworldbooks**.co.uk

BOOKS BY MARTIN GILBERT

The Appeasers (with Richard Gott)
The European Powers, 1900–1945
The Roots of Appeasement
Children's Illustrated Bible Atlas
Atlas of British Charities
The Holocaust: Maps and Photographs
The Jews of Arab Lands: Their History in Maps
The Jews of Russia: Their History in Maps
Sir Horace Rumbold: Portrait of a Diplomat
Jerusalem: Rebirth of a City
Jerusalem in the Twentieth Century
Exile and Return: The Struggle for Jewish
  Statehood
Israel: A History
The Story of Israel
Auschwitz and the Allies
The Jews of Hope: The Plight of Soviet Jewry
  Today
Shcharansky: Hero of Our Time
The Holocaust: The Jewish Tragedy
Kristallnacht: Prelude to Destruction
The Boys: Triumph over Adversity
The First World War
Somme: The Heroism and Horror of War

The Second World War
D-Day
The Day the War Ended
Empires in Conflict: A History of the Twentieth
  Century, 1900–1933
Descent into Barbarism: A History of the
  Twentieth Century, 1934–1951
Challenge to Civilization: A History of the
  Twentieth Century, 1952–1999
Never Again: A History of the Holocaust
The Jews in the Twentieth Century: An
  Illustrated History
Letters to Auntie Fori: The 5,000-Year History
  of the Jewish People and Their Faith
The Righteous: The Unsung Heroes of the
  Holocaust
In Ishmael's House: the 1,400-Year History of
  Jews under Muslim Rule
In Search of Churchill
Churchill and America
Churchill and the Jews
The Will of the People: Churchill and
  Parliamentary Democracy

THE CHURCHILL BIOGRAPHY

Volume III: The Challenge of War, 1914–1916
  Document Volume III (in two parts)
Volume IV: World in Torment, 1917–1922
  Document Volume IV (in three parts)
Volume V: The Coming of War, 1922–1939
Document Volume V: The Exchequer Years,
  1922–1929
Document Volume V: The Wilderness Years,
  1929–1935
Document Volume V: The Coming of War,
  1936–1939

Volume VI: Finest Hour, 1939–1941
Churchill War Papers I: At the Admiralty,
  September 1939–May 1940
Churchill War Papers II: Never Surrender,
  May–December 1940
Churchill War Papers III: The Ever-Widening
  War, 1941
Volume VII: Road to Victory, 1941–1945
Volume VIII: Never Despair, 1945–1965
Churchill: A Photographic Portrait
Churchill: A Life

ATLASES

Atlas of American History
Atlas of the Arab–Israeli Conflict
Atlas of British History
Atlas of the First World War
Atlas of the Holocaust

Historical Atlas of Jerusalem
Atlas of Jewish History
Atlas of Russian History
Atlas of the Second World War

EDITIONS OF DOCUMENTS

Britain and Germany between the Wars
Plough My Own Furrow: The Life of Lord Allen
  of Hurtwood
Servant of India: Diaries of the Viceroy's Private
  Secretary, 1905–1910

Surviving the Holocaust: The Kovno Ghetto
  Diary of Avraham Tory
Winston Churchill and Emery Reves:
  Correspondence 1937–1964

CHURCHILL:
THE POWER OF WORDS

His remarkable life
recounted through his writings and speeches

200 readings
selected, edited and introduced by

MARTIN GILBERT

BANTAM PRESS

LONDON • TORONTO • SYDNEY • AUCKLAND • JOHANNESBURG

TRANSWORLD PUBLISHERS
61–63 Uxbridge Road, London W5 5SA
A Random House Group Company
www.transworldbooks.co.uk

First published in Great Britain
in 2012 by Bantam Press
an imprint of Transworld Publishers

A CIP catalogue record for this book
is available from the British Library.

ISBNs 9780593070086 (cased)
9780593070116 (tpb)

Addresses for Random House Group Ltd companies outside the UK
can be found at: www.randomhouse.co.uk
The Random House Group Ltd Reg. No. 954009

The Random House Group Limited supports the Forest Stewardship Council (FSC®), the
leading international forest-certification organization. Our books carrying the FSC label are
printed on FSC®-certified paper. FSC is the only forest-certification scheme endorsed by
the leading environmental organizations, including Greenpeace. Our paper procurement
policy can be found at www.randomhouse.co.uk/environment.

Typeset in Minion Pro by Falcon Oast Graphic Art Ltd.
Printed in Great Britain by
Clays Ltd, St Ives plc

2 4 6 8 10 9 7 5 3 1

MIX
Paper from
responsible sources
FSC
www.fsc.org   FSC® C016897

CONTENTS

PREFACE

President John F. Kennedy, in making Winston Churchill an Honorary Citizen of the United States in April 1963, said of him: 'He mobilised the English language and sent it into battle.'

Churchill died in 1965, a few weeks after his ninetieth birthday. Throughout his six decades in the public eye and in public life, he understood and wielded the power of words. In his speeches, books, and newspaper and magazine articles, he expressed his feelings and laid out his vision for the future. From his first experiences of war between 1895 and 1900, his vivid narrative style and thoughtful reflections were read with fascination in Britain and beyond. While still in his twenties, he was a much sought-after speaker in Britain and the United States.

I have chosen 200 extracts from his books, articles and speeches that seem to me to express the essence of his thoughts, and to describe – in his own words – the main adventures of his life, the main crises of his career, his main parliamentary interventions and initiatives, and his philosophy of life and human existence. These extracts range from his memories of his childhood and schooldays to his contributions, during more than fifty years, to debates on social policy and on war. They cover his contributions to the discourse and events of two world wars, and his hopes and efforts to see the world emerge a better place.

Churchill used words for different purposes: to argue for moral and political causes, to advocate courses of action in the social, national and international spheres, and to tell the story of his own life and that of Britain and its place in the world. He was the author of fifty-eight books: seven books of memoirs, sixteen volumes of history (which contained within them his personal memories of both world wars), twenty-two volumes of his own speeches, four selections of his newspaper and magazine articles, two volumes of essays, six biographical volumes (four about his illustrious military ancestor John Churchill, first Duke of Marlborough, and two about his father Lord Randolph Churchill) and one novel (from which the first reading in this collection is taken).

Churchill's newspaper and magazine articles have never been published in book form in their totality. He wrote 842 articles in all, 212 of them his eye-witness reports from theatres of war in Cuba, the North-West Frontier, Sudan and South Africa. The first, sent from Cuba, was published in London on 13 December 1895, two weeks after his twenty-first birthday.

Churchill was an accomplished storyteller. He loved the ebb and flow of narrative, and in many of his books, and also in his speeches, portrayed the dramatic events that he had witnessed, and had often been a part of. His summary of Britain's role in the Second World War, in his broadcast on 13 May 1945, six days after the German surrender, is a masterpiece of concision combined with emotion.

The extracts that I have chosen are my favourites; ones through which I came to see the range and impact of Churchill's interests, concerns, and contributions to British life and to the international conflicts and hopes of the first half of the twentieth century. I began collecting this material in 1962, the year in which I first began work on the Churchill biography as a young research assistant to Churchill's son Randolph, whom I succeeded as biographer on his death in 1968.

I have put the extracts in chronological order, and in their context, so that, read sequentially, they form a biographical narrative. Read in whatever order, they give a flavour of Churchill's wide-ranging interests and involvement in national and world events, both as an observer and as a participant, often at the centre of government or at its head as Prime Minister. His broadcast of 16 June 1941 to the United States is published here in full, with a note of the words and phrases he changed.

Churchill's published writings span every aspect of his life and career, in peace and in war. His speeches, in Parliament and in public, reflect the conflicts and controversies with which he was involved during his long years of public life. 'If I found the right words', he told those gathered in Westminster Hall to celebrate his eightieth birthday in 1954, 'you must remember that I have always earned my living by my pen and by my tongue.'

As one of the highest-paid journalists of his generation, and as a candidate – five times unsuccessfully – at twenty-one parliamentary electoral contests between 1899 and 1955, Churchill could write amid the storm of the battlefield and in the calm of his study, and speak in the cut and thrust of vigorous public and parliamentary debate. Words were his most persuasive weapon. Each of the extracts in these pages adds to our understanding of Churchill's life and thought, and provides an insight into how he made his mark on the British and the world stage. I hope you enjoy reading – and re-reading – them as much as I have.

Martin Gilbert
10 January 2012

A NOTE ON SOURCES

These readings are taken from a range of sources in which one can find Churchill's actual words, written or spoken; details of these sources are given in the 'Sources for each of the readings' at the end of the book.

The largest single number of Churchill's speeches – those that he made in the House of Commons between 1901 and 1955 – are to be found in *Hansard* (the verbatim record of debates in the House of Commons). His speeches elsewhere were mostly printed in contemporary national and local newspapers, in his own collected volumes of speeches, and in *Winston S. Churchill: His Complete Speeches, 1897–1963*, edited by Robert Rhodes James (eight volumes, 1974). Churchill's speech to the officers of his battalion in Flanders in 1916 is in a letter that he wrote to his wife on the following day; this letter, and his speech notes on the 'terrible' twentieth century, are in the Churchill Papers at the Churchill Archives Centre, Churchill College, Cambridge. His speech of 4 October 1901 is from a press cutting in the Churchill Papers. His speech notes for his broadcast of 16 June 1941 to the United States are from a private collection.

Many of Churchill's own published books contain his personal memories and reflections. Among these books are *The Story of the Malakand Field Force* (1898), *The River War* (1899), *London to Ladysmith via Pretoria* (1900), *The World Crisis* (five volumes, 1923–31), *My Early Life* (1930) and *The Second World War* (six volumes, 1948–53).

Churchill's letter of resignation in November 1915 was published in the British national newspapers at the time. His description of a commander-in-chief on the Western Front in the First World War – a little-known portrayal of Field Marshal Sir Douglas Haig – is tucked discreetly away in Volume Two of his four-volume biography, *Marlborough: His Life and Times.*

Churchill's retort to Ambassador Kennedy's defeatism on the eve of war in 1939 was recorded by two of those present, Harold Nicolson and Walter Lippmann, in their diaries. His remarks in 1942 about General de Gaulle in a Secret Session speech in the House of Commons – remarks that Churchill decided to omit from the speech when it was published after the war – are in the Churchill Archives Centre at Churchill College, Cambridge, as are the recollections of Sir Murland de Grasse Evans of a conversation with Churchill at Harrow in 1891.

ACKNOWLEDGEMENTS

I am grateful first of all to the Hon. Randolph Churchill MBE (Military Division), for whom I worked as one of his research assistants between 1962 and his death in 1968; it was he who encouraged me to read aloud from his father's writings, and to do so standing at the desk that had once belonged to Disraeli, and later to Winston Churchill. 'Reading aloud' was a regular feature of evenings at Randolph Churchill's house in Suffolk. Many of the extracts that I have chosen in this book were ones to which I was introduced at that time. Others were ones that I chose with Professor Jim Merriweather, of the University of South Carolina; he and I spent many evenings reading them aloud during my sabbatical term in the United States in 1965. In the forty-six years since then, I have enjoyed reading each of the extracts in this book both on my own and with numerous friends, including that master of oral military history, my North London neighbour Max Arthur.

I am grateful for textual material provided by Preeti Chavda, The Civic Centre Reference Library, Harrow; by Mr Allen Packwood and Dr Lynsey Robertson, Churchill Archives Centre, Churchill College, Cambridge; and by the Churchill bibliographer, Ronald I. Cohen, whose work is indispensable for anyone working in the Churchill vineyard. Richard Langworth CBE (Hon.) is, as always, a wise guide on sources. Cameron Hazlehurst gave me the benefit of his wide knowledge of Churchill's early political career.

For help in transcribing many of these extracts, I am grateful to Ela Gottwald and Kay Thomson. The final text gained immensely from the eagle eye of Gillian Somerscales, and the selection of photographs from the skill and enthusiasm of Sheila Lee.

At every stage in the compilation of what has been a most fulfilling task, I am indebted to my wife Esther for her enthusiasm and encouragement.

LIST OF READINGS

'The trials of our latter-day generals', 1917–18
'I, who saw him on twenty occasions', 1917–18
'The toils, perils, sufferings and passions of millions of men', 1917–18
'The meaning of war with the American Union', 6 April 1917
'The country is in danger', 11 December 1917
'The most tremendous cannonade I shall ever hear', 21 March 1918
'An utter absence of excitement or bustle', 28 March 1918
'Such a tyrant and such a champion', 28 March 1918
'A great actor on the stage', 30 March 1918
'There was no rigmarole or formalism', 1918
'Victory had come after all the hazards', 11 November 1918
'The ache for those who would never come home', 11 November 1918
'The dauntless and devoted people', 1914–18
'Rebuild the ruins. Heal the wounds', 26 November 1918
'The heart of the Russian people', 19 February 1919
'The future was heavy with foreboding', 1919
'A frightful and overwhelming force', 18 July 1919
'The agony of Russia', 20 January 1920
'The clemency of the conqueror', 8 July 1920
'Thoroughly tired of war', 28 July 1920
'A measureless array of toils and perils', 4 August 1920
'From the confusion of tyranny to a reign of law', 16 February 1922
'Destructive tendencies have not yet run their course',
    11 November 1922
'I am not going to be muzzled', 13 November 1922
'I have always stuck to the middle road', 27 November 1923
'I am too old a campaigner to be disheartened', 19 March 1924
'The powers now in the hands of man', September 1924
'The ambulances of State aid', 28 April 1925
'What shall I do with all my books?' December 1925
'Will our children bleed and gasp again?', 1927
'It is equally vain to prophesy or boast', 15 April 1929
'An unlimited capacity of adaptiveness', 1930
'Alarming and also nauseating', 23 February 1931
'I certainly suffered every pang', 12 December 1931
'We of the English-speaking lands', 1932
'These bands of sturdy Teutonic youths', 23 November 1932

LIST OF ILLUSTRATIONS

First section

1   Churchill as a schoolboy at Harrow
2   The swimming pool at Harrow
3   Churchill as a soldier in South Africa, May 1900
4   *The River War*, 1899
5   *London to Ladysmith via Pretoria*, 1900
6   Churchill as a prisoner of the Boers, 1899
7   'How I escaped from Pretoria', 1899
8   Announcement of lecture in Cardiff, November 1900
9–11 Speaking to munition workers at Enfield, 18 September 1915
12, 13 At Dundee, after his appendicitis, 11 November 1922
14   Addressing supporters at Victoria Palace, London,
        19 March 1924
15   On his way to his first Budget, 28 April 1925
16   On his way to his fifth Budget, 15 April 1929
17   Speaking outside the City of London Recruiting Centre,
        24 April 1939
18, 19 At work in his study at Chartwell, 25 February 1939
20   In his study at Chartwell, 25 February 1939
21   Making his first wartime broadcast, 1 October 1939

Second section

22   Addressing the crew of HMS *Exeter*, 15 February 1940
23   The Anglo-French Supreme War Council, 31 May 1940
24   Exhortation against 'alarm and despondency', 4 July 1940
25   Inspecting bomb damage in the Blitz, 10 September 1940
26   Visiting the ruins of the Guildhall, 31 December 1940
27, 28 Speaking to both Houses of Congress, Washington,
        26 December 1941

LIST OF MAPS

THE READINGS

'THE LOVE OF A FOSTER-MOTHER'

Winston Churchill was born on 30 November 1874, in Blenheim Palace, Oxfordshire. His father, Lord Randolph Churchill, was the son of a duke, and had political ambitions: first entering Parliament in the year of Winston's birth, he rose in eleven years to Cabinet rank, eventually serving as Chancellor of the Exchequer. His mother was American, born Jennie Jerome in Brooklyn. From the age of two until the age of seven, Churchill was looked after by his nurse, Mrs Everest, who was devoted to him, and to whom he was in turn devoted. His mother, he wrote in *My Early Life*, 'shone for me like the Evening Star. I loved her dearly – but at a distance . . . My nurse was my confidante. Mrs Everest it was who looked after me and tended all my wants. It was to her I poured out my many troubles.' Mrs Everest remained a welcome source of support and advice to Churchill until his teens. In the only novel that he wrote, *Savrola*, published in 1900, he described a moment when the hero's nurse enters the room:

> His thoughts were interrupted by the entrance of the old woman with a tray. He was tired, but the decencies of life had to be observed; he rose, and passed into the inner room to change his clothes and make his toilet.
>
> When he returned, the table was laid; the soup he had asked for had been expanded by the care of his housekeeper into a more elaborate meal. She waited on him, plying him the while with questions and watching his appetite with anxious pleasure.
>
> She had nursed him from his birth up with a devotion and care which knew no break. It is a strange thing, the love of these women. Perhaps it is the only disinterested affection in the world. The mother loves her child; that is maternal nature. The youth loves his sweetheart; that too may be explained. The dog loves his master; he feeds him; a man loves his friend; he has stood by him perhaps at doubtful moments. In all there are reasons; but the love of a foster-mother for her charge appears absolutely irrational. It is one of the few proofs, not to be explained even by the association of ideas, that the nature of mankind is superior to mere utilitarianism, and that his destinies are high.
>
> The light and frugal supper finished, the old woman departed with the plates, and he fell to his musings again.

'THIS HATEFUL SERVITUDE'

Four weeks before his eighth birthday, Churchill's parents sent him to a boarding school, St George's, Ascot, outside London. He recalled his time at that school in his book *My Early Life*:

How I hated this school, and what a life of anxiety I lived – there for more than two years. I made very little progress at my lessons, and none at all at games. I counted the days and the hours to the end of every term, when I should return home from this hateful servitude and range my soldiers in line of battle on the nursery floor.

The greatest pleasure I had in those days was reading. When I was nine and a half my father gave me *Treasure Island*, and I remember the delight with which I devoured it. My teachers saw me at once backward and precocious, reading books beyond my years and yet at the bottom of the Form. They were offended. They had large resources of compulsion at their disposal, but I was stubborn. Where my reason, imagination or interest were not engaged, I would not or I could not learn. In all the twelve years I was at school no one ever succeeded in making me write a Latin verse or learn any Greek except the alphabet. I do not at all excuse myself for this foolish neglect of opportunities procured at so much expense by my parents and brought so forcibly to my attention by my Preceptors. Perhaps if I had been introduced to the ancients through their history and customs, instead of through their grammar and syntax, I might have had a better record.

'AN ELEMENT OF KINDNESS'

As a young boy Churchill suffered from repeated bouts of ill-health, so much so that the family doctor advised that he should leave St George's (which Churchill called St James's in his memoirs) and go to a school by the sea. This was a boarding school at Brighton, of which Churchill later wrote in *My Early Life*:

I fell into a low state of health at St. James's School, and finally after a serious illness my parents took me away. Our family doctor, the celebrated Robson Roose, then practised at Brighton; and as I was now supposed to be very delicate, it was thought desirable that I should be under his constant care. I was accordingly, in 1883, transferred to a school at Brighton kept by two ladies.

This was a smaller school than the one I had left. It was also cheaper and less pretentious. But there was an element of kindness and of sympathy which I had found conspicuously lacking in my first experiences. Here I remained for three years; and though I very nearly died from an attack of double pneumonia, I got gradually much stronger in that bracing air and gentle surroundings. At this school I was allowed to learn things which interested me: French, History, lots of Poetry by heart, and above all Riding and Swimming. The impression of those years makes a pleasant picture in my mind, in strong contrast to my earlier schoolday memories.

'I WAS STARTLED TO SEE A FURIOUS FACE EMERGE'

Churchill's next school was Harrow, chosen for him by his parents – again on their doctor's advice – as it was set on a hill and thus considered healthier than Eton, by the River Thames. Churchill lived at Harrow as a boarder, from 1888, when he was thirteen, until he was eighteen, in 1892. There he excelled at History and English, and won both the Harrow School and Public Schools fencing championships. As he wrote in *My Early Life*:

I first went to Harrow in the summer term. The school possessed the biggest swimming bath I had ever seen. It was more like the bend of a river than a bath, and it had two bridges across it. Thither we used to repair for hours at a time, and bask between our dips, eating enormous buns, on the hot asphalt margin. Naturally it was a good joke to come up behind some naked friend, or even enemy, and push him in. I made quite a habit of this with boys of my own size or less.

One day when I had been no more than a month in the school, I saw a boy standing in a meditative posture wrapped in a towel on the very brink. He was no bigger than I was, so I thought him fair game. Coming stealthily behind, I pushed him in, holding on to his towel out of humanity, so that it should not get wet. I was startled to see a furious face emerge from the foam, and a being evidently of enormous strength making its way by fierce strokes to the shore. I fled; but in vain. Swift as the wind my pursuer overtook me, seized me in a ferocious grip and hurled me into the deepest part of the pool. I soon scrambled out on the other side, and found myself surrounded by an agitated crowd of younger boys. 'You're in for it,' they said. 'Do you know what you have done? It's Amery; he's in the Sixth Form. He is Head of his House; he is champion at Gym; he has got his football colours.'

They continued to recount his many titles to fame and reverence, and to dilate upon the awful retribution that would fall upon me. I was convulsed not only with terror, but with the guilt of sacrilege. How could I tell his rank when he was in a bath-towel and so small? I determined to apologise immediately. I approached the potentate in lively trepidation. 'I am very sorry,' I said. 'I mistook you for a Fourth Form boy. You are so small.' He did not seem at all placated by this; so I added in a most brilliant recovery, 'My father, who is a great man, is also small'. At this he laughed, and after some general remarks about my 'cheek' and how I had better be careful in the future, signified that the incident was closed.

I have been fortunate to see a good deal more of him, in times when three years' difference in age is not so important as it is at school. We were afterwards to be Cabinet colleagues for a good many years.

'I SHALL SAVE LONDON AND ENGLAND FROM DISASTER'

In 1891, while at Harrow, the sixteen-year-old Churchill would often speak about his future with the other boys, one of whom, Murland (later Sir Murland) de Grasse Evans – who was Churchill's age, and lived to see him become Prime Minister – later recalled a conversation one Sunday evening after chapel: 'We frankly discussed our futures. After placing me in the Diplomatic Service, perhaps because of my French descent from Admiral de Grasse who was defeated by Lord Rodney in the Battle of the Saints, 1782; or alternatively in finance, following my father's career, we came to his own future':

'Will you go into the army?' I asked.

'I don't know, it is probable, but I shall have great adventures beginning soon after I leave here.'

'Are you going into politics? Following your famous father?'

'I don't know, but it is more than likely because, you see, I am not afraid to speak in public.'

'You do not seem at all clear about your intentions or desires.'

'That may be, but I have a wonderful idea of where I shall be eventually. I have dreams about it.'

'Where is that?' I enquired.

'Well, I can see vast changes coming over a now peaceful world; great upheavals, terrible struggles; wars such as one cannot imagine; and I tell you London will be in danger – London will be attacked and I shall be very prominent in the defence of London.'

'How can you talk like that?' I said; 'we are for ever safe from invasion, since the days of Napoleon.'

'I see further ahead than you do. I see into the future. This country will be subjected somehow, to a tremendous invasion, by what means I do not know, but (warming up to his subject) I tell you I shall be in command of the defences of London and I shall save London and England from disaster.'

'Will you be a general then, in command of the troops?'

'I don't know; dreams of the future are blurred but the main objective is clear. I repeat – London will be in danger and in the high position I shall occupy, it will fall to me to save the Capital and save the Empire.'

'TO PLUNGE OR NOT TO PLUNGE, THAT WAS THE QUESTION'

Churchill was to have several narrow escapes from death during his life: at school when he almost succumbed to pneumonia, in the Army, while flying, in the water, and while crossing the street in New York. The second of these escapes – following the pneumonia – took place early in 1893, when he was eighteen, as he described in *My Early Life*:

My aunt, Lady Wimborne, had lent us her comfortable estate at Bournemouth for the winter. Forty or fifty acres of pine forest descended by sandy undulations terminating in cliffs to the smooth beach of the English Channel. It was a small, wild place and through the middle there fell to the sea level a deep cleft called a 'chine'. Across this 'chine' a rustic bridge nearly 50 yards long had been thrown. I was just 18 and on my holidays. My younger brother aged 12 and a cousin aged 14 proposed to chase me. After I had been hunted for twenty minutes and was rather short of breath, I decided to cross the bridge. Arrived at its centre I saw to my consternation that the pursuers had divided their forces. One stood at each end of the bridge; capture seemed certain. But in a flash there came across me a great project. The chine which the bridge spanned was full of young fir trees.

Their slender tops reached to the level of the footway. 'Would it not' I asked myself 'be possible to leap on to one of them and slip down the pole-like stem, breaking off each tier of branches as one descended, until the fall was broken?' I looked at it. I computed it. I meditated. Meanwhile I climbed over the balustrade. My young pursuers stood wonder-struck at either end of the bridge. To plunge or not to plunge, that was the question! In a second I had plunged, throwing out my arms to embrace the summit of the fir tree. The argument was correct; the data were absolutely wrong. It was three days before I regained consciousness and more than three months before I crawled from my bed.

The measured fall was 29 feet on to hard ground. But no doubt the branches helped. My mother, summoned by the alarming message of the children, 'He jumped over the bridge and he won't speak to us,' hurried down with energetic aid and inopportune brandy. It was an axiom with my parents that in serious accident or illness the highest medical aid should be invoked, regardless of cost. Eminent specialists stood about my bed.

Later on when I could understand again, I was shocked and also flattered to hear of the enormous fees they had been paid. My father travelled over at full express from Dublin where he had been spending his Christmas at one of old Lord Fitzgibbon's once-celebrated parties. He brought the greatest of London surgeons with him. I had among other injuries a ruptured kidney. It is to the surgeon's art and to my own pronounced will-to-live that the reader is indebted for this story. But for a year I looked at life round a corner.

'NOW I SAW DEATH AS NEAR AS I BELIEVE I HAVE EVER SEEN HIM'

Churchill's next narrow escape from death came eighteen months later, in the summer of 1894, when he was once again on holiday, this time with his brother Jack, on Lake Geneva. Churchill, then nineteen, was an army cadet at Sandhurst. He described what happened in *My Early Life*, not mentioning that the 'boy a little younger than myself' was his brother:

I went for a row with another boy a little younger than myself. When we were more than a mile from the shore, we decided to have a swim, pulled off our clothes, jumped into the water and swam about in great delight. When we had had enough, the boat was perhaps 100 yards away. A breeze had begun to stir the waters. The boat had a small red awning over its stern seats. This awning acted as a sail by catching the breeze. As we swam towards the boat, it drifted farther off. After this had happened several times we had perhaps halved the distance. But meanwhile the breeze was freshening and we both, especially my companion, began to be tired.

Up to this point no idea of danger had crossed my mind. The sun played upon the sparkling blue waters; the wonderful panorama of mountains and valleys, the gay hotels and villas still smiled. But I now saw Death as near as I believe I have ever seen him. He was swimming in the water at our side, whispering from time to time in the rising wind which continued to carry the boat away from us at about the same speed we could swim. No help was near. Unaided we could never reach the shore. I was not only an easy, but a fast swimmer, having represented my House at Harrow, when our team defeated all comers.

I now swam for life. Twice I reached within a yard of the boat and each time a gust carried it just beyond my reach; but by a supreme effort I caught hold of its side in the nick of time before a still stronger gust bulged the red awning again. I scrambled in, and rowed back for my companion who, though tired, had not apparently realised the dull yellow glare of mortal peril that had so suddenly played around us. I said nothing to the tutor about this serious experience; but I have never forgotten it; and perhaps some of my readers will remember it too.

'A RAGGED VOLLEY RANG OUT FROM THE EDGE OF THE FOREST'

Churchill's father died on 24 January 1895, three weeks before his forty-sixth birthday. Churchill was just twenty years old. Four weeks after his father's death, Churchill entered the cavalry as a second lieutenant. That October he and a fellow officer went to Cuba, as guests of the Spanish Army, to witness the Spanish attempt to crush the Cuban nationalist rebellion. Churchill was also given an intelligence task by the British Army: to report on the penetrating power of a new Spanish bullet. On 2 December 1895, in Cuba, he was in action for the first time, describing the scene in one of his regular reports back to London for the *Daily Graphic*:

Behold next morning a distinct sensation in the life of a young officer! It is still dark, but the sky is paling. We are in what a brilliant though little-known writer has called 'The dim mysterious temple of the Dawn.' We are on our horses, in uniform; our revolvers are loaded. In the dusk and half-light, long files of armed and laden men are shuffling off towards the enemy. He may be very near; perhaps he is waiting for us a mile away. We cannot tell; we know nothing of the qualities either of our friends or foes. We have nothing to do with their quarrels. Except in personal self-defence we can take no part in their combats. But we feel it is a great moment in our lives – in fact, one of the best we have ever experienced. We think that something is going to happen; we hope devoutly that something will happen; yet at the same time we do not want to be hurt or killed.

What is it then that we do want? It is that lure of youth – adventure, and adventure for adventure's sake. You might call it tomfoolery. To travel thousands of miles with money one could ill afford, and get up at four o'clock in the morning in the hope of getting into a scrape in the company of perfect strangers, is certainly hardly a rational proceeding. Yet we knew there were very few subalterns in the British Army who would not have given a month's pay to sit in our saddles.

[⋯]

On this day when we halted for breakfast every man sat by his horse and ate what he had in his pocket. I had been provided with half a skinny chicken. I was engaged in gnawing the drumstick when suddenly, close at hand, almost in our faces it seemed, a ragged volley rang out from the edge of the forest. The horse immediately behind me – not my horse – gave a bound. There was excitement and commotion. A party of soldiers rushed to the place whence the volley had been fired, and of course found nothing except a few empty cartridge cases.

Meanwhile I had been meditating upon the wounded horse. It was a chestnut. The bullet had struck between his ribs, the blood dripped on the ground, and there was a circle of dark red on his bright chestnut coat about a foot wide. He hung his head, but did not fall. Evidently however he was going to die, for his saddle and bridle were soon taken off him. As I watched these proceedings I could not help reflecting that the bullet which had struck the Chestnut had certainly passed within a foot of my head. So at any rate I had been 'under fire.' That was something. Nevertheless, I began to take a more thoughtful view of our enterprise than I had hitherto done.

[···]

The next day:

The day was hot, and my companion and I persuaded a couple of officers on the Staff to come with us and bathe in the river. The water was delightful, being warm and clear, and the spot very beautiful. We were dressing on the bank when, suddenly, we heard a shot fired. Another and another followed; then came a volley.

The bullets whistled over our heads. It was evident that an attack of some sort was in progress. A sentry, sitting on a tree about fifty yards higher up stream, popped over it, and, kneeling down behind, began to fire at the advancing enemy, who were now not 200 yards away. We pulled on our clothes anyhow, and one of the officers, in a half-dressed state, ran and collected about fifty men who were building shelters for the night close by. Of course they had their rifles, in this war no soldier ever goes a yard without his weapon, and these men doubled up in high delight and gave the rebels a volley from their Mausers which checked the enemy's advance.

We retired along the river as gracefully as might be, and returned to the general's quarters. When we arrived there was a regular skirmish going on half a mile away, and the bullets were falling over the camp. The rebels, who use Remingtons, fired independently, and the deep note of their pieces contrasted strangely with the shrill rattle of the magazine rifles of the Spaniards. After about half an hour the insurgents had enough, and went off carrying their wounded and dead away with them.

At eleven that night they came back and fired at us for about an hour. This time they employed volleys, and killed and wounded several soldiers about the camp. One bullet came through the thatch of the hut in which we were sleeping and another wounded an orderly just outside.

'A SHARP AND PECULIAR WRENCH'

On 11 September 1896, Second Lieutenant Churchill sailed with his regiment to India. Three weeks later, on October 1, his ship reached Bombay. In *My Early Life*, he recalled his arrival:

A shoal of tiny boats had been lying around us all day long, rising and falling with the swell. We eagerly summoned some of these. It took about a quarter of an hour to reach the quays of the Sassoon Dock. Glad I was to be there; for the lively motion of the skiff to which I and two friends had committed ourselves was fast becoming our main preoccupation.

We came alongside of a great stone wall with dripping steps and iron rings for hand-holds. The boat rose and fell four or five feet with the surges. I put out my hand and grasped at a ring; but before I could get my feet on the steps the boat swung away, giving my right shoulder a sharp and peculiar wrench. I scrambled up all right, made a few remarks of a general character, mostly beginning with the earlier letters of the alphabet, hugged my shoulder and soon thought no more about it.

Let me counsel my younger readers to beware of dislocated shoulders. In this, as in so many other things, it is the first step that counts. Quite an exceptional strain is required to tear the capsule which holds the shoulder joint together; but once the deed is done, a terrible liability remains. Although my shoulder did not actually go out, I had sustained an injury which was to last me my life, which was to cripple me at polo, to prevent me from ever playing tennis, and to be a grave embarrassment in moments of peril, violence and effort. Since then, at irregular intervals my shoulder has dislocated on the most unexpected pretexts; sleeping with my arm under the pillow, taking a book from the library shelves, slipping on a staircase, swimming, etc. Once it very nearly went out through a too expansive gesture in the House of Commons, and I thought how astonished the members would have been to see the speaker to whom they were listening, suddenly for no reason throw himself upon the floor in an instinctive effort to take the strain and leverage off the displaced arm-bone.

This accident was a serious piece of bad luck. However, you never can tell whether bad luck may not after all turn out to be good luck. Perhaps if in the charge of Omdurman I had been able to use a sword, instead of having to adopt a modern weapon like a Mauser pistol, my story might not have got so far as the telling. One must never forget when misfortunes come that it is quite possible they are saving one from something much worse; or that when you make some great mistake, it may very easily serve you better than the best-advised decision. Life is a whole, and luck is a whole, and no part of them can be separated from the rest.

'I RESOLVED TO READ HISTORY, PHILOSOPHY, ECONOMICS'

As a soldier in India, based in Bangalore, Churchill spent several hours each day reading. He had asked his mother to send him books on history, politics and political economy. In *My Early Life* he recalled:

I had always liked history at school. But there we were given only the dullest, driest, pemmicanised forms like *The Student's Hume*. Once I had a hundred pages of *The Student's Hume* as a holiday task. Quite unexpectedly, before I went back to school, my father set out to examine me upon it. The period was Charles I. He asked me about the Grand Remonstrance; what did I know about that? I said that in the end the Parliament beat the King and cut his head off. This seemed to me the grandest remonstrance imaginable. It was no good. 'Here', said my father, 'is a grave parliamentary question affecting the whole structure of our constitutional history, lying near the centre of the task you have been set, and you do not in the slightest degree appreciate the issues involved.'

I was puzzled by his concern; I could not see at the time why it should matter so much. Now I wanted to know more about it. So I resolved to read history, philosophy, economics, and things like that; and I wrote to my mother asking for such books as I had heard of on these topics. She responded with alacrity, and every month the mail brought me a substantial package of what I thought were standard works.

In history I decided to begin with Gibbon. Someone had told me that my father had read Gibbon with delight; that he knew whole pages of it by heart, and that it had greatly affected his style of speech and writing. So without more ado I set out upon the eight volumes of Dean Milman's edition of Gibbon's *Decline and Fall of the Roman Empire*. I was immediately dominated both by the story and the style. All through the long glistening middle hours of the Indian day, from when we quitted stables till the evening shadows proclaimed the hour of Polo, I devoured Gibbon. I rode triumphantly through it from end to end and enjoyed it all. I scribbled all my opinions on the margins of the pages, and very soon found myself a vehement partisan of the author against the disparagements of his pompous-pious editor. I was not even estranged by his naughty footnotes.

[...]

So pleased was I with *The Decline and Fall* that I began at once to read Gibbon's *Autobiography*, which luckily was bound up in the same edition. When I read his reference to his old nurse: 'If there be any, as I trust there are some, who rejoice that I live, to that dear and excellent woman their gratitude is due', I thought of Mrs. Everest [Churchill's nanny]; and it shall be her epitaph.

'THE RISING TIDE OF TORY DEMOCRACY'

In May 1897, Churchill returned to Britain for three months' leave from India. On reaching London, he informed Conservative Central Office that he would welcome an early opportunity of becoming a parliamentary candidate. He later wrote, in *My Early Life*: 'It appeared there were hundreds of indoor meetings and outdoor fetes, of bazaars and rallies all of which were clamant for speakers. I surveyed this prospect with the eye of an urchin looking through a pastry cook's window. Finally we selected Bath as the scene of my (official) maiden effort.' On 26 July 1897, he spoke at Claverton Manor (now the American Museum) near Bath. According to *The Lady* magazine ten days later: 'An auspicious debut on the platform was made the other day by Mr Winston Churchill, elder son of the late Lord Randolph Churchill. He spoke at a large Primrose League meeting, and delighted his audience by the force and mental agility he displayed. Mr Churchill, who is only twenty-three, aspires to a seat in Parliament. He is in the 4th Hussars at present, and is strikingly like his late father in features and colouring.' Churchill – in fact only twenty-two – told his first political audience, speaking first about the Conservatives' Workmen's Compensation Bill:

> When the Radicals brought in their Bill and failed, they called it an Employers' Liability Bill. Observe how much better the Tories do these things. They call this Bill the Workmen's Compensation Bill, and that is a much nicer name.

> [···]

> I do not say that workmen have not been treated well in the past by the kindness and consideration of their employers, but this measure removes the question from the shifting sands of charity and places it on the firm bedrock of law.
> So far the Bill only applies to dangerous trades. Radicals, and Liberals, always liberal with other people's money, asked why it was not applied to all trades. This was just like a Radical, just the slapdash,

wholesale, harum-scarum policy of the Radical. It reminds me of the man who, on being told that ventilation was an excellent thing, went and smashed every window in his house. That is not Conservative policy. Conservative policy is essentially a tentative policy, a look-before-you-leap policy, and it is a policy of don't leap at all if there is a ladder.

[···]

British workmen have more to hope for from the rising tide of Tory Democracy than from the dried-up drainpipe of Radicalism.

One of the questions which politicians have to face is how to avoid disputes between Capital and Labour. I hope that ultimately the labourer may become a shareholder in the profits and may not be unwilling to share the losses of a bad year because he shared the profits of a good one.

In 1880 the Tory Party was crushed, broken, dispirited. Its great leader, Lord Beaconsfield, was already touched by the finger of Death. Its principles were unpopular; its numbers were few; and it appeared on the verge of extinction. Observe it now. That struggling remnant of Toryism has swollen into the strongest Government of modern times. And the great Liberal Party which in 1882 was vigorous, united, supreme, is shrunk to a few discordant factions of discredited faddists, without numbers, without policy, without concord, without cohesion, around whose necks is bound the millstone of Home Rule. In all this revolution of public opinion the Primrose League has borne its share. It has kept pegging away, driving the principles of the Tory Party into the heads of the people of this country, and, though the task has been heavy and the labour long, they have had in the end a glorious reward.

'DELIGHTED TO GET SAFE HOME AGAIN'

Three weeks after speaking at Bath, Churchill was back in India, in Bangalore. On 28 August 1897, breaking off work on a novel that he was writing, entitled *Savrola* – a political romance stimulated by his

Cuban experiences – he left Bangalore for the North-West Frontier of India, where a rebellion had broken out by those whom he described in a letter to his mother as 'fierce wild warlike tribes of Afghan stock'. Churchill was in action on the North-West Frontier for five weeks in September and October 1897. The impressions that those five weeks fighting the Pashtun tribesmen in the Mohmand Valley made on him were vivid, as was his sense of the ideals for which the tribesmen were fighting. He set down his thoughts in his book *The Story of the Malakand Field Force*:

> I would that it were in my power to convey to the reader, who has not had the fortune to live with troops on service, some just appreciation of the compensations of war. The healthy, open-air life, the vivid incidents, the excitement, not only of realisation, but of anticipation, the generous and cheery friendships, the chances of distinction which are open to all, invest life with keener interests, and rarer pleasures.
>
> The uncertainty and importance of the present reduce the past and future to comparative insignificance, and clear the mind of minor worries. And when all is over, memories remain which few men do not hold precious. As to the hardships, these though severe may be endured. Ascetics and recluses have in their endeavours to look beyond the grave suffered worse things. Nor will the soldier in the pursuit of fame and the enjoyment of the pleasures of war be exposed to greater discomforts than Diogenes in his tub, or the Trappists in their monastery. Besides all this, his chances of learning about the next world are infinitely greater.
>
> And yet, when all has been said, we are confronted with a mournful but stubborn fact. In this contrary life, so prosaic is the mind of man, so material his soul, so poor his spirit, that there is no one who has been six months on active service who is not delighted to get safe home again, to the comfortable monotonies of peace.

Reflecting on the adversaries of Britain on the North-West Frontier, he wrote:

Yet the life even of these barbarous people is not without moments when the lover of the picturesque might sympathise with their hopes and fears. In the cool of the evening, when the sun has sunk behind the mountains of Afghanistan, and the valleys are filled with a delicious twilight, the elders of the village lead the way to the chenar trees by the water's side, and there, while the men are cleaning their rifles, or smoking their hookas, and the women are making rude ornaments from beads, and cloves, and nuts, the Mullah drones the evening prayer.

Few white men have seen, and returned to tell the tale. But we may imagine the conversation passing from the prices of arms and cattle, the prospects of the harvest, or the village gossip, to the great Power, that lies to the southward, and comes nearer year by year. Perhaps some former Sepoy, of Beluchis or Pathans, will recount his adventures in the bazaars of Peshawar, or tell of the white officers he has followed and fought for in the past.

He will speak of their careless bravery and their strange sports; of the far-reaching power of the Government, that never forgets to send his pension regularly as the months pass by; and he may even predict to the listening circle the day when their valleys will be involved in the comprehensive grasp of that great machine, and judges, collectors and commissioners shall ride to sessions at Ambeyla, or value the land tax on the soil of Nawagai.

Then the Mullah will raise his voice and remind them of other days when the sons of the prophet drove the infidel from the plains of India, and ruled at Delhi, as wide an Empire as the Kafir holds today: when the true religion strode proudly through the earth and scorned to lie hidden and neglected among the hills: when mighty princes ruled in Baghdad, and all men knew that there was one God, and Mahomet was His prophet.

And the young men hearing these things will grip their Martinis, and pray to Allah, that one day He will bring some Sahib – best prize of all – across their line of sight at seven hundred yards so that, at least, they may strike a blow for insulted and threatened Islam.

'THE COLLISION WAS PRODIGIOUS'

Leaving India in July 1898, Churchill joined the Expeditionary Force against the Muslim Dervish insurgents in the Sudan. On September 2, at Omdurman, he took part in the cavalry charge by the 21st Lancers against the Dervish lines, a charge that he described in his book *The River War*, which was published a year later:

Two hundred and fifty yards away the dark-blue men were firing madly in a thin film of light-blue smoke. Their bullets struck the hard gravel into the air, and the troopers, to shield their faces from the stinging dust, bowed their helmets forward, like the Cuirassiers at Waterloo. The pace was fast and the distance short. Yet, before it was half covered, the whole aspect of the affair changed. A deep crease in the ground – a dry watercourse, a khor – appeared where all had seemed smooth, level plain; and from it there sprang, with the suddenness of a pantomime effect and a high-pitched yell, a dense white mass of men nearly as long as our front and about twelve deep.

A score of horsemen and a dozen bright flags rose as if by magic from the earth. Eager warriors sprang forward to anticipate the shock. The rest stood firm to meet it. The Lancers acknowledged the apparition only by an increase of pace. Each man wanted sufficient momentum to drive through such a solid line. The flank troops, seeing that they overlapped, curved inwards like the horns of a moon. But the whole event was a matter of seconds. The riflemen, firing bravely to the last, were swept head over heels into the khor, and jumping down with them, at full gallop and in the closest order, the British squadrons struck the fierce brigade with one loud furious shout.

The collision was prodigious. Nearly thirty Lancers, men and horses, and at least two hundred Arabs were overthrown. The shock was stunning to both sides and for perhaps ten wonderful seconds no man heeded his enemy. Terrified horses wedged in the crowd of bruised and shaken men, sprawling in heaps, struggled, dazed and stupid, to their feet, panted, and looked about them. Several fallen Lancers had even time to remount. Meanwhile the impetus of the cavalry carried them on. As a rider tears through a bullfinch, the officers forced their way through the press; and as an iron rake might be drawn through a heap of shingle, so the regiment followed. They shattered the Dervish array, and, their pace reduced to a walk, scrambled out of the khor on the further side, leaving a score of troopers behind them, and dragging on with the charge more than a thousand Arabs. Then, and not till then, the killing began; and thereafter each man saw the world along his lance, under his guard, or through the backsight of his pistol; and each had his own strange tale to tell.

Stubborn and unshaken infantry hardly ever meet stubborn and unshaken cavalry. Either the infantry run away and are cut down in flight, or they keep their heads and destroy nearly all the horsemen by their musketry. On this occasion two living walls had actually crashed. The Dervishes fought manfully. They tried to hamstring the horses. They fired their rifles, pressing the muzzles into the very bodies of their opponents. They cut reins and stirrup leathers. They flung their throwing-spears with great dexterity. They tried every device of cool, determined men practised in war and familiar with cavalry; and, besides, they swung sharp, heavy swords which bit deep.

The hand-to-hand fighting on the further side of the khor lasted for perhaps one minute. Then the horses got into their stride again, the pace increased, and the Lancers drew out from among their antagonists. Within two minutes of the collision every living man was clear of the Dervish mass. All who had fallen were cut at with swords till they stopped quivering, but no artistic mutilations were attempted. Two hundred yards away the regiment halted, rallied, faced about, and in less than five minutes were re-formed and ready for a second charge. The men were anxious to cut their way back through their enemies. We were alone together – the cavalry regiment and the Dervish brigade.

The ridge hung like a curtain between us and the army. The general battle was forgotten, as it was unseen. This was a private quarrel. The other might have been a massacre; but here the fight was fair, for we too fought with sword and spear. Indeed the advantage of ground and numbers lay with them. All prepared to settle the debate at once and for ever. But some realisation of the cost of our wild ride began to come to those who were responsible. Riderless horses galloped across the plain. Men, clinging to their saddles, lurched helplessly about, covered with blood from perhaps a dozen wounds. Horses, streaming from tremendous gashes, limped and staggered with their riders. In 120 seconds five officers, 65 men, and 119 horses out of fewer than 400 had been killed or wounded.

The Dervish line, broken by the charge, began to reform at once. They closed up, shook themselves together, and prepared with constancy and courage for another shock. But on military considerations it was desirable to turn them out of the khor first and thus deprive them of their vantage-ground. The regiment again drawn up, three squadrons in line and the fourth in column, now wheeled to the right, and, galloping round the Dervish flank, dismounted and opened a heavy fire with their magazine carbines. Under the pressure of this fire the enemy changed front to meet the new attack, so that both sides were formed at right angles to their original lines. When the Dervish change of front was completed, they began to advance against the dismounted men. But the fire was accurate, and there can be little doubt that the moral effect of the charge had been very great, and that these brave enemies were no longer unshaken. Be this as it may, the fact remains that they retreated swiftly, though in good order, towards the ridge of Surgham Hill, where the Khalifa's Black Flag still waved, and the 21st Lancers remained in possession of the ground – and of their dead.

'AT SUCH SIGHTS THE TRIUMPH OF VICTORY FADED ON THE MIND'

What Churchill saw after the Battle of Omdurman shocked and appalled him. He described the scene on the battlefield in *The River War*:

All over the ground – on the average three yards apart – were dead men, clad in the white and patched smocks of faithful Dervishes. Three days of burning sun had done their work. The bodies were swollen to almost gigantic proportions. Twice as large as living men, they appeared in every sense monstrous. The more advanced corpses hardly resembled human beings, but rather great bladders such as natives use to float down the Nile on. Frightful gashes scarred their limbs, and great black stains, once crimson, covered their garments. The sight was appalling. The smell redoubled the horror.

We galloped on. A strong, hot wind blew from the west across the great plain and hurried foul and tainted to the river. Keeping to wind-ward of the thickest clusters, we picked our way, and the story of the fight unfolded itself. Here was where the artillery had opened on the swarming masses. Men had fallen in little groups of five or six to each shell. Nearer to the zeriba – about 1,000 yards from it – the musketry had begun to tell, and the dead lay evenly scattered about – one every ten yards. Two hundred yards further the full force of the fire – artillery, Maxims, and rifles – had burst on them. In places desperate rushes to get on at all costs had been made by devoted, fearless men. In such places the bodies lay so thickly as to hide the ground. Occasionally there were double layers of this hideous covering. Once I saw them lying three deep. In a space not exceeding a hundred yards square more than 400 corpses lay festering.

It is difficult to imagine the postures into which man, once created in the image of his Maker, had been twisted. It is not wise to try, for he who succeeds will ask himself with me: 'Can I ever forget?'

I have tried to gild war, and to solace myself for the loss of dear and gallant friends, with the thought that a soldier's death for a cause that he believes in will count for much, whatever may be beyond this world. When the soldier of a civilised Power is killed in action, his limbs are composed and his body is borne by friendly arms reverently to the grave. The wail of the fifes, the roll of the drums, the triumphant words of the Funeral Service, all divest the act of its squalor, and the spectator sympathises with, perhaps almost envies, the comrade who has found this honourable exit. But there was nothing dulce et decorum about the Dervish dead; nothing of the dignity of unconquerable manhood; all was filthy corruption. Yet these were as brave men as ever walked the earth. The conviction was borne in on me that their claim beyond the grave in respect of a valiant death was not less good than that which any of our

countrymen could make. The thought may not be original; it may
happily be untrue; it seemed certainly most unwelcome.

[···]

The white-clad bodies of the men were intermingled with the brown
and bay horses, so that this part of the field looked less white-
speckled than the rest. They had ridden straight at the solid line of
bayonets and in the teeth of the storm of projectiles. Every man had
galloped at full speed, and when he fell he shot many lengths in front
of his horse, rolling over and over – destroyed, not conquered by
machinery.

At such sights the triumph of victory faded on the mind and a
mournful feeling of disgust grew stronger. All this was bad to see, but
worse remained; after the dead, the wounded. The officer or soldier
who escapes from the field with a wound has a claim on his country.
To the private it may mean a pension; to the officer a gratuity, perhaps
a 'mention in despatches', certainly advancement in his profession.
The scar may even, when the stink has departed, be a source of pride
– an excuse to retell the story. To soothe the pain there are
anaesthetics; to heal the injury the resources of science are at hand. It
was otherwise with the Dervish wounded.

Would the reader be further sickened with the horrors of the field?
There was a man that had crawled a mile in three days, but was yet
two miles from the river. He had one foot; the other remained behind.
I wonder if he ever reached the water he had struggled so hard to
attain! There was a man with both legs shattered; he had dragged
himself along in a sitting posture, making perhaps four hundred
yards a day. The extraordinary vitality of these poor wretches only
prolonged their torments.

So terrible were the sights and smells that the brain failed to realise
the suffering and agony they proclaimed. As a man faints and his
body refuses to suffer beyond a certain degree under torture, so the
mind was unable to appreciate that an arrangement of line and colour
lying on the ground was a human being, partly putrefied but still
alive. Perhaps stern Nature, more merciful than stern civilisation, lent
a kindly delirium. But I must record the fact that most of the men I
saw were sane and capable of feeling every pang. And meanwhile they

all struggled towards the Nile, the great river of their country, without which the invaders could never have come upon them, but which they nevertheless did not reproach. One man had reached it and lay exhausted, but content, on the bank. Another had attained the water and had died at its brim. Let us hope he had his drink first.

The statement that 'the wounded Dervishes received every delicacy and attention' is so utterly devoid of truth that it transcends the limits of mendacity and passes into the realms of the ridiculous. I was impatient to get back to the camp. There was nothing to be gained by dallying on the field, unless a man were anxious to become quite callous, so that no imaginable misery which could come to human flesh would ever have moved him again. I may have written in these pages something of vengeance and of the paying of a debt. It may be that vengeance is sweet, and that the gods forbade vengeance to men because they reserved for themselves so delicious and intoxicating a drink. But no one should drain the cup to the bottom. The dregs are often filthy-tasting.

[· · ·]

So as the haze deepened into the gloom of the night, and the uncertain outlines of the distant hills faded altogether from the view, we rode back to camp – 'home to Omdurman' and left the field of battle to its silent occupants. There they lie, those valiant warriors of a false faith and fallen domination; their only history preserved by their conquerors; their only monument, their bones – and these the drifting sand of the desert will bury in a few short years. Three days before I had seen them rise – eager, confident, resolved. The roar of their shouting had swelled like the surf on a rocky shore. The flashing of their blades had displayed their numbers, their vitality, their ferocity. They were confident in their strength, in the justice of their cause, in the support of their religion.

Now only the heaps of corruption in the plain, and the fugitives dispersed and scattered in the wilderness, remained. The terrible machinery of scientific war had done its work. The Dervish host was scattered and destroyed. Their end, however, only anticipates that of the victors; for Time, which laughs at science, as science laughs at valour, will in due course contemptuously brush both combatants away.

'ODD AND BIZARRE POTENTATES'

In *The River War*, Churchill, aged twenty-four, reflected on those rulers against whom Britain was fighting throughout its vast Empire:

We may consider how strange and varied are the diversions of an Imperial people. Year after year, and stretching back to an indefinite horizon, we see the figures of the odd and bizarre potentates against whom the British arms continually are turned. They pass in a long procession: The Akhund of Swat; Cetewayo, brandishing an assegai as naked as himself; Kruger, singing a psalm of victory; Osman Digna, the Immortal and the Irretrievable; Theebaw, with his Umbrella; Lobengula, gazing fondly at the pages of Truth; Prempeh, abasing himself in the dust; the Mad Mullah, on his white ass; and, latest of all, the Khalifa in his coach of state. It is like a pantomime scene at Drury Lane. These extraordinary foreign figures, each with his complete set of crimes, horrible customs, and 'minor peculiarities', march one by one from the dark wings of barbarism up to the bright footlights of civilisation.

For a space their names are on the wires on the world and the tongues of men. The Sovereign on the Throne, the Minister in his Cabinet, the General in his tent, pronounce or mispronounce their styles and titles. A thousand compositors make the same combination of letters. The unusual syllables become household words. The street-boy bellows them in our ears. The artisan laughs over them at night in his cottage. The child in the nursery is cajoled into virtue or silence by the repetition of the dread accents.

And then the world-audience clap their hands, amused yet impatient, and the potentates and their trains pass on, some to exile, some to prison, some to death – for it is a grim jest for them – and their conquerors, taking their possessions, forget even their names. Nor will history record such trash. Perhaps the time will come when the supply will be exhausted, and there will be no more royal freaks to conquer. In that gloomy period there will be no more of these nice expeditions – 'the image of war without its guilt and only five-and-twenty percent its danger'; no more medals for the soldiers, no more peerages for the Generals, no more copy for the journalists. The good old times will have passed away, and the most cynical philosopher will be forced to admit that, though the world may be much more prosperous, it can scarcely be so merry.

'NO STRONGER RETROGRADE FORCE EXISTS IN THE WORLD'

In *The River War*, the young Churchill set down his thoughts on Islam, which he had seen in action both on the North-West Frontier of India and in the Sudan, and about which he had developed decisive views, which he decided to put before his readers:

How dreadful are the curses which Mohammedanism lays on its votaries. Besides the fanatical frenzy, which is as dangerous in a man as hydrophobia in a dog, there is this fearful fatalistic apathy. The effects are apparent in many countries. Improvident habits, slovenly systems of agriculture, sluggish methods of commerce, and insecurity of property exist wherever the followers of the Prophet rule or live. A degraded sensualism deprives this life of its grace and refinement; the next of its dignity and sanctity. The fact that in a Mohammedan law every woman must belong to some man as his absolute property – either as a child, a wife or a concubine – must delay the final extinction of slavery until the faith of Islam has ceased to be a great power among men.

Individual Moslems may show splendid qualities. Thousands become the brave and loyal soldiers of the Queen; all know how to die; but the influence of religion paralyses the social development of those who follow it. No stronger retrograde force exists in the world. Far from being moribund, Mohammedanism is a militant and proselytising faith. It has already spread throughout Central Africa, raising fearless warriors at every step; and were it not that Christianity is sheltered in the strong arms of science – the science against which it had vainly struggled – the civilisation of modern Europe might fall, as fell the civilisation of ancient Rome.

'DEATH STOOD BEFORE ME, GRIM SULLEN DEATH'

In March 1899, Churchill gave up soldiering – as he thought, for ever – and in July 1899 he stood for Parliament, as a Conservative, for the largely working-class constituency of Oldham. He was defeated, but only narrowly, and determined to stand again at the next possible opportunity. That September he was asked to go to South Africa as a war correspondent for the *Morning Post*, to report on the second Anglo-Boer War. On November 15, two weeks before his twenty-fifth birthday, he was accompanying an armoured train when, at Frere, near Estcourt, it was ambushed by the Boers. As he described in his book *London to Ladysmith via Pretoria*, he helped rescue those trapped on the train, and then returned to see if there was more he could do:

I found myself alone in a shallow cutting and none of our soldiers, who had all surrendered on the way, to be seen. Then suddenly there appeared on the line at the end of the cutting two men not in uniform. 'Platelayers', I said to myself, and then, with a surge of realisation, 'Boers'. My mind retains a momentary impression of these tall figures, full of animated movement, clad in dark flapping clothes, with slouch, storm-driven hats posing on their rifles hardly a hundred yards away. I turned and ran between the rails of the track, and the only thought I achieved was this, 'Boer marksmanship'.

Two bullets passed, both within a foot, one on either side. I flung myself against the banks of the cutting. But they gave no cover. Another glance at the figures; one was now kneeling to aim. Again I darted forward. Movement seemed the only chance. Again two soft kisses sucked in the air, but nothing struck me. This could not endure. I must get out of the cutting – that damnable corridor. I scrambled up the bank. The earth sprang up beside me, and something touched my hand, but outside the cutting was a tiny depression. I crouched in this, struggling to get my wind. On the other side of the railway a horseman galloped up, shouting to me and waving his hand. He was scarcely forty yards off. With a rifle I could have killed him easily.

I knew nothing of white flags, and the bullets had made me savage. I reached down for my Mauser pistol. 'This one at least,' I said, and indeed it was a certainty; but alas! I had left the weapon in the cab of the engine in order to be free to work at the wreckage. What then? There was a wire fence between me and the horseman. Should I continue to fly? The idea of another shot at such a short range decided me. Death stood before me, grim sullen Death without his light-hearted companion, Chance. So I held up my hand, and like Mr. Jorrocks's foxes, cried 'Capivy'. Then I was herded with the other prisoners in a miserable group, and about the same time I noticed that my hand was bleeding, and it began to pour with rain.

Two days before I had written to an officer in high command at home, whose friendship I have the honour to enjoy: 'There has been a great deal too much surrendering in this war, and I hope people who do so will not be encouraged.' Fate had intervened, yet though her tone was full of irony she seemed to say, as I think Ruskin once said, 'It matters very little whether your judgments of people are true or untrue, and very much whether they are kind or unkind,' and repeating that I will make an end.

'I THEREFORE RESOLVED TO ESCAPE'

Taken prisoner in the railway cutting near Estcourt, Churchill was taken by train to Pretoria where he was confined in the States Model School, a prisoner-of-war camp. Despite his protest that he was a journalist (as indeed he was) when captured, and not therefore a combatant, his request for release was rejected. On 12 December 1899 – after twenty-seven days in captivity, including his twenty-fifth birthday – he escaped, making his way with great difficulty and amid much danger to the safety of the Indian Ocean port of Lourenço Marques, in Portuguese East Africa. From there, he telegraphed an article to London. It appeared in *Pearson's Illustrated War News* on 30 December 1899, with the editorial note: 'The Morning Post has received the following telegram from Mr Winston Spencer Churchill, its war correspondent, who was taken prisoner by the Boers and escaped from Pretoria.' The article was dated and timed: 'Lourenço Marques, December 21st, 10 p.m.':

I was concealed in a railway truck under great sacks.

I had a small store of good water with me.

I remained hidden, chancing discovery.

The Boers searched the train at Komati Poort, but did not search deep enough, so after sixty hours of misery I came safely here.

I am very weak, but I am free.

I have lost many pounds weight, but I am lighter in heart.

I shall also avail myself of every opportunity from this moment to urge with earnestness an unflinching and uncompromising prosecution of the war.

On the afternoon of the 12th the Transvaal Government's Secretary for War informed me that there was little chance of my release.

I therefore resolved to escape the same night, and left the State Schools Prison at Pretoria by climbing the wall when the sentries' backs were turned momentarily.

I walked through the streets of the town without any disguises, meeting many burghers, but I was not challenged in the crowd.

I got through the pickets of the Town Guard, and struck the Delagoa Bay Railroad.

I walked along it, evading the watchers at the bridges and culverts.

I waited for a train beyond the first station.

The out 11.10 goods train from Pretoria arrived, and before it had reached full speed I boarded with great difficulty, and hid myself under coal sacks.

I jumped from the train before dawn, and sheltered during the day in a small wood, in company with a huge vulture, who displayed a lively interest in me.

I walked on at dusk.

There were no more trains that night.

The danger of meeting the guards of the railway line continued; but I was obliged to follow it, as I had no compass or map.

I had to make wide *détours* to avoid the bridges, stations and huts.

My progress was very slow, and chocolate is not a satisfying food.

The outlook was gloomy, but I persevered, with God's help, for five days.

The food I had was very precarious.

I was lying up at daylight, and walking on at night time, and, meanwhile, my escape had been discovered and my description telegraphed everywhere.

All the trains were searched.

Everyone was on the watch for me.

Four wrong people were arrested.

But on the sixth day I managed to board a train beyond Middelburg, whence there is a direct service to Delagoa.

'I HAD BETTER TELL YOU THE TRUTH'

Churchill was unable to include in his telegram the most extraordinary episode of his escape: how, as he wandered about the veldt, lost and hungry, and fearful of discovery by the Boers, he found shelter in a coal mine. He wrote nothing about this at the time in order to protect the mine-owner and others who had hidden him deep underground until he could smuggle himself aboard a goods train out of Boer-held territory to Lourenço Marques, and from there by ship to British-held Durban. Thirty years later, in *My Early Life*, he described his arrival in the middle of the night at what he first thought were the lights of a native village:

After about an hour or an hour and a half they still seemed almost as far off as ever. But I persevered, and presently between two and three o'clock in the morning I perceived that they were not the fires of a Kaffir kraal. The angular outline of buildings began to draw out against them, and soon I saw that I was approaching a group of houses around the mouth of a coal-mine. The wheel which worked the winding gear was plainly visible, and I could see that the fires which had led me so far were from the furnaces of the engines. Hard by, surrounded by one or two slighter structures, stood a small but substantial stone house two storeys high.

I halted in the wilderness to survey this scene and to revolve my action. It was still possible to turn back. But in that direction I saw nothing but the prospect of further futile wanderings terminated by hunger, fever, discovery, or surrender. On the other hand, here in front was a chance. I had heard it said before I escaped that in the mining district of Witbank and Middelburg there were a certain number of English residents who had been suffered to remain in the country in order to keep the mines working. Had I been led to one of these? What did this house which frowned dark and inscrutable upon me contain? A Briton or a Boer; a friend or a foe? Nor did this exhaust the possibilities. I had my seventy-five pounds in English notes in my pocket. If I revealed my identity, I thought that I could give reasonable assurance of a thousand. I might find some indifferent neutral-minded person who out of good nature or for a large sum of money would aid me in my bitter and desperate need. Certainly I would try to make what bargain I could now – now while I still had the strength to plead my cause and perhaps to extricate myself if the results were adverse. Still the odds were heavy against me, and it was with faltering and reluctant steps that I walked out of the shimmering gloom of the veldt into the light of the furnace fires, advanced towards the silent house, and struck with my fist upon the door.

There was a pause. Then I knocked again. And almost immediately a light sprang up above and an upper window opened.

'Wer ist da?' cried a man's voice.

I felt the shock of disappointment and consternation to my fingers.

'I want help; I have had an accident,' I replied.

Some muttering followed. Then I heard steps descending the stairs, the bolt of the door was drawn, the lock was turned. It was opened abruptly, and in the darkness of the passage a tall man hastily attired, with a pale face and dark moustache, stood before me.

'What do you want?' he said, this time in English.

I had now to think of something to say. I wanted above all to get into parley with this man, to get matters in such a state that instead of raising an alarm and summoning others he would discuss things quietly.

'I am a burgher,' I began. 'I have had an accident. I was going to join my commando at Komati Poort. I have fallen off the train. We were skylarking. I have been unconscious for hours. I think I have dislocated my shoulder.'

It is astonishing how one thinks of these things. This story leapt out as if I had learnt it by heart. Yet I had not the slightest idea what I was going to say or what the next sentence would be.

The stranger regarded me intently, and after some hesitation said at length, 'Well, come in.' He retreated a little into the darkness of the passage, threw open a door on one side of it, and pointed with his left hand into a dark room. I walked past him and entered, wondering if it was to be my prison. He followed, struck a light, lit a lamp, and set it on the table at the far side of which I stood. I was in a small room, evidently a dining room and office in one. I noticed besides the large table, a roll desk, two or three chairs, and one of those machines for making soda-water, consisting of two glass globes set one above the other and encased in thin wire-netting. On his end of the table my host had laid a revolver, which he had hitherto presumably been holding in his right hand.

'I think I'd like to know a little more about this railway accident of yours,' he said, after a considerable pause.

'I think,' I replied, 'I had better tell you the truth.'

'I think you had,' he said, slowly.

So I took the plunge and threw all I had upon the board.

'I am Winston Churchill, War Correspondent of the *Morning Post*. I escaped last night from Pretoria. I am making my way to the frontier.' (Making my way!) 'I have plenty of money. Will you help me?'

There was another long pause. My companion rose from the table slowly and locked the door. After this act, which struck me as unpromising, and was certainly ambiguous, he advanced upon me and suddenly held out his hand.

'Thank God you have come here! It is the only house for twenty miles where you would not have been handed over. But we are all British here, and we will see you through.'

It is easier to recall across the gulf of years the spasm of relief which swept over me, than it is to describe it. A moment before I had thought myself trapped; and now friends, food, resources, aid, were all at my disposal. I felt like a drowning man pulled out of the water and informed he has won the Derby!

My host now introduced himself as Mr. John Howard, manager of the Transvaal Collieries. He had become a naturalised burgher of the Transvaal some years before the war. But out of consideration for his British race and some inducements which he had offered to the local Field Cornet, he had not been called up to fight against the British. Instead he had been allowed to remain with one or two others on the mine, keeping it pumped out and in good order until coal cutting could be resumed. He had with him at the mine-head, besides his secretary, who was British, an engine-man from Lancashire and two Scottish miners. All these four were British subjects and had been allowed to remain only upon giving their parole to observe strict neutrality. He himself as burgher of the Transvaal Republic would be guilty of treason in harbouring me, and liable to be shot if caught at the time or found out later on.

'Never mind,' he said, 'we will fix it up somehow.' And added, 'The Field Cornet was round here this afternoon asking about you. They have got the hue and cry out all along the line and all over the district.'

I said that I did not wish to compromise him.

Let him give me food, a pistol, a guide, and if possible a pony, and I would make my own way to the sea, marching by night across country far away from the railway line or any habitation.

He would not hear of it. He would fix up something. But he enjoined the utmost caution. Spies were everywhere. He had two Dutch servant-maids actually sleeping in the house. There were many Kaffirs employed about the mine premises and on the pumping-machinery of the mine. Surveying these dangers, he became very thoughtful.

Then: 'But you are famishing.'

I did not contradict him. In a moment he had bustled off into the kitchen, telling me meanwhile to help myself from a whisky bottle and the soda-water machine which I have already mentioned. He returned after an interval with the best part of a cold leg of mutton and various other delectable commodities, and, leaving me to do full justice to these, quitted the room and let himself out of the house by a back door.

Nearly an hour passed before Mr. Howard returned. In this period my physical well-being had been brought into harmony with the improvement in my prospects. I felt confident of success and equal to anything.

'It's all right,' said Mr. Howard. 'I have seen the men, and they are all for it. We must put you down the pit tonight, and there you will have to stay till we can see how to get you out of the country. One difficulty,' he said, 'will be the skoff (food). The Dutch girl sees every mouthful I eat. The cook will want to know what has happened to her leg of mutton. I shall have to think it all out during the night. You must get down the pit at once. We'll make you comfortable enough.'

Accordingly, just as the dawn was breaking, I followed my host across a little yard into the enclosure in which stood the winding-wheel of the mine. Here a stout man, introduced as Mr. Dewsnap, of Oldham, locked my hand in a grip of crushing vigour.

'They'll all vote for you next time,' he whispered.

A door was opened and I entered the cage. Down we shot into the bowels of the earth. At the bottom of the mine were the two Scottish miners with lanterns and a big bundle which afterwards proved to be a mattress and blankets. We walked for some time through the pitchy labyrinth, with frequent turns, twists, and alterations of level, and finally stopped in a sort of chamber where the air was cool and fresh. Here my guide set down his bundle, and Mr. Howard handed me a couple of candles, a bottle of whisky, and a box of cigars.

'There's no difficulty about these,' he said. 'I keep them under lock and key. Now we must plan how to feed you tomorrow.'

'Don't you move from here, whatever happens,' was the parting injunction. 'There will be Kaffirs about the mine after daylight, but we shall be on the look-out that none of them wanders this way. None of them has seen anything so far.'

My four friends trooped off with their lanterns, and I was left alone. Viewed from the velvety darkness of the pit, life seemed bathed in rosy light. After the perplexity and even despair through which I had passed I counted upon freedom as certain. Instead of a humiliating recapture and long months of monotonous imprisonment, probably in the common jail, I saw myself once more rejoining the Army with a real exploit to my credit, and in that full enjoyment of freedom and keen pursuit of adventure dear to the heart of youth. In this comfortable mood, and speeded by intense fatigue, I soon slept the sleep of the weary – but of the triumphant.

'I BECAME FOR THE TIME QUITE FAMOUS'

On his arrival in Durban, Churchill discovered that he was suddenly famous. As he recalled in *My Early Life*:

I found that during the weeks I had been a prisoner of war my name had resounded at home. The part I had played in the armoured train had been exaggerated by the railway men and the wounded who had come back safely on the engine. The tale was transmitted to England with many crude or picturesque additions by the Press correspondents gathered at Estcourt. The papers had therefore been filled with extravagant praise of my behaviour. The news of my escape coming on the top of all this, after nine days' suspense and rumours of recapture, provoked another outburst of public eulogy.

Youth seeks Adventure. Journalism requires Advertisement. Certainly I had found both. I became for the time quite famous. The British nation was smarting under a series of military reverses such as are so often necessary to evoke the exercise of its strength, and the news of my outwitting the Boers was received with enormous and no doubt disproportionate satisfaction. This produced the inevitable reaction, and an undercurrent of disparagement, equally undeserved, began to mingle with the gushing tributes.

'AH, HORRIBLE WAR'

From Durban, Churchill travelled by train to Pietermaritzburg, where he rejoined the British Army as a lieutenant in the South African Light Horse. Once more, as in India and the Sudan, he found himself in action, sending detailed reports to the *Morning Post* after each battle; these were later reprinted in his book *London to Ladysmith via Pretoria*. On 22 January 1900 he reported on the aftermath of that week's battle:

> Then we searched the ground, finding ten dead or dying and twenty loose horses, ten dead and eight badly wounded men. The soldiers crowded round these last, covering them up with blankets or mackintoshes, propping their heads with saddles for pillows, and giving them water and biscuits from their bottles and haversacks.
>
> Anger had turned to pity in an instant. The desire to kill was gone. The desire to comfort replaced it. A little alert officer – Hubert Gough, now a captain, soon to command a regiment – came up to me. Two minutes before his eyes were bright and joyous with the excitement of the man hunt. He had galloped a mile – mostly under fire – to bring the reinforcements to surround the Boers. 'Bag the lot, you know.' Now he was very sad. 'There's a poor boy dying up there – only a boy, and so cold – who's got a blanket?' So the soldiers succoured the Boer wounded, and we told the prisoners that they would be shown courtesy and kindness worthy of brave men and a famous quarrel. The Boer dead were collected and a flag of truce was sent to the enemy's lines to invite a burying and identification party at dawn.
>
> I have often seen dead men, killed in war – thousands at Omdurman – scores elsewhere, black and white, but the Boer dead aroused the most painful emotions. Here by the rock under which he had fought lay the Field Cornet of Heilbronn, Mr de Mentz – a grey-haired man of over sixty years, with firm aquiline features and a short beard. The stony face was grimly calm, but it bore the stamp of unalterable resolve; the look of a man who had thought it all out, and was quite certain that his cause was just, and such as a sober citizen might give his life for.

Nor was I surprised when the Boer prisoners told me that Mentz had refused all suggestions of surrender, and that when his left leg was smashed by a bullet he had continued to load and fire until he bled to death; and they found him, pale and bloodless, holding his wife's letter in his hand. Beside him was a boy of about seventeen shot through the heart. Further on lay our own two poor riflemen with their heads smashed like eggshells; and I suppose they had mothers or wives far away at the end of the deep-sea cables. Ah, horrible war, amazing medley of the glorious and the squalid, the pitiful and the sublime, if modern men of light and leading saw your face closer, simple folk would see it hardly ever.

'WE WERE NEARLY THROUGH THE DANGEROUS GROUND'

On 28 February 1900, Churchill was among the first British soldiers to enter Ladysmith, which had been besieged by the Boer forces for four months. Churchill's report to the *Morning Post* was published on March 3 (and later reprinted in his book *London to Ladysmith via Pretoria*):

Never shall I forget that ride. The evening was deliciously cool. My horse was strong and fresh, for I had changed him at midday. The ground was rough with many stones, but we cared little for that. Beyond the next ridge, or the rise beyond that, or around the corner of the hill, was Ladysmith – the goal of all our hopes and ambitions during weeks of almost ceaseless fighting. Ladysmith – the centre of the world's attention, the scene of famous deeds, the cause of mighty efforts – Ladysmith was within our reach at last. We were going to be inside the town within an hour.

The excitement of the moment was increased by the exhilaration of the gallop. Onward wildly, recklessly, up and down hill, over the boulders through the scrub, Hubert Gough with his two squadrons,

Mackenzie's Natal Carabineers and the Imperial Light Horse, were clear of the ridges already. We turned the shoulder of a hill, and there before us lay the tin houses and dark trees we had come so far to see and save. The British guns on Caesar's Camp were firing steadily in spite of the twilight.

What was happening? Never mind, we were nearly through the dangerous ground. Now we were all on the flat. Brigadier, staff, and troops let their horses go. We raced through the thorn bushes by Intombi Spruit. Suddenly there was a challenge. 'Halt, who goes there?' 'The Ladysmith Relief Column', and thereat from out of trenches and rifle pits artfully concealed in the scrub a score of tattered men came running, cheering feebly, and some were crying. In the half-light they looked ghastly pale and thin. A poor, white-faced officer waved his helmet to and fro, and laughed foolishly, and the tall, strong colonial horsemen, standing up in their stirrups, raised a loud resounding cheer, for then we knew we had reached the Ladysmith picket line.

'REVENGE MAY BE SWEET, BUT IT IS ALSO MOST EXPENSIVE'

In an article published in the *Natal Witness* on 29 March 1900, Churchill reflected on the demand in Britain for revenge against the Boer enemy:

A cry, growing into a clamouring, which I can perfectly understand, has arisen that stern retribution should be meted out to these guilty and miserable people. I read your newspapers and the reports of recent meetings industriously and all reveal the same spirit. 'Give them a lesson they will never forget.' 'Make an example.' 'Condign punishment.' 'Our turn now.' These are the phrases or ideas which recur. It is the spirit of revenge. It is wrong, first of all because it is morally wicked; and secondly because it is practically foolish. Revenge may be sweet, but it is also most expensive.

While we continue to prosecute the war with tireless energy and remorselessly beat down all who resist – to the last man if necessary – we must also make it easy for the enemy to accept defeat. We must tempt as well as compel. On the one hand the Dutchman may see vast armies equipped with all the terrible machinery of war advancing irresistibly; on the other the quiet tin-roofed farm half buried in the trees far from the roar of conflict and the dread of death.

'BARREN SPOILS'

In an article published in the *Morning Post* on 31 March 1900, Churchill warned his fellow-Britons against the demand for revenge against the Boers. His warning ended:

Lastly, beware of driving men to desperation: even a cornered rat is dangerous.

We desire a speedy peace, and the last thing we want is that this war should enter on a guerrilla phase.

Those who demand 'an eye for an eye and a tooth for a tooth' should ask themselves whether such barren spoils are worth five years' bloody partisan warfare.

Peace and happiness can only come to South Africa through the union and concord of the Dutch and British races, who must for ever live side by side under the supremacy of Great Britain.

We have fought this war because it was certain that as long as the Boer Republics existed their malignant influence would prevent all fusion.

The Boer Republics, and with them the dream of Dutch dominion, will soon have vanished into the shades of the past.

Already we may see a nobler and wealthier South Africa, serene and prosperous in the sunlight of peace.

'I HAVE ZEALOUSLY TRIED TO AVOID ALL DANGER'

Churchill's many near-escapes from death, including in three savage wars – in India, Sudan and South Africa – led him to sombre reflection on the dangers he had faced and his own survival. While serving as a war correspondent with General Sir Ian Hamilton's army in South Africa, he had an experience of which he wrote to his mother: 'I do not think I have ever been so near destruction.' He described his reflections, and the incident itself, in one of his letters to the *Morning Post*:

Whether I am to see the white cliffs of Dover again I know not, nor will I attempt to predict. But it seems that my fortunes in this land are to be a succession of adventures and escapes, any one of which would suffice for a personal experience of the campaign. I acquit myself of all desire to seek for these. Indeed, I have zealously tried to avoid all danger except what must attend a War Correspondent's precarious existence. This I recognise as a necessary evil, for the lot of the writer in the field is a hard and heavy one. 'All the danger of war and one-half per cent, the glory': such is our motto, and that is the reason why we expect large salaries. But these hazards swoop on me out of a cloudless sky, and that I have hitherto come unscathed through them, while it fills my heart with thankfulness to God for His mercies, makes me wonder why I must be so often thrust to the brink and then withdrawn.

[···]

Churchill then described the episode:

We arrived at a wire fence 100 yards – to be accurate, 120 yards – from the crest of the kopje, dismounted, and, cutting the wire, were about to seize the precious rocks when – as I had seen them in the railway cutting at Frere, grim, hairy, and terrible – the heads and shoulders of a dozen Boers appeared; and how many more must be close behind them?

41

There was a queer, almost inexplicable, pause, or perhaps there was no pause at all; but I seem to remember much happening. First the Boers – one fellow with a long, drooping, black beard, and a chocolate-coloured coat, another with a red scarf round his neck. Two scouts cutting the wire fence stupidly. One man taking aim across his horse, and McNeill's voice, quite steady: 'Too late; back to the other kopje. Gallop!'

Then the musketry crashed out, and the 'swish' and 'whirr' of the bullets filled the air. I put my foot in the stirrup. The horse, terrified at the firing, plunged wildly. I tried to spring into the saddle; it turned under the animal's belly. He broke away, and galloped madly off. Most of the scouts were already 200 yards off. I was alone, dismounted, within the closest range, and a mile at least from cover of any kind.

One consolation I had – my pistol. I could not be hunted down unarmed in the open as I had been before. But a disabling wound was the brightest prospect. I turned, and, for the second time in this war, ran for my life on foot from the Boer marksmen, and I thought to myself, 'Here at last I take it.' Suddenly, as I ran, I saw a scout. He came from the left, across my front; a tall man, with skull and cross-bones badge, and on a pale horse. Death in Revelation, but life to me.

I shouted to him as he passed: 'Give me a stirrup.' To my surprise he stopped at once. 'Yes,' he said shortly. I ran up to him, did not bungle in the business of mounting, and in a moment found myself behind him on the saddle.

Then we rode. I put my arms round him to catch a grip of the mane. My hand became soaked with blood. The horse was hard hit; but, gallant beast, he extended himself nobly. The pursuing bullets piped and whistled – for the range was growing longer – overhead.

'Don't be frightened,' said my rescuer; 'they won't hit you.' Then, as I did not reply, 'My poor horse, oh, my poor horse; shot with an explosive bullet. The devils! But their hour will come. Oh, my poor horse!'

I said, 'Never mind, you've saved my life.' 'Ah,' he rejoined, 'but it's the horse I'm thinking about.' That was the whole of our conversation.

Judging from the number of bullets I heard I did not expect to be hit after the first 500 yards were covered, for a galloping horse is a difficult target, and the Boers were breathless and excited. But it was with a feeling of relief that I turned the corner of the further kopje and found I had thrown double sixes again.

'THE RESULTS WERE SUBSTANTIAL'

Churchill left South Africa, and soldiering, on 7 July 1900. Two weeks later he was back in England, and five days after that he was adopted as the prospective Conservative candidate for Oldham at the coming General Election. He was determined to reverse his narrow defeat there in July 1899. There was great excitement during his election speech at the Theatre Royal: after he had described how Mr Dewsnap of Oldham had wound him down the mine seven months earlier, the audience shouted 'His wife's in the gallery!', whereupon, as Churchill recalled, there was 'general jubilation'.

On 1 October 1900, Churchill was elected to Parliament. Then, five weeks before his twenty-sixth birthday, he embarked on an extended lecture tour of Britain, the United States and Canada, talking about his South African experiences. His British tour was in two parts, from 25 October to 30 November 1900, and from 5 March to 8 May 1901 (see Map 12). While in Washington, he was invited to the White House to meet President McKinley – who was soon afterwards to be assassinated. In *My Early Life* Churchill recalled:

For five weeks I had what seemed to me a triumphal progress through the country. The party managers selected the critical seats, and quite a lot of victories followed in my train. I was twenty-six. Was it wonderful that I should have thought I had arrived? But luckily life is not so easy as all that: otherwise we should get to the end too quickly.

There seemed however to be still two important steps to be taken. The first was to gather sufficient money to enable me to concentrate my attention upon politics without having to do any other work. The sales of *The River War* and of my two books of war correspondence from South Africa, together with the ten months' salary amounting to £2,500 from the *Morning Post*, had left me in possession of more than

£4,000. An opportunity of increasing this reserve was now at hand. I had planned to lecture all the autumn and winter at home and in America.

The English tour began as soon as the election was over. Having already spoken every night for five weeks, I had now to undergo two and a half months of similar labours interrupted only by the week's voyage across the ocean. The lectures in England were successful. Lord Wolseley presided over the first, and the greatest personages in the three kingdoms on both sides of politics took the chair as I moved from one city to another. All the largest halls were crowded with friendly audiences to whom, aided by a magic lantern, I unfolded my adventures and escape, all set in the general framework of the war. I hardly ever earned less than £100 a night, and often much more. At the Philharmonic Hall in Liverpool I gathered over £300. Altogether in the month of November I banked safely over £4,500, having toured little more than half of Great Britain.

Parliament was to meet in the opening days of December, and I longed to take my seat in the House of Commons. I had however instead, to cross the Atlantic to fulfil my engagements. A different atmosphere prevailed in the United States. I was surprised to find that many of these amiable and hospitable Americans who spoke the same language and seemed in essentials very like ourselves, were not nearly so excited about the South African War as we were at home. Moreover a great many of them thought the Boers were in the right; and the Irish everywhere showed themselves actively hostile.

The audiences varied from place to place. At Baltimore only a few hundreds assembled in a hall which would have held 5,000. At Boston, on the other hand, an enormous pro-British demonstration was staged, and even the approaches to the Fremont Hall were thronged. The platform here was composed of 300 Americans in red uniforms belonging to an Anglo-American Society, and the aspect of the meeting was magnificent. In Chicago I encountered vociferous opposition. However, when I made a few jokes against myself, and paid a sincere tribute to the courage and humanity of the Boers, they were placated. On the whole I found it easy to make friends with American audiences. They were cool and critical, but also urbane and good-natured.

Throughout my journeyings I received the help of eminent Americans. Mr. Bourke Cockran, Mr. Chauncey Depew, and other leading politicians presided, and my opening lecture in New York was under the auspices of no less a personage than 'Mark Twain' himself. I was thrilled by this famous companion of my youth. He was now very old and snow-white, and combined with a noble air a most delightful style of conversation. Of course we argued about the war. After some interchanges I found myself beaten back to the citadel 'My country right or wrong'. 'Ah', said the old gentleman, 'When the poor country is fighting for its life, I agree. But this was not your case.' I think however I did not displease him; for he was good enough at my request to sign every one of the thirty volumes of his works for my benefit; and in the first volume he inscribed the following maxim intended, I daresay, to convey a gentle admonition: 'To do good is noble; to teach others to do good is nobler, and no trouble.'

All this quiet tolerance changed when we crossed the Canadian border. Here again were present the enthusiastic throngs to which I had so easily accustomed myself at home. Alas, I could only spend ten days in these inspiring scenes. In the middle of January I returned home and resumed my tour of our cities. I visited every one of them. When I spoke in the Ulster Hall, the venerable Lord Dufferin introduced me. No one could turn a compliment so well as he. I can hear him now saying with his old-fashioned pronunciation, 'And this young man – at an age when many of his contemporaries have hardly left their studies – has seen more active service than half the general *officers* in Europe.' I had not thought of this before. It was good.

When my tour came to an end in the middle of February, I was exhausted. For more than five months I had spoken for an hour or more almost every night except Sundays, and often twice a day, and had travelled without ceasing, usually by night, rarely sleeping twice in the same bed. And this had followed a year of marching and fighting with rarely a roof or a bed at all. But the results were substantial. I had in my possession nearly £10,000. I was entirely independent and had no need to worry about the future, or for many years to work at anything but politics.

'WE HAVE NO CAUSE TO BE ASHAMED'

Churchill had been elected to Parliament on 1 October 1900. He took his seat in the House of Commons, on the Conservative benches, on 14 February 1901. He was twenty-six years old. Four days later, he made his maiden speech, during a debate on the conduct of the Boer War. Churchill's words, the *Morning Post* reported, were listened to by an audience 'which very few members have commanded', including two future Liberal Prime Ministers, Henry Campbell-Bannerman and H. H. Asquith, under both of whom Churchill would later serve. Churchill spoke immediately after one of the war's principal parliamentary critics, the young Liberal MP David Lloyd George:

> I understood that the hon. Member to whose speech the House has just listened, had intended to move an Amendment to the Address. The text of the Amendment, which had appeared in the papers, was singularly mild and moderate in tone; but mild and moderate as it was, neither the hon. Member nor his political friends had cared to expose it to criticism or to challenge a division upon it, and, indeed, when we compare the moderation of the Amendment with the very bitter speech which the hon. Member has just delivered, it is difficult to avoid the conclusion that the moderation of the Amendment was the moderation of the hon. Member's political friends and leaders, and that the bitterness of his speech is all his own.
>
> It has been suggested to me that it might perhaps have been better, upon the whole, if the hon. Member, instead of making his speech without moving his Amendment, had moved his Amendment without making his speech. I would not complain of any remarks of the hon. Member were I called upon to do so.
>
> In my opinion, based upon the experience of the most famous men whose names have adorned the records of the House, no national emergency short, let us say, of the actual invasion of this country itself ought in any way to restrict or prevent the entire freedom of Parliamentary discussion. Moreover, I do not believe that the Boers would attach particular importance to the utterances of the hon. Member. No people in the world received so much verbal

sympathy and so little practical support as the Boers.

If I were a Boer fighting in the field – and if I were a Boer I hope I should be fighting in the field – I would not allow myself to be taken in by any message of sympathy, not even if it were signed by a hundred hon. Members.

The hon. Member dwelt at great length upon the question of farm burning. I do not propose to discuss the ethics of farm burning now; but hon. Members should, I think, cast their eyes back to the fact that no considerations of humanity prevented the German army from throwing its shells into dwelling houses in Paris, and starving the inhabitants of that great city to the extent that they had to live upon rats and like atrocious foods in order to compel the garrison to surrender.

I venture to think His Majesty's Government would not have been justified in restricting their commanders in the field from any methods of warfare which are justified by precedents set by European and American generals during the last fifty or sixty years. I do not agree very fully with the charges of treachery on the one side and barbarity on the other. From what I saw of the war – and I sometimes saw something of it – I believe that as compared with other wars, especially those in which a civil population took part, this war in South Africa has been on the whole carried on with unusual humanity and generosity.

The hon. Member for Carnarvon Boroughs has drawn attention to the case of one general officer, and although I deprecate debates upon the characters of individual general officers who are serving the country at this moment, because I know personally General Bruce Hamilton, whom the hon. Member with admirable feeling described as General Brute Hamilton, I feel unable to address the House without offering my humble testimony to the fact that in all His Majesty's Army there are few men with better feeling, more kindness of heart, or with higher courage than General Bruce Hamilton.

There is a point of difference which has been raised by the right hon. Gentleman the Leader of the Opposition upon the question of the policy to be pursued in South Africa after this war has been brought to a conclusion. So far as I have been able to make out the difference between the Government and the Opposition on this question is that whereas His Majesty's Government propose that when hostilities are brought to a conclusion there shall be an interval of civil government before full representative rights are extended to the peoples of these countries, on the other hand the right hon. Gentleman the Leader of the Opposition believes that these representative institutions will be more quickly obtained if the military government be prolonged as a temporary measure and no interval of civil government be interposed. I hope I am not misinterpreting the right hon. Gentleman in any way. If I am, I trust he will not hesitate to correct me, because I should be very sorry in any way to misstate his views. If that is the situation, I will respectfully ask the House to allow me to examine these alternative propositions.

I do not wish myself to lay down the law, or thrust my views upon hon. Members. I have travelled a good deal about South Africa during the last ten months under varying circumstances, and I should like to lay before the House some of the considerations which have been very forcibly borne in upon me during that period.

In the first place I would like to look back to the original cause for which we went to war. We went to war – I mean of course we were gone to war with – in connection with the extension of the franchise. We began negotiations with the Boers in order to extend the franchise to the people of the Transvaal. When I say the people of the Transvaal, I mean the whole people of the Transvaal, and not necessarily those who arrived there first. At that time there were nearly two and a half times as many British and non-Dutch as there were Boers, but during the few weeks before the outbreak of the war every train was crowded with British subjects who were endeavouring to escape from the approaching conflict, and so it was that the Uitlanders were scattered all over the world.

It seems to me that when the war is over we ought not to forget the original object with which we undertook the negotiations which led to the war. If I may lay down anything I would ask the House to establish the principle that they ought not to extend any representative institutions to the people of the Transvaal until such time as the population has regained its ordinary level. What could be more dangerous, ridiculous or futile, than to throw the responsible government of a ruined country on that remnant of the population, that particular section of the population, which is actively hostile to the fundamental institutions of the State? I think there ought to be no doubt and no difference of opinion on the point that between the firing of the last shot and the casting of the first vote there must be an appreciable interval. I invite the House to consider which form of government – civil government or military government – is most likely to be conducive to the restoration of the banished prosperity of the country and most likely to encourage the return of the population now scattered far and wide. I understand that there are hon. Members who are in hopes that representative institutions may directly follow military government, but I think they cannot realise thoroughly how very irksome such military government is.

I have the greatest respect for British officers, and when I hear them attacked, as some hon. Members have done in their speeches, it makes me very sorry, and very angry too. Although I regard British officers in the field of war, and in dealing with native races, as the best officers in the world, I do not believe that either their training or their habits of thought qualify them to exercise arbitrary authority over civil populations of European race.

I have often myself been very much ashamed to see respectable old Boer farmers – the Boer is a curious combination of the squire and the peasant, and under the rough coat of the farmer there are very often to be found the instincts of the squire – I have been ashamed to see such men ordered about peremptorily by young subaltern officers, as if they were private soldiers. I do not hesitate to say that as long as you have anything like direct military government there will be no revival of trade, no return of the Uitlander population, no influx of immigrants from other parts of the world – nothing but despair and discontent on the part of the Boer population, and growing resentment on the part of our own British settlers.

If there was a system of civil government on the other hand, which I think we have an absolute moral right to establish if only from the fact that this country through the Imperial Exchequer will have to provide the money – if you had a civil government under such an administrator as Sir Alfred Milner – [Cries of 'Hear, hear,' and 'Oh'] – it is not for me to eulogise that distinguished administrator, I am sure he enjoys the confidence of the whole of the Conservative Party, and there are a great many Members on the other side of the House who do not find it convenient in their own minds to disregard Sir Alfred Milner's deliberate opinion on South African affairs.

As soon as it is known that there is in the Transvaal a government under which property and liberty are secure, so soon as it is known that in these countries one can live freely and safely, there would be a rush of immigrants from all parts of the world to develop the country and to profit by the great revival of trade which usually follows war of all kinds. If I may judge by my own experience there are many Members of this House who have received letters from their constituents asking whether it was advisable to go out to South Africa. When this policy of immigration is well advanced we shall again have the great majority of the people of the Transvaal firmly attached and devoted to the Imperial connection, and when you can extend representative institutions to them you will find them reposing securely upon the broad basis of the consent of the governed, while the rights of the minority will be effectively protected and preserved by the tactful and judicious intervention of the Imperial authority. May I say that it was this prospect of a loyal and Anglicised Transvaal turning the scale in our favour in South Africa, which must have been the original 'good hope' from which the Cape has taken its name.

It is not for me to criticise the proposals which come from such a distinguished authority as the Leader of the Opposition, but I find it impossible not to say that in comparing these two alternative plans one with the other I must proclaim my strong preference for the course His Majesty's Government propose to adopt. I pass now from the question of the ultimate settlement of the two late Republics to the immediate necessities of the situation. What ought to be the present policy of the Government? I take it that there is a pretty general consensus of opinion in this House that it ought to be to make it easy and honourable for the Boers to surrender, and painful and perilous for them to continue in the field. Let the Government proceed on both those lines concurrently and at full speed.

I sympathise very heartily with my hon. friend the senior Member for Oldham, who, in a speech delivered last year, showed great anxiety that everything should be done to make the Boers understand exactly what terms were offered to them, and I earnestly hope that the right hon. Gentleman the Colonial Secretary will leave nothing undone to bring home to those brave and unhappy men who are fighting in the field that whenever they are prepared to recognise that their small independence must be merged in the larger liberties of the British Empire, there will be a full guarantee for the security of their property and religion, an assurance of equal rights, a promise of representative institutions, and last of all, but not least of all, what the British Army would most readily accord to a brave and enduring foe – all the honours of war. I hope the right hon. Gentleman will not allow himself to be discouraged by any rebuffs which his envoys may meet with, but will persevere in endeavouring to bring before these people the conditions on which at any moment they may obtain peace and the friendship of Great Britain. Of course, we can only promise, and it rests with the Boers whether they will accept our conditions. They may refuse the generous terms offered them, and stand or fall by their old cry, 'Death or independence!' [Nationalist cheers.]

I do not see anything to rejoice at in that prospect, because if it be so, the war will enter upon a very sad and gloomy phase. If the Boers remain deaf to the voice of reason, and blind to the hand of friendship, if they refuse all overtures and disdain all terms, then, while we cannot help admiring their determination and endurance, we can only hope that our own race, in the pursuit of what they feel to be a righteous cause, will show determination as strong and endurance as lasting.

It is wonderful that hon. Members who form the Irish party should find it in their hearts to speak and act as they do in regard to a war in which so much has been accomplished by the courage, the sacrifices, and, above all, by the military capacity of Irishmen. There is a practical reason, which I trust hon. Members will not think it presumptuous in me to bring to their notice, which is that they would be well advised cordially to co-operate with His Majesty's Government in bringing the war to a speedy conclusion, because they must know that no Irish question or agitation can possibly take any hold on the imagination of the people of Great Britain so long as all our thoughts are with the soldiers who are fighting in South Africa.

What are the military measures we ought to take? I have no doubt that other opportunities will be presented to the House to discuss them, but so far as I have been able to understand the whispers I have heard in the air there are, on the whole, considerable signs of possible improvement in the South African situation. There are appearances that the Boers are weakening, and that the desperate and feverish efforts they have made so long cannot be indefinitely sustained. If that be so, now is the time for the Government and the Army to redouble their efforts. It is incumbent on Members like myself, who represent large working class constituencies, to bring home to the Government the fact that the country does not want to count the cost of the war until it is won. I think we all rejoiced to see the announcement in the papers that 30,000 more mounted men were being despatched to South Africa. I cannot help noticing with intense satisfaction that, not content with sending large numbers of men, the Secretary of State for War has found some excellent Indian officers, prominent among whom is Sir Bindon Blood, who will go out to South Africa and bring their knowledge of guerilla warfare on the Indian frontier to bear on the peculiar kind of warfare – I will not call it guerilla warfare – now going on in South Africa. I shall always indulge the hope that, great as these preparations are, they will not be all, and that some fine afternoon the Secretary of State for War will come down to the House with a brand-new scheme, not only for sending all the reinforcements necessary for keeping the Army up to a fixed standard of 250,000 men, in spite of the losses by battle and disease, but also for increasing it by a regular monthly quota of 2,000 or 3,000 men, so that the Boers will be compelled, with ever-diminishing resources, to make head against ever-increasing difficulties, and will not only be exposed to the beating of the waves, but to the force of the rising tide.

Some hon. Members have seen fit, either in this place or else-where, to stigmatise this war as a war of greed. I regret that I feel bound to repudiate that pleasant suggestion. If there were persons who rejoiced in this war, and went out with hopes of excitement or the lust of conflict, they have had enough and more than enough to-day. If, as the hon. Member for Northampton has several times suggested, certain capitalists spent money in bringing on this war in the hope that it would increase the value of their mining properties, they know now that they made an uncommonly bad bargain. With the mass of the nation, with the whole people of the country, this war from beginning to end has only been a war of duty. They believe, and they have shown in the most remarkable manner that they believe, that His Majesty's Government and the Colonial Secretary have throughout been actuated by the same high and patriotic motives. They know that no other inspiration could sustain and animate the Regulars and Volunteers, who through all these hard months have had to bear the brunt of the public contention. They may indeed have to regret, as I myself have, the loss of a great many good friends in the war. We cannot help feeling sorry for many of the incidents of the war, but for all that I do not find it possible on reflection to accuse the general policy which led to the war; we have no cause to be ashamed of anything that has passed during the war, nor have we any right to be doleful or lugubrious.

I think if any hon. Members are feeling unhappy about the state of affairs in South Africa I would recommend them a receipt from which I myself derived much exhilaration. Let them look to the other great dependencies and colonies of the British Empire and see what the effect of the war has been there. Whatever we may have lost in doubtful friends in Cape Colony we have gained ten times, or perhaps twenty times, over in Canada and Australia, where the people – down to the humblest farmer in the most distant provinces – have by their effective participation in the conflict been able to realise, as they never could realise before, that they belong to the Empire, and that the Empire belongs to them.

I cannot sit down without saying how very grateful I am for the kindness and patience with which the House has heard me, and which have been extended to me, I well know, not on my own account, but because of a certain splendid memory which many hon. Members still preserve.

'THE WARS OF PEOPLES WILL BE MORE TERRIBLE THAN THOSE OF KINGS'

On 13 May 1901, to the alarm of his own Conservative Party leaders, Churchill spoke critically in the House of Commons of the Conservative Government's desire to raise the size of the British Army:

> We must not regard war with a modern Power as a kind of game in which we may take a hand, and with good luck and good management may play adroitly for an evening and come safe home with our winnings. It is not that, and I rejoice that it cannot be that. A European war cannot be anything but a cruel, heart-rending struggle, which, if we are ever to enjoy the bitter fruits of victory, must demand, perhaps for several years, the whole manhood of the nation, the entire suspension of peaceful industries, and the concentrating to one end of every vital energy in the community.
>
> I have frequently been astonished since I have been in this House to hear with what composure and how glibly Members, and even Ministers, talk of a European war. I will not expatiate on the horrors of war, but there has been a great change which the House should not omit to notice. In former days, when wars arose from individual causes, from the policy of a Minister or the passion of a King, when they were fought by small regular armies of professional soldiers, and when their course was retarded by the difficulties of communication and supply, and often suspended by the winter season, it was possible to limit the liabilities of the combatants. But now, when mighty populations are impelled on each other, each individual severally embittered and inflamed, when the resources of science and civilisation sweep away everything that might mitigate their fury, a European war can only end in the ruin of the vanquished and the scarcely less fatal commercial dislocation and exhaustion of the conquerors. Democracy is more vindictive than Cabinets. The wars of peoples will be more terrible than those of kings.

[· · ·]

Foreign nations know what war is. There is scarcely a capital in Europe which has not been taken in the last one hundred years, and it is the lively realisation of the awful consequences of war which maintains the peace of Europe. We do not know what war is. We have had a glimpse of it in South Africa. Even in miniature it is hideous and appalling; but, for all our experience, war to us does not mean what it means to the Frenchman, or the German, or the Austrian. Are we not arming ourselves with their weapons without being under their restraints?

What I fear is that these three costly and beautiful army corps which are to be kept ready almost at a moment's notice for foreign war will develop in the country, if they need developing, feelings of pride and power, which will not only be founded in actual military superiority, but also on the appearance of it. And in these days, when popular newspapers, appealing with authority to countless readers, are prepared almost every morning to urge us into war against one or other and sometimes several of the Great Powers of the earth, surely we ought not to make it seem so easy, and even attractive, to embark on such terrible enterprises, or to think that with the land forces at our disposal we may safely intermeddle in the European game?

'NEVER TO LET THE WAR PASS OUT OF YOUR MINDS FOR A DAY'

On 4 October 1901, in a speech at Saddleworth in Yorkshire, Churchill criticised the public lack of interest in the continuing war in South Africa. President McKinley, whom Churchill had met in Washington less than a year earlier, had died on September 14, eight days after being shot by an anarchist. Churchill's remarks were reported by a local newspaper:

Now there is a most perilous apathy. We seem to regard the war as chronic. Public attention is often diverted from it. The visit of an Emperor to a neighbouring State, the murder of a President on the other side of the Atlantic; yes, even such things as the racing of pleasure yachts, turn the minds of thousands from the great public undertaking which we are pledged to carry through.

Gentlemen, I appeal to you never to let the war pass out of your minds for a day. Think what it means to us all. Friends, brothers, or sons, fighting and toiling, ragged and hungry, while the weeks pass by, while summer grows out of spring, and autumn withers into winter. How many are there here to-night who may look in the newspaper tomorrow morning to find, as I found last week, some familiar name, and learn that some bright eye known and trusted is closed for ever.

Then there is the money, the wealth of the nation, draining away, drip, drip, drip – enough to buy every month four of the largest battleships in the world. There is India. Nearly thirty thousand men detained beyond their contract with the State, impatiently await relief in India.

Every day increases the strain on your military organisation, and the embarrassment of your finances. The loyal districts of South Africa sicken in the grip of martial law; the gulf of hatred between Boer and Briton grows wider; and every day devastation and ruin rule over larger areas.

Surely, if ever a supreme effort were needed to terminate or curtail this time of trouble, it is needed now.

'AN ENGLAND OF WISE MEN'

On 31 May 1904, disillusioned with many aspects of Conservative Party policy – above all the party's move away from Free Trade to Protection and Tariffs – Churchill crossed the floor of the House of Commons and took his place on the Liberal Party benches. In the General Election held over several weeks in January 1906 he was elected to Parliament, on January 13, for a Liberal Party constituency, Manchester North-West. That year, eleven years after his father's death, saw the publication of Churchill's two-volume biography *Lord Randolph Churchill*, in which he expressed his own feelings about party politics:

Lord Randolph Churchill's name will not be recorded upon the bead-roll of either party. The Conservatives, whose forces he so greatly strengthened, the Liberals, some of whose finest principles he notably sustained, must equally regard his life and work with mingled feelings. A politician's character and position are measured in his day by party standards. When he is dead, all that he achieved in the name of party, is at an end. The eulogies and censures of partisans are powerless to affect his ultimate reputation. The scales wherein he was weighed are broken. The years to come bring weights and measures of their own.

There is an England which stretches far beyond the well-drilled masses who are assembled by party machinery to salute with appropriate acclamation the utterances of their recognised fuglemen; an England of wise men who gaze without self-deception at the failings and follies of both political parties; of brave and earnest men who find in neither faction fair scope for the effort that is in them; of 'poor men' who increasingly doubt the sincerity of party philanthropy. It was to that England that Lord Randolph Churchill appealed; it was that England he so nearly won; it is by that England he will be justly judged.

'THE CAUSE OF THE POOR AND THE WEAK ALL OVER THE WORLD'

Following the Liberal Party victory at the General Election of January 1906, the new Prime Minister, Sir Henry Campbell-Bannerman, invited Churchill to enter the Government as Under-Secretary of State for the Colonies. He was thirty-one years old. Given the task of introducing responsible government to both the Transvaal Colony and the Orange River Colony – the defeated Boer republics – he introduced the respective measures to Parliament after copious and diligent preparation. Presenting the Transvaal Bill to the House of Commons on 31 July 1906, he said of the Liberal and Conservative Parties' roles in the measure: 'We can only make it the gift of Party.

They can make it the gift of England.' On 17 December 1906, Churchill introduced the Orange Free State Bill, telling the House:

> By the Treaty of Vereeniging, Great Britain promised full self-government to the peoples of the two Boer Republics which had been conquered and annexed as the result of the war. This intention of giving responsible government did not arise out of the terms of peace, although it is, of course, solemnly expressed in them. It has always been the settled and successful colonial policy of this country during the last fifty years to allow great liberties of self-government to distant communities under the Crown, and no responsible statesman and no British Cabinet, so far as I know, ever contemplated any other solution of the South African problem but that of full self-government.
>
> The idea which I have seen put forward in some quarters, that in order to get full satisfaction for the expense and the exertions to which we were put in the war we are bound to continue governing those peoples according to our pleasure and against their will, and that that is, as it were, an agreeable exercise which is to be compensation for our labours, is an idea which no doubt finds expression in the columns of newspapers, but to which I do not think any serious person ever gave any countenance. No, Sir, the ultimate object was not lost sight of even in the height of the war, namely, the bestowal of full self-government; and as all parties were agreed that some interval for reconstruction must necessarily intervene, the only questions at issue between us have been questions of manner and questions of time.
>
> [...]
>
> We have tried in South Africa to deal fairly between man and man, to adjust conflicting interests and overlapping claims. We have tried so far as possible to effect a broad-bottomed settlement of the question which should command the assent of people even beyond the great party groupings which support us. We do not ask hon. Gentlemen opposite to share our responsibility. All we ask of the Opposition is not to add to our difficulties, but to give the policy which has been determined on as good a chance as possible

of success. The responsibilities of the Government are heavy. They now pass in a large measure to the members of the new Parliaments. Other liberties besides their own will be enshrined in those Parliaments.

The people of these Colonies, and, in a special measure, the Boers, will become the trustees of freedom all over the world. We have tried to act with fairness and good feeling. If by any chance our counsels of reconciliation should come to nothing, if our policy should end in mocking disaster, then the resulting evil would not be confined to South Africa.

Our unfortunate experience would be trumpeted forth all over the world wherever despotism wanted a good argument for bayonets, whenever an arbitrary Government wished to deny or curtail the liberties of imprisoned nationalities.

But if, on the other hand, as we hope and profoundly believe, better days are in store for South Africa, if the long lane which it has been travelling has reached its turning at last, if the words of President Brand, 'All shall come right', are at length to be fulfilled, and if the near future should unfold to our eyes a tranquil, prosperous, consolidated Afrikaner nation under the protecting ægis of the British crown, then, I say, the good as well as the evil will not be confined to South Africa; then, I say, the cause of the poor and the weak all over the world will have been sustained; and everywhere small peoples will get more room to breathe, and everywhere great empires will be encouraged by our example to step forward – and it only needs a step – into the sunshine of a more gentle and a more generous age.

'TIME TO SEE THEIR HOMES BY DAYLIGHT'

On 8 April 1908, H. H. Asquith succeeded Campbell-Bannerman as Prime Minister of the Liberal administration. On the following day, at the age of thirty-three, Churchill entered the Cabinet as President of the Board of Trade, responsible for social policy. On 6 July 1908, introducing a Bill in the House of Commons to reduce working hours in the coal mines, he set out his social philosophy:

> The general march of industrial democracy is not towards inadequate hours of work, but towards sufficient hours of leisure. That is the movement among the working people all over the country. They are not content that their lives should remain mere alternations between bed and the factory. They demand time to look about them, time to see their homes by daylight, to see their children, time to think and read and cultivate their gardens – time, in short, to live. That is very strange, perhaps, but that is the request they have made and are making with increasing force and reason as years pass by.
>
> No one is to be pitied for having to work hard, for nature has contrived a special reward for the man who works hard. It gives him an extra relish, which enables him to gather in a brief space from simple pleasures a satisfaction in search of which the social idler wanders vainly through the twenty-four hours. But this reward, so precious in itself, is snatched away from the man who has won it, if the hours of his labour be too severe to leave any time for him to enjoy what he has won.

'HUMANITY WILL NOT BE CAST DOWN'

Under the rules of that time, a newly appointed Cabinet Minister had to seek re-election. Churchill duly did so, and just six days after his appointment, on April 14, was defeated in his own constituency, Manchester North-West. In order to take up his Cabinet post, he needed a new constituency; on May 9 he was elected as Liberal Member of Parliament for the Scottish city of Dundee. Speaking in Dundee to his new constituents on October 10 about his vision for social justice, he described – in a speech reprinted the following year in his book *Liberalism and the Social Problem* – the 'measure of great and cardinal importance' that, under the oversight of the newly appointed Chancellor of the Exchequer, David Lloyd George, he was helping to pilot through the House of Commons. In his speech, Churchill set out his wider vision for the people of Britain:

Surely no one will deny the magnitude and significance of the step which has been taken in the establishment of a system of Old Age Pensions. It marks the assertion in our social system of an entirely new principle in regard to poverty, and that principle, once asserted, cannot possibly be confined within its existing limits.

Old Age Pensions will carry us all a very long way. They have opened a door which will not soon or easily be closed. The members of both Houses of Parliament have been led to the verge of the cruel abyss of poverty, and have been in solemn session assembled to contemplate its depths and its gloom. All alike have come to gaze; none has remained unmoved. There are some distinguished and eminent men, men whose power and experience I cannot impugn, who have started back appalled by what they have seen, and whose only idea is to slam the door on the grim and painful prospect which has been revealed to their eyes.

But that is not the only spirit which has been awakened in our country; there are others, not less powerful, and a greater number, who will never allow that door to be closed; they have got their feet in it, they are resolved that it shall be kept open. Nay, more, they are prepared to descend into the abyss, and grapple with its evils – as sometimes you see after an explosion at a coalmine a rescue party advancing undaunted into the smoke and steam. Now there is the issue on which the future of this Parliament hangs – 'Forward or back?' Voices sound loud and conflicting in our ears; the issue, the sharpest and simplest, the most tremendous that can be put to a generation of men – 'Forward or backward?' – is the issue which confronts us at the present time, and on it the future of the Government is staked. There are faint-hearted friends behind; there are loud-voiced foes in front. The brewer's dray has been pulled across the road, and behind it are embattled a formidable confederation of vested interests. A mountainous obstacle of indifference and apathy bars our advance. What is your counsel? Forward or back?

[· · ·]

The social machinery at the basis of our industrial life is deficient, ill-organised, and incomplete. While large numbers of persons enjoy great wealth, while the mass of the artisan classes are abreast of and in advance of their fellows in other lands, there is a minority, considerable in numbers, whose condition is a disgrace to a scientific and professedly Christian civilisation, and constitutes a grave and increasing peril to the State. Yes, in this famous land of ours, so often envied by foreigners, where the grace and ease of life have been carried to such perfection, where there is so little class hatred and jealousy, where there is such a wide store of political experience and knowledge, where there are such enormous moral forces available, so much wisdom, so much virtue, so much power, we have not yet succeeded in providing that necessary apparatus of insurance and security without which our industrial system is not merely incomplete but actually inhumane.

[...]

If the first vicious condition which I have mentioned to you is lack of industrial organisation, if the second is the evil of casual labour, there is a third not less important. I mean the present conditions of boy labour. The whole underside of the labour market is deranged by the competition of boys or young persons who do men's work for boys' wages, and are turned off so soon as they demand men's wages for themselves. That is the evil so far as it affects the men; but how does it affect the boys, the youth of our country, the heirs of all our exertion, the inheritors of that long treasure of history and romance, of science and knowledge – aye, of national glory, for which so many valiant generations have fought and toiled – the youth of Britain, how are we treating them in the twentieth century of the Christian era? Are they not being exploited? Are they not being demoralised? Are they not being thrown away?

[...]

I agree most whole-heartedly with those who say that in attempting to relieve distress or to regulate the general levels of employment, we must be most careful not to facilitate the very disorganisation of industry which causes distress. But I do not agree with those who say that every man must look after himself, and that the intervention by the State in such matters as I have referred to will be fatal to his self-reliance, his foresight, and his thrift.

We are told that our non-contributory scheme of old-age pensions, for instance, will be fatal to thrift, and we are warned that the great mass of the working classes will be discouraged thereby from making any effective provision for their old age. But what effective provision have they made against old age in the past? If terror be an incentive to thrift, surely the penalties of the system which we have abandoned ought to have stimulated thrift as much as anything could have been stimulated in this world. The mass of the labouring poor have known that unless they made provision for their old age betimes they would perish miserably in the workhouse. Yet they have made no provision; and when I am told that the institution of old-age pensions will prevent the working classes from making provision for their old age, I say that cannot be, for they have never been able to make such provision. And I believe our scheme, so far from preventing thrift, will encourage it to an extent never before known.

It is a great mistake to suppose that thrift is caused only by fear; it springs from hope as well as from fear; where there is no hope, be sure there will be no thrift. No one supposes that five shillings a week is a satisfactory provision for old age. No one supposes that seventy is the earliest period in a man's life when his infirmities may overwhelm him. We have not pretended to carry the toiler on to dry land; it is beyond our power. What we have done is to strap a lifebelt around him, whose buoyancy, aiding his own strenuous exertions, ought to enable him to reach the shore.

And now I say to you Liberals of Scotland and Dundee two words – 'Diligence and Daring'. Let that be your motto for the year that is to come.

'Few,' it is written, 'and evil are the days of man.' Soon, very soon, our brief lives will be lived. Soon, very soon, we and our affairs will have passed away. Uncounted generations will trample heedlessly upon our tombs. What is the use of living, if it be not to strive for noble causes and to make this muddled world a better place for those who will live in it after we are gone? How else can we put ourselves in harmonious relation with the great verities and consolations of the infinite and the eternal? And I avow my faith that we are marching towards better days. Humanity will not be cast down. We are going on – swinging bravely forward along the grand high road – and already behind the distant mountains is the promise of the sun.

'THE DARK WATERS OF A FRIENDLESS WORLD'

The social reforms undertaken by Churchill as President of the Board of Trade were wide-ranging. They included a Standing Court of Arbitration in labour disputes, Labour Exchanges to help those looking for work, Trade Boards to prosecute employers who were exploiting their workers, a minimum wage for the low paid, and the right of all workers to breaks for meals and refreshment. A high point of his social policy was the introduction of compulsory State-supported unemployment insurance, of which he declared, in the Free Trade Hall in Manchester on 23 May 1909:

> If I had my way I would write the word 'Insure' over the door of every cottage, and upon the blotting-book of every public man, because I am convinced that by sacrifices which are inconceivably small, which are all within the power of the very poorest man in regular work, families can be secured against catastrophes which otherwise would smash them up for ever.
>
> I think it is our duty to use the strength and the resources of the State to arrest the ghastly waste not merely of human happiness but of national health and strength which follows when a working man's home which has taken him years to get together is broken up and scattered through a long spell of unemployment, or when, through the death, the sickness, or the invalidity of the breadwinner, the frail boat in which the fortunes of the family are embarked founders, and the women and children are left to struggle helplessly on the dark waters of a friendless world.

'THE UNNATURAL GAP BETWEEN RICH AND POOR'

In the midst of his work on social reform, Churchill was married, on 12 September 1908, to Clementine Hozier, 'my darling Clementine'. She was to be at his side at many of his public speeches, and to be a staunch supporter of his vision for a fairer society. When he spoke at Leicester on 5 September 1909 – in a speech reprinted in *Liberalism and the Social Problem* – that vision, and the obstacles to its fulfilment, were much in his mind, as he spoke about poverty in Britain. He also spoke of the power of the House of Lords to veto any budgetary expenditure. The Liberal Government's social reform policies depended on expenditure that had to be approved not only by the House of Commons but by the House of Lords. When it became clear that a majority of the Upper House would throw out David Lloyd George's Budget, Churchill took a leading part in the Liberal Party's campaign to end the Lords' power of veto over the Budget:

The social conditions of the British people in the early years of the twentieth century cannot be contemplated without deep anxiety. The anxiety is keen because it arises out of uncertainty. It is the gnawing anxiety of suspense. What is the destiny of our country to be? Nothing is settled either for or against us. We have no reason to despair; still less have we any reason to be self-satisfied. All is still in our hands for good or for ill. We have the power today to choose our fortune, and I believe there is no nation in the world, perhaps there never has been in history, any nation which at one and the same moment was confronted with such opposite possibilities, was threatened on the one hand by more melancholy disaster, and cheered on the other by more bright, yet not unreasonable hopes.

The two roads are open. We stand at the crossways. If we go on in the old happy-go-lucky way – the richer classes ever growing in wealth and in number, and the very poor remaining plunged or plunging ever deeper in helpless, hopeless misery – then I think there is nothing before us but savage strife between class and class, with the increasing disorganisation, with increasing waste of human strength and human virtue, nothing but that dual degeneration which comes from the simultaneous waste of extreme wealth and extreme want.

[· · ·]

The greatest danger to the British Empire and to the British people is not to be found among the enormous fleets and armies of the European Continent, nor in the solemn problems of Hindustan; it is not the Yellow peril nor the Black peril nor any danger in the wide circuit of colonial and foreign affairs.

No, it is here in our midst, close at home, close at hand in the vast growing cities of England and Scotland, and in the dwindling and cramped villages of our denuded countryside.

It is there you will find the seeds of Imperial ruin and national decay – the unnatural gap between rich and poor, the divorce of the people from the land, the want of proper discipline and training in our youth, the exploitation of boy labour, the physical degeneration which seems to follow so swiftly on civilised poverty, the awful jumbles of an obsolete Poor Law, the horrid havoc of the liquor traffic, the constant insecurity in the means of subsistence and employment which breaks the heart of many a sober, hard-working man, the absence of any established minimum standard of life and comfort among the workers, and, at the other end, the swift increase of vulgar, joyless luxury – here are the enemies of Britain. Beware lest they shatter the foundations of her power.

[· · ·]

There is a Budget every year and, memorable as the Budget of my right hon. friend may be, far-reaching as is the policy depending upon it, the Finance Bill, after all, is in its character only an annual affair. But the rejection of the Budget by the House of Lords would not be an annual affair. It would be a violent rupture of constitutional custom and usage extending over three hundred years and recognised during all that time by the leaders of every Party in the State. It would involve a sharp and sensible breach with the traditions of the past; and what does the House of Lords depend upon if not upon the traditions of the past? It would amount to an attempt at revolution not by the poor but by the rich; not by the masses but by the privileged few; not in the name of progress but in that of reaction; not for the purpose of broadening the framework of the State but of greatly narrowing it.

Such an attempt, whatever you may think of it, would be historic in its character, and the result of the battle fought upon it, whoever wins, must inevitably be not of an annual but of a permanent and final character. The result of such an election must mean an alteration of the veto of the House of Lords; if they win they will have asserted their right, not merely to reject legislation of the House of Commons, but to control the finances of the country, and if they lose, we will deal with their veto once and for all.

We do not seek the struggle, we have our work to do; but if it is to come, it could never come better than now. Never again perhaps, certainly not for many years, will such an opportunity be presented to the British democracy. Never will the ground be more favourable; never will the issues be more clearly or more vividly defined. Those issues will be whether the new taxation, which is admitted on all sides to be necessary, shall be imposed upon luxuries, superfluities, and monopolies, or upon the prime necessaries of life; whether you shall put your tax upon the unearned increment on land or upon the daily bread of labour; whether the policy of constructive social reform on which we are embarked, and which expands and deepens as we advance, shall be carried through and given a fair chance, or whether it shall be brought to a dead stop and all the energies and attention of the State devoted to jingo armaments and a senseless foreign adventure.

And, lastly, the issue will be whether the British people in the year of grace 1909 are going to be ruled through a representative Assembly, elected by six or seven millions of voters, about which almost everyone in the country, man or woman, has a chance of being consulted, or whether they are going to allow themselves to be dictated to and domineered over by a minute minority of titled persons who represent nobody, who are answerable to nobody, and who only scurry up to London to vote in their party interests, in their class interests, and in their own interests.

These will be the issues, and I am content that the responsibility for such a struggle, if it should come, should rest with the House of Lords themselves. But if it is to come, we shall not complain, we shall not draw back from it. We will engage in it with all our hearts and with all our might, it being always clearly understood that the fight will be a fight to the finish, and that the fullest forfeits which are in accordance with the national welfare shall be exacted from the defeated foe.

'THE DARK ANGEL'

In September 1909, when President of the Board of Trade, Churchill was invited as the guest of the German Kaiser to German Army manoeuvres near Würzburg in Bavaria. The next military review that he saw in Germany was in 1919, when, as Secretary of State for War, he took the march-past of 40,000 British troops in Cologne 'in', as he later wrote, 'the solemn glitter of unchallengeable victory', adding: 'But I did not expect ever to witness such a spectacle when I left Würzburg in 1909. Indeed no fancy could have seemed more wild.' Recalling the Würzburg manoeuvres some fifteen years later, when the Kaiser was in exile at Doorn in Holland, cutting wood on his estate in enforced isolation, Churchill wrote:

Upon how many of those who marched and cantered in that autumn sunlight had the dark angel set his seal! Violent untimely death, ruin and humiliation worse than death, privation, mutilation, despair to the simple soldier, the downfall of their pride and subsistence to the chiefs: such were the fates – could we but have read them – which brooded over thousands and tens of thousands of these virile figures.

All the Kings and Princes of Germany, all the Generals of her Empire, clustered round the banqueting-tables. Ten years were to see them scattered, exiled, deposed, in penury, in obloquy – the victims of a fatal system in which they were inextricably involved.

And for the Kaiser, that bright figure, the spoilt child of fortune, the envy of Europe – for him in the long series of heart-breaking disappointments and disillusions, of failure and undying self-reproach, which across the devastation of Europe was to lead him to the wood-cutter's block at Doorn – there was surely reserved the sternest punishment of all.

'WE PROPOSE TO TAX NOT WAGES BUT WEALTH'

On 30 November 1909, Churchill's thirty-fifth birthday, the House of Lords used its veto power to reject the Liberal Government's social reform Budget, and did so by 350 votes to 75. Four days later, Asquith prorogued Parliament and called a General Election. On 8 January 1910, during the election campaign, Churchill spoke in Leven, in Asquith's East Fife constituency:

> We are gathered together in the close grip of a well fought and, as I think we have every reason to believe, a victorious battle. (Cheers.) The country has been plunged into a constitutional crisis of rare significance and importance. Mr. Asquith, who for twenty-two years has unbrokenly represented East Fife, happens to be Prime Minister. His duties call upon him to fight in all parts of the field. He has gone south to fight for the cause, which is your cause and was the cause of your forefathers before you, the good old cause of Liberalism and Free Trade. (Cheers.)
>
> By a series of terse, clear, straightforward, and forcible speeches the Prime Minister is laying antagonists on their backs in every quarter, and he has already wiped the floor with Mr. Balfour. (Laughter and cheers.) In the meanwhile, he relies upon his faithful friends and comrades here while he fights for them elsewhere, and I believe you will not fall below the level of the great responsibility entrusted to you. (Cheers.)
>
> It looks as if things are going on very well in East Fife, and I am glad to participate in what will be a victory. By returning this powerful friend of progress, for the sixth time, by a substantially

increased margin, you will honour yourselves and will forward alike the highest ideals for which we have laboured and the most material interests which sustain you and your families. (Loud cheers.)

What is the cause of the Budget which has produced this turmoil? It is want of money. Sixteen millions of money are required to meet the needs of the State. That fact does not suggest unwise or profligate expenditure. The money is needed for legitimate and worthy objects – first for old age pensions and secondly for imperial defence. (Cheers.)

The Conservatives are not in a position to challenge either of these causes of expenditure. They won the election of 1895 by promising old age pensions. They were in power for ten years and never gave them. Mr. Chamberlain promised them again in 1903, when he began his fiscal campaign; but his Conservative friends were indignant and forced Mr. Chamberlain to write to the papers and say that old age pensions did not form part of his Tariff scheme. The Liberals did not promise old age pensions at the last General Election. Instead of promising them the Liberals gave them. (Cheers.) As to the Navy, the Liberal Government have made adequate provision for its un-questioned supremacy.

The Conservative Party, who are not looking to the security of the country but to a party advantage, are trying to make political capital out of a Navy scare. This is the party whose one defence of the House of Lords is that they wish the people to be consulted, and now that the people are being consulted they are bringing in outside issues to raise a new scare . . . it is upon the Navy that they base their highest hopes as a red herring to draw the people off the real issues – the land, the Budget, and the Lords. (Cheers.) So far, therefore, from being able to impeach the Government for the heavy burdens we are asking the electors to bear for the proper maintenance of British sea power, the Conservative party will be found to ask for an amount far in excess of what is needed for national security, but as a foundation for a braggart and sensational display of armaments. (Cheers.)

How is the deficit to be met? The Government put forward our plan, not in the vague, nebulous, and loose fashion in which Tariff 'Reform' speakers are accustomed to unfold the many glories of their infallible panacea. The Government have not depended on perorations of speeches and cryptic pronouncements on half-sheets of notepaper; we have put our plan in the precise clauses and chapters of a statute, which has been examined and discussed with minute care by the House of Commons for many months.

We propose to tax not wages but wealth, but we do not propose to lay any taxes on the wealthy classes which could not be justified in equity or which could not be borne without trenching on their comforts or even elegances. We, in short, propose to tax luxuries, monopolies, and superfluities, but we scrupulously avoid taxing the necessaries of life.

Our taxes will yield not only the money necessary for this year; next year and the year after these taxes, without any addition, will bring in a larger yield, and this expanding revenue the Government intend to devote to financing a very extensive and carefully thought out scheme of social organisation. (Cheers.)

In the centre of this scheme stands the great principle of national insurance against unemployment, invalidity, sickness, infirmity, and the death of the breadwinner. (Renewed cheers.) This is linked with the system of national labour exchanges, now being established, and with large projects for reforming the Poor Law, for rescuing children from the workhouse, for providing for the proper treatment of the feeble-minded, for inebriates, and others in places specially suited for their care, and for discriminating between the honest worker in search of a job and the idle loafer in search of a tip. (Laughter and cheers.)

It is also linked with the Development Act, which provides for an extensive system of economic development. This is the Government plan, and after all the labour of the Ministry and the House of Commons in working out the measure necessary to finance it that measure was kicked incontinently and contemptuously out of Parliament by an unrepresentative party Chamber, who in order to strike a blow at popular representation and to save their own pockets had not hesitated to break with the old usage of the Constitution, upon which alone their own positions as legislators depend. (Cheers.)

The money must be found before 31 March. Another Budget will soon be on its way for the expenses of the next financial year. The process is simple. The Crown demands the money, the Commons grants the supplies, and the Lords assent; indeed, the Lords are forced to assent to the grant, for they have no right to refuse the request of the Crown.

The House of Lords is an unrepresentative body. No estimates are laid before them, and no financial statement is made to them. They cannot authorise the spending of a single penny or regulate the expenditure. If they destroy one Budget, they cannot replace it by another. All they can do is to put a stone on the line and throw the train off the rails, and that is what they have done.

The electors must not underestimate the constitutional question. It is a matter of life and death to representative institutions. The electors choose the Chamber which chooses the Government. If you allow the power over the nation's finance to be taken away from the House of Commons your votes will no longer have the same virtue: the assembly you elect will no longer be able to settle the fortunes of the Government of the day.

Every man with the smallest flavour of democracy in his composition should stand like a rock against this invasion of his rights. If you allow those rights to be fooled away by apathy there will cease to be a democratic Government, and when your children in future years find themselves ruled by a capitalist oligarchy they will look at their fathers with justifiable reproach. (Cheers.)

The rejection of the Budget is an insolent thing. Indeed, the whole attitude of Lord Lansdowne is one of aristocratic insolence. The other night he said: 'Twenty years ago who would ever have thought a Lloyd George likely?' I reply: 'Twenty years hence who will ever think a Lansdowne possible.' (Laughter and cheers.)

What is Mr. Lloyd George representative of? The democratic freedom of the British Constitution, which enables a man of merit and parts to rise from a village school to a position of the highest consequence under the Crown. (Cheers.) It is an example of that glory of the British Constitution which has made it possible for every son of our soil to enjoy, with the consent and by the authority of his fellow-citizens, great honour, power, and distinction in the land. (Cheers.) That is what Mr. Lloyd George's career represents.

What does Lord Lansdowne's career represent? It represents privilege and favour from beginning to end. It represents consistent and unbroken spoon-feeding from start to finish. (Cheers.) It represents the royal road to favour and employment. And what does Lord Lansdowne's political action represent? It represents not the authority of the people, but the partisanship of a faction and of a class. It represents a small group of hereditary legislators, who are in close alliance with the caucus of the Tory Party.

Lord Lansdowne takes his instructions from the managers of the Conservative Party, and on their instructions he does not hesitate to throw out legislation which comes to him from great majorities in the people's Chamber. Sometimes he goes through the form of holding a meeting in his back parlour, to which he invites some select hundreds of his coroneted friends, and he goes through the form of a public or semi-public discussion. At another time, 'a nod is as good as a wink'. (Laughter.) A letter is written to the Licensed Victuallers' Association, who are assured that their cause will not be lost sight of. The party agents are asked what is the gossip in the public houses, and on this decisions are taken which will make a memorable mark on British history. (Cheers.)

Let the electors contrast what these two men represent to the masses of British citizens. One represents all that is encouraging and dignified to the ordinary voter and elector: the other represents a played-out, obsolete anachronistic assembly, the survival of a feudal arrangement which has utterly passed out of its original meaning, a force long since passed away, and which only now requires a smashing blow from the electors to finish it for ever. (Loud cheers.) That is the main issue of this election. The veto of the House of Lords is an abuse. It has long been used in a partisan interest, and now that the Lords have violated the Constitution it is well that they should be dealt with once for all.

The Government ask the electors to give us the power to carry the Budget and the social legislation upon the Budget. More important, we ask the electors to support us in abolishing, absolutely and for ever, the power of the Lords to interfere with finance and effectually to restrain their power over other legislation, so that the will of the House of Commons shall prevail in the lifetime of a Parliament. (Loud cheers.)

'THE NOBLE STATUS OF CITIZENSHIP'

On 30 May 1910, Churchill spoke in the House of Commons in support of a Government Bill to protect the trades unions against what he regarded as the unfair bias of judges against them:

We have endeavoured to achieve a two-fold object in this Bill. First, we have tried to secure for individual workmen freedom of political opinion. Secondly, we have tried to secure for the trade union organisations of the country freedom from the embarrassment of that perpetual litigation to which in the last decade they have so harshly and vexatiously been subjected.

This Bill we believe will achieve both these results. I should like to say that no one in any quarter of the House has disputed the necessity of the Bill.

[···]

I should have no hesitation in saying that it is quite impossible to prevent trade unions from entering the political field. The sphere of industrial and political activity is often indistinguishable, always overlaps, and representation in Parliament is absolutely necessary to trade unions, even if they confine themselves to the most purely industrial forms of action, and the moment you touch representation you reach the very heart and centre of controversial political life, because the disputes as to representation raise every question of general politics and party politics which can be imagined.

The problem therefore as the Government have considered it, is how to render possible the participation of trade unions in politics without doing violence to the conscientious convictions of individual trade unionists. That is the problem as we have regarded it, and I think it will be found as this Bill is studied, and I think it has emerged from this Debate as it has progressed that we have honestly laboured to give effect to both those purposes, and that we have succeeded in producing genuine safeguards and a practical procedure on both points.

Let us take the case of the workman first. It is highly important that the workman should be assigned the noble status of citizenship in all our legislation. We must in the House of Commons never lend ourselves to the view that a workman has not got the same rights to conscientious scruples or convictions in political or religious matters as any other class of the community or that his convictions are not as important to him, and not as important to our society of the present day, as the convictions of individuals in any other class. If we were to fail to recognise that we should take a most disastrous conception of democracy.

A man may be poor; he may have nothing at all except his labour to sell; he may be a manual worker for a weekly wage, but in a free commonwealth he must enjoy as good a right as any lord, or prelate, or capitalist in the country to the integrity of his own political convictions. I hope the House of Commons will never consent to say that a workman must put his opinions in his pocket if they clash with his personal interests, or that the majority must decide once and for all what his political action must be, or that he must not arrogate to himself an independence above his class, or that political independence of judgment is the privilege and the perquisite of the well-to-do. Any assertion or demand of that kind in the House of Commons would, I am sure, be most injurious to the foundations of our whole political system.

I quite agree that in practice there is a great deal too much of this sort of pressure operative upon working people and employés generally throughout the country. The contrast which exists in our system between the unequalled sovereignty so freely assigned in speeches to democracy and the actual facts of the situation, and especially the economic situation as they present themselves to the individual worker may afford a fertile field for political cynicism, but the House of Commons cannot sanction or give any countenance to a suggestion that the workman has not the fullest political discretion, and has not the fullest right to express freely his own opinions. We must resist and we must repudiate that in whatever form it manifests itself.

The whole foundation of our political system is the equality of rights and the equal importance and value of the political rights enjoyed by persons in every class. I quite agree the difficulty is one of theory rather than of practice. In the great majority of cases workmen do not feel injured even if their very small contributions are taken to support trade union politics, with which they do not agree. They do not in the great majority of cases object. Many of them do not think very much about it. Very few workmen, luckily for them, are cursed with logical or theological subtleties of mind. They do not mind, in practice and as a general rule in the great majority of cases, paying for their union politics, which they regard as advancing the interests of their class, and then voting for a different political party which they regard as advancing political affairs upon another road at the same time. There is a great deal more sense and deep reason and sagacity in that lack of logical subtlety than might appear upon the surface. I think the workman will not often raise the point. He has often voted against a candidate to whom his trade union subscription has gone without being conscious of any injury to himself in his own personal integrity.

Where there is no sense of injury in this field there is no injury. Where a man is not conscious of the fact that he has been made to take sides against his personal convictions there is no injury which need trouble the legislature. But where there is a sense of injury, that sense of injury is fundamental.

If the workman objects it is imperative that he should have a right to object, and it is imperative that the House of Commons, which stands on the foundation of the common people of these realms, should make it clear to him that he has a right to object. To deny that he has a right to object would be an unmistakable insult to the moral and civic status of labouring men, which undoubtedly would be fatal in the end to their future political advancement. I hope hon. Gentlemen below the Gangway, who are deeply concerned in all these matters, will consider that to adopt the position of saying, as I am afraid the hon. Member (Mr. Ramsay MacDonald) did, that all this is mere humanitarian balderdash about the rights of the individual in regard to the trade union is to place the great mass of the working-class electors in this country, many of whom belong to trade union organisations, more and more of whom, I trust, will belong to such organisations as the years pass by, in a position which is undoubtedly humiliating to their status as citizens.

No one can say, as my hon. Friend the senior Member for Leicester

(Mr. Crawshay-Williams) pointed out, that if the workman does not like the decision of the majority of his trade union he can leave the union. You might as well say he can leave the earth. He cannot leave the trade union, and he ought not to leave it. In a great many great trades in this country, the best and most highly organised trades, to leave the union would involve leaving the only means by which he could earn his living.

What we want is to encourage people to join trade unions and not to force them to leave them. I consider that every workman is well advised to join a trade union. I cannot conceive how any man standing undefended against the powers that be in this world could be so foolish, if he can possibly spare the money from the maintenance of his family, not to associate himself with an organisation to protect the rights and interests of labour, and I think there could be no greater injury to trade unionism than that the unions should either be stripped of a great many strong and independent spirits, because it is only the strong and independent men, in most cases, who stand upon these subjects, or that they should split into rival bodies and that attempts should be made to make party trade unions – Liberal and Socialist party trade unions – and so break the homogeneity and solidarity of the great trade union movement.

It would be a great disadvantage to the movement that individuals should be forced out of trade unions because of their political opinions, or that the advantages of trade unions should be reserved for persons of one political creed. We make it clear by law that a man may not be deprived of the immense benefits of trade unionism – after all, apart from politics, 90 per cent. of the work of trade unionism lies in the industrial field – because of the peculiar views he holds on politics or religion. An hon. Member asked how you can enable him to enforce these rights. He can take action in the courts, and action has been effectively taken in the courts by individuals; in fact, so far as individuals are concerned, in their actions in the courts against trade unionism it must be said that the advantage in every case rests with the individual who has taken action rather than with the trade union.

[···]

I was going to say, that nothing you can put into an Act of Parliament will prevent a certain element of illegitimate pressure existing in all societies, in all communities, on all sorts of subjects about which people feel keenly. But I say this: there never was a time in the history of this country when intolerance or bigotry of any kind, harshness or bullying of individuals for their opinions, or the persecuting of humble people for their political or religious views was more generally and universally condemned.

There never was a time when public opinion was more vigilant, when publicity was more searching, and when intolerance in all its forms was so absolutely lacking in defenders of any kind, and any attempt to trample upon the political convictions of individuals, whether it be an attempt by a landlord – that happens sometimes – or by a trade union, or by a Government, as we are told, or by Party Whips, or by an employer of labour, or by a university caste, or by a club, or by a bench of magistrates, or by a religious body – any attempt to bully, to persecute, to harry individuals in the tolerant exercise and expression of their opinions is more severely censured and condemned, and more effectively pilloried at the present time than it ever has been in any other country or circumstances of which we have any record.

There is your safeguard, your only effective safeguard against abuses of this character. It is no good to amend the Bill. You will have to amend human nature if you wish to arrive at any absolute prevention. No doubt occasional abuses will occur in every party and in all circles, but public opinion is the only safeguard, and it is a safeguard whose power is constantly growing.

[· · ·]

The machinery of the Bill is designed to be as convenient as possible. It is quite true that we do not allow a man just to do anything. We think that if he dissents from the general policy of the union he ought to take the step of giving formal notice that he intends to do so. We provide him with an opportunity of giving formal notice that affords no ground or occasion for altercation of any sort. We do not ask him, as proposed in many cases, to pay his money and afterwards to reclaim it. We give him an effective and convenient method in regard to his subscription which is not unfair, which does not stone-wall the trade union with indifference, and which does not expose the individual who wishes to dissent to undue pressure.

It is not at all invidious that a man should decline to pay to a particular political effort, because, by the separation of the fund he will not get any part of the management of it unless he has contributed to it.

I turn now to the second main object of the Bill. As I have said, the first is the effective protection of the rights of the individual workman in regard to his conscientious opinions or convictions, and the second is to relieve trade unions from the harassing litigation to which they have been exposed and set them free to develop and do their work without the perpetual check and uncertainty of frequent trials and without being brought constantly into contact with the courts.

It is a very unseemly thing, and indeed in the House of Commons we must regard it as such, to have the spectacle we have witnessed these last few years of these workmen's guilds, trade union organisations, being enmeshed, harassed, worried, and checked at every step and at every turn by all kinds of legal decisions, which came with the utmost surprise to the greatest lawyers in the country. It is not good for trade unions that they should be brought in contact with the courts, and it is not good for the courts.

The courts hold justly a high and, I think, unequalled prominence in respect of the world in criminal cases, and in civil cases between man and man, no doubt, they deserve and command the respect and admiration of all classes in the community, but where class issues are involved, and where party issues are involved, it is impossible to pretend that the courts command the same degree of general confidence. On the contrary, they do not, and a very large number of our population have been led to the opinion that they are, unconsciously, no doubt, biased. [HON MEMBERS: 'No, no,' and 'Withdraw,' and interruption.]

[···]

[Mr CHURCHILL:] ... I have not the slightest intention of withdrawing, and I repeat what I said, that it is unfortunate that these collisions occur between the courts and the great trade union bodies. [HON. MEMBERS: 'Withdraw.']

I have only got two or three more words to say, and I am quite indifferent to the interruptions. It is for those reasons that we have sought to find in our Bill some bulwark which will stand between the trade unions and the courts. Some authority which will be able— [HON. MEMBERS: 'Withdraw.'] We have tried to discover some authority— [An HON. MEMBER: 'We do not attack the judges.']

[. . .]

Although it may be very difficult to define in law what is or what is not a trade union, most people of common sense know a trade union when they see one. It is like trying to define a rhinoceros: it is difficult enough, but if one is seen, everybody can recognise it.

The decision of the party opposite not to divide against this Bill is a measure of the general acceptance by this House of the value and usefulness of trade unions. We know perfectly well that the trade union movement ought to develop, ought not to be stereotyped, ought to have power to enter a new field, and to make new experiments. We do not wish to tie up or to trammel it, but we wish to remove it from the area of uncertainty in which it has been placed. We wish to separate it from the perpetual contact with the courts, from the sort of warfare between the great hierarchy of the law and the workmen's guilds. We wish to do that in such a way that the work of trade unions may proceed on a reasonable and practicable basis, without injury to or intruding upon the rights of individual workmen or their conscientious convictions or scruples, which are guarded to the full.

We wish to set the trade unions free to develop their efforts, to build up in this country a minimum standard of life and labour, and to secure the happiness of the people, which, after all, in spite of party feeling, is the goal and object which earnest men in all parties, by different roads I do not doubt, are increasingly labouring to attain.

'A CONSTANT HEART-SEARCHING'

On 15 February 1910, following the General Election, the Liberal Party was returned to power. That day, Churchill was appointed Home Secretary, with responsibility for the police, prisons and prisoners. He at once set about reforming the prison system, drastically reducing the number of young people in prison, reducing the numbers liable to solitary confinement, challenging what he saw as excessive prison sentences, and improving prison conditions. On 20 July 1910 he set out in the House of Commons his view of crime and punishment:

The mood and temper of the public in regard to the treatment of crime and criminals is one of the most unfailing tests of the civilization of any country. A calm and dispassionate recognition of the rights of the accused against the State, and even of convicted criminals against the State, a constant heart-searching by all charged with the duty of punishment, a desire and eagerness to rehabilitate in the world of industry all those who have paid their dues in the hard coinage of punishment, tireless efforts towards the discovery of curative and regenerating processes, and an unfaltering faith that there is a treasure, if you can only find it, in the heart of every man – these are the symbols which in the treatment of crime and criminals mark and measure the stored-up strength of a nation, and are the sign and proof of the living virtue in it.

[···]

We must not forget that when every material improvement has been effected in prisons, when the temperature has been adjusted, when the proper food to maintain health and strength has been given, when the doctors, chaplains, and prison visitors have come and gone, the convict stands deprived of everything that a free man calls life. We must not forget that all these improvements, which are sometimes salves to our consciences, do not change that position.

'A CATASTROPHE IN OUR NATIONAL LIFE'

In the first week of November 1910, a coal strike broke out in the Rhondda Valley. In the village of Tonypandy, rioters attacked shops. The Chief Constable of Glamorgan, with only 1,400 county policemen at his disposal, asked the Army to send 400 soldiers from London to South Wales by train. As soon as this was reported to Churchill at the Home Office, he ordered the troops halted at Swindon, and sent in their place 200 London police constables and 70 mounted police, all unarmed. On the following day, Churchill was attacked in the Conservative newspapers for not sending troops to Tonypandy. According to *The Times*: 'Mr Churchill hardly seems to understand that an acute crisis has arisen, which needs decisive handling.' In a stormy debate in the House of Commons on 17 February 1911, he defended his action in recalling the troops:

> Law and order must be preserved, but I am confident that the House will agree with me that it is a great object of public policy to avoid a collision between soldiers and crowds of persons engaged in industrial disputes. All such collisions attended, as they must be, by loss of life and by the use of firearms, do great harm to the Army, which is a volunteer Army, and whose relation with the civil forces of the country must be carefully safeguarded, and they also cause feuds and resentments which last for a generation. For soldiers to fire on the people would be a catastrophe in our national life.
>
> Alone among the nations, or almost alone, we have avoided for a great many years that melancholy and unnatural experience. And it is well worth while, I venture to think, for the Minister who is responsible to run some risk of broken heads or broken windows, to incur expense and an amount of inconvenience in the police arrangements, and to accept direct responsibility in order that the shedding of British blood by British soldiers may be averted, as, thank God, it has been successfully averted in South Wales.

'AN ISLAND WELL-GUARDED HITHERTO, AT LAST DEFENCELESS'

In the summer of 1911, the German Government sent a gunboat to the port of Agadir, on the Atlantic coast of Morocco. Seven years earlier, Britain had recognised Morocco as being within the French sphere of influence. The Chancellor of the Exchequer, David Lloyd George, speaking at the Mansion House on July 21, warned that 'peace at any price would be a humiliation intolerable for a great country like ours to endure'. In his multi-volume history of the First World War, *The World Crisis*, Churchill wrote:

> They sound so very cautious and correct, these deadly words. Soft, quiet voices purring, courteous, grave, exactly measured phrases in large peaceful rooms. But with less warning cannons had opened fire and nations had been struck down by this same Germany. So now the Admiralty wireless whispers.
>
> It is nothing. It is less than nothing. It is too foolish, too fantastic to be thought of in the twentieth century. Or is it fire and murder leaping out of the darkness at our throats, torpedoes ripping the bellies of half-awakened ships, a sunrise on a vanished naval supremacy, and an island well-guarded hitherto, at last defenceless?
>
> No, it is nothing. No one would do such things. Civilization has climbed above such perils. The interdependence of nations in trade and traffic, the sense of public law, the Hague Convention, Liberal principles, the Labour Party, high finance, Christian charity, common sense have rendered such nightmares impossible.
>
> Are you quite sure? It would be a pity to be wrong. Such a mistake could only be made once – once for all.

'THE ENORMOUS NUMBER OF HAZARDS'

In October 1911, five weeks before his thirty-seventh birthday, Churchill was appointed First Lord of the Admiralty. As well as being in charge of the Royal Navy, he had responsibility for the newly established Royal Naval Air Service. At the beginning of 1913 he asked the Royal Naval Air Service pilots to teach him to fly. In his book *Thoughts and Adventures* he described his flying lessons:

> Once I had started flying from motives in which a sense of duty, as well as excitement and curiosity, played its part, I continued for sheer joy and pleasure. I went up in every kind of machine and at every air station under the Admiralty. The 'vol plané' or descending glide with the engine off was in those days a comparative novelty, and I must say its silent downward rush through the soft air, amid the glories of the sunset and with the earth as a map spread beneath, was a delightful experience when first enjoyed.
>
> I soon became ambitious to handle these machines myself, and took many lessons both at the Naval and Military Schools. Dual-control machines were developing fast in 1913, and I had one made where pilot and passenger could sit side by side and take control alternately. In this machine, the type of which was particularly useful for instructional purposes, I made many delightful flights, and it was ultimately the means of revealing in an exceedingly unpleasant manner the dangers of a particular form of rudder and spin which we thereafter avoided.
>
> Curiously enough my apprehensions about going into the air were apparently confirmed by a long series of dangerous or fatal accidents in which I narrowly missed being involved. The young Pilot Instructor who gave me my first lesson at Eastchurch was killed the day after we had been flying together. I was sitting in the Treasury Board Room, discussing the details of the Naval Estimates of 1913 with the Chancellor of the Exchequer, when a slip of paper was put before me acquainting me with the fact that my companion of yesterday had perished in the same machine in which we had been practising for two or three hours.
>
> A few weeks later a seaplane of a new and experimental type was produced in Southampton Water, and I made a prolonged flight in it

while it was being tested. It manoeuvred perfectly under every condition, and I sailed away in the Admiralty yacht *Enchantress* to Sheerness. I had no sooner arrived than I learnt that the machine had nose-dived into the sea with three officers, all of whom were killed. I was going out to fly, as I frequently did, in the sociable dual-control machine which I have mentioned, and was prevented by press of public business. The machine, having flown perfectly all the morning, suddenly took it into its head to plunge into a spin of a kind then quite unknown, and smashed itself to pieces on the ground, thereby gravely injuring the two officers, both personal friends of mine, who were flying it.

As I began to know more about flying, I began to understand the enormous number of hazards which beset every moment of the airman's flight – I suppose it is all different now – and I noticed on several occasions defects in the machine in which we had been flying – a broken wire, a singed wing, a cracked strut – which were the subject of mutual congratulation between my pilot and myself once we had returned safely to terra firma. However, having been thoroughly bitten, I continued to fly on every possible occasion when my other duties permitted.

'AN ULTIMATUM SUCH AS HAD NEVER BEEN PENNED IN MODERN TIMES'

On 28 June 1914, the Archduke Franz Ferdinand of Austria and his wife were assassinated in Sarajevo by a Serb nationalist. The Austro-Hungarian government sent a note to Serbia, demanding recompense. In Britain, the Irish question dominated public debate throughout the summer. The Liberal Government was committed to bringing in Home Rule for Ireland. The determination of the Protestants of Ulster to remain in the United Kingdom had led to the prospect of civil war. In the summer of 1914, Churchill, who that spring had sent the Royal Navy to confront the Ulster gun-runners, was one of the government negotiators at the Buckingham Palace Conference seeking a compromise between the Irish Nationalists and the Ulster Unionists. On 25 July 1914 the Cabinet met at 10 Downing Street to discuss the narrowing area of disagreement. Churchill recalled that Cabinet meeting in *The World Crisis*:

> The Cabinet on Friday afternoon sat long revolving the Irish problem. The Buckingham Palace Conference had broken down. The disagreements and antagonisms seemed as fierce and as hopeless as ever, yet the margin in dispute, upon which such fateful issues hung, was inconceivably petty. The discussion turned principally upon the boundaries of Fermanagh and Tyrone. To this pass had the Irish factions in their insensate warfare been able to drive their respective British champions. Upon the disposition of these clusters of humble parishes turned at that moment the political future of Great Britain. The North would not agree to this, and the South would not agree to that.
>
> Both the leaders wished to settle; both had dragged their followers forward to the utmost point they dared. Neither seemed able to give an inch. Meanwhile, the settlement of Ireland must carry with it an immediate and decisive abatement of party strife in Britain, and those schemes of unity and co-operation which had so and intensely appealed to the leading men on both sides, ever since Mr Lloyd George had mooted them in 1910, must necessarily have come forward into the light of day. Failure to settle on the other hand meant something very like civil war and the plunge into depths of which no one could make any measure.
>
> And so, turning this way and that in search of an exit from the deadlock, the Cabinet toiled around the muddy byways of Fermanagh and Tyrone. One had hoped that the events of April at the Curragh and in Belfast would have shocked British public opinion, and formed a unity sufficient to impose a settlement on the Irish factions. Apparently they had been insufficient. Apparently the conflict would be carried one stage further by both sides with incalculable consequences before there would be a recoil. Since the days of the Blues and the Greens in the Byzantine Empire, partisanship had rarely been carried to more absurd extremes. An all-sufficient shock was, however, at hand.
>
> The discussion had reached its inconclusive end, and the Cabinet was about to separate, when the quiet grave tones of Sir Edward

Grey's voice were heard reading a document which had just been brought to him from the Foreign Office. It was the Austrian note to Serbia. He had been reading or speaking for several minutes before I could disengage my mind from the tedious and bewildering debate which had just closed.

We were all very tired, but gradually as the phrases and sentences followed one another, impressions of a wholly different character began to form in my mind. This note was clearly an ultimatum; but it was an ultimatum such as had never been penned in modern times. As the reading proceeded it seemed absolutely impossible that any State in the world could accept it, or that any acceptance, however abject, would satisfy the aggressor. The parishes of Fermanagh and Tyrone faded back into the mists and squalls of Ireland, and a strange light began immediately, but by perceptible gradations, to fall and grow upon the map of Europe.

'THE WAR WILL BE LONG AND SOMBRE'

Britain declared war on Germany on 4 August 1914, following the German advance through Belgium – an essential part of the German plan to conquer France. For the first six weeks of the war, German troops swept towards Paris. The British Expeditionary Force, sent to Belgium to halt them, and facing the Germans at Mons, was driven back more than one hundred miles, together with the French forces, to the River Marne, less than forty miles from Paris. On September 8, the British and French troops on the Marne halted the German advance and began to push the Germans back. The race was then on to reach the Channel and North Sea ports. On September 11, after spending twenty-four hours examining the defences at Dunkirk, Churchill spoke to an anxious audience at the London Opera House, his words widely reported in the newspapers:

We meet here together in serious times, but I come to you tonight in good heart (cheers), and with good confidence for the future and for the task upon which we are engaged. It is too soon to speculate upon the results of the great battle which is waging in France. Everything that we have heard during four long days of anxiety seems to point to a marked and substantial turning of the tide.

We have seen the forces of the French and British Armies strong enough not only to contain and check the devastating avalanche which had swept across the French frontier, but now at last, not for an hour or for a day, but for four long days in succession, it has been rolled steadily back. (Cheers.)

With battles taking place over a front of 100 or 150 miles one must be very careful not to build high hopes on results which are achieved even in a great area of the field of war. We are not children looking for light and vain encouragement, but men engaged upon a task which has got to be put through. Still, when every allowance has been made for the uncertainty with which these great operations are always enshrouded, I think it only fair and right to say that the situation to-night is better, far better, than cold calculation of the forces available on both sides before the war should have led us to expect at this early stage. (Cheers.)

It is quite clear that what is happening now is not what the Germans planned (laughter), and they have yet to show that they can adapt themselves to the force of circumstances created by the military power of their enemies with the same efficiency that they have undoubtedly shown in regard to plans long preferred, methodically worked out, and executed with the precision of deliberation. The battle, I say, gives us every reason to meet together tonight in good heart. But let me tell you frankly that if this battle had been as disastrous as, thank God, it appears to be triumphant, I should come before you with unabated confidence and with the certainty that we have only to continue in our efforts to bring this war to the conclusion which we wish and intend.

We did not enter upon the war with the hope of easy victory; we did not enter upon it in any desire to extend our territory, or to advance and increase our position in the world; or in any romantic desire to shed our blood and spend our money in Continental quarrels. We entered upon this war reluctantly after we had made every effort compatible with honour to avoid being drawn in, and we entered upon it with a full realization of the sufferings, losses, disappointments, vexations, and anxieties, and of the appalling and sustaining exertions which would be entailed upon us by our action.

The war will be long and sombre. It will have many reverses of fortune and many hopes falsified by subsequent events, and we must derive from our cause and from the strength that is in us, and from the traditions and history of our race, and from the support and aid of our Empire all over the world the means to make this country overcome obstacles of all kinds and continue to the end of the furrow, whatever the toil and suffering may be.

[· · ·]

The nose of the bulldog has been slanted backwards so that he can breathe with comfort without letting go.

[· · ·]

Some thought there would be a German war, some did not; but no one supposed that a great military action would exhibit all the vices of military organization without those redeeming virtues which, God knows, are needed to redeem warlike operations from the taint of shame. We have been confronted with an exhibition of ruthlessness and outrage enforced upon the weak, enforced upon women and children. We have been confronted with repeated breaches of the law of enlightened warfare, practices analogous to those which in the private life are regarded as cheating, and which deprive persons or country adopting them, or condoning them, of the credit and respect due to honourable soldiers. We have been confronted with all this. Let us not imitate it. (Cheers.)

Let us not try to make small retaliations and reprisals here and there. Let us concentrate upon the simple, obvious task of creating a military force so powerful that the war, even in default of any good fortune, can certainly be ended and brought to a satisfactory conclusion. However the war began, now that it is started it is a war of self-preservation for us. Our civilization, our way of doing things, our political and Parliamentary life, with its voting and its thinking, our party system, our party warfare, the free and easy tolerance of British life, our method of doing things and of keeping ourselves alive and self-respecting in the world – all these are brought into contrast, into collision, with the organized force of bureaucratic Prussian militarism.

[· · ·]

That is the struggle which is opened now and which must go forward without pause or abatement until it is settled decisively and finally one way or the other. On that there can be no compromise or truce. It is our life or it is theirs. We are bound, having gone so far, to go forward without flinching to the very end.

[· · ·]

Years ago the elder Pitt urged upon his countrymen the compulsive invocation, 'Be one people'. It has taken us till now to obey his appeal, but now we are together, and while we remain one people there are no forces in the world strong enough to beat us down or break us up. (Cheers.)

I hope even in this dark hour of strife and struggle, that the unity which has been established in our country under the pressure of war will not cease when the great military effort upon which we are engaged and the great moral causes which we are pursuing have been achieved. I hope, and I do not think my hope is a vain one, that the forces which have come together in our islands and throughout our Empire may continue to work together, not only in a military struggle, but to try to make our country more quickly a more happy and more prosperous land, where social justice and free institutions are more firmly established than they have been in the past. (Cheers.) If that is so we shall not have fought in vain at home as well as abroad. With these hopes and in this belief I would urge you, laying aside all hindrance, thrusting away all private aims, to devote yourselves unswervingly and unflinchingly to the vigorous and successful prosecution of the war.

'NO REASON TO DESPAIR'

On 2 October 1914, as German troops drew closer to the North Sea and Channel ports, Churchill left London for Antwerp, where for four days he encouraged the Belgians to hold the Germans at bay for as long as they could, helped by a force of British Royal Marines. By the time Antwerp surrendered to the Germans on October 10, the resistance had enabled the British and French forces to regroup and protect Dunkirk, which remained an Allied port for the rest of the war. At sea, the worst British maritime disaster of the war took place on 1 November 1914, off Coronel on the Pacific coast of Chile, with 1,500 sailors drowned. That week, Churchill learned of the death on the Western Front of his cousin Norman Leslie, and a week later of the death of his friend Hugh Dawnay, who had been with him in action at Omdurman and in South Africa. On November 27 – three days before his fortieth birthday – Churchill told the House of Commons, in answer to criticism that details of the war at sea were being withheld, and in order to combat public 'nervousness, anxiety, or alarm':

The Prime Minister in times like these is the servant of the Crown directly and personally responsible that the withholding of information in the public interest shall not be abused by the Departments of State and Ministers specially affected. It is also the desire of the Admiralty to give as much information as is possible on all these matters without prejudice to the interests to which I have referred, and I think we have done so. I think we have done it, and we shall continue to do so whenever the opportunity offers and the season presents itself.

Once information has been given about any action or incident I am of opinion that comment upon it should be perfectly free. Criticism is always advantageous. I have derived continued benefit from criticism at all periods of my life, and I do not remember any time when I was ever short of it. But there is a salutary rule about criticism which applies in time of peace as well as in time of war, in private as well as in public things, and that is that criticism should be very restrained when the party criticised is not able to reply, and it is especially so when he is not able to reply without disclosing facts which would do harm to the critic as well as the party criticised if they were disclosed.

But I recognise the great difficulties of the Press during the present War, and I sympathise very keenly with them in the prohibitions and limitations which fence them about on every side, and which from day to day deny them the opportunity of publishing quantities of information which reach them – information which is most interesting and which may have been collected in many cases with great trouble and expense. There is often a tendency to underrate the acute discomfort under which our great newspapers are living at the present time, and speaking as one of the heads of one of the combatant Departments I feel bound to say that we owe the Press a very great debt, so far as this War has proceeded, for the way in which it has helped, with inconsiderable exceptions and with only momentary lapses, the course of the military operations, and has upheld the interests of the country.

I would like to say that I greatly appreciate the kindness and confidence with which the House during this Session has treated the Admiralty and its representatives in not pressing for information on many matters in which the keenest interest is taken, and upon which there is a natural desire to arrive at conclusions and to pronounce judgment.

Ultimately, and as soon as possible, all the facts connected with past operations, and with the administration of the Navy, now and immediately before the War, will be made public in a form in which they can be studied and weighed by the nation. For my part I look forward hopefully to that day.

There is, however, one other reason why I think it is not desirable to dwell too much on particular incidents at the present time. The incidents which are seen are a very small proportion of the work which is going forward all over the world, and it would be a great pity if the mind of the public were disproportionately concerned with particular incidents, and if the departments concerned were occupied in defending themselves or in justifying themselves in regard to these incidents. We are waging this War, on which from day to day our vital safety depends, and no one who is concerned with military departments ought to have his attention drawn away from the immediate needs of the military and naval operations for the purpose of going at undue length into matters which lie in the past.

[· · ·]

Two years ago I set up a Committee of the Admiralty to go into the whole question of the acceleration of new construction immediately after the outbreak of war so that the greatest possible number of deliveries could be made in the shortest possible time and very elaborate reports were furnished, and a complete system was worked out in every detail. In carrying out this system we have been aided by the patriotism and energy of the workmen in all the yards, who have strained their physical strength to the utmost, and have, by so doing, made themselves, in fact, the comrades of their fellow citizens who are fighting in the trenches at the front. During this period – between the beginning of the War and the end of 1915 – while the Germans will be receiving an accession of three ships we shall receive [. . .] fifteen ships in all. All these ships are, of course, of the greatest power of any vessels that have ever been constructed in naval history, and it is no exaggeration to say that we could afford to lose a super-Dreadnought every month for twelve months without any loss occurring to the enemy and yet be in approximately as good a position of superiority as we were at the declaration of the War.

I hope that these facts will be of comfort to nervous people during the months that lie before us. They prove that so far as any policy of attrition is concerned the results so far, and the forecast so far as we may judge it, are not unsatisfactory to us: nor is there any attrition by wear and tear. The refits of the Fleet and flotillas are being regularly conducted. The health of the sailors is nearly twice as good as in time of peace. Six hundred thousand pounds has been spent by the Admiralty on warm clothing, and I have every reason to believe that the arrangements are thoroughly satisfactory, though, of course, if friends like to send additional comforts, arrangements are made for their reception and distribution. The sailors have received with warm gratitude the separation allowance which the Navy had, always hitherto, been completely denied.

The conduct of the Fleet is exemplary, and any crime there is arises mainly among men who have been a long time in civil life, and who have not fully remembered the excellent precepts of their naval training. In the Grand Fleet the conduct of the men is almost perfect. The whole personnel of the Navy consists of a most intelligent class of skilled workmen and mechanicians. They have studied fully the conditions of the War, and they follow with the closest interest the heroic struggles of our soldiers in the field, and the zeal and enthusiasm with which they are discharging their duties inspires those who lead them with the utmost confidence.

I have thought it right to offer these few remarks of a general character to the House because despondent views are prejudicial to the public interest, and ought not to be tolerated by persons in the responsible position of Members of Parliament while they are in any public situation. There is absolutely no reason whatever for nervousness, anxiety, or alarm. We are now separating for an adjournment of some weeks, which will probably be very important weeks in the history of this War. There is every reason for complete confidence in the power of the Navy to give effect to the wishes and the purposes of the State and the Empire. We have powerful Allies on the seas. The Russian Navy is developing in strength; the French Navy has complete command of the Mediterranean, and the Japanese Navy has effective command of the Pacific, and the utmost cordiality characterises the working of the Admiralties of the four countries.

But even if we were single-handed, as we were in the days of the Napoleonic wars, we should have no reason to despair of our capacity – no doubt we should suffer discomfort and privation and loss – but we should have no reason to despair of our capacity to go on indefinitely, drawing our supplies from wherever we needed them, and transporting our troops wherever we required them, and to continue this process with a strength which would grow stronger with each month the War continued until, in the end, and perhaps not at any very distant date, the purposes for which we are fighting are achieved.

'ANXIETY WILL MAKE ITS ABODE IN OUR BRAIN'

The setbacks and defeats of the first six months of the war were made much of by the Conservative opposition in the House of Commons and in several newspapers. The Germans had successfully defended the line of trenches that ran from the North Sea coast east of Dunkirk to the Swiss Alps; the daily death toll on the Western Front caused growing unease in Britain. When Churchill proposed, in strictest secrecy, a method to break the trench stalemate – what was to become the tank – the War Office was sceptical. The war that was to have ended by Christmas 1914 was dragging on, with no end in sight. The defeat on 28 August 1914 of units of the German High Sea Fleet, in action with Admiral Sir David Beatty's battlecruisers in the Heligoland Bight (with 712 German and 35 British sailors killed), raised British morale, as did a British naval victory in the Falklands on 8 December 1914; but the bulk of the German High Sea Fleet was still undefeated, and the North Sea still a potential route for a German invasion of Britain. When Churchill spoke in the House of Commons on 15 February 1915, he sought to calm the parliamentary and public mood of unease:

We have never been a military nation, though now we are going to take a hand in that. We have always relied for our safety on naval power, and in that respect it is not true to say we entered on this War unprepared. On the contrary, the German Army was not more ready for an offensive war on a gigantic scale than was the British Fleet for national defence. The credit for this is due to the House, which, irrespective of party interests, has always by overwhelming, and in later years by unchallengeable majorities, supported the Government and the Minister in every demand made for naval defence. Indeed, such disputes as we have had from time to time have only been concerned with the margins of superiority, and have turned on comparatively small points respecting them. For instance, we have discussed at enormous length what percentages of 'Dreadnought' superiority would be available in particular months in future years, and we have argued whether the 'Lord Nelsons' should be counted as 'Dreadnoughts' or not. The House of Commons as a whole has a right to claim the Navy as its child and as the unchanging object of its care and solicitude; and now after six months of war, with new dangers and new difficulties coming into view, we have every right to feel content with the results of our labours.

[···]

The great sailors of the past, the men of the Revolutionary and Napoleonic Wars, would have been astounded. During those two great wars, which began in 1793 and ended, after a brief interval, in 1814, 10,871 British merchant ships were captured or sunk by the enemy. Even after the decisive battle of Trafalgar, when we had the undisputed command of the sea so far as it can be tactically and strategically attained, the loss of British ships went on at a rate of over 500 ships a year. In 1806, 519 ships were sunk or captured – that is, the year after Trafalgar; in 1807, 559; in 1808, 469; in 1809, 571; and in 1810, 619. Our total losses on the high seas in the first six months of the present War, including all ships other than trawlers engaged in mine-sweeping – including losses by mines and vessels scuttled by submarines – our losses in the whole of that period are only sixty-three.

Of course, we must always be on the lookout for another attempt by the enemy to harass the trade routes. Although the oceans offer rather a bleak prospect to the German cruisers, and the experience of their consorts is not encouraging, the Admiralty must be fully prepared for that possibility, and we shall be able to meet any new efforts with advantages and resources incomparably superior to those which were at our disposal at the beginning of the War. The truth is that steam and the telegraph have enormously increased, as compared with sailing days, the thoroughness and efficiency of super-ior sea power. Coaling, communications, and supplies are vital and constant needs, and once the upper hand has been lost they become operations of almost insuperable difficulty to the weaker navy. Credit is due to our outlying squadrons and to the Admiralty organisation by which they have been directed. It must never be forgotten that the situation on every sea, even the most remote, is dominated and decided by the influence of Sir John Jellicoe's Fleet – lost to view amid the northern mists, preserved by patience and seamanship in all its strength and efficiency, silent, unsleeping, and, as yet, unchallenged.

[· · ·]

We have now moved by sea, at home and abroad, including wounded brought back from the front, including Belgian wounded, including Belgian and French troops, moved here and there as circumstances required, often at the shortest possible notice, with constant changes of plan, across oceans threatened by the enemy's cruisers and across channels haunted by submarines, to and fro from India and Egypt, from Australia, New Zealand, Canada, China, South Africa, from every fortress and Possession under the Crown, approximately 1,000,000 men without, up to the present, any accident or loss of life. If that is 'incapacity' I hope there will be an inexhaustible supply of that quality.

[· · ·]

With regard to the Army, it should be remembered that we are supplying across the sea, in the teeth of the enemy's opposition, an Army almost as large as the Grand Army of Napoleon, only vastly more complex in organisation and equipment. We are also preparing other Armies still larger in number. I do not know on what day or at what hour the Secretary of State for War will ask the Admiralty to move 20,000 or it may be 40,000 men. It may be at very short notice. He does not know, until we tell him, how we shall move them, by what route or to what ports. Plans are frequently changed on purpose at the very last moment; it is imperative for the safety of our soldiers and the reinforcement of our Armies and the conduct of the War.

We have at the present moment a powerful and flexible machinery which can move whole Armies with celerity wherever it is desired in a manner never before contemplated or dreamt of, and I warn the House most solemnly against allowing grounds of commercial advantage or financial economy to place any hampering restriction or impediment upon these most difficult and momentous operations. Careful and prudent administration does not stop at the outbreak of war. Everything in our power will be done to enforce it and avoid extravagance.

[· · ·]

It is my duty in this House to speak for the Navy, and the truth is that it is sound as a bell all through. I do not care where or how it may be tested; it will be found good and fit and keen and honest. It will be found to be the product of good management and organisation, of sound principle in design and strategy, of sterling workmen and faithful workmanship, and careful clerks and accountants, and skilful engineers, and painstaking officers, and hardy tars.

The great merit of Admiral Sir David Beatty's action is that it shows us and the world that there is at present no reason to assume that, ship for ship, gun for gun, and man for man, we cannot give a very good account of ourselves. It shows that at five to four in representative ships – because the quality of the ships on either side is a very fair representation of the relative qualities of the lines of battle – the Germans did not think it prudent to engage, that they accepted without doubt or hesitation their inferiority, that they thought only of flight just as our men thought only of pursuit, that they were wise in the view they took, and that if they had taken any other view they would, unquestionably, have been destroyed. That is the cruel fact, which no falsehood – and many have been issued – no endeavour to sink by official communiqués vessels they could not stay to sink in war, can obscure.

[···]

If any mood or tendency of public opinion arises, or is fostered by the newspapers, or given countenance in this House, which makes too much of our losses, even if they are cruel losses, and even if it may be said that they are in some respects avoidable losses, then I say you will have started on a path which, pressed to its logical conclusion, would leave our Navy cowering in its harbours, instead of ruling the seas. When I think of the great scale of our operations, the enormous target we expose, the number of ships whose movements have to be arranged for, the novel conditions to which I have referred, it is marvellous how few have been our losses, and how great the care and vigilance exercised by the admirals afloat and by the Admiralty Staff, and it appears to me, and it will certainly be regarded by those who study this War in history, as praiseworthy in the highest degree.

The tasks which lie before us are anxious and grave. We are, it now appears, to be the object of a kind of warfare which has never before been practised by a civilised State. The scuttling and sinking at sight, without search or parley, of merchant ships by submarine agency is a wholly novel and unprecedented departure. It is a state of things which no one had ever contemplated, and which would have been universally reprobated, and repudiated, before this War. But it must not be supposed because the attack is extraordinary that a good defence and a good reply cannot be made. The statutes of ancient Rome contained no provision for the punishment of parricide, but when the first offender appeared it was found that satisfactory arrangements could be made to deal with him. Losses no doubt will be incurred – of that I give full warning – but we believe that no vital injury can be done. If our traders put to sea regularly and act in the spirit of the gallant captain of the merchant ship *Laertes*, whose well merited honour has been made public this morning, and if they take the precautions which are proper and legitimate, we expect that the losses will be confined within manageable limits, even at the outset, when the enemy must be expected to make his greatest effort to produce an impression.

[···]

I thank the House for the attention with which they have listened to me. The stresses and strains of this War are not imperceptible to those who are called on to bear a part in the responsibility for the direction of the tremendous and terrible events which are now taking place. They have a right to the generous and indulgent judgment and support of their fellow countrymen, and to the goodwill of the House of Commons.

We cannot tell what lies before us, or how soon or in what way the next great developments of the struggle will declare themselves, or what the state of Europe and the world will be at its close. But this, I think, we can already say, as far as the British Navy is concerned, that although no doubt new dangers and perplexities will come upon us continuously, and anxiety will make its abode in our brain, yet the dangers and anxieties which now are advancing upon us will not be more serious or more embarrassing than those through which we have already successfully made our way. For during the months that are to come the British Navy and the sea power which it exerts will increasingly dominate the general situation, will be the main and unfailing reserve of the allied nations, will progressively paralyse the fighting energies of our antagonists, and will, if need be, even in default of all other favourable forces, ultimately by itself decide the issue of the War.

'AN EVENT SHOCKING AND UNNATURAL IN ITS CHARACTER'

When, in October 1914, the Ottoman Empire joined the war on the side of Germany, Churchill favoured an immediate naval attack at the Dardanelles. This was not approved by the War Council until January 1915. The Anglo-French naval attempt to push through the Dardanelles to the Sea of Marmara took place on 18 March 1915. The attack was unsuccessful. A French battleship, the *Bouvet*, was sunk and more than six hundred French sailors drowned. Three British battleships, *Inflexible*, *Irresistible* and *Ocean*, were sunk, but most of the sailors were saved, although twenty-nine on *Inflexible* were drowned. Churchill urged the British naval officer commanding, Admiral de Robeck, to try a second attack; the Admiral declined. Although Churchill was much angered at the time by the refusal, he later wrote, in *The World Crisis*:

> One must, however, make great allowances for the Admiral and for the naval point of view which he represented. To statesmen or soldiers, ships in time of war possess no sentimental value. They are engines of war to be used, risked, and if necessary expended in the common cause and for the general policy of the State. To such minds the life of a soldier was every whit as precious as that of a sailor, and an old battleship marked for the scrap heap was an instrument of war to be expended in a good cause as readily as artillery ammunition is fired to shelter and support a struggling infantry attack.
>
> But to an Admiral of this standing and upbringing, these old ships were sacred. They had been the finest ships afloat in the days when he as a young officer had first set foot upon their decks. The discredit and even disgrace of casting away a ship was ingrained deeply by years of mental training and outlook. The spectacle of this noble structure on which so many loyalties centred, which was the floating foothold of daily life, foundering miserably beneath the waves, appeared as an event shocking and unnatural in its character.
>
> Whereas a layman or soldier might have rejoiced that so important an action as that of March 18 could have been fought with a loss

of less than thirty British lives and two or three worthless ships, and that so many valuable conclusions had been attained at such a slender cost, Admiral de Robeck was saddened and consternated to the foundations of his being. These emotions were also present around the Admiralty table in Whitehall.

'THE SORROW OF YOUTH ABOUT TO DIE'

Among those for whom Churchill obtained a commission in the Royal Naval Volunteer Reserve was the poet Rupert Brooke, who sailed with the Mediterranean Expeditionary Force to the Dardanelles in February 1915. While in reserve on the Greek island of Skyros, awaiting orders to go into action, Brooke was bitten by a mosquito. The wound became infected and he died on board a French hospital ship in Skyros Bay on April 23. He was twenty-seven years old. Churchill's obituary of Brooke was published in *The Times* three days later:

Rupert Brooke is dead. A telegram from the Admiral at Lemnos tells us that this life has closed at the moment when it seemed to have reached its springtime. A voice had become audible, a note had been struck, more true, more thrilling, more able to do justice to the nobility of our youth in arms engaged in this present war, than any other – more able to express their thoughts of self-surrender, and with a power to carry comfort to those who watch them so intently from afar. The voice has been swiftly stilled. Only the echoes and the memory remain; but they will linger.

During the last few months of his life, months of preparation in gallant comradeship and open air, the poet-soldier told with all the simple force of genius the sorrow of youth about to die, and the sure triumphant consolations of a sincere and valiant spirit. He expected to die; he was willing to die for the dear England whose beauty and majesty he knew; and he advanced towards the brink in perfect serenity, with absolute conviction of the rightness of his country's cause and a heart devoid of hate for fellow men.

The thoughts to which he gave expression in the very few incomparable war sonnets which he has left behind will be shared by many thousands of young men moving resolutely and blithely forward into this, the hardest, the cruellest, and the least-rewarded of all the wars that men have fought. They are a whole history and revelation of Rupert Brooke himself. Joyous, fearless, versatile, deeply instructed, with classic symmetry of mind and body, ruled by high undoubting purpose, he was all that one would wish England's noblest sons to be in days when no sacrifice but the most precious is acceptable, and the most precious is that which is most freely proffered.

'RUGGED KINDNESS AND WARM-HEARTED COURTESY'

Following the failure of the naval attack at the Dardanelles on 18 March 1915, a military landing was carried out on the Gallipoli Peninsula on 25 April 1915, under the authority and control of the Secretary of State for War, Field Marshal Lord Kitchener of Khartoum. The landing came at the moment when a political crisis, the scandal of a grave shell shortage in the British forces in France and Flanders, led to Conservative Party demands for a Coalition Government. One of the Conservative conditions was that Churchill leave the Admiralty. They had not forgiven him his pre-war support for Irish Home Rule, or the dispatch of naval forces in March 1914 to disarm the Ulster Unionists. On 21 May 1915, Churchill learned that he was no longer to be First Lord of the Admiralty. The next day, while waiting to learn what new, inevitably less senior, post would be his, Churchill was visited at the Admiralty by Kitchener – whose harsh attitude towards the defeated Dervishes in 1898 he had criticised publicly in *The River War*. Of Kitchener's visit to him in 1915, he later wrote in *The World Crisis*:

It was during this interval that I had the honour of receiving a visit of ceremony from Lord Kitchener. I was not at first aware of what it was about. We had differed strongly and on a broad front at the last meeting of the War Council. Moreover, no decision of any importance on naval and military affairs could be taken during the hiatus. We talked about the situation. After some general remarks he asked me whether it was settled that I should leave the Admiralty. I said it was. He asked what I was going to do. I said I had no idea; nothing was settled. He spoke very kindly about our work together. He evidently had no idea how narrowly he had escaped my fate.

As he got up to go he turned and said, in the impressive and almost majestic manner which was natural to him, 'Well, there is one thing at any rate they cannot take from you. The Fleet was ready.' After that he was gone. During the months that we were still to serve together in the new Cabinet I was condemned often to differ from him, to oppose him and to criticize him. But I cannot forget the rugged kindness and warm-hearted courtesy which led him to pay me this visit.

'TRUST THE PEOPLE'

On 23 May 1915, Churchill was offered, and accepted, the post of Chancellor of the Duchy of Lancaster. In this capacity he retained his seat both in the Cabinet and on the War Council, where he was free to continue his advocacy of a more active war policy, but with no authority to give effect to it, and no War Staff (as at the Admiralty) to examine, elaborate or carry out his plans. On 5 June 1915, he went to Dundee to give his constituents an account of the turn in his fortunes. The *Dundee Courier* reported his remarks:

I thought it right to take an opportunity of coming here to my constituency in view of all the events which have recently taken place, and also of the fact that considerably more than a year has passed since I have had the opportunity of speaking in Dundee. I have not come here to trouble you with personal matters, or to embark on explanations or to indulge in reproaches or recriminations. In wartime a man must do his duty as he sees it, and take his luck as it comes or goes. I will not say a word here or in Parliament which I cannot truly feel will have a useful bearing upon the only thing that matters, upon the only thing I care about, and the only thing I want you to think about – namely, the waging of victorious war upon the enemy. (Cheers.)

I was sent to the Admiralty in 1911, after the Agadir crisis had nearly brought us into war, and I was sent with the express duty laid upon me by the Prime Minister to put the Fleet in a state of instant and constant readiness for war in case we were attacked by Germany. (Cheers.) Since then, for nearly four years, I have borne the heavy burden of being, according to the time-honoured language of my patent, 'responsible to Crown and Parliament for all the business of the Admiralty', and when I say responsible, I have been responsible in the real sense, that I have had the blame for everything that has gone wrong. (Laughter and cheers.) These years have comprised the most important period in our naval history – a period of preparation for war, a period of vigilance and mobilization, and a period of actual war under conditions of which no man has any experience. I have done my best (cheers), and the archives of the Admiralty will show in the utmost detail the part I have played in all the great transactions that have taken place. It is to them I look for my defence. I look also to the general naval situation. The terrible dangers of the beginning of the war are over. The seas have been swept clear: the submarine menace has been fixed within definite limits; the personal ascendancy of our men, the superior quality of our ships on the high seas, has been established beyond doubt or question; our strength has greatly increased, actually and relatively from what it was in the beginning of the war, and it grows continually every day by leaps and bounds in all the classes of vessels needed for the special purpose of the war.

Between now and the end of the year, the British Navy will receive reinforcements which would be incredible if they were not actual facts. Everything is in perfect order. Nearly everything has been foreseen, all our supplies, stores, ammunition, and appliances of every kind, our supplies and drafts of officers and men – all are there. Nowhere will you be hindered. You have taken the measure of your foe, you have only to go forward with confidence. On the whole surface of the seas of the world no hostile flag is flown.

[· · ·]

I have two things to say to you about the Dardanelles. First, you must expect losses both by land and sea; but the Fleet you are employing there is your surplus Fleet, after all other needs have been provided for. Had it not been used in this great enterprise, it would have been lying idle in your southern ports. A large number of the old vessels of which it is composed have to be laid up, in any case, before the end of the year, because their crews are wanted for the enormous reinforcements of new ships which the industry of your workshops is hurrying into the water. Losses of ships, therefore, as long as the precious lives of the officers and men are saved, as in nearly every case they have been – losses of that kind, I say, may easily be exaggerated in the minds both of friend and foe.

And military operations will also be costly, but those who suppose that Lord Kitchener (loud cheers) has embarked upon them without narrowly and carefully considering their requirements in relation to all other needs and in relation to the paramount need of our Army in France and Flanders – such people are mistaken and, not only mistaken, they are presumptuous.

My second point is this: in looking at your losses squarely and soberly, you must not forget, at the same time, the prize for which you are contending. The Army of Sir Ian Hamilton, the Fleet of Admiral de Robeck, are separated only by a few miles from a victory such as this war has not yet seen. When I speak of victory, I am not referring to those victories which crowd the daily placards of many newspapers. I am speaking of victory in the sense of a brilliant and formidable fact, shaping the destinies of nations and shortening the duration of the war. Beyond those few miles of ridge and scrub on which our soldiers, our French comrades, our gallant Australians, and our New Zealand fellow-subjects are now battling, lie the downfall of a hostile empire, the destruction of an enemy's fleet and army, the fall of a world-famous capital, and probably the accession of powerful Allies. The struggle will be heavy, the risks numerous, the losses cruel; but victory when it comes will make amends for all.

[···]

There never was a great subsidiary operation of war in which a more complete harmony of strategic, political, and economic advantages has combined, or which stood in truer relation to the main decision which is in the central theatre. Through the narrows of the Dardanelles and across the ridges of the Gallipoli Peninsula lie some of the shortest paths to a triumphant peace.

[···]

It is the duty of all in times like these to give loyalty and confidence to their leaders, be they the soldiers in the active sphere or the statesmen who sit in anxious council here at home, to give them loyalty and confidence, not only when all goes smoothly, for that is easy, but to make them feel that they will not be blamed for necessary losses incurred in valiant enterprise or rounded on in reproach at the first check or twist of fortune. Then you will get from your leaders, be they military or civilian, you will get from them the courage, the energy, the audacity, and readiness to run all risks and shoulder the responsibilities without which no great result in war can ever be achieved. (Cheers.)

Now I would like to say something which will get me into trouble. (Laughter.) I do not think that the newspapers ought to be allowed to attack the responsible leaders of the nation (loud cheers), whether in the field or at home, or to write in a manner which is calculated to spread doubts and want of confidence in them or in particular operations, or to write anything which is calculated to make bad blood between them. I apply this not only to the Admirals and Generals, but to the principal Ministers at home, and especially the heads of the great fighting departments.

No other nation now at war would allow the newspapers such a licence in the present time, and if there is to be criticism, if there must be criticism, first, it should be only the loyal criticism of earnest intention. But if there is to be criticism, let it be in Parliament. If the speeches are such that we cannot allow the enemy to be a party to our discussions, then let Parliament, as is its right, sit for the time being with closed doors. But it seems imperative, in the interests of the

1 Left A photograph of Churchill as a schoolboy at Harrow.

2 Below The swimming pool at Harrow School, known as 'The Ducker', into which Churchill pushed a more senior boy.

3 Left Churchill as a soldier in South Africa, a photograph taken in Bloemfontein, May 1900.

4 Below left Churchill's book *The River War*, published on 6 November 1899.

5 Below right Churchill's book of his South African War newspaper despatches, *London to Ladysmith via Pretoria*, published on 15 May 1900.

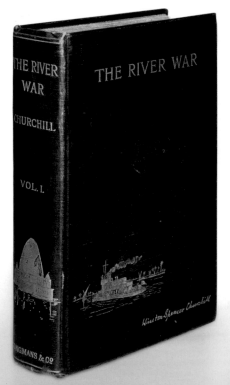

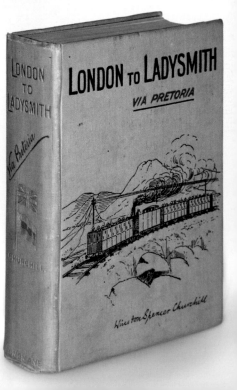

HOW I ESCAPED
FROM PRETORIA.
By Winston Churchill.

The *Morning Post* has received the following telegram from Mr. Winston Spencer Churchill, its war correspondent, who was taken prisoner by the Boers and escaped from Pretoria.

LOURENÇO MARQUES, December 21st, 10 p.m.

I was concealed in a railway truck under great sacks. I had a small store of good water with me. I remained hidden, chancing discovery. The Boers searched the train at Komati Poort, but did not search deep enough, after sixty hours of misery I came safely here. I am very weak, but I am free. I have lost many pounds weight, but I am lighter in heart. I shall also avail myself of every opportunity from this moment to urge with experiences as undiscning and uncompromising prosecution of the war. On the afternoon of the 12th the Transvaal Government's Secretary for War informed me that there was little chance of my release. I therefore resolved to escape the same night, and left the State Schools Prison Pretoria by climbing the wall when the sentries' backs were turned momentarily. I walked through the streets of the town without any disguise, meeting many burghers, but I was not challenged in the crowd. I got through the pickets of the Town Guard, and struck the Delagoa Bay railroad.

I walked along it, eluding the watchers at the bridges and culverts. I waited for a train beyond the first station. The out 11.10 goods train from Pretoria arrived, and before it had reached full speed I boarded with great difficulty, and hid myself under coal sacks. I jumped from the train before dawn, and sheltered during the day in a small wood, in company with a huge vulture, who displayed a lively interest in me. I walked on at dusk. There were no more trains that night. The danger of meeting the guards of the railway line continued; but I was obliged to follow it, as I had no compass or map. I had to make wide detours to avoid the bridges, stations, and huts. My progress was very slow, and chocolate is not a satisfying food. The outlook was gloomy, but I persevered, with God's help, for five days. The food I had to have was very precarious. I was lying up all daylight, and walking on at night time, and, meanwhile, my escape had been discovered and my description telegraphed everywhere. All the trains were searched. Everyone was on the watch for me. Four wrong people were arrested. But on the sixth day I managed to board a train beyond Middleburg, whence there is a direct service to Delagoa.

PARK HALL, CARDIFF.

The Committee of the Cardiff Naturalists Society beg to announce that Mr.

Winston Churchill, M.P.

Will give his deeply interesting Lecture, entitled :

"THE WAR AS I SAW IT"

ON

THURSDAY EVENING, NOVEMBER 29th, 1900, at 8.

The Lecture will be illustrated by Lantern Slides from Photos.

Mr. J. J. NEALE (*President of the Cardiff Naturalists Society*). will preside.

Doors open at 7.30. Lecture at 8. Carriages at 9.45.

RESERVED SEATS—Balcony, Front Row, 7/6; [Other Seats in Balcony, 5/-; Area, 3/6; UNRESERVED SEATS, 2/-.

Plan of the Hall may be seen and Tickets obtained at Mr. Wm. Lewis's, Duke Street.

6 Top Churchill, far right, a newspaper correspondent in captivity, with British soldiers captured by the Boers, Pretoria, 18 November 1899.

7 Above Churchill's telegram about his escape from Boer captivity, published in London on 30 December 1899.

8 Right Announcement of one of Churchill's British lectures on his experiences in South Africa, Cardiff, 29 November 1900.

9 **Left** Churchill speaking to munition workers at Enfield, 18 September 1915. His wife Clementine looks on.

10 **Below** Enfield, 18 September 1915, making a point.

11 **Bottom** Enfield, 18 September 1915, a well-received joke.

12 Left Churchill, in pain following an operation for appendicitis, is led to the platform at Dundee on 11 November 1922, during the General Election campaign. He is wearing his North-West Frontier, Sudan, South Africa and First World War military medals.

13 Below On the podium at Dundee, 11 November 1922, waiting to speak. Clementine sits below him on the platform, immediately to his left.

14 Bottom Churchill at the Victoria Palace Theatre, addressing his supporters in the Abbey Division of Westminster, 19 March 1924, on learning that he has been defeated by the narrowest of margins. Clementine watches as he speaks.

15 Left Churchill as Chancellor of the Exchequer leaving 11 Downing Street for the House of Commons, to deliver his first Budget, 28 April 1925.

16 Above Churchill walking down Whitehall, to the House of Commons, to deliver his fifth Budget, 15 April 1929. To his left are his wife Clementine, his daughter Sarah and his son Randolph.

17 Below Churchill speaking outside the City of London Recruiting Centre for the Territorial Army, Mansion House, London, 24 April 1939.

18 **Above** Churchill in his study at Chartwell, 25 February 1939, working at his upright desk.

19 **Below** Churchill in his study at Chartwell, 25 February 1939, dictating by the fireplace. His bedroom is beyond. Below the portrait of himself is a painting of his father, Lord Randolph Churchill.

NOW THEY LISTEN TO CHURCHILL

Kept out of Conservative Cabinets for years, Winston Churchill comes back as a political power because his warnings proved true.

20 Above Churchill at Chartwell, a photograph taken on 25 February 1939 and published in the *New York Times* magazine on 13 August 1939.

21 Below Churchill making his first wartime broadcast, 1 October 1939.

country for the future, and for the safety and success of our arms, that irresponsible or malicious carping should not continue.

We in this country are the firm supporters of a free Press. A free Press is a natural and healthy feature in national life, so long as you have also a free Parliament and a free platform; but when, owing to war conditions, Parliament observes a voluntary but severe restraint, and when many of the subjects cannot be freely discussed without giving information to the enemy, then the balance of society is no longer true and grave injury results from the unrestricted action of the newspapers.

[...]

A new Government has been formed, old opponents have laid aside their differences, personal interests and party interests have been adjusted or suppressed, and the Administration may now claim to represent the political energies and abilities and to command the loyalties of a united nation. (Cheers.) To support that Government, to make it a success, to make it an efficient instrument for waging war, to be loyal to it, to treat it fairly, and judge it with consideration and respect is not a matter of likes and dislikes, not a matter of ordinary political choice or option. It is for all of us a matter of self-preservation. (Cheers.) For nearly three weeks the country has had its attention diverted from the war by the business of Cabinet making and the dividing of offices and honours, and all those commonplace but necessary details of our political system which are so entertaining in time of peace. (Laughter.)

Now that is all over. It has taken long enough, but it is over, and I ask myself this question – What does the nation expect of the new National Government? I can answer my question. I am going to answer it in one word – action. (Loud cheers.) That is the need, that is the only justification, that there should be a stronger national sentiment, a more powerful driving force, a greater measure of consent in the people, a greater element of leadership and design in the rulers – that is what all parties expect and require in return for the many sacrifices which all parties have after due consideration made from their particular interests and ideals. Action – action, not hesitation; action, not words; action, not agitation. The nation awaits its orders.

The duty lies upon the Government to declare what should be done, to propose it to Parliament, and to stand or fall by the result. That is the message which you wish me to take back to London – Act; act now; act with faith and courage. Trust the people. They have never failed you yet.

[···]

We are confronted with a foe who would without the slightest scruple extirpate us, man, woman, and child, by any method open to him if he had the opportunity. We are fighting a foe who would not hesitate one moment to obliterate every single soul in this great country this afternoon if it could be done by pressing a button. We are fighting a foe who would think as little of that as a gardener would think of smoking out a wasps' nest. Let us recognize that this is a new fact in the history of the world – (cheers) – or, rather, it is an old fact, sprung up out of the horrible abysses of the past. We are fighting with a foe of that kind, and we are locked in mortal struggle. To fail is to be enslaved, or, at the very best, to be destroyed. Not to win decisively is to have all this misery over again after an uneasy truce, and to fight it over again, probably under less favourable circumstances and, perhaps, alone. Why, after what has happened, there could never be peace in Europe until the German military system has been so shattered and torn and trampled that it is unable to resist by any means the will and decision of the conquering Power. (Loud cheers.) For this purpose our whole nation must be organized (cheers) – must be socialized, if you like the word, must be organized and mobilized, and I think there must be asserted in some form or other – I do not attempt to prejudge that – but I think there must be asserted in some form or other by the Government, a reserve power to give the necessary control and organizing authority and to make sure that every one of every rank and condition, men and women as well, do, in their own way, their fair share. (Cheers.) Democratic principles enjoin it, social justice requires it, national safety demands it, and I shall take back to London, with your authority, the message 'Let the Government act according to its faith.' (Cheers.)

Above all, let us be of good cheer. (Cheers, and a voice, 'Shame the devil and to hell with the Huns'.) Let us be of good cheer. I have told you how the Navy's business has been discharged. You see for your-selves how your economic life and energy have been maintained without the slightest check, so that it is certain you can realize the full strength of this vast community. The valour of our soldiers has won general respect in all the Armies of Europe. (Cheers.) The word of Britain is now taken as the symbol and the hall mark of international good faith. The loyalty of our Dominions and Colonies vindicates our civilization, and the hate of our enemies proves the effectiveness of our warfare. Yet I would advise you from time to time, when you are anxious or depressed, to dwell a little on the colour and light of the terrible war pictures now presented to the eye. See Australia and New Zealand smiting down in the last and finest crusade the combined barbarism of Prussia and of Turkey. General Louis Botha holding South Africa for the King. See Canada defending to the death the last few miles of shattered Belgium. Look further, and, across the smoke and carnage of the immense battlefield, look forward to the vision of a united British Empire on the calm background of a liberated Europe.

Then turn again to your task. Look forward, do not look back-ward. Gather afresh in heart and spirit all the energies of your being, bend anew together for a supreme effort. The times are harsh, need is dire, the agony of Europe is infinite, but the might of Britain hurled united into the conflict will be irresistible. We are the grand reserve of the Allied cause, and that grand reserve must now march forward as one man.

'I SEIZED THE LARGEST BRUSH AND FELL UPON MY VICTIM'

Having left Admiralty House in Whitehall, the home of the First Lord of the Admiralty, Churchill moved with his wife and children into a house in London's Cromwell Road with his mother, his brother Jack, and Jack's family. He also rented a farm, Hoe Farm, near Godalming. There he spent as many weekends as he could with his wife and three children, Diana (born 1909), Randolph (born 1911) and Sarah (born 1914). At the suggestion of Jack's wife, Lady Gwendeline, during a summer weekend in June 1915 he took up painting, to soothe his intense frustration at having no ministerial responsibilities; and in the first weekend of July he returned to Hoe Farm, and to painting. In an article in *Strand* magazine (later reprinted in *Thoughts and Adventures*, and then in *Painting as a Pastime*), he recalled how his attachment to painting – which was to bring him so much solace – began:

I shall now relate my personal experience. When I left the Admiralty at the end of May, 1915, I still remained a member of the Cabinet and of the War Council. In this position I knew everything and could do nothing. The change from the intense executive activities of each day's work at the Admiralty to the narrowly measured duties of a counsellor left me gasping. Like a sea-beast fished up from the depths, or a diver too suddenly hoisted, my veins threatened to burst from the fall in pressure.

I had great anxiety and no means of relieving it; I had vehement convictions and small power to give effect to them. I had to watch the unhappy casting-away of great opportunities, and the feeble execution of plans which I had launched and in which I heartily believed. I had long hours of utterly unwonted leisure in which to contemplate the frightful unfolding of the War. At a moment when every fibre of my being was inflamed to action, I was forced to remain a spectator of the tragedy, placed cruelly in a front seat. And then it was that the Muse of Painting came to my rescue – out of charity and out of chivalry, because after all she had nothing to do with me – and said, 'Are these toys any good to you? They amuse some people.'

Some experiments one Sunday in the country with the children's paint-box led me to procure the next morning a complete outfit for painting in oils.

Having bought the colours, an easel, and a canvas, the next step was to begin. But what a step to take! The palette gleamed with beads of colour; fair and white rose the canvas; the empty brush hung poised, heavy with destiny, irresolute in the air. My hand seemed arrested by a silent veto. But after all the sky on this occasion was unquestionably blue, and a pale blue at that. There could be no doubt that blue paint mixed with white should be put on the top part of the canvas. One really does not need to have had an artist's training to see that. It is a starting point open to all. So very gingerly I mixed a little blue paint on the palette with a very small brush, and then with infinite precaution made a mark about as big as a bean upon the affronted snow-white shield.

It was a challenge, a deliberate challenge; but so subdued, so halting, indeed so cataleptic, that it deserved no response. At that moment the loud approaching sound of a motorcar was heard in the drive. From this chariot there stepped swiftly and lightly none other than the gifted wife of Sir John Lavery. 'Painting! But what are you hesitating about? Let me have a brush – the big one.'

Splash into the turpentine, wallop into the blue and the white, frantic flourish on the palette – clean no longer – and then several large, fierce strokes and slashes of blue on the absolutely cowering canvas. Anyone could see that it could not hit back. No evil fate avenged the jaunty violence. The canvas grinned in helplessness before me. The spell was broken. The sickly inhibitions rolled away. I seized the largest brush and fell upon my victim with Berserk fury. I have never felt any awe of a canvas since.

'THIS UNHAPPY BUT NOT INGLORIOUS GENERATION'

Churchill remained a member of the Cabinet and of the War Council – renamed the Dardanelles Committee – from May to October 1915. He often spoke in the committee about the Gallipoli campaign, but policy was made by others: by the Prime Minister, Asquith; by the Secretary of State for War, Lord Kitchener; and by Churchill's successor as First Lord of the Admiralty, Arthur Balfour. They endorsed the continuing battle on the Gallipoli Peninsula, and authorised a second landing there – at Suvla Bay – on 6 August 1915.

There, as at the landings at Cape Helles and Anzac Cove on April 25, the troops succeeded in getting ashore, but made little headway on land, and failed to take their objective, the high ground overlooking the Dardanelles. On the Western Front, the fighting and the stalemate continued. On 18 September 1915, Churchill spoke, at his wife Clementine's request, at Enfield Lock munitions works, where she had established one of a number of canteens on behalf of the YMCA. He spoke twice, first to the men about to go on the night shift, and then to the men coming off the day shift:

Our situation is a serious one. We have it in our power by our exertions to carry this war to a successful and a decisive conclusion, but we have it in our power to do so only if we exert our strength to the utmost limit of human and national capacity.

After all we did not seek this struggle. We did not desire as a nation, or as a generation, to have imposed upon us this terrible ordeal. We cannot understand the inscrutable purposes which have plunged these evils upon the world, and have involved all the nations of Europe in a catastrophe measureless in its horror. But we know that if in this time of crisis and strain we do our duty, we shall have done all that it is in human power to do – and we shall so bear ourselves in this period – all of us, whatever part we play on the stage of the world's history – we shall bear ourselves so that those who come after us will find amid the signs and scars of this great struggle that the liberties of Europe and of Britain are still intact and inviolate; when those looking back upon our efforts, such as they have been, will say of this unhappy but not inglorious generation, placed in a position of extraordinary trial, that it did not fail in the test, and that the torch which it preserved lights the world for us today.

I cannot but express most sincerely my gratitude for all the exertions which are being made, and I earnestly trust you will not flag or slacken in these, so that by your efforts our country may emerge from this period of darkness and peril once more into the sunlight of a peaceful time.

'I HAVE A CLEAR CONSCIENCE'

At the end of October 1915, the Prime Minister, H. H. Asquith, announced that the inner War Cabinet would no longer be the five-man Dardanelles Committee – on which Churchill had served for the previous six months – but a smaller policy-making body of three, the Cabinet War Committee, headed by Asquith as Prime Minister, with Kitchener and Balfour as the other two members. Churchill was excluded. On October 30 he offered his resignation from the Cabinet, asking Asquith if he could be made Governor-General and Commander-in-Chief of British East Africa. The Conservative leader, Andrew Bonar Law, supported Churchill's request, but Asquith rejected it. On November 11, Churchill formally resigned from the Cabinet. His resignation letter was published two days later in all the newspapers:

My dear Asquith,

When I left the Admiralty five months ago, I accepted an office with few duties in order at your request to take part in the work of the War Council, and to assist new Ministers with the knowledge of current operations which I then possessed in a special degree. The counsels which I have offered are upon record in the minutes of the Committee of Imperial Defence, and in the memoranda I have circulated to the Cabinet: and I draw your attention at the present time to these.

I am in cordial agreement with the decision to form a small War Council. I appreciated the intention you expressed to me six weeks ago to include me among its members. I foresaw then the personal diffi-culties which you would have to face in its composition, and I make no complaint at all that your scheme should be changed. But with that change my work in the Government comes naturally to a close.

Knowing what I do about the present situation, and the instru-ment of executive power, I could not accept a position of general responsibility for war policy without any effective share in its guidance and control. Even when decisions of principle are rightly taken, the speed and method of their execution are factors which determine the result. Nor do I feel in times like these able to remain in well-paid inactivity. I therefore ask you to submit my resignation to the King. I am an officer, and I place myself unreservedly at the disposal of the military authorities, observing that my regiment is in France.

I have a clear conscience which enables me to bear my responsibility for past events with composure.

Time will vindicate my administration of the Admiralty, and assign me my due share in the vast series of preparations and operations which have secured us the command of the seas.

With much respect, and unaltered personal friendship, I bid you good-bye.

> Yours very sincerely
> Winston S. Churchill

'WE ARE PASSING THROUGH A BAD TIME NOW'

On 15 November 1915, four days after resigning from the Cabinet, Churchill made a personal statement to the House of Commons, the right accorded any Minister who has resigned. His tone was a positive one:

There is no reason to be discouraged about the progress of the war. We are passing through a bad time now and it will probably be worse before it is better, but that it will be better, if we only endure and persevere, I have no doubt whatever. The old wars were decided by their episodes rather than by their tendencies. In this war the tendencies are far more important than the episodes. Without winning any sensational victories we may win this war. We may win it even during a continuance of extremely disappointing and vexatious events. It is not necessary for us in order to win the war to push the German lines back over all the territory they have absorbed, or to pierce them. While the German lines extend far beyond her frontiers, and while her flag flies over conquered capitals and subjugated provinces, while all the appearances of military success attend her arms, Germany may be defeated more fatally in the second and third year of the war than if the Allied Armies had entered Berlin in the first.

[···]

All through this year I have offered the same counsel to the Government – undertake no operation in the West which is more costly to us in life than to the enemy; in the East, take Constantinople; take it by ships if you can; take it by soldiers if you must; take it by whichever plan, military or naval, commends itself to your military experts, but take it, and take it soon, and take it while time remains.

The situation is now entirely changed, and I am not called upon to offer any advice upon its new aspects. But it seems to me that if there were any operations in the history of the world which, having been begun, it was worth while to carry through with the utmost vigour and fury, with a consistent flow of reinforcements, and an utter disregard of life, it was the operations so daringly and brilliantly begun by Sir Ian Hamilton in the immortal landing of the 25th April.

[···]

It is no doubt disconcerting for us to observe the Government of a State like Bulgaria convinced, on an impartial survey of the chances, that victory will rest with the Central Powers. Some of these small States are hypnotised by German military pomp and precision. They see the glitter, they see the episode; but what they do not see or realise is the capacity of the ancient and mighty nations against whom Germany is warring to endure adversity, to put up with disappointment and mismanagement, to recreate and renew their strength, to toil on with boundless obstinacy through boundless suffering to the achievement of the greatest cause for which men have fought.

'IT WAS A COMFORT TO BE WITH THESE FINE TROOPS'

On 18 November 1915, Churchill left London for the Western Front, in the uniform of a major in the Queen's Own Oxfordshire Hussars, the regiment with which he had served as a Territorial officer until the outbreak of war, attending its annual military camp. Reaching Boulogne, he found a car waiting to take him to General Sir John French, Commander-in-Chief of the British Expeditionary Force, who offered him command of an infantry brigade, some four thousand men, with the rank of brigadier general. Churchill accepted, but asked if he could have some experience of trench warfare first; the Commander-in-Chief agreed, and Churchill was then attached, as a major, to the Grenadier Guards. Churchill recalled, in *The World Crisis*:

> The closing scenes at the Dardanelles proceeded while I was serving with the 2nd Battalion of the Grenadier Guards near Laventie. I was not without information on the course of affairs from my friends both in the Cabinet and at General Headquarters. It was a comfort to be with these fine troops at such a time, to study their methods, unsurpassed in the Army, of discipline and trench warfare, and to share from day to day their life under the hard conditions of the winter and the fire of the enemy.
>
> The kindness with which I was received during my period of instruction with the Guards Division will ever be gratefully remembered by me. As in the shades of a November evening, I for the first time led a platoon of grenadiers across the sopping fields which gave access to our trenches, while here and there the bright flashes of the guns or the occasional whistle of a random bullet accompanied our path, the conviction came into my mind with absolute assurance that the simple soldiers and their regimental officers, armed with their cause, would by their virtues in the end retrieve the mistakes and ignorances of Staffs and Cabinets, of Admirals, Generals and politicians – including, no doubt, many of my own.
>
> But, alas, at what a needless cost! To how many slaughters,

through what endless months of fortitude and privation would these men, themselves already the survivors of many a bloody day, be made to plod before victory was won!

'SENDING THE WOUNDED SOLDIERS BACK THREE OR FOUR TIMES'

On New Year's Day 1916, Churchill learned that he was to command, not a brigade of some four thousand men, with the rank of brigadier general, but a battalion of a thousand men, with the rank of lieutenant colonel. The battalion was the 6th Royal Scots Fusiliers, which he joined in their reserve billets on 5 January 1916. On the evening of January 13, while Churchill was with his battalion in reserve at Ploegsteert on the Western Front, he read in a copy of *The Times* that had just reached him that the Gallipoli Peninsula had been evacuated four days earlier, without loss of life. 'There is no culminating catastrophe,' he wrote that night to his wife, 'only a cruel tale of wasted effort, life & treasure, & opportunity – priceless and unique – gone forever.' Churchill later wrote, in *The World Crisis*:

The end of the Dardanelles campaign closed the second great period of the struggle. There was nothing left on land now but the war of exhaustion – not only of armies but of nations. No more strategy, very little tactics; only the dull wearing down of the weaker combination by exchanging lives; only the multiplying of machinery on both sides to exchange them quicker.

The continuous front now stretched not only from the Alps to the Seas, but across the Balkan Peninsula, across Palestine, across Mesopotamia. The Central Empires had successfully defended their southern flank in the Balkans and in Turkey. Their victory quelled simultaneously all likelihood of any attempt against their northern flank upon the Baltic. All such ideas had received their quietus. Good, plain, straightforward frontal attacks by valiant flesh and blood against wire and machine guns, 'killing' Germans while

Germans killed Allies twice as often, calling out the men of forty, of fifty, and even of fifty-five, and the youths of eighteen, sending the wounded soldiers back three or four times over into the shambles – such were the sole manifestations now reserved for the military art.

And when at the end, three years later, the throng of uniformed functionaries who in the seclusion of their offices had complacently presided over this awful process, presented Victory to their exhausted nations, it proved only less ruinous to the victor than to the vanquished.

'IF YOU CAN'T GRIN KEEP OUT OF THE WAY TILL YOU CAN'

On the evening of 26 January 1916, Churchill called all the officers of his battalion together and spoke to them for an hour. On the following day he wrote to his wife (using his regular abbreviations), setting down the advice he had given them:

Don't be careless about yourselves – on the other hand not too careful.

Keep a special pair of boots to sleep in & only get them muddy in a real emergency.

Use alcohol in moderation but don't have a great parade of bottles in yr dugouts.

Live well but do not flaunt it.

Laugh a little, & teach your men to laugh – gt good humour under fire – war is a game that is played with a smile.

If you can't smile grin.

If you can't grin keep out of the way till you can.

'A DEFINITE AND PRACTICAL PROPOSAL TO MAKE'

While commanding his battalion on the Western Front, Churchill fretted and fumed at his inability to influence British war policy, particularly naval policy. Learning that a debate on the Naval Estimates was imminent, he returned to London on 2 March 1916, and was in the House of Commons for the debate on March 7. During his five days in London, he had been encouraged – his closest friends said he had been incited – by Admiral of the Fleet Lord Fisher to challenge the Government's naval policy. It was Fisher whose sudden resignation and physical disappearance from the Admiralty as First Sea Lord in May 1915 had precipitated the crisis that led to Churchill's departure from the Admiralty. But when Churchill spoke in the debate, he was to astonish all who heard him by calling for Fisher's return as First Sea Lord. Up to his concluding remarks, Churchill's speech – the first time in twelve years that he had spoken in the House of Commons as a critic of government policy – was a measured survey and criticism of naval policy, addressed to his successor as First Lord of the Admiralty, Arthur Balfour:

We do not know what Germany has done. An impenetrable veil, as the right hon. Gentleman knows, has fallen for eighteen months over the German dockyards, naval and commercial. The right hon. Gentleman says he does not know what progress is being made there. That is a serious statement – not one in connection with which I make any reproach, but it is a grave fact which we must bear in mind that we do not know what is going on there. But let us be sure of this: something is in progress there.

[...]

Can we conceive that the German Government, as we know it to our cost, would be content to allow that Navy to lie impotent and derided in the Kiel Canal without any hope of action? If there were any possibility within the range of their extraordinary military intelligences by which it could be rendered a really effective factor in the course of the struggle, is it likely that they would have acquiesced in the total loss of utility and of all the efforts, organisation, and resources which have made them the second naval Power? We should be most imprudent if we were to act on such an assumption. We are bound to assume that Germany has completed every vessel begun before the War. It may not be so – I dare say it is not so – but we must assume it.

We have not only reached a period in the War when all the capital ships begun before the War can certainly be completed, but we are just entering upon a period when new capital ships begun since the War may be ready on either side. Here, again, I know of course what we have done, and that secret is jealously guarded; but we cannot tell what Germany has done. We have left the region of the known, of the declared or defined; we have left the region of naval annuals and almanacs; and we have entered the sphere of the uncertain. We have entered a sphere which is within certain limits not merely uncertain but incalculable. For this reason we cannot afford to allow any delay to creep into the execution of our programme, because we must from now on provide, not only against the known and against the declared ships, but against what will be a continually increasing element of the unknown.

[· · ·]

The War is full of surprises to all of us; but so far the Admiralty has kept ahead. But that has not been done – I am very anxious to couch my argument in language which will not be offensive or vexing to my right hon. Friend, whose courtesy I have always experienced, but I must say that it has not been done – by easy methods. It was done by rough and harsh and even violent methods, and by a tireless daily struggle. Remember, everything else is in movement too. We see our own great expansion, but remember, everything else around us is expanding and developing at the same time. You cannot afford to indulge even for the shortest period of time in resting on your oars. You must continually drive the vast machine forward at its utmost speed. To lose momentum is not merely to stop, but to fall.

We have survived, and we are recovering from a shortage of munitions for the Army. At a hideous cost in life and treasure we have regained control, and ascendancy lies before us at no great distance. A shortage in naval material, if it were to occur from any cause, would give no chance of future recovery. Blood and money, however lavishly poured out, would never repair the consequences of what might be even an unconscious relaxation of effort.

[···]

A strategic policy for the Navy, purely negative in character, by no means necessarily implies that the path of greatest prudence is being followed. I wish to place on record that the late Board would certainly not have been content with an attitude of pure passivity during the whole of the year 1916.

[···]

We hear a great deal about air raids. A great remedy against Zeppelin raids is to destroy the Zeppelins in their sheds. I cannot understand myself why all these many months, with resources far greater than those which Lord Fisher and I ever possessed, it has not been found possible to carry on the policy of raiding which, in the early days even, carried a handful of naval pilots to Cologne, Düsseldorf, and Friedrichshafen, and even to Cuxhaven itself.

[···]

But I have not spoken today without intending to lead up to a conclusion. I have not used words of warning without being sure first that they are spoken in time to be fruitful, and secondly, without having a definite and practical proposal to make.

When in November 1914, Prince Louis of Battenberg told me he felt it his duty to retire and lay down the charge he had executed so faithfully, I was certain that there was only one man who could succeed him. I knew personally all the high officers of the Navy, and I was sure that there was no one who possessed the power, the insight, and energy of Lord Fisher. I therefore made it plain that I would work with no other First Sea Lord. In this way the oppositions, naval and otherwise, which have always, perhaps not unnaturally, obstructed Lord Fisher's faithful footsteps, were overcome. He returned to his old place, and the six months of war administration which followed will,

I believe, rank as one of the remarkable periods in the history of the Royal Navy.

I did not believe it possible that our very cordial and intimate association would be ruptured, but the stress and shocks of this War are tremendous, and the situations into which men are plunged expose them to strain beyond any that this generation have had experience of.

We parted on a great enterprise upon which the Government had decided and to which they were committed and in which the fortunes of a struggling and ill-supported Army were already involved; it stood between us as a barrier. I therefore should have resisted, on public grounds, the return of Lord Fisher to the Admiralty – and I have on several occasions expressed this opinion in the strongest terms to the Prime Minister and the First Lord of the Admiralty.

We have now reached an entirely different situation, and I have no doubt whatever what it is my duty to say now. There was a time when I did not think that I could have brought myself to say it, but I have been away for some months, and my mind is now clear. The times are crucial. The issues are momentous. The great War deepens and widens and expands around us. The existence of our country and of our cause depend upon the Fleet. We cannot afford to deprive ourselves or the Navy of the strongest and most vigorous forces that are available. No personal consideration must stand between the country and those who can serve her best.

I feel that there is in the present Admiralty administration, for all their competence, loyalty, and zeal, a lack of driving force and mental energy which cannot be allowed to continue, which must be rectified while time remains and before evil results, and can only be rectified in one way. I am sure the nation and the Navy expect that the necessary step will be taken.

I urge the First Lord of the Admiralty without delay to fortify himself, to vitalise and animate his Board of Admiralty by recalling Lord Fisher to his post as First Sea Lord.

'THERE CAN BE NO EXCUSE'

Churchill's 'definite and practical proposal' for the return of Lord
Fisher as First Sea Lord was the object of much immediate ridicule
and sarcasm. On 13 March 1916 he returned to his battalion on the
Western Front. Then, on May 7, after another seven weeks facing the
daily perils of trench warfare, he finally returned to London and
resumed his seat in Parliament. On 17 May 1916, ten days after his
return, he spoke in the House of Commons about air power:

> Why, after a whole year of limitless money, of accumulated experi-
> ence, and of multiplying resources, has it not been possible to
> continue this system of attack upon the enemy's air bases?
>
> Why has it not been possible to construct the special types of
> machines that may be required for each particular objective? No
> doubt the difficulties have increased, and the enemy's means of
> defence is continually improving. All the more condemnation to you,
> I say, for losing so much valuable time, and perhaps for letting such
> precious opportunities slip by!
>
> [···]
>
> Complete, unquestionable supremacy in the air would give an over-
> whelming advantage to the artillery of the Armies that enjoyed it. It
> would confer the greatest benefits upon the Fleet that enjoyed it.
>
> You have not got, in spite of what the right hon. Gentleman has
> said, that complete supremacy now. You have not even got equality.
> On the contrary, in many respects the Germans have the advantage,
> and you have lost the superiority which, at the outbreak of war, it was
> admitted we possessed. But you can recover it. There is nothing to
> prevent your recovering it.
>
> At sea, the increased power of the defensive in mines and
> submarines has largely robbed the stronger Navy of its rights. On
> land, we are in the position of having lost our ground before the
> modern defensive was thoroughly understood, and having to win it
> back when the offensive has been elevated into a fine art. But the air
> is free and open. There are no entrenchments there. It is equal for the
> attack and for the defence. It is equal for all comers.

The resources of the whole world are at our disposal and command. Nothing stands in the way of our obtaining the aerial supremacy in the War but yourselves. There is no reason, and there can be no excuse, for failure to obtain that aerial supremacy, which is, perhaps, the most obvious and the most practical step towards a victorious issue from the increasing dangers of the War.

'WHATEVER IS DONE MUST BE DONE IN THE COLD LIGHT OF SCIENCE'

On 23 May 1916, six days after his speech on air power, in which he urged a more active British policy – and hoped, in vain, that he might be given a ministerial post in charge of air warfare – Churchill spoke again in the House of Commons, about what he saw as a failure in the military policy of renewed offensives on the Western Front:

The trench population lives almost continuously under the fire of the enemy. It returns again and again, after being wounded twice and sometimes three times, to the front and to the trenches, and it is continually subject, without respite, to the hardest of tests that men have ever been called upon to bear, while all the time the non-trench population scarcely suffers at all, and has good food and good wages, higher wages in a great many cases than are drawn by the men under fire every day, and their share of the decorations and rewards is so disproportionate that it has passed into a byword.

I wish to point out to the House this afternoon that the part of the Army that really counts for ending the War is this killing, fighting, suffering part.

I say to myself every day, what is going on while we sit here, while we go away to dinner, or home to bed? Nearly 1,000 men – Englishmen, Britishers, men of our own race – are knocked into bundles of bloody rags every twenty-four hours, and carried away to hasty graves or to field ambulances, and the money of which the Prime Minister has spoken so clearly is flowing away in its broad stream. Every measure must be considered, and none put aside while there is hope of obtaining something from it.

[···]

Many of our difficulties in the West at the present time spring from the unfortunate offensive to which we committed ourselves last autumn. My right hon. Friend knows that this is no new view of mine taken after the event.

Let us look back now. Only think if we had kept that tremendous effort ever accumulating for the true tactical moment. Think if we had kept that rammer compressed ready to release when the time came – if we had held in reserve the energies which were expended at Loos, Arras, and in Champagne – kept them to discharge at some moment during the protracted and ill-starred German attack on Verdun! Might we not then have recovered at a stroke the strategic initiative without which victory lags long on the road?

Let us not repeat that error. Do not let us be drawn into any course of action not justified by purely military considerations. The argument which is used that 'it is our turn now' has no place in military thought. Whatever is done must be done in the cold light of science.

When you are able to gather round the frontiers of Germany and Austria armies which show a real, substantial preponderance of strength, then the advantage of their interior situation will be swamped and overweighed, and then the hour of decisive victory will be at hand. This hour is bound to come if patience is combined with energy, and if all the resources at the disposal of the Allies are remorselessly developed to their extreme capacity.

'MARTYRS NOT LESS THAN SOLDIERS'

The Battle of the Somme opened on 1 July 1916. On the first day almost 20,000 British soldiers were killed. When the battle ended that November, more than 130,000 British and Commonwealth soldiers and 170,000 German soldiers had been killed. In *The World Crisis*, Churchill reflected on the battle:

A young army, but the finest we have ever marshalled; improvised at the sound of the cannonade, every man a volunteer, inspired not only by love of country but by a widespread conviction that human freedom was challenged by military and Imperial tyranny, they grudged no sacrifice however unfruitful and shrank from no ordeal however destructive. Struggling forward through the mire and filth of the trenches, across the corpse-strewn crater fields, amid the flaring, crashing, blasting barrages and murderous machine-gun fire, conscious of their race, proud of their cause, they seized the most formidable soldiery in Europe by the throat, slew them and hurled them unceasingly backward.

If two lives or ten lives were required by their commanders to kill one German, no word of complaint ever rose from the fighting troops. No attack however forlorn, however fatal, found them without ardour. No slaughter however desolating prevented them from returning to the charge. No physical conditions however severe deprived their commanders of their obedience and loyalty. Martyrs not less than soldiers, they fulfilled the high purpose of duty with which they were imbued.

The battlefields of the Somme were the graveyards of Kitchener's Army. The flower of that generous manhood which quitted peaceful civilian life in every kind of workaday occupation, which came at the call of Britain, and as we may still hope, at the call of humanity, and came from the most remote parts of her Empire, was shorn away for ever in 1916. Unconquerable except by death, which they had conquered, they have set up a monument of native virtue which will command the wonder, the reverence and the gratitude of our island people as long as we endure as a nation among men.

'THE TRIALS OF OUR LATTER-DAY GENERALS'

On 18 July 1917 Churchill became Minister of Munitions in Lloyd George's Coalition Government. Over the next four months he made many visits to France, including twenty to the headquarters of Field

Marshal Sir Douglas Haig, Commander-in-Chief since January 1916 of the British Armies in France. When, fifteen years after the end of the war, Churchill published a four-volume biography of his military ancestor John Churchill, first Duke of Marlborough – *Marlborough: His Life and Times* – he recalled the atmosphere at Haig's headquarters, and slipped into his eighteenth-century narrative a reflection on 'our latter-day generals' – in fact, Haig himself. Churchill's reference to 'when twenty thousand men are falling every day' was to the first day of the Battle of the Somme, fought when Haig's headquarters château was at Val Vion, eight miles from the front line:

> The task of the commander in Marlborough's wars was direct . . . In the midst of the scene of carnage, with its drifting smoke clouds, scurrying fugitives, and brightly coloured lines, squares, and oblongs of men, he sat on his horse, often in the hottest fire, holding in his mind the position and fortunes of every unit in his army from minute to minute and giving his orders aloud. We must picture him in those days when the Signal Corps was non-existent, attended not only by three or four generals of high rank, but by at least twenty young officers specially trained and specially mounted, men who were capable of following the event with intelligent eyes, who watched the field incessantly, and who knew where to find the subordinate commanders, their brigades and regiments. For short distances or less important orders the runners we see in the tapestries with their long brass-headed staves of authority were used. Thus in the space of four or five hours perhaps thirty or forty thousand men were killed or wounded on the two sides, and another fearful but glorious name was inscribed in the annals of war.
>
> All this was quite different from the trials of our latter-day generals. We will not belittle them, but they were the trials of mind and spirit working in calm surroundings, often beyond even the sound of the cannonade. There are no physical disturbances: there is no danger: there is no hurry. The generalissimo of an army of two million men, already for ten days in desperate battle, has little or nothing to do except to keep himself fit and cool. His life is not different, except in its glory, from that of a painstaking, punctual

public official, and far less agitating than that of a Cabinet Minister who must face an angry Chamber on the one hand or an offended party upon the other. There is no need for the modern commander to wear boots and breeches: he will never ride a horse except for the purposes of health. In the height of his largest battles, when twenty thousand men are falling every day, time will hang heavy on his hands. The heads of a dozen departments will from hour to hour discreetly lay significant sheets of paper on his desk. At intervals his staff will move the flags upon his map, or perhaps one evening the Chief of the Staff himself will draw a blue line or a brown line or make a strong arrow upon it.

His hardest trials are reduced to great simplicity. 'Advance', 'Hold', or 'Retreat'. 'There are but ten divisions left in reserve: shall we give three today to the beseeching, clamouring battle-zone, or keep them back till to-morrow or the day after? Shall we send them in trains to the north or to the south?' His personal encounters are limited to an unpleasant conversation with an army commander who must be dismissed, an awkward explanation to a harassed Cabinet, or an interview with a representative of the neutral Press. Time is measured at least by days and often by weeks. There is nearly always leisure for a conference even in the gravest crises.

It is not true that the old battle has merely been raised to a gigantic scale. In the process of enlargement the sublime function of military genius – perhaps happily – has been destroyed for ever.

'I, WHO SAW HIM ON TWENTY OCCASIONS'

As the German Army swept westward in the spring of 1918, Field Marshal Haig issued, on April 11, a Special Order of the Day, known as his 'Backs to the Wall' communiqué, to all ranks of the British Army in France and Flanders. In it he declared: 'There is no other course open to us but to fight it out. Every position must be held to the last man: there must be no retirement. With our backs to the wall and believing in the justice of our cause each one of us must fight on to the end.' Ten months after Haig's death in January 1928, Churchill published another assessment of him as Commander-in-Chief in *Nash's – Pall Mall* magazine, later reprinted in his book *Great Contemporaries*:

Napoleon and the great Captains before him rode on the field amid their troops in the ardour of battle, and amid the perils of the storm. How gladly would Haig have welcomed the chance to mount his horse as he had done when a mere Corps Commander in the First Ypres, and ride slowly forward among the exploding shells! But all this is supposed to be forbidden to the modern Commander-in-Chief. He is lucky if even an aeroplane bomb, or some long-range projectile near Headquarters, relieves at rare intervals by its physical reminder the inward stress of mind. No anodyne of danger, no relief in violent action; nothing but anxiety, suspense, perplexing and contradictory information; weighing the imponderable, assigning proportions to what cannot be measured, intricate staff duties, difficult personal negotiations, and the mutterings of far-distant guns.

But he endured it all; and with such impassivity and matter-of-fact day-to-day routine that I, who saw him on twenty occasions – some of them potentially fatal – doubted whether he was not insensitive and indurated to the torment and drama in the shadow of which he dwelt.

But when I saw after the War was over, for the first time, the historic 'Backs to the Wall' document written before sunrise on that fateful April morning in 1918, and that it was no product of some able staff officer in the bureau, but written with his own precise hand, pouring out without a check or correction the pent-up passion of his heart, my vision of the man assumed a new scale and colour. The Furies indeed contended in his soul; and that arena was large enough to contain their strife.

'THE TOILS, PERILS, SUFFERINGS AND PASSIONS OF MILLIONS OF MEN'

While British, Commonwealth, French and – from 1917 – American troops battled with the Germans on the Western Front, a no less bloody conflict was taking place on the Eastern Front, where Russia confronted Germany and Austria-Hungary. Churchill wrote about this distant battlefield in his fifth volume of *The World Crisis, The Unknown War – The Eastern Front*:

If for a space we obliterate from our minds the fighting in France and Flanders, the struggle upon the Eastern Front is incomparably the greatest war in history. In its scale, in its slaughter, in the exertions of the combatants, in its military kaleidoscope, it far surpasses by magnitude and intensity all similar human episodes.

It is also the most mournful conflict of which there is record. All three empires, both sides, victors and vanquished, were ruined. All the Emperors or their successors were slain or deposed. The Houses of Romanov, Hapsburg and Hohenzollern woven over centuries of renown into the texture of Europe were shattered and extirpated. The structure of three mighty organisms built up by generations of patience and valour and representing the traditional groupings of noble branches of the European family, was changed beyond all semblance.

These pages recount dazzling victories and defeats stoutly made good. They record the toils, perils, sufferings and passions of millions of men. Their sweat, their tears, their blood bedewed the endless plain. Ten million homes awaited the return of the warriors. A hundred cities prepared to acclaim their triumphs. But all were defeated; all were stricken; everything that they had given was given in vain. The hideous injuries they inflicted and bore, the privations they endured, the grand loyalties they exemplified, all were in vain. Nothing was gained by any. They floundered in the mud, they perished in the snowdrifts, they starved in the frost. Those that survived, the veterans of countless battle-days, returned, whether with the laurels of victory or tidings of disaster, to homes engulfed already in catastrophe.

We may make our pictures of this front from Napoleon's campaigns. Hard and sombre war; war of winter; bleak and barren regions; long marches forward and back again under heavy burdens; horses dying in the traces; wounded frozen in their own blood; the dead uncounted, unburied; the living pressed again into the mill. Eylau; Aspern; Wagram; Borodino; The Beresina – all the sinister impressions of these names revive, divested of their vivid flash of pomp, and enlarged to a hideous size. Here all Central Europe tore itself to pieces and expired in agony, to rise again, unrecognizable.

'THE MEANING OF WAR WITH THE AMERICAN UNION'

On 9 January 1917, in an attempt to turn the course of the war in its favour, the German High Command ordered unrestricted German submarine attacks on all shipping, Allied and neutral, including that of the neutral United States. On 2 April 1917, President Woodrow Wilson asked Congress to declare war on Germany. Four days later, on April 6, the United States entered the war, and began recruiting and training an army of more than two million men, to be sent to Europe. Churchill later reflected, in *The World Crisis*, on this turn of events:

Of all the grand miscalculations of the German High Command none is more remarkable than their inability to comprehend the meaning of war with the American Union. It is perhaps the crowning example of the unwisdom of basing a war policy upon the computation of material factors alone.

The war effort of 120,000,000 educated people, equipped with science, and possessed of the resources of an unattackable Continent, nay, of a New World, could not be measured by the number of drilled soldiers, of trained officers, of forged cannon, of ships of war they happened to have at their disposal. It betokens ignorance of the elemental forces resident in such a community to suppose they could be permanently frustrated by a mechanical instrument called the U-boat. How rash to balance the hostile exertions of the largest, if not the leading, civilized nation in the world against the chance that they would not arrive in time upon the field of battle! How hard to condemn the war-worn, wearied, already outnumbered heroic German people to mortal conflict with this fresh, mighty, and once aroused, implacable antagonist!

There is no need to exaggerate the material assistance given by the United States to the Allies. All that could be sent was given as fast and as freely as possible, whether in manhood, in ships or in money. But the war ended long before the material power of the United States could be brought to bear as a decisive or even as a principal factor. It ended with over 2,000,000 American soldiers on the soil of France. A campaign in 1919 would have seen very large American armies continually engaged, and these by 1920 might well have amounted to 5,000,000 of men. Compared to potentialities of this kind, what would have been the value of, let us say, the capture of Paris? As for the 200 U-boats, the mechanical hope, there was still the British Navy, which at this period, under the aegis of an overwhelming battle fleet, maintained upwards of 3,000 armed vessels on the seas.

But if the physical power of the United States was not in fact applied in any serious degree to the beating down of Germany; if for instance only a few score thousand Germans fell by American hands; the moral consequence of the United States joining the Allies was indeed the deciding cause in the conflict.

The war had lasted nearly three years; all the original combatants were at extreme tension; on both sides the dangers of the front were matched by other dangers far behind the throbbing lines of contact. Russia has succumbed to these new dangers; Austria is breaking up; Turkey and Bulgaria are wearing thin; Germany herself is forced even in full battle to concede far-reaching Constitutional rights and franchise to her people; France is desperate; Italy is about to pass within an ace of destruction; and even in stolid Britain there is a different light in the eyes of men. Suddenly a nation of one hundred and twenty millions unfurls her standard on what is already the stronger side; suddenly the most numerous democracy in the world, long posing as a judge, is hurled, nay, hurls itself into the conflict. The loss of Russia was forgotten in this new reinforcement. Defeatist movements were strangled on the one side and on the other inflamed. Far and wide through every warring nation spread these two opposite impressions – 'The whole world is against us' – 'The whole world is on our side.'

'THE COUNTRY IS IN DANGER'

By November 1917 the German spring offensive had been halted and thrown back, but in the Third Battle of Ypres the Allied advance had been halted at the village of Passchendaele with heavy losses. Also that November, a Bolshevik government came to power in Russia, committed to ending the war on the Eastern Front by negotiation and massive territorial surrender, thus freeing millions of German troops and their weaponry to turn westward in 1918. Churchill spoke of the dangers, and of the challenges, in a speech in the House of Commons on 11 December 1917:

Two months ago I stated in London that the war was entering upon its sternest phase, but I must admit that the situation at this moment is more serious than it was reasonable two months ago to expect. The country is in danger as it has not been since the battle of the Marne saved Paris, and the battles of Ypres and of the Yser saved the Channel ports. The cause of the Allies is now in danger. The future of the British Empire, and of democracy, and of civilization hang, and will continue to hang for a considerable period, in a balance and an anxious suspense. It is impossible, even if it were desirable, to conceal these facts from our enemies. It would be folly not to face them boldly ourselves.

Anyone can see for himself what has happened in Russia. Russia has been thoroughly beaten by the Germans. Her great heart has been broken, not only by German might, but by German intrigue; not only by German steel, but by German gold. Russia has fallen on the ground prostrate in exhaustion and in agony. No one can tell what fearful vicissitudes will come to Russia, or how or when she will arise, but arise she will. It is this melancholy event which has prolonged the war, that has robbed the French, the British and the Italian armies of the prize that was perhaps almost within their reach this summer, it is this event, and this event alone, that has exposed us to perils and sorrows and sufferings which we have not deserved, which we cannot avoid, but under which we shall not bend.

There never was a moment in this war when the practical steps which we ought to take showed themselves more plainly, or when the choice presented to us was so brutally clear as it is to-night, or when there was less excuse for patriotic men to make the mistake of being misled by sophistries and dangerous counsels.

[···]

What is the one great practical step we must take without a day's delay? We must raise the strength of our army to its highest point. A heavier strain will be thrown upon this army than it has ever had to bear before. We must see that it is stronger than it has ever been before. Do not put too heavy a burden on those heroic men by whose valiant efforts we exist from day to day. Husband their lives, conserve and accumulate their force.

Every division of our army must be raised to full strength; every service – the most scientific, the most complex – must be thoroughly provided; we must make sure that in the months to come a large proportion of our army is resting, refreshing, and training behind the front line ready to spring like leopards upon the German hordes. Masses of guns, mountains of shells, clouds of aeroplanes – all must be ready, all must be there; we have only to act together, and we have only to act at once.

'THE MOST TREMENDOUS CANNONADE I SHALL EVER HEAR'

Churchill's work as Minister of Munitions often took him to France, where he established several munitions factories around Paris and a tank factory at Châteauroux. While he was in France in March 1918, he went to the front to visit his friend Major General Hugh Tudor, who was at Nurlu, commanding the 9th Scottish Division. At that very moment, on 21 March 1918, the Germans launched their spring offensive. In *The World Crisis*, he recalled:

I woke up in a complete silence at a few minutes past four and lay musing. Suddenly, after what seemed about half an hour, the silence was broken by six or seven very loud and very heavy explosions several miles away. I thought they were our 12-inch guns, but they were probably mines. And then, exactly as a pianist runs his hands across the keyboard from treble to bass, there rose in less than one minute the most tremendous cannonade I shall ever hear. 'At 4.30 a.m.,' says Ludendorff in his account, 'our barrage came down with a crash.' Far away, both to the north and to the south, the intense roar and reverberation rolled upwards to us, while through the chinks in the carefully papered window the flame of the bombardment lit like flickering firelight my tiny cabin.

I dressed and went out. On the duckboards outside the Mess I met Tudor. 'This is <u>it</u>,' he said. 'I have ordered all our batteries to open. You will hear them in a minute.' But the crash of the German shells bursting on our trench lines eight thousand yards away was so overpowering that the accession to the tumult of nearly two hundred guns firing from much nearer to us could not be even distinguished. From the Divisional Headquarters on the high ground of Nurlu one could see the front line for many miles. It swept around us in a wide curve of red leaping flame stretching to the north far along the front of the Third Army, as well as of the Fifth Army on the south and quite unending in either direction.

There were still two hours to daylight, and the enormous explosions of the shells upon our trenches seemed almost to touch each other, with hardly an interval in space or time. Among the bursting shells there rose at intervals, but almost continually the much larger flames of exploding magazines. The weight and intensity of the bombardment surpassed anything which anyone had ever known before.

Only one gun was firing at the Headquarters. He belonged to the variety called 'Percy', and all his shells fell harmlessly a hundred yards away. A quarter of a mile to the south along the Péronne road a much heavier gun was demolishing the divisional canteen. Daylight super-vened on pandemonium, and the flame picture pulsated under a pall of smoke from which great fountains of the 'dumps' rose mushroom-headed. It was my duty to leave these scenes; and at ten o'clock, with mingled emotions, I bade my friends farewell and motored without misadventure along the road to Péronne.

'AN UTTER ABSENCE OF EXCITEMENT OR BUSTLE'

On 21 March 1918, as the German Army drove back both the British and French forces on the Western Front, Churchill went back from the front to Haig's Headquarters at St Omer, where he spent March 22 in conference at the Chemical Warfare School. On March 23, Nurlu, where he had been with General Tudor when the German attack began, was overrun by German forces. That day, Churchill returned to England. On March 28, as the German advance continued, Lloyd George asked Churchill to return to France and to report on the situation at first hand. He did so at once, going first to Montreuil, ten miles from the Channel coast, where Haig had set up his new Headquarters. Churchill later recalled, in his book *Great Contemporaries*:

The rain streamed down in torrents in the silent, empty streets of this peaceful little old-world town. From this point sixty British divisions – more than half in bloody action – were being directed. From La Bassée southward the battle was at its intensest pitch. The remains of the Fifth Army were streaming back across the old crater fields of the Somme towards Amiens. Byng with the Third Army was in full grapple.

From every part of the British front, from every depot and school in the rear, every division of which could be spared, every reserve that could be discovered, every man who could shoulder a rifle, were

being scraped together and rushed forward by rail and motor to stop
the terrible tide of German advance.

All this I knew. Yet how oddly the calm, almost somnolence, of
this supreme nerve centre of the Army contrasted with the gigantic
struggle shattering and thundering on a fifty thousand yard front fifty
or sixty miles away. The ordinary routine of the bureaus was
proceeding. There was an utter absence of excitement or bustle. The
Commander-in-Chief was taking his afternoon ride. No one not
acquainted with the conditions of the Great War would have believed
it possible that one of the largest and most bloody and critical battles
in the history of the world was in fact being skilfully and effectively
conducted from this spot.

'SUCH A TYRANT AND
SUCH A CHAMPION'

From Haig's new headquarters at Montreuil Churchill drove that
same day, March 28, to Paris, where that evening, only a week since
he had been at the front when the Germans launched their spring
offensive, he called on the 76-year-old French Prime Minister,
Georges Clemenceau (who was to use words that evening that gave
Churchill the inspiration for his defiant clarion call of 4 June 1940).
Churchill's arrival in Paris coincided with what he later called 'the
supreme crisis' for Britain and France. As he recalled in *Great
Contemporaries*:

The Germans were again on the Marne. From the heights of
Montmartre the horizon could be seen alive with the flashes of
artillery. The Americans were pitchforked in at Château-Thierry. I
had important munition and aeroplane factories all around Paris: we
had to prepare to move them and to improvise shelters farther south:
so I was much in the French capital.

Before a war begins one should always say, 'I am strong, but so
is the enemy.' When a war is being fought one should say, 'I am

exhausted, but the enemy is quite tired too.' It is almost impossible to say either of these two things at the time they matter.

Until the Germans collapsed, they seemed unconquerable; but so was Clemenceau. He uttered to me in his room at the Ministry of War the words he afterwards repeated in the tribune: 'I will fight in front of Paris; I will fight in Paris; I will fight behind Paris.' Everyone knew this was no idle boast. Paris might have been reduced to the ruins of Ypres or Arras. It would not have affected Clemenceau's resolution. He meant to sit on the safety valve, till he won or till all his world blew up. He had no hope beyond the grave; he mocked at death; he was in his seventy-seventh year.

Happy the nation which when its fate quivers in the balance can find such a tyrant and such a champion.

'A GREAT ACTOR ON THE STAGE'

The Prime Minister, David Lloyd George, had instructed Churchill to see the situation on all sectors of the battered front line, and to report back daily. Travelling with Clemenceau, Churchill went on 30 March 1918 to see General Ferdinand Foch at Beauvais. Four days earlier, Foch had been appointed Supreme Commander of the Allied Armies, authorised by all the Allies to co-ordinate all their military activities. Churchill later recalled the scene in his book *Thoughts and Adventures*:

General Foch seized a large pencil as if it were a weapon, and without the slightest preliminary advanced upon the map and proceeded to describe the situation. I had heard of his extraordinary methods of exposition; his animation, his gestures, his habit of using his whole body to emphasise and illustrate as far as possible the action which he was describing or the argument which he was evolving, his vivid descriptiveness, his violence and vehemence of utterance. For this style he had been long wondered at, laughed at, and admired in all the schools of war in which he had been Professor or Chief.

He spoke so quickly and jumped from point to point by such large and irregular leaps that I could not make any exact translation of his words. But the whole impression was conveyed to the mind with perfect clearness by his unceasing pantomime and by his key phrases. I cannot attempt to reproduce his harangue, but this was his theme.

'Following the fighting of the 21st, the Germans broke through on the 22nd. See where they went. First stage of the invasion. Oh! oh! oh! How big!' He pointed to a line on the map.

'On the 23rd they advanced again. Deuxième journée d'invasion. Ah! ah!' Another enormous stride. 'On the 24th. Troisième journée. Aié'! Aié?!'

But the fourth day there was a change. The lines on the map showed that the amount of territory gained by the enemy on the fourth day was less than that which they had gained on the third day. The famous Commander turned towards us and swayed from side to side, using his hands as if they were the scales of a balance.

'Oho!' he said. 'Quatrième journée. Oho! Oho!'

We all knew that something had happened to the advancing flood. When he came to the fifth day, the zone was distinctly smaller. The sixth and the seventh zones were progressively smaller still. Foch's voice had dropped almost to a whisper. It was sufficient for him to point to the diminishing zones and with a wave of the hand or a shrug of the shoulder to convey the moral and meaning which he intended.

Until finally, 'Hier, dernière journée d'invasion,' and his whole attitude and manner flowed out in pity for this poor, weak, miserable little zone of invasion which was all that had been achieved by the enemy on the last day. One felt what a wretched, petty compass it was compared to the mighty strides of the opening days. The hostile effort was exhausted. The mighty onset was coming to a standstill. The impulse which had sustained it was dying away. The worst was over. Such was the irresistible impression made upon every mind by his astonishing demonstration, during which every muscle and fibre of the General's being had seemed to vibrate with excitement and passion of a great actor on the stage.

And then suddenly in a loud voice 'Stabilisation. Sure, certain, soon. And afterwards. Ah, afterwards. That is my affair.'

He stopped. Everyone was silent.

Then Clemenceau, advancing, 'Alors, Général, il faut que je vous embrasse.'

'THERE WAS NO RIGMAROLE OR FORMALISM'

As Minister of Munitions from July 1917 to November 1918, Churchill provided vast quantities of arms, tanks and warplanes for the United States forces about to go into action on the Western Front. United States troops were first in action during the crisis that broke with the German spring offensive in March 1918. Nine years after the end of the war, in *The World Crisis*, Churchill reflected:

To fight in defence of his native land is the first duty of the citizen. But to fight in defence of some one else's native land is a different proposition. It may also be a sacred obligation, but it involves a higher conception. Willingly to cross the ocean and fight for strangers, far from home, upon an issue in the making of which one has had no say, requires a wide outlook upon human affairs and a sense of world responsibility. Canada, Australia, New Zealand, drawn by common citizenship under the Crown, had from the outset revealed this noble power of comprehension, and had made their decision good across broader spaces on the battlefields of three years. They had endured slaughters which no American army was destined to know, and their achievements are upon record. But the decision which in the emergency President Wilson took to remedy the consequences of previous long delay involved personal deprivations of a peculiar kind for the soldiers of the United States.

To serve in one's national army, under one's own leader, amid a great mass of men animated by a common spirit is one ordeal. To serve in isolated divisions or brigades or even regiments under the orders of foreign Generals, flanked on either side by troops of different race and language and of unknown comradeship or quality, is another. Amid the hardships and terrors of war the soldier is accustomed to find his last remaining comfort of mind in being with his own friends and fellow-countrymen, sustained by the esprit de corps at least of 'The Battalion'. But in the dire need of the great struggle and in a loyal desire to share the tribulations of their allies, American soldiers by scores of thousands readily obeyed orders from their Government to serve, albeit under the general supervision of Pershing, as isolated companies or even platoons in British or French units in order that the largest number might come under the fire of the enemy at an earlier period.

Such conduct required from the Allies the utmost loyal exertions to equip the forces so trustfully sent. At this I laboured incessantly. My duties brought me into intimate and constant contact with the leading representatives in Europe of the United States Supply Services, as well as with General Bliss and upon occasion with General Pershing. From the first we worked together without a single misunderstanding or disagreement.

[...]

The arrangements worked excellently. We 'carried on the war in common' in every sense of the expression. We transferred masses of every kind of material, in every stage of production, from one ledger to the other in accordance with our very different needs as easily as two friends might share a luncheon-basket. There was no rigmarole or formalism in our affairs. We ransacked our cupboards to find anything the American troops in France required, and the Americans on the other hand, once the case was clearly explained in conversation, drew without hesitation from their own remoter programmes for our more urgent needs. We built common factories for tanks and aviation material. The Americans offered us their earliest supply of mustard gas.

At the end I accepted from Mr. Stettinius a contract of over £100,000,000 sterling to supply the whole requirements of the United States Army in medium artillery (6-inch guns and howitzers) for the campaign of 1919. The principles of this contract were simple. We guaranteed the United States we would make no profit, and they guaranteed us we should suffer no loss, however the event might turn.

'VICTORY HAD COME AFTER
ALL THE HAZARDS'

The First World War came to an end with the German Armistice of 11 November 1918. Austria-Hungary, Bulgaria and Turkey had already surrendered: with the German Armistice the fighting was over on all the war fronts. Churchill was working that day in London, in his office in the Ministry of Munitions. He recalled nine years later, in the third volume of *The World Crisis*:

It was a few minutes before the eleventh hour of the eleventh day of the eleventh month. I stood at the window of my room looking up Northumberland Avenue towards Trafalgar Square, waiting for Big Ben to tell that the War was over. My mind strayed back across the scarring years to the scene and emotions of the night at the Admiralty when I listened for these same chimes in order to give the signal of war against Germany to our Fleets and squadrons across the world. And now all was over! The unarmed and untrained island nation, who with no defence but its Navy had faced unquestioningly the strongest manifestation of military power in human record, had completed its task. Our country had emerged from the ordeal alive and safe, its vast possessions intact, its war effort still waxing, its institutions unshaken, its people and Empire united as never before.

Victory had come after all the hazards and heart-breaks in an absolute and unlimited form. All the Kings and Emperors with whom we had warred were in flight or exile. All their Armies and Fleets were destroyed or subdued. In this Britain had borne a notable part, and done her best from first to last.

The minutes passed. I was conscious of reaction rather than elation. The material purposes on which one's work had been centred, every process of thought on which one had lived, crumbled into nothing. The whole vast business of supply, the growing outputs, the careful hoards, the secret future plans – but yesterday the whole duty of life – all at a stroke vanished like a nightmare dream, leaving a void behind.

My mind mechanically persisted in exploring the problems of demobilization. What was to happen to our three million Munition workers? What would they make now? How would the roaring factories be converted? How in fact are swords beaten into plough shares? How long would it take to bring the Armies home? What would they do when they got home? We had of course a demobilization plan for the Ministry of Munitions. It had been carefully worked out, but it had played no part in our thoughts. Now it must be put into operation. The levers must be pulled – Full Steam Astern. The Munitions Council must meet without delay.

And then suddenly the first stroke of the chime. I looked again at the broad street beneath me. It was deserted. From the portals of one of the large hotels absorbed by Government Departments darted the slight figure of a girl clerk, distractedly gesticulating while another stroke resounded. Then from all sides men and women came scurrying into the street. Streams of people poured out of all the buildings. The bells of London began to clash. Northumberland Avenue was now crowded with people in hundreds, nay, thousands, rushing hither and thither in a frantic manner, shouting and screaming with joy. I could see that Trafalgar Square was already swarming.

Around me in our very headquarters, in the Hotel Metropole, disorder had broken out. Doors banged. Feet clattered down corridors. Everyone rose from the desk and cast aside pen and paper. All bounds were broken. The tumult grew. It grew like a gale, but from all sides simultaneously. The street was now a seething mass of humanity. Flags appeared as if by magic. Streams of men and women flowed from the Embankment. They mingled with torrents pouring down the Strand on their way to acclaim the King. Almost before the last stroke of the clock had died away, the strict, war-straitened, regulated streets of London had become a triumphant pandemonium. At any rate it was clear that no more work would be done that day.

Yes, the chains which had held the world were broken. Links of imperative need, links of discipline, links of brute force, links of self-sacrifice, links of terror, links of honour which had held our nation, nay, the greater part of mankind, to grinding toil, to a compulsive cause – every one had snapped upon a few strokes of the clock. Safety, freedom, peace, home, the dear one back at the fireside – all after fifty-two months of gaunt distortion. After fifty-two months of making burdens grievous to be borne and binding them on men's backs, at last, all at once, suddenly and everywhere the burdens were cast down. At least so for the moment it seemed.

'THE ACHE FOR THOSE WHO WOULD NEVER COME HOME'

Churchill watched as Londoners, and all Britain, rejoiced that the First World War was over. Eleven years later, in the fourth volume of *The World Crisis*, he reflected on the scenes in London on Armistice Day:

Who shall grudge or mock these overpowering entrancements? Every Allied nation shared them. Every victorious capital or city in the five continents reproduced in its own fashion the scenes and sounds of London. These hours were brief, their memory fleeting; they passed as suddenly as they had begun.

Too much blood had been spilt. Too much life-essence had been consumed. The gaps in every home were too wide and empty. The shock of an awakening and the sense of disillusion followed swiftly upon the poor rejoicings with which hundreds of millions saluted the achievement of their hearts' desire.

There still remained the satisfactions of safety assured, of peace restored, of honour preserved, of the comforts of fruitful industry, of the home-coming of the soldiers; but these were in the background; and with them all there mingled the ache for those who would never come home.

'THE DAUNTLESS AND
DEVOTED PEOPLE'

Before the First World War, Churchill had a central role in the establishment of the British Secret Service. Peacetime and wartime espionage were at different times his Ministerial responsibility. In the Foreword to a book by a British First World War spy, Marthe McKenna, he set down his thoughts on the perils and ethics of spying. It was Churchill who, as Secretary of State for War in 1919, signed Marthe McKenna's notification of Mentioned in Despatches by Field Marshal Haig 'for gallant and distinguished services in the Field':

> Self-preservation has forced States and armies in every age to exact the penalty of death from a spy. The elaborate deceit which is the essence of espionage also casts its slur upon those who undertake it.
>
> Nevertheless, a Secret Service agent who is not actuated by any sordid motive, but inspired by patriotism, and ready to pay the well-known forfeit, deserves respect and honour from those he serves so faithfully.
>
> The courage of a soldier advancing in a forlorn hope is not greater, and his ordeal is far less trying, than that of the man – or woman – who, sometimes for years, dwells in the midst of the enemy with his life hanging upon every chance word or action.
>
> The fortitude required for the endurance of these prolonged Strains is equal to anything demanded of the bravest fighting troops, and the services which can be rendered to King and Country may sometimes far exceed in importance the results of the most splendid acts of devotion in the field.
>
> Many were the dauntless and devoted people who sacrificed their lives unhonoured and unsung for the Allied cause.
>
> It is often the fashion of our countrymen to belittle their own efficiency in matters of this kind, and to exult the superior craft and ability of foreigners.
>
> But I believe it to be unquestionably true that the British Secret

Service before and during the Great War was more skilfully organised, more daringly pursued and achieved more important results than that of any other country, friend or foe.

'REBUILD THE RUINS.
HEAL THE WOUNDS'

In his first public speech after the Armistice, Churchill told his constituents in Dundee, on 26 November 1918, as recorded in the *Dundee Courier*:

Why should war be the only purpose capable of uniting us in comradeship? Why should war be the only cause large enough to call forth really great and fine sacrifices? Look at the wonderful superb things people will do to carry on a war and to win a victory. Look what they will give up. Look what toils they achieve, what risks, what sufferings, what marvellous ingenuity, and what heroic and splendid qualities they display. All for war.

Nothing is too good for war. Why cannot we have some of it for peace? Why is war to have all the splendours, all the nobleness, all the courage and loyalty? Why should peace have nothing but the squabbles and the selfishness and the pettiness of daily life? Why if men and women, all classes, all parties, are able to work together for five years like a mighty machine to produce <u>destruction</u>, can they not work together for another five years to produce <u>abundance</u>?

All the arts and science that we used in war are standing by us now ready to help us in peace. All the organised power which moved the fleets and armies, which hunted the submarines in the depths of the sea, which made us the victors in the air, which produced unlimited munitions of every intricate kind – all the clever brains, true brave hearts, strong unwearied hands – all are available. Only one thing do we require – a common principle of action, a plain objective, that everyone can understand and work for, as he worked to beat the German. Without this we cannot succeed. But surely we have a common purpose? Surely this period of reconstruction may be looked upon as if it were a part of the war? Surely if the sense of self-preservation enabled us to combine to conquer, the same sense of self-preservation should enable us to restore and revive our prosperity?

[···]

Five years of concerted effort by all classes, like what we have given in the war, but without its tragedies, would create an abundance and prosperity in this land, aye, throughout the world, such as has never yet been known or dreamt of. Five years of faction, of bickering, of class jealousies and Party froth, will not merely not give us prosperity, it will land us in utter and universal privation.

The Choice is in our own hands. Like the Israelites of old, blessing and cursing is set before us. Today we can have the greatest failures or the greatest triumph as we choose. There is enough for all. The earth is a generous mother. Never, never did science offer such fairy gifts to man. Never did their knowledge and organisation stand so high. Repair the waste. Rebuild the ruins. Heal the wounds. Crown the victors. Comfort the broken and broken-hearted. There is the battle we have now to fight. There is the victory we have now to win. Let us go forward together.

'THE HEART OF THE RUSSIAN PEOPLE'

Following the Bolshevik Revolution in November 1917, Churchill became a leading advocate of Allied military intervention against the Bolsheviks. Then, as Secretary of State for War, appointed in January 1919, he proposed that the British troops then in Russia give what support they could to the many anti-Bolshevik armies that, as they advanced from the west during 1919 to the outskirts of Petrograd and drove from the south towards Moscow, hoped to destroy the new regime. With Cabinet support, Churchill authorised the British troops then in Russia to aid the anti-Bolshevik armies. On February 19 he told the House of Commons:

If Russia is to be saved, as I pray she may be saved, she must be saved by Russians. It must be by Russian manhood and Russian courage and Russian virtue that the rescue and regeneration of this once mighty nation and famous branch of the European family can alone be achieved.

The aid which we can give to these Russian Armies – who we do not forget were called into the field originally during the German war to some extent by our inspiration and who are now engaged in fighting against the foul baboonery of Bolshevism – can be given by arms, munitions, equipment, and technical services raised upon a voluntary basis. But Russia must be saved by Russian exertions, and it must be from the heart of the Russian people and with their strong arm that the conflict against Bolshevism in Russia must be mainly waged.

'THE FUTURE WAS HEAVY WITH FOREBODING'

As a young boy, Churchill had been taken by his father, when they were passing through Paris, to see the statues representing the two French provinces of Alsace and Lorraine in the Place de la Concorde. Both statues were covered in black crepe, to signify the annexation of the territories by Germany in 1871. As a schoolboy, Churchill had been impressed by the words of the French patriot Léon Gambetta about the loss of Alsace and Lorraine: 'Think of it always, speak of it never.' In 1919, Churchill understood that Germany's defeat did not automatically mean the end of the conflict between France and Germany. As he wrote in the first volume of his Second World War memoirs:

Nearly a million and a half Frenchmen had perished defending the soil of France on which they stood against the invader. Five times in a hundred years, in 1814, 1815, 1870, 1914, and 1918, had the towers of Nôtre Dame seen the flash of Prussian guns and heard the thunder of the cannonade. Now for four horrible years thirteen provinces of France had lain in the rigorous grip of Prussian military rule. Wide regions had been systematically devastated by the enemy or pulverized in the encounter of the armies. There was hardly a cottage nor a family from Verdun to Toulon that did not mourn its dead or shelter its cripples.

To those Frenchmen, and there were many in high authority, who had fought and suffered in 1870, it seemed almost a miracle that France should have emerged victorious from the incomparably more terrible struggle which had just ended. All their lives they had dwelt in fear of the German Empire. They remembered the preventive war which Bismarck had sought to wage in 1875; they remembered the brutal threats which had driven Delcassé from office in 1905; they had quaked at the Moroccan menace in 1906, at the Bosnian dispute of 1908, and at the Agadir crisis of 1911. The Kaiser's 'mailed fist' and 'shining armour' speeches might be received with ridicule in England and America. They sounded a knell of horrible reality in the hearts of the French. For fifty years almost they had lived under the terror of the German arms. Now, at the price of their life-blood, the long oppression had been rolled away. Surely here at last was peace and safety. With one passionate spasm the French people cried 'Never again!'

But the future was heavy with foreboding. The population of France was less than two-thirds that of Germany. The French population was stationary, while the German grew. In a decade or less the annual flood of German youth reaching the military age must be double that of France. Germany had fought nearly the whole world, almost single-handed, and she had almost conquered. Those who knew the most knew best the several occasions when the result of the Great War had trembled in the balance, and the accidents and chances which had turned the fateful scale. What prospect was there in the future that the Great Allies would once again appear in their millions upon the battlefields of France or in the East? Russia was in ruin and convulsion, transformed beyond all semblance of the past. Italy might be upon the opposite side. Great Britain and the United States were separated by the seas or oceans from Europe. The British Empire itself seemed knit together by ties which none but its citizens could understand.

What combination of events could ever bring back again to France and Flanders the formidable Canadians of the Vimy Ridge; the glorious Australians of Villers-Bretonneux; the dauntless New Zealanders of the crater-fields of Passchendaele; the steadfast Indian Corps which in the cruel winter of 1914 had held the line by Armentières? When again would peaceful, careless, anti-militarist Britain tramp the plains of Artois and Picardy with armies of two or three million men? When again would the ocean bear two millions of the splendid manhood of America to Champagne and the Argonne?

Worn down, doubly decimated, but undisputed masters of the hour, the French nation peered into the future in thankful wonder and haunting dread. Where then was that SECURITY without which all that had been gained seemed valueless, and life itself, even amid the rejoicings of victory, was almost unendurable? The mortal need was Security at all costs and by all methods, however stern or even harsh.

On Armistice Day the German Armies had marched homeward in good order. 'They fought well', said Marshal Foch, Generalissimo of the Allies, with the laurels bright upon his brow, speaking in soldierly mood: 'let them keep their weapons'. But he demanded that the French frontier should henceforth be the Rhine. Germany might be disarmed; her military system shivered in fragments; her fortresses dismantled: Germany might be impoverished; she might be loaded with measureless indemnities; she might become a prey to internal feuds: but all this would pass in ten years or in twenty. The in-destructible might 'of all the German tribes' would rise once more and the unquenched fires of warrior Prussia glow and burn again. But the Rhine, the broad, deep, swift-flowing Rhine, once held and forti-fied by the French Army, would be a barrier and a shield behind which France could dwell and breathe for generations.

Very different were the sentiments and views of the English-speaking world, without whose aid France must have succumbed. The territorial provisions of the Treaty of Versailles left Germany practically intact. She still remained the largest homogeneous racial block in Europe. When Marshal Foch heard of the signing of the Peace Treaty of Versailles he observed with singular accuracy: 'This is not Peace. It is an Armistice for twenty years.'

'A FRIGHTFUL AND OVERWHELMING FORCE'

Despite his wife Clementine's reluctance that Churchill should continue his flying lessons, following the fatal crashes before the war of two of his flying instructors, in 1919 Churchill asked a pilot friend, Colonel Jack Scott, for some more instruction. Scott, an air ace who had shot down thirteen German aircraft in the war, had damaged his legs so badly in a flying accident that he had to be lowered into the cockpit every time he flew. Churchill was then forty-four. In his book *Thoughts and Adventures*, published thirteen years later, he described his flight on 18 July 1919:

It was not, and still is not, common for men over forty to become good and trustworthy pilots. Youth with its extraordinary quickness and aptitudes was almost always the first qualification for the attainment of 'Flying Sense'. I persevered, however, in my endeavours and continued, as I thought, to make steady progress. I was thus fated to have a much more melancholy adventure before I decided to relinquish, at any rate for the time being, the fascinating study of the art of flight. This event occurred in the summer of 1919. I had had a long day's work at the War Office, and motored down with Colonel Scott to the Croydon Aerodrome for an evening flight.

I took the machine off the ground myself. The engine was pulling well, and we rose to 70 or 80 feet smoothly and swiftly. The Croydon Aerodrome was in those days bordered at several points by high elm trees, and it was necessary to make two half circles, first to the right and then to the left, in order to gain a safe height to pass over these.

The machine took its first turn perfectly, and the dial marked over sixty miles an hour, a thoroughly trustworthy flying speed. I now turned her to the left, as I had so often done before, and having put her on her bank, I began to centre the guiding-stick slowly and gently in order to resume an even keel. Anyone who has handled an aeroplane knows how delicate are its controls and how instantaneously it responds when all is well to the smallest movement.

To my surprise the stick came home at least a foot without

producing the slightest effect. The aeroplane remained inclined at about 45 degrees and began gradually to increase its list. 'She is out of control,' I said through the microphone to my pilot. Instantly I felt the override of his hand and feet on stick and rudders, as by a violent effort he sought to plunge the machine head-downwards in the hope of regaining our lost flying speed. But it was too late.

We were scarcely 90 feet above the ground, just the normal height for the usual side-slip fatal accident, the commonest of all. The machine rushed earthwards helplessly. Above two hundred feet there would have been no danger; in fact at a thousand or fifteen hundred feet we had over and over again deliberately stalled the machine, made it fall out of control, waited till the side-slip turned (as all side-slips do) into the ultimate nose-dive, and then, as the speed increased to eighty or a hundred miles an hour and the controls began again to answer, had pulled her gently out into a normal flight.

But there was no time now. I saw the sunlit aerodrome close beneath me, and the impression flashed through my mind that it was bathed in a baleful yellowish glare. Then in another flash a definite thought formed in my brain, 'This is very likely Death.' And swift upon that I felt again in imagination the exact sensations of my smash on the Buc Aerodrome a month before. Something like that was going to happen NOW! I record these impressions exactly as they occurred, and they probably occupied in reality about the same time as they take to read. Apart from the sinister impression of a differently lighted world, there was no time for fear. Luckily we can only take in a certain amount at a time, whatever happens.

The aeroplane was just turning from its sideslip into the nose-dive when it struck the ground at perhaps fifty miles an hour with terrific force. Its left wing crumpled, and its propeller and nose plunged into the earth. Again I felt myself driven forward, as if in some new dimension by a frightful and overwhelming force, through a space I could not measure. There was a sense of unendurable oppression across my chest as the belt took the strain. Streams of petrol vapour rushed past in the opposite direction. I felt, as a distinct phase, the whole absorption of the shock. Suddenly the pressure ceased, the belt parted, and I fell forward quite gently on to the dial board in front of me. Safe! was the instantaneous realization.

I leapt out of the shattered fuselage and ran to my companion. He was senseless and bleeding. I stood by, ready to try and pull him out should the machine catch fire. Otherwise it was better to leave him till skilled help arrived.

No fire or explosion followed the crash.

'THE AGONY OF RUSSIA'

During the last six months of 1919, Churchill, as Secretary of State for War, withdrew all British combat troops from Russia, and limited Britain's support for the anti-Bolshevik Russian armies to providing munitions and a few military advisers. When one of those armies embarked on a series of pogroms against Jews, he threatened to halt all British supplies unless the killing of Jews were stopped. In mid-October 1919 it looked as if the anti-Bolshevik Russian forces would enter Petrograd and Moscow, but within a month the tide had turned. By the end of 1919 the Bolsheviks had regained control of much of Russia. Churchill – one of whose friends, Captain Francis Cromie, the British Naval Attaché in Russia, had been murdered in the British Embassy in Petrograd in August 1918 by a Bolshevik mob – despaired for Russia's future, telling an audience in Sunderland on 20 January 1920:

Was there ever a more awful spectacle in the whole history of the world than is unfolded by the agony of Russia?

This vast country, this mighty branch of the human family, not only produced enough food for itself, but before the war, it was one of the great granaries of the world, from which food was exported to every country. It is now reduced to famine of the most terrible kind, not because there is no food – there is plenty of food – but because the theories of Lenin and Trotsky have fatally, and it may be finally, ruptured the means of intercourse between man and man, between workman and peasant, between town and country; because they have scattered the systems of scientific communication by rail and river on which the life of great cities depends; because they have raised class against class and race against race in fratricidal war; because they have given vast regions where a little while ago were smiling villages or prosperous townships back to the wolves and the bears; because they have driven man from civilization to a barbarism worse than the Stone Age, and have left him the most awful and pitiable spectacle in human experience, devoured by vermin, racked by pestilence, and deprived of hope.

And this is progress, this is liberty. This is Utopia! What a monstrous absurdity and perversion of the truth it is to represent the communistic theory as a form of progress, when, at every step and at every stage, it is simply marching back into the dark ages.

'THE CLEMENCY OF THE CONQUEROR'

In April 1919, while Churchill was Secretary of State for War, a British general in India, Major General Reginald Dyer, opened fire on a large crowd of unarmed Indians in a confined space, the Jallianwalla Bagh, in the city of Amritsar. More than three hundred Indians were killed. When General Dyer was censured by a War Office commission of inquiry, many Members of Parliament were appalled by the criticism of a senior British officer. Churchill defended the decision to censure General Dyer when he spoke in the House of Commons on 8 July 1920, recalling at one point in his speech scenes from the First World War on the Western Front:

Over and over again we have seen British officers and soldiers storm entrenchments under the heaviest fire, with half their number shot down before they entered the position of the enemy, the certainty of a long, bloody day before them, a tremendous bombardment crashing all around – we have seen them in these circumstances taking out their maps and watches, and adjusting their calculations with the most minute detail, and we have seen them show, not merely mercy, but kindness, to prisoners, observing restraint in the treatment of them, punishing those who deserved to be punished by the hard laws of war, and sparing those who might claim to be admitted to the clemency of the conqueror.

We have seen them exerting themselves to show pity and to help, even at their own peril, the wounded. They have done it thousands of times, and in requiring them, in moments of crisis, dealing with civil riots, when the danger is incomparably less, to consider these broad, simple guides, really I do not think we are taxing them beyond their proved strength.

There is surely one general prohibition which we can make. I mean a prohibition against what is called 'frightfulness'. What I mean by frightfulness is the inflicting of great slaughter or massacre upon a particular crowd of people, with the intention of terrorising not merely the rest of the crowd, but the whole district or the whole country.

[A Conservative Member of Parliament interrupted with the question.

'Was not the frightfulness started three days before? Was not the frightfulness on the other side?'

Churchill ignored the question and continued with his speech:]

We cannot admit this doctrine in any form. Frightfulness is not a remedy known to the British pharmacopoeia.

[···]

On the contrary, as we contemplate the great physical forces and the power at the disposal of the British Government in their relations with the native population of India, we ought to remember the words of Macaulay – 'and then was seen what we believe to be the most frightful of all spectacles, the strength of civilisation without its mercy'.

Our reign in India or anywhere else has never stood on the basis of physical force alone, and it would be fatal to the British Empire if we were to try to base ourselves only upon it. The British way of doing things, as my right hon. Friend the Secretary of State for India, who feels intensely upon this subject, has pointed out, has always meant and implied close and effectual co-operation with the people of the country. In every part of the British Empire that has been our aim, and in no part have we arrived at such success as in India, whose princes spent their treasure in our cause, whose brave soldiers fought side by side with our own men, whose intelligent and gifted people are co-operating at the present moment with us in every sphere of government and of industry.

'THOROUGHLY TIRED OF WAR'

During his two years as Secretary of State for War – between January 1919 and January 1921 – Churchill often spoke in public, and wrote in newspaper articles, about the Great War that was such a recent memory, and about the continuing European conflicts. In the summer of 1920, in an article published in the *Evening News* on July 28, Churchill reflected on the nature of the First World War, on the Polish advance eastward deep into Soviet Ukraine in early 1920, on the Soviet counter-attack deep into the territory of newly independent Poland – a counter-attack that was taking place as Churchill was writing his article – and on the future of Germany in Europe. The article was entitled 'The Poison Peril from the East':

The Great War through which we have passed differed from all ancient wars in the immense power of the combatants and their fearful agencies of destruction, and from all modern wars in the utter ruthlessness with which it was fought. All the horrors of all the ages were brought together, and not only armies but whole populations were thrust into the midst of them. The mighty educated States involved conceived with reason that their very existence was at stake. Germany having let Hell loose kept well in the van of terror; but she was followed step by step by the desperate and ultimately avenging nations she had assailed.

Every outrage against humanity or international law was repaid by reprisals often on a greater scale and of longer duration. No truce or parley mitigated the strife of the armies. The wounded died between the lines: the dead mouldered into the soil. Merchant ships and neutral ships and hospital ships were sunk on the seas and all on board left to their fate, or killed as they swam. Every effort was made to starve whole nations into submission without regard to age or sex. Cities and monuments were smashed by artillery.

Bombs from the air were cast down indiscriminately. Poison gas in many forms stifled or seared the soldiers. Liquid fire was projected upon their bodies. Men fell from the air in flames, or were smothered, often slowly, in the dark recesses of the sea. The fighting strength of armies was limited only by the manhood of their countries. Europe and large parts of Asia and Africa became one vast battlefield on which after years of struggle not armies but nations broke and ran.

When all was over, Torture and Cannibalism were the only two expedients that the civilized, scientific, Christian States had been able to deny themselves: and these were of doubtful utility.

But nothing daunted the valiant heart of man. Son of the Stone Age, vanquisher of nature with all her trials and monsters, he met the awful and self-inflicted agony with new reserves of fortitude. Freed in the main by his intelligence from mediaeval fears, he marched to death with sombre dignity. His nervous system was found in the twentieth century capable of enduring physical and moral stresses before which the simpler natures of primeval times would have collapsed. Again and again to the hideous bombardment, again and again from the hospital to the front, again and again to the hungry submarines, he strode unflinching. And withal, as an individual, preserved through these torments the glories of a reasonable and compassionate mind.

No country wants peace in the world more than Great Britain. It is her heart's desire. It is also her main interest. Her people are thoroughly tired of war. They have learnt during five bitter years too much of its iron slavery, its squalor, its mocking disappointment, its ever-dwelling sense of loss.

Moreover, we have emerged victoriously and safely from the appalling conflict in which so many powerful States were dashed to pieces, and the British Empire, united, extended, erect, occupies at this moment a leading place among the Governments of men and the most glorious pinnacle ever reached in all our history. Small wonder we desire peace for ourselves and for every nation.

There is no reason why the world should not obtain and enjoy that long and indefinite period of peace which is now the general wish and the universal need. A wise, careful, yet decided policy pursued by the leading nations in common during the next few years ought to give that consolidation and tranquillization which are required to usher in a brilliant sunlit era.

Such a policy demands, however, that we should recognize and understand the formidable dangers which, foolishly handled or supinely disregarded, might ruin the fair prospect of the future and undo the great achievements of the past.

It is from this point of view of securing and preserving our world peace that the case of Poland must be considered.

Poland is the lynch-pin of the Treaty of Versailles. This ancient State, torn into three pieces by Austria, Prussia and Russia, has been liberated from its oppressors and reunited in its integrity after 150 years of bondage and partition.

We ask ourselves: how has the Polish national character and spirit been affected by this prolonged and melancholy experience? What has Poland learnt from her vicissitudes? What has she lost in her captivity?

As far as we can judge by what has happened in the last eighteen months, 150 years of adversity have neither broken the spirit of Poland, nor taught her wisdom. The doors of the 'Bastille' were broken down. Its towers and battlements were overthrown in the supreme convulsion, and from the ruins there emerged this prisoner of the Eighteenth Century, long cut from light and air, limbs dislocated by the rack, with a nature as gifted, a heart as proud and a head as impracticable as ever. But justice to Poland requires a fair recognition of her extraordinary difficulties.

[· · ·]

While she was still dazzled by the newly found sunshine, before she could brace herself to the atmosphere of this modern age, there rushed upon her a series of perils, perplexities and embarrassments which might well have baffled the veteran sagacity and trained experience even of England.

To the westward lay terrific Germany, half stunned, half chained, but still endowed with those tremendous faculties and qualities which had enabled her almost single-handed to wage an obstinate war against nearly the whole world at once.

Eastward, also prostrate, also in dire confusion, lay the huge mass of Russia – not a wounded Russia only, but a poisoned Russia, an infected Russia, a plague-bearing Russia; a Russia of armed hordes smiting not only with bayonet and with cannon, but accompanied and preceded by the swarms of typhus-bearing vermin which slay the bodies of men, and political doctrines which destroy the health and even the soul of nations.

And between these two agonized Empires, reacted upon continually by their convulsions, stood Poland, comparatively weak, comparatively small, quite inexperienced, without organization, without structure, short of food, short of weapons, short of money, brandishing her indisputable and newly reaffirmed title deeds to freedom and independence.

A reasonable comprehension of Poland's difficulties is indispensable to a true view of Poland's peril.

It is easy for those who live a long way from the Russian Bolshevists – especially those who are protected by a good strip of salt water, and who stand on the firm rock of an active political democracy – to adopt a cool and airy view of their Communist doctrines and machinations.

But a new, weak, impoverished, famishing State like Poland, itself quaking internally, is placed in hourly jeopardy by close and continuous contact with such neighbours.

The Bolshevist aim of world revolution can be pursued equally in peace or war. In fact, a Bolshevist peace is only another form of war. If they do not for the moment overwhelm with armies, they can undermine with propaganda. Not a shot may be fired along the whole front, not a bayonet may be fixed, not a battalion may move, and yet invasion may be proceeding swiftly and relentlessly. The peasants are roused against the landlords, the workmen against their employers, the railways and public services are induced to strike, the soldiers are incited to mutiny and kill their officers, the mob are raised against the middle classes to murder them, to plunder their houses, to steal their belongings, to debauch their wives and carry off their children, an elaborate network of secret societies entangles honest political action; the Press is bought wherever possible.

This was what Poland dreaded and will now have reason to dread still more; and this was the cause, even more than the gathering of the Russian armies on the Polish front, continuous for nearly a year, that led the Poles to make that desperate military sally or counterstroke which English Liberal opinion has so largely misunderstood, and which Socialist opinion has so successfully misrepresented.

But the Polish point of view is not the only point of view. We have also to think of British interests, of the interests of France, of the main results gained by the war and embodied in the Treaty of Versailles.

All these interests would be gravely and even vitally affected by the overrunning of Poland by the Bolshevist armies or by the subversion of the Polish State by Bolshevist propaganda and conspiracy.

It was hoped by those who framed the Treaty of Versailles to create in Poland a living, healthy, vigorous organism which should form a peaceful barrier between Germany and Russia and between Russian Bolshevism and Western Europe.

The ruin and collapse of Poland, either from external violence or internal subversion, and the incorporation of Poland as a whole in the Russian Bolshevist system, would sweep away the barrier on which so much depends and would bring Russia and Germany into direct and immediate contact.

Should such an event unhappily take place, it is necessary to realize that an awful, yet in some ways a wonderful, choice will be presented to Germany.

Beaten as they have been in the war, powerless as they are in so many matters, the German people will have it in their hands either to renew and redouble the miseries of Europe, or to render a service to civilization of the very highest order.

It will be open to the Germans either to sink their own social structure in the general Bolshevist welter and spread the reign of chaos far and wide throughout the Continent; or, on the other hand, by a supreme effort of sobriety, of firmness, of self-restraint and of courage – undertaken, as most great exploits have to be, under conditions of peculiar difficulty and discouragement – to build a dyke of peaceful, lawful, patient strength and virtue against the flood of red barbarism flowing from the East, and thus safeguard their own interests and the interests of their principal antagonists in the West.

If the Germans were able to render such a service, not by vain-glorious military adventure or with ulterior motives, they would unquestionably have taken a giant step upon that path of self-redemption which would lead them surely and swiftly as the years pass by back to their own great place in the councils of Christendom, and would have rendered easier that sincere co-operation between Britain, France and Germany on which the very salvation of Europe depends.

'A MEASURELESS ARRAY OF TOILS AND PERILS'

On 4 August 1920, the Bolshevik armies, advancing deep into Poland, stood within a few miles of the Polish capital, Warsaw. That morning, Churchill was in the Cabinet Room at 10 Downing Street when the Prime Minister, Lloyd George, summoned two Soviet emissaries and gave them a formidable ultimatum. It was six years to the day since Britain had delivered its ultimatum to Germany. In the fourth volume of *The World Crisis*, Churchill recalled the scene:

On August 4 Mr Lloyd George warned Kamenev and Krassin that 'if the Soviet armies advanced further into Poland, a rupture with the Allies would be inevitable.' On that famous anniversary, as we sat in the Cabinet room upon this serious communication, my mind's eye roamed back over the six years of carnage and horror through which we had struggled.

Was there never to be an end? Was even the most absolute victory to afford no basis for just and lasting peace? Out of the unknown there seemed to march a measureless array of toils and perils. Again it was August 4, and this time we were impotent. Public opinion in England and France was prostrate. All forms of military intervention were impossible. There was nothing left but words and gestures.

'FROM THE CONFUSION OF TYRANNY TO A REIGN OF LAW'

In January 1921, Lloyd George appointed Churchill as Secretary of State for the Colonies. For the next two years, Churchill worked to secure peace between Southern Ireland and the counties of Ulster, and to give Southern Ireland its independence. It was a hard task, but Churchill was determined to end the Anglo-Irish quarrel. On 16 February 1922, he introduced the Irish Free State Bill to the House of Commons:

> If you want to see Ireland degenerate into a meaningless welter of lawless chaos and confusion, delay this Bill. If you wish to see increasingly serious bloodshed all along the borders of Ulster, delay this Bill. If you want this House to have on its hands, as it now has, the responsibility for peace and order in Southern Ireland, without the means of enforcing it, if you want to impose those same evil conditions upon the Irish Provisional Government, delay this Bill. If you want to enable dangerous and extreme men, working out schemes of hatred and subterranean secrecy, to undermine and over-turn a Government which is faithfully doing its best to keep its word with us and enabling us to keep our word with it, delay this Bill. If you want to proclaim to all the world, week after week, that the British Empire can get on just as well without law as with it, then you will delay this Bill.
>
> But if you wish to give a fair chance to a policy to which Parliament has pledged itself, and to Irish Ministers to whom you are bound in good faith, so long as they act faithfully with you, to give fair play and a fair chance, if you wish to see Ireland brought back from the confusion of tyranny to a reign of law, if you wish to give logical and coherent effect to the policy and experiment to which we are committed, you will not impede, even for a single unnecessary week, the passage of this Bill.
>
> [···]
>
> I remember on the eve of the Great War we were gathered together at a Cabinet meeting in Downing Street, and for a long time, an hour or

an hour and a half, after the failure of the Buckingham Palace Conference, we discussed the boundaries of Fermanagh and Tyrone. Both of the great political parties were at each other's throats. The air was full of talk of civil war. Every effort was made to settle the matter and bring them together. The differences had been narrowed down, not merely to the counties of Fermanagh and Tyrone, but to parishes and groups of parishes inside the areas of Fermanagh and Tyrone, and yet, even when the differences had been so narrowed down, the problem appeared to be as insuperable as ever, and neither side would agree to reach any conclusion.

Then came the Great War. Every institution, almost, in the world was strained. Great Empires have been overturned. The whole map of Europe has been changed. The position of countries has been violently altered. The modes of thought of men, the whole outlook on affairs, the grouping of parties, all have encountered violent and tremendous changes in the deluge of the world, but as the deluge subsides and the waters fall short we see the dreary steeples of Fermanagh and Tyrone emerging once again. The integrity of their quarrel is one of the few institutions that has been unaltered in the cataclysm which has swept the world.

That says a lot for the persistency with which Irish men on the one side or the other are able to pursue their controversies. It says a great deal for the power which Ireland has, both Nationalist and Orange, to lay their hands upon the vital strings of British life and politics, and to hold, dominate, and convulse, year after year, generation after generation, the politics of this powerful country.

'DESTRUCTIVE TENDENCIES HAVE NOT YET RUN THEIR COURSE'

On 19 October 1922, the Conservative Party decided to withdraw from Lloyd George's peacetime coalition, in which they had served for almost four years. That afternoon, Lloyd George, who was dependent on the Conservative Members of Parliament for his majority, resigned. Andrew Bonar Law, the leader of the Conservative Party, became Prime Minister, and a General Election was called for mid-November. Churchill, in hospital with appendicitis, was unable to take any part in these dramatic political events, or to persuade the Conservatives, as he had earlier tried to do, to remain in the coalition. Too ill to campaign when the election date was announced, he had to wait until November 10 to be well enough to set off for Dundee to address his constituents. The notes of his first speech to them – made on Armistice Day, 11 November 1922 – survive in the Churchill Papers in the 'speech form', or 'psalm form' as he knew it and as it was known among his secretaries, with its customary abbreviations, in which he wrote them out, and from which he spoke:

> What a disappointment the Twentieth Century has been.
> How terrible & how melancholy
>   is long series of disastrous events
>   wh. have darkened its first 20 years.
> We have seen in ev. country a dissolution,
>   a weakening of those bonds,
>   a challenge to those principles
>   a decay of faith
>   an abridgement of hope
>   on wh. structure & ultimate existence
>   of civilized society depends.
> We have seen in ev. part of globe
>   one gt. country after another
>   wh. had erected an orderly, a peaceful
>   a prosperous structure of civilised society,
>   relapsing in hideous succession
>   into bankruptcy, barbarism or anarchy.
>
> This process is not to be explained
>   entirely by the Gt. War.
> It had begun before Gt. War.
> It is continuing or threatening
>   now that Gt. War is over
>   in countries scarcely affected by Gt. War.

Gt., fertile, beautiful countries
    like China & Mexico
        had sunk into confusion before ever a shot was fired.

Then you have havoc of the war.
In Germany, in Austria, throughout Balkans
    & throughout Turkish Empire,
        you have havoc wh. extends to-day
        as far away as Persia & Mesopotamia.

The sufferings of Russia in war were grievous,
    but all that those 180 mil. Russians
        suffered at hands of enemy
          was petty compared to what they have suffered
          in grip of that little sect of Communist criminals
          who have exterminated
            mils. of the Russian people
            & crushed the life & freedom
            out of whole of Russia
            as they wd. crush it if they cd.
            out of rest of world

I shall have to speak to you later abt. Ireland;
    but here even at our own doors
        there is enormous retrogression
        of civilisation & of Christianity,
          & the Govt. of Irish Free State struggling
        not merely for honour & freedom
          but for vy. existence of the Irish people.

In India & in Egypt
    same sort of tendencies are rife;
& we see among mils. of people hitherto shielded
    by superior science & superior law
        a desire to shatter structure by wh. they live
        & to return blindly & heedlessly
        to primordial chaos.

Can you doubt, my faithful friends
    as you survey this sombre panorama,
        that mankind is passing through a period marked
            not only by an enormous destruction
                & abridgement of human species,
                not only by a vast impoverishment
                        & reduction in means of existence
            but also that destructive tendencies
                have not yet run their course ?

And only intense, concerted & prolonged efforts
    among all nations
            can avert further & perhaps even greater calamities.

'I AM NOT GOING TO BE MUZZLED'

For five days during the General Election campaign, Churchill campaigned in his constituency as best he was able. When he spoke on 13 November 1922, two days before polling, he was in considerable physical pain. The *Dundee Courier* gave a full account:

I have not had much opportunity, he began, to prosecute – (A Voice – 'Why don't you go to Manchester this time? – (laughter) – my campaign in Dundee. A lot of people have been criticising me – (A Voice – 'You deserve it') – but whether I deserve it or not I have a right to make my answer. (Cheers.)

Continued interruptions were accompanied by cries of 'Shut up' from the other section of the audience.

Mr Churchill said no man was condemned unheard in Britain. The election campaign had been in progress for nearly three weeks, and he was only able to come here last Saturday, and this was the second great meeting he had had the chance of addressing, and as the poll was on Wednesday – (A Voice – 'You will be at the bottom of the poll'.) 'If I am going to be at the bottom of the poll', interjected Mr Churchill, 'why don't you allow me my last dying kick'. (Cheers.) He had only got three days in which to state his case to the electors of Dundee. It was perfectly clear when they were very crowded, when many of them, he feared – (A Voice – 'You are a political failure.' laughter) – were very uncomfortable and crowded together, it was perfectly clear they could not conduct a public meeting – (interruptions) – unless everyone looked after one (A Voice – 'Do be serious'. laughter.) 'If they do', continued Mr Churchill, 'we can have an important political discussion; and if they don't we can have a bear garden'. (Uproar.)

[···]

'This I do say to you. As a matter of fair bargain, if you are going to let me speak at all, you must let me say whatever I choose. I am not going to be muzzled and to be told that I am going to attack this man or that; that I must not say anything against this candidate and that candidate. Not at all. If anybody has got a shrewd rejoinder to make let them make it, but let us at any rate survey broadly the situation.'

Churchill could go no further. From the audience came the cry: 'What about the Dardanelles?' When Churchill replied that he was not going to try to put any arguments forward unless he was listened to 'in silence', there was another howl from the audience, and then Churchill spoke again, turning his attention to the Communist Party candidate, William Gallacher, and his followers:

'If about a hundred young men and women in the audience choose to spoil the whole meeting, and if about a hundred of these young reptiles – (cheers and uproar) – choose to deny to democracy, the masses of the people, the power to conduct great assemblies, the fault is with them, the blame is with them, and the punishment will be administered to them by the electors. (Cheers and booing.) Now you see what the Gallacher crowd are worth. (Cheers and uproar.) Now you see the liberty you have if the country were run by them – (cheers and interruptions) – no sense, no brains, just breaking up a meeting that they would not have the wit to address. (Cheers.) The electors will know how to deal with a party whose only weapon is idiotic clamour.' (Cheers.)

At this stage pandemonium broke out anew, and when

comparative quietness again prevailed Mr Churchill said he had addressed public meetings for the last five and twenty years, and he never remembered having addressed one which was not willing to listen to a political argument. 'Perhaps you would like to hear some other speaker for the time being, in which case I will be glad to give way. I am quite willing to listen to some other speaker.'

Subsequent interruptions lasted for nearly five minutes. Mr. Churchill waited patiently, remarking – 'They will soon get tired.' ('Send him home', cried a voice.)

Churchill could say no more. He abandoned his speech, and suggested that he answer questions instead. There was at once a 'fusillade of questions', and it was some minutes before speakers could be persuaded to ask their questions one at a time. Five questioners managed to make themselves heard above the catcalls and uproar. Then the spate of questions increased. No single one could be heard among the others. 'The howling mob intensified their efforts in producing a perfect rabble of vocal discord', the *Dundee Courier* reported. Churchill remained seated during the outcry. Finally, while the noise continued unabated, he rose, in the hope of saying a few concluding words. According to the *Dundee Courier*:

His opening sentence was marked by an effort to sing the 'Red Flag', but it soon died away.

He said – Ladies and gentlemen, I thank you most sincerely for the attentive hearing – (applause) – you have given me, and I think you have vindicated in a most effective manner the devotion of the Socialist party to free speech. You have shown, it has been shown, clearly that a handful of rowdies can break up a great meeting, and can then prevent ten times their number from transacting their public business. (Applause.) We may be interrupted here tonight, but we will carry out our purpose at the poll. (Applause.) We will stand up for the rights of British citizens, the rights and liberties of British citizens against the supporters of the Socialist candidates who, if they have their way, would reduce – (uproar) – this great country to the same bear garden to which they have reduced this great meeting. (Applause, and booing.)

'I HAVE ALWAYS STUCK TO THE MIDDLE ROAD'

On 16 November 1922, Churchill was defeated at Dundee – by a Prohibitionist and a Labour candidate. For the first time since 1900, he was without a seat in Parliament. The new Conservative Government had no interest in finding him one or offering him a Cabinet post; indeed, although the Liberal Party had been drastically reduced in strength, he was still determined to stand as a Liberal. In November 1923 the new Conservative Prime Minister, Stanley Baldwin, called a General Election. Churchill had been out of Parliament for a year. Seven local Liberal Associations asked him to be their candidate. He agreed to stand at West Leicester, and on 27 November 1923 spoke in his new constituency for the first time:

> I shall certainly not reproach the electors, whatever the result of the contest may be. The idea of sweeping away, as the result of a fortnight's electioneering, the Free Trade system on which the industries of this country, tier upon tier, have been built for nearly 100 years is to my mind repulsive, a criminal idea which gives no real heed to the vital consequences to, and needs of, the mass of people of this country. Mr. Baldwin has not thought out any of his proposals. The Prime Minister, who is inviting the electors to embark on this astonishing gamble, has not taken the trouble to reach definite conclusions in his own mind as to what he really intends to do, or, if he has reached such conclusions, he has shown himself totally incapable of expressing them to the public.
>
> Mr. Baldwin does not say whether the tariff is to be permanent or temporary. He carefully shrouds that in mystery, so that Lord Derby can run about Lancashire and say it is only to meet a temporary need, while the Prime Minister can say at Worcester that we will want it in the remote future. (Laughter.) Nor have we been told whether the tariff is to be high or low. We have a right to be informed on that point, upon which the whole, or nearly the whole, argument depends. (Cheers.)
>
> We have to consider whether we should scrap the commercial foundations of the country, and start under the leadership of the

March Hare and the Mad Hatter into some unexpected project of Protection. (Cheers.) It is the intention to rush a decision that I resent more than anything else. We are asked to give a blank cheque to an unknown man. Mr. Baldwin describes himself as a plain, blunt man, although he is as rich as any man in Leicester, and certainly is not a representative at all of the toiling millions, whose livelihood and homes are at stake in this fierce party quarrel. (Cheers.) England is a great exporting country, and it is no use for an exporting country to protect the home market. In cotton goods the imports are 5 millions and the exports 148 millions; in iron and steel, imports are 11 millions and the exports 68 millions; in woollen goods, imports are 8 millions and exports 53 millions. (Cheers.)

What is the use of pretending that this greatest of all exporting nations has got to lie down pusillanimously behind a network of tariffs, cowering in our own markets, living by taking in each other's washing, feeding like a dog on its own tail (laughter), nursing the last glimmers of the fires of British prosperity, when we are actually breaking down this barrier and that, and sending our goods in British ships to all lands?

[···]

I see the dreary Socialist circus has arrived. It is made up of about half the local Labour Party, and they rush breathlessly around on bicycles to Liberal meetings instead of looking in at their own. Now we shall hear their carefully prepared interruptions and their stock questions, which they repeat parrot-like wherever they go—

[A Girl's Voice]: Yes, but we have to earn our bread by the sweat of our brow in the factories.

[Mr. Churchill]: Well, you seem to have a lot of the sweat of your brow still to spare after your day's labour.

[···]

Socialism will mean that the Government will be obliged to try that which no Government have ever yet attempted, namely, to prescribe for everyone in the whole country their daily task and duty.

[···]

Odd as it may seem, I have always stuck to the middle road equally against Protection on the one hand and the capital levy on the other. How do we know that standing on the middle road we will not find a lot of sensible people gathered together who do not believe that anyone has a quick remedy for curing human ills?

[···]

I left the Conservative Party in opposition to Protection twenty years ago because I believed Protection would inflict terrible injury on the wellbeing of this country. The electors are entitled to more notice, and to more solid reasoning before they are called upon to alter the whole system under which the country has built up its industry. It is a remarkable fact that we have gained the leadership of the shipping of the whole world through the fact that our ports are free. If we protect the home market we shall lose more than we gain. Protection will be a gross invasion of the simple rights and necessities of the great mass of the working-class people of this country.

[···]

The Labour Party is a new party just starting out in the world and ought not to forget the past, because there are no great measures of social reform and betterment which have not been driven through by the Liberal Party.

[A voice]: 'What about the Dardanelles?'

What do you know about that? You throw that retort out without having given consideration to the question. The Dardanelles might have saved millions of lives. (Dissent.) I am sure the gentleman is not one who would wish to introduce prejudice into a discussion of this kind.

People who in the war filled positions of awful responsibility and had to take terrible decisions have the right to be judged leniently and generously by their fellow-countrymen. I believe history will show they acted for the best, and will record its opinion that this was the right thing to do, and that if one could have got more power and influence to push it through with vigour it would have made an enormous difference and would have saved us the torments and tortures of the last two years of the war. Don't imagine I am running away from the Dardanelles. I glory in it.

'I AM TOO OLD A CAMPAIGNER
TO BE DISHEARTENED'

The General Election was held on 6 December 1923, a week after
Churchill's forty-ninth birthday. Churchill stood at West Leicester and
failed to get elected. A Labour Government came to power, with
Ramsay MacDonald as Prime Minister, dependent on Liberal Party
members to maintain his power. Churchill, disillusioned that his
fellow Liberals were enabling a Labour Government to rule, next
stood for Parliament not as a Liberal, but as an Independent, at a
by-election in the Abbey Division of Westminster in March 1924. He
asked the leader of the Conservative Party, Stanley Baldwin, to let
him stand unopposed by the Conservatives in what was one of the
most prized Conservative seats in the country. Baldwin agreed, but
was unable to dissuade the local Conservative Association from
putting up its own candidate. Polling took place on 19 March 1924. It
was the ninth parliamentary election of Churchill's career. As the final
packet of votes was counted, Churchill was told that he had been
elected with a majority of a hundred, a result that was passed by the
wire services to all the London clubs. In fact, Churchill had been
defeated by forty-three votes. In his speech after the true results were
known, he set out for his supporters his political and personal
position:

> The three-Party system could never again produce majority govern-
> ment. The idea of a coalition or centre Party does not reign or rule
> today. The only practical step which can be taken is to make a united
> Conservative Party with large numbers of Liberals in all parts of the
> country.
>
> The date of the poll was fixed for the minimum period of time
> which the law allowed, and this adversely affected my chances in
> what from the beginning was an extraordinary and astonishing
> attempt.
>
> Another day – certainly another two or three days – would have
> produced the result at which we were aiming. We were gaining
> ground every hour. It took us four or five days to create this extra-

ordinarily efficient organisation, which came into being almost at the stroke of a wand, and it was not until a week ago that we really began to function effectively. That is a fact which must, I think, be taken into consideration by me and by others in considering what will be my future relations with this great constituency. (Cheers, and a voice, 'Stand next time.')

I am too old a campaigner to be disheartened (cheers) by the ups and downs of political life. It was not on personal grounds or for personal reasons that I came forward to make this effort. I have been considering throughout what was the real need of this country and of the stable forces of this country on which it must increasingly rely in future years.

Although the deadweight of a strong party machine, aided by the exertions of two other party machines, has proved effective against a single individual, I believe that we have roused the attention of the whole country to an aspect of their political affairs which merited their urgent attention. We have succeeded in setting on foot a movement and in proclaiming a policy which will exercise a material, a potent, and possibly a decisive influence upon the immediate future of our political affairs.

I do not believe that the Conservative Party can afford to reject and repulse the forces which are represented in the 8,000 votes for an Independent Anti-Socialist candidate. I do not believe that narrow, bitter, party views or weak, incoherent party action will receive the approval of the mass of patriotic, loyal, progressive British men and women throughout the land, who see very clearly the direction in which the leaders of the historic parties ought to lead their followers. I am content to let this lesson be studied in all parts of the country, and I predict that the course of events in the next few months, and certainly within a year, will show very clearly the foresight, the clarity of judgment, the patriotic resolution, which has animated all those who have fought this contest on my side.

It is to that day to which I look forward, when you will see the great Conservative Party in its senses and still occupying a broad and progressive platform, united with large numbers of Liberals in all parts of the country. You will see these combined forces repulsing the Socialist attack which is levelled at our institutions, and you will see the inauguration of a Government worthy to rank with the Governments of the Unionist Party in the days of the great Lord Salisbury, and capable of affording a stable foundation for the administration and conduct of our affairs at home and abroad.

'THE POWERS NOW IN THE HANDS OF MAN'

In an article entitled 'Shall We All Commit Suicide?', published first in *Nash's – Pall Mall* magazine in September 1924, then reprinted as a pamphlet, and later published in his book of essays *Thoughts and Adventures*, Churchill looked to the future with foreboding:

The war stopped as suddenly and as universally as it had begun. The world lifted its head, surveyed the scene of ruin, and victors and vanquished alike drew breath. In a hundred laboratories, in a thousand arsenals, factories, and bureaux, men pulled themselves up with a jerk and turned from the task in which they had been absorbed. Their projects were put aside unfinished, unexecuted; but their knowledge was preserved; their data, calculations, and discoveries were hastily bundled together and docketed 'for future reference' by the War Offices in every country. The campaign of 1919 was never fought; but its ideas go marching along. In every army they are being explored, elaborated, refined under the surface of peace, and should war come again to the world it is not with the weapons and agencies prepared for 1919 that it will be fought, but with developments and extensions of these which will be incomparably more formidable and fatal.

It is in these circumstances that we entered upon that period of exhaustion which has been described as Peace. It gives us, at any rate, an opportunity to consider the general situation. Certain sombre facts emerge, solid, inexorable, like the shapes of mountains from drifting mist. It is established that henceforward whole populations will take part in war, all doing their utmost, all subjected to the fury of the enemy. It is established that nations who believe their life is at stake will not be restrained from using any means to secure their existence. It is probable – nay, certain – that among the means which will next time be at their disposal will be agencies and processes of destruction wholesale, unlimited, and perhaps, once launched, uncontrollable.

Mankind has never been in this position before. Without having improved appreciably in virtue or enjoying wiser guidance, it has got into its hands for the first time the tools by which it can unfailingly accomplish its own extermination. That is the point in human destinies to which all the glories and toils of men have at last led them. They would do well to pause and ponder upon their new responsibilities. Death stands at attention, obedient, expectant, ready to serve, ready to shear away the peoples en masse; ready, if called on, to pulverise, without hope of repair, what is left of civilisation. He awaits only the word of command. He awaits it from a frail, bewildered being, long his victim, now – on one occasion only – his Master.

Let it not be thought for a moment that the danger of another explosion in Europe is passed. For the time being the stupor and the collapse which followed the World War ensure a sullen passivity, and the horror of war, its carnage and its tyrannies, has sunk into the soul, has dominated the mind, of every class in every race. But the causes of war have been in no way removed; indeed they are in some respects aggravated by the so-called Peace Treaties and the reactions following thereupon. Two mighty branches of the European family will never rest content with their existing situation. Russia, stripped of her Baltic Provinces, will, as the years pass by, brood incessantly upon the wars of Peter the Great.

From one end of Germany to the other an intense hatred of France unites the whole population. The enormous contingents of German youth growing to military manhood year by year are inspired by the fiercest sentiments, and the soul of Germany smoulders with dreams of a War of Liberation or Revenge. These ideas are restrained at the present moment only by physical impotence. France is armed to the teeth. Germany has been to a great extent disarmed and her military system broken up. The French hope to preserve this situation by their technical military apparatus, by their shield of fortresses, by their black troops, and by a system of alliances with the smaller States of Europe; and for the present at any rate overwhelming force is on their side. But physical force alone, unsustained by world opinion, affords no durable foundation for security. Germany is a far stronger entity than France, and cannot be kept in permanent subjugation.

'Wars,' said a distinguished American to me some years ago, 'are fought with Steel: weapons may change, but Steel remains the core of all modern warfare. France has got the Steel of Europe, and Germany has lost it. Here, at any rate, is an element of permanency.' 'Are you sure,' I asked, 'that the wars of the future will be fought with Steel?' A few weeks later I talked with a German. 'What about Aluminium?' he replied. 'Some think,' he said, 'that the next war will be fought with Electricity.' And on this a vista opens out of electrical rays which could paralyse the engines of a motor car, could claw down aeroplanes from the sky, and conceivably be made destructive of human life or human vision.

Then there are Explosives. Have we reached the end? Has Science turned its last page on them? May there not be methods of using explosive energy incomparably more intense than anything heretofore discovered? Might not a bomb no bigger than an orange be found to possess a secret power to destroy a whole block of buildings – nay, to concentrate the force of a thousand tons of cordite and blast a township at a stroke? Could not explosives even of the existing type be guided automatically in flying machines by wireless or other rays, without a human pilot, in ceaseless procession upon a hostile city, arsenal, camp, or dockyard?

As for Poison Gas and Chemical Warfare in all its forms, only the first chapter has been written of a terrible book. Certainly every one of these new avenues to destruction is being studied on both sides of the Rhine, with all the science and patience of which man is capable. And why should it be supposed that these resources will be limited to Inorganic Chemistry? A study of Disease – of Pestilences methodically prepared and deliberately launched upon man and beast – is certainly being pursued in the laboratories of more than one great country. Blight to destroy crops, Anthrax to slay horses and cattle,

Plague to poison not armies only but whole districts, such are the lines along which military science is remorselessly advancing.

It is evident that, whereas an equally contested war under such conditions might work the ruin of the world and cause an immeasurable diminution of the human race, the possession by one side of some overwhelming scientific advantage would lead to the complete enslavement of the unwary party. Not only are the powers now in the hands of man capable of destroying the life of nations, but for the first time they afford to one group of civilized men the opportunity of reducing their opponents to absolute helplessness.

'THE AMBULANCES OF STATE AID'

When a General Election was called for 29 October 1924, Churchill stood as a Constitutionalist. Stanley Baldwin gave him a safe Conservative seat in Epping and this time ensured that no Conservative candidate would stand against him. Churchill defeated both a Liberal and a Labour challenger to win the seat, which he was to hold for the rest of his parliamentary life – a period of almost forty years. The result of the General Election was a victory for the Conservatives, who obtained 419 seats, as against 151 for Labour and a mere 40 for the once all-powerful Liberal Party, of which only ten months earlier Churchill had been a parliamentary candidate and a leading member. On 5 November 1924, Churchill was asked by Stanley Baldwin to become Chancellor of the Exchequer. He agreed to do so, and agreed also to rejoin the Conservative Party, which he did a few days after his fiftieth birthday on 30 November 1924. Five months later, on 28 April 1925, in the House of Commons, he made his first Budget Speech from the Government Front Bench:

The average British workman in good health, full employment and standard wages, does not regard himself and his family as an object of compassion. But when exceptional misfortune descends upon the cottage home with the slender margin upon which it is floated, or there is a year of misfortune, distress, or unemployment, or, above all, the loss of the breadwinner, it leaves this once happy family in the grip of the greatest calamity.

Although the threat of adversity has been active all these years, no effective provision has been made by the great mass of the labouring classes for their widows and families in the event of death. I am not reproaching them, but it is the greatest need at the present time.

If I may change to a military metaphor, it is not the sturdy marching troops that need extra reward and indulgence. It is the stragglers, the exhausted, the weak, the wounded, the veterans, the widows and orphans to whom the ambulances of State aid should be directed.

[···]

I cherish the hope, Sir, that by liberating the production of new wealth from some of the shackles of taxation the Budget may stimulate enterprise and accelerate industrial revival, and that by giving a far greater measure of security to the mass of wage-earners, their wives and children, it may promote contentment and stability, and make our Island more truly a home for all these people.

'WHAT SHALL I DO WITH
ALL MY BOOKS?'

Churchill had a remarkable library, comprising more than ten thousand books, several hundred of them signed by their authors. Within it was a substantial collection of books on Napoleon, about whom he hoped to write a biography (though he never did). He wrote about his books in an article for *Nash's – Pall Mall* magazine in December 1925, later published in *Painting as a Pastime*:

'What shall I do with all my books?' was the question; and the answer, 'Read them,' sobered the questioner. But if you cannot read them, at any rate handle them and, as it were, fondle them. Peer into them. Let them fall open where they will. Read on from the first sentence that arrests the eye. Then turn to another. Make a voyage of discovery, taking soundings of uncharted seas. Set them back on their shelves with your own hands. Arrange them on your own plan, so that if you do not know what is in them, you at least know where they are. If they cannot be your friends, let them at any rate be your acquaintances. If they cannot enter the circle of your life, do not deny them at least a nod of recognition.

It is a mistake to read too many good books when quite young. A man once told me that he had read all the books that mattered. Cross-questioned, he appeared to have read a great many, but they seemed to have made only a slight impression. How many had he understood? How many had entered into his mental composition? How many had been hammered on the anvils of his mind and afterwards ranged in an armoury of bright weapons ready to hand?

Choose well, choose wisely, and choose one. Concentrate upon that one. Do not be content until you find yourself reading in it with real enjoyment.

'WILL OUR CHILDREN BLEED AND GASP AGAIN?'

On his visits to France in the first decade after the Great War, including while he was Chancellor of the Exchequer, Churchill witnessed the changes that were taking place in the war-shattered landscape, and was troubled by sombre thoughts, writing in 1927, in the third volume of *The World Crisis*:

The curtain falls upon the long front in France and Flanders. The soothing hands of time and nature, the swift repair of peaceful industry, have already almost effaced the crater fields and the battle lines which in a broad belt from the Vosges to the sea lately blackened the smiling fields of France. The ruins are rebuilt. The riven trees are replaced by new plantations. Only the cemeteries, the monuments and stunted steeples, with here and there a mouldering trench or huge mine-crater lake, assail the traveller with the fact that twenty-five millions of soldiers fought here and twelve millions shed their blood or perished in the greatest of all human contentions less than ten years ago. Merciful oblivion draws its veils; the crippled limp away; the mourners fall back into the sad twilight of memory. New youth is here to claim its rights, and the perennial stream flows forward even in the battle zone, as if the tale were all a dream.

Is this the end? Is it to be merely a chapter in a cruel and senseless story? Will a new generation in their turn be immolated to square the black accounts of Teuton and Gaul? Will our children bleed and gasp again in devastated lands? or will there spring from the very fires of conflict that reconciliation of the three giant combatants, which would unite their genius and secure to each in safety and freedom a share in rebuilding the glory of Europe?

'IT IS EQUALLY VAIN TO PROPHESY OR BOAST'

On 15 April 1929, Churchill introduced his fifth and final Budget Speech in the House of Commons. Only four previous Chancellors of the Exchequer – Walpole, Pitt, Peel and Gladstone – had made five Budget Speeches; each either was or was to become Prime Minister. Churchill spoke for three hours. On the following day, Stanley Baldwin wrote to him: 'I have never heard you speak better, and that's saying a great deal . . . I congratulate you with both hands.' In the course of his speech, Churchill said:

It is usual, in opening the Budget, to compare the current year with the last, but on this occasion, in presenting a fifth Budget, at the close of a Parliament, I feel entitled to look back over the whole period for which we have been responsible. It has been a chequered story. The difficulties have been more prominent than the good fortune. The immense industrial disaster of 1926 has cut a deep gash across the statistical record of our national life. I thought at one time, and I so informed the House of Commons three years ago, that the finances of the Parliament would have been completely ruined by a loss to the Exchequer, which, including the coal subsidy of 1926, was certainly not less than £80,000,000. However, on a review of the past five years, I must admit that matters have worked out a good deal better than I hoped or expected. [An HON. MEMBER: 'Or deserved.']

No one has more interest in things going well than the Government of the day and the Minister responsible for the finances of the country. In spite of the injury to every form of national life by the follies of 1926 we have realised a respectable and, as I shall show, a solid surplus in the year that has closed. The material prosperity of this country, whether judged by the condition of its finances, by the volume of its trade or by the saving and consuming power of its people, has maintained a steady advance. For more than two years now we have enjoyed a lucid interval without a general strike or a period of general elections, or a general war. That is the longest lucid interval that I can remember since 1914. Two years' recuperation is quite a long time for this country to allow itself between its ordeals, and, naturally, after two years of peace and quiet there must be a sensible improvement in the general situation.

[...]

We may console ourselves among present discontents by observing that London, in spite of the immense sacrifices made by Great Britain in the War, has regained effectually its solid international pre-eminence in the world, by observing that we are still the greatest international market, that we are able to maintain money rates which are lower than those prevailing in New York, and that the bill of exchange on London, which after the War was seriously menaced, has, in the last few years, regained its time-honoured position as the favourite international instrument and token of commerce.

But I will own that an equally great attraction for me, in the pursuance of this policy, has been that decline in the cost of living which was definitely promised as the result of our allegiance to sound money. I spoke earlier about the increased consumption of tea and sugar. Everyone knows the argument in favour of a free breakfast table, but what is the burden of these remaining taxes on tea and sugar compared to the relief afforded to the consuming public by a decline of 18 points in the cost of living? The identifiable increase in the purchasing power of the wages of insured wage and salary earners alone is equivalent to a remission of indirect taxation of £160,000,000 a year. This takes no account of the proportionate advantages reaped by the enormous number of persons, including the poorest in our midst, unorganised and uncatalogued, from the improvement in the purchasing power of the humble incomes upon which they depend.

[···]

I place these two surpluses, so to speak, upon the mantelpiece, where they can be admired or deplored according to Party inclination. Naturally, I am very pleased that the realised surplus should have exceeded, by £8,500,000, the forecast figures which I gave Parliament last year. But the revenue upon which the prospective surplus of 1929 is based has a special charm and virtue of its own. This year there are no adventitious aids and no windfalls of any consequence. We have passed through that period of fortunate but lucky expedients. We stand once more on the basis of permanent and continuing revenue. Moribund taxes have passed out of existence; revenue has become independent of temporary aids, or raids if you like to call them so; and I can present a balanced Budget with a reasonable prospect of a surplus upon the basis of the revenues which will live and grow.

[···]

I have never had much fiscal sympathy with the consumer of luxuries, and particularly of foreign luxuries. It is to the primary comforts and to some extent virtual necessities of the mass of the population that we should now turn our attention. I have already spoken of the immense boon of at least £160,000,000 a year conferred upon the wage earners by the reduction in the cost of living. Compared with that universal easement, anything the present surplus can bestow must necessarily be small. We reduced last year the tax on sugar at a cost of £3,000,000 of revenue, and it is to tea that I now turn with feelings of good will. The Committee know, from the annual Debates in this House, that I have long desired to effect some reduction in the Tea Duty. There is no other comfort which enters so largely into the budget of the cottage home, or the still humbler budgets of the old, the weak, and the poor.

The reduction or the removal of the tax on tea has been asked for in a long succession of Parliaments. Its mitigation would always have been regarded by social reformers of every party as an auspicious milestone in the history of the Custom House. There has been a tax on tea ever since the reign of Queen Elizabeth, and I am glad to think that the reign of His Majesty King George the Fifth will witness the total, immediate, and, I believe, final abolition:

> And while the bubbling and loud-hissing urn
> Throws up a steamy column, and the cups
> That cheer but not inebriate wait on each,
> So let us welcome peaceful evening in.

I said that the remission would be total and I have said so advisedly, and, although over three-quarters of the tea drunk in these islands is produced within the British Empire, Javanese tea enters to a great extent into the cheapest blends used by the poorest people. To maintain for preferential reasons a tax on this foreign tea would therefore exclude from the benefits of remission the very class for whose sake, most of all, this serious sacrifice of revenue is being made.

[···]

I feel that the corner in our economic fortunes may well now have been turned. There are no causes, apart from fresh causes of our own making, which should prevent the next four or five years being easier and more fruitful than those through which we have made our way.

The future lies freely in our hands. Reviving trade, lower unemployment, expanding revenues, cheaper money, more favourable conditions for debt conversion, lie before us at this moment as reasonable and tangible probabilities. We can by wisdom and public spirit bring them nearer and realise these long sought for advantages. We can by faction, violence, and folly drive them far away again.

The future is inscrutable, and it is equally vain to prophesy or boast, but for my part I have faith in the fair play and august common sense of the British nation, and to their judgment now, and in later years, I submit with confidence the financial record of a Conservative Administration.

'AN UNLIMITED CAPACITY OF ADAPTIVENESS'

In the General Election of May 1929, the Conservative Government was defeated and a Labour Government came to power. Churchill, having retained his parliamentary seat, set off on an extended visit to Canada and the United States, studying the political systems in both countries. On his return, during a lecture at Oxford University in 1930 on 'Parliamentary Democracy and the Economic Problem' – published that year as a booklet, *Parliamentary Government and the Economic Problem* – he spoke of his enduring allegiance, informed by three decades' experience, to the Westminster model of government:

I see the Houses of Parliament – and particularly the House of Commons – alone among the senates and chambers of the world a living and ruling entity; the swift vehicle of public opinion; the arena – perhaps fortunately the padded arena – of the inevitable class and social conflict; the College from which the Ministers of State are chosen, and hitherto the solid and unfailing foundation of the executive power.

I regard these parliamentary institutions as precious to us almost beyond compare. They seem to give by far the closest association yet achieved between the life of the people and the action of the State. They possess apparently an unlimited capacity of adaptiveness, and they stand an effective buffer against every form of revolutionary and reactionary violence.

It should be the duty of faithful subjects to preserve these institutions in their healthy vigour, to guard them against the encroachment of external forces, and to revivify them from one generation to another from the springs of national talent, interest, and esteem.

'ALARMING AND ALSO NAUSEATING'

Churchill was uneasy at the plans being made by the British Government to grant India self-rule – then called Dominion Status. He argued that this would be followed by an Indian demand for full independence, which he opposed, and which was not the policy of the British Government. He also feared Hindu–Muslim communal violence, and felt that the Indian 'untouchables' would remain outcasts. When Mahatma Gandhi pressed for a greater degree of independence than the British Government wanted to concede, Churchill warned, in speech after speech, against giving in to Gandhi's demands. On 23 February 1931 he told the Council of the West Essex Conservative Association:

It is alarming and also nauseating to see Mr Gandhi, a seditious Middle Temple lawyer, now posing as a fakir of a type well-known in the East, striding half-naked up the steps of the Viceregal palace, while he is still organising and conducting a defiant campaign of civil disobedience, to parley on equal terms with the representative of the King-Emperor. Such a spectacle can only increase the unrest in India and the danger to which white people there are exposed. It can only encourage all the forces which are hostile to British authority.

What good can possibly come of such extraordinary negotiations? Gandhi has said within the last few weeks that he demands the substance of independence, though he kindly adds that the British may keep the shadow. He declares that the boycott of foreign cloth must be continued until either prohibition or a prohibitive tariff can be put up against it by an Indian national Parliament. This, if accepted, would entail the final ruin of Lancashire. He has also pressed for the repudiation of the Indian loans, and has laid claim to the control of the Army and foreign affairs. These are his well-known aims. Surely they form a strange basis for heart-to-heart discussions – 'sweet' we are told they were – between this malignant, subversive fanatic and the Viceroy of India.

'I CERTAINLY SUFFERED EVERY PANG'

At the end of 1931, Churchill, having lost heavily in the Wall Street economic collapse of 1929, and hoping to recoup his losses, agreed to undertake a strenuous lecture tour through the United States (see Map 16). On the evening of December 12, the day after his first lecture, he was crossing the road in New York when, looking the wrong way, he was knocked down by a car and badly hurt. After a week in hospital, he had to postpone his remaining lectures while he recuperated. On December 28 he was well enough to telegraph an account of his experience for a British newspaper, the *Daily Mail*. His account was syndicated all over the world:

I certainly suffered every pang, mental and physical, that a street accident or, I suppose, a shell wound can produce. None is un-endurable. There is neither the time nor the strength for self-pity. There is no room for remorse or fears. If at any moment in this long series of sensations a grey veil deepening into blackness had descended upon the sanctum I should have felt or feared nothing additional.

Nature is merciful and does not try her children, man or beast, beyond their compass. It is only where the cruelty of man intervenes that hellish torments appear. For the rest – live dangerously; take things as they come; dread naught, all will be well.

'WE OF THE ENGLISH-SPEAKING LANDS'

After recuperating in the Bahamas for a month, Churchill resumed his lecture tour of the United States on 28 January 1932. He spoke in nineteen cities between January 28 and February 21, earning in that short time more than the annual salary of a British Prime Minister. One of his themes was the Anglo-American relationship:

> We hear always when we draw closer together in international affairs the whisper, (and sometimes the cry) 'Ah, look! The English and Americans are working together!'
>
> Well, why should we be ashamed of that? Why should we not frankly recognize that there must be some source of doctrine and authority to rescue the nations from confusion?
>
> Remember, I beg of you, that, vast as our resources are, there is another power coming into being which makes its appeal to certain classes in all countries and which has its agents in all countries. I mean the force of international communism.
>
> I see two imminent forces that will be brought to bear in the shaping of mankind's destiny – the armed Asiatic conception of communism and the English-speaking ideal of individualism. Our disunion may make the struggle end the wrong way.
>
> May it therefore not be our time now to raise together, with our united hands, the standards of the home, of the family, of individualism, of God? This we can do, not with our hands raised against the rest of mankind but with our hands clasped.
>
> Moving in harmony with that spirit, we of the English-speaking lands will travel more prosperously and travel further if we tread the path together, like good companions.

'THESE BANDS OF STURDY
TEUTONIC YOUTHS'

In the summer of 1932, Churchill was in southern Germany,
researching the biography of his military ancestor John Churchill,
first Duke of Marlborough, who had defeated the French and
Bavarians in 1704 at the Battle of Blenheim, in Bavaria. While staying
in Munich during the course of his researches, Churchill witnessed
a Nazi procession. Speaking to the House of Commons on
23 November 1932, just ten weeks before Hitler came to power in
Germany – he recalled his experience, and, making particular
reference to the threat to Belgium, Poland, Rumania, Czechoslovakia
and Yugoslavia – he warned:

> Do not delude yourselves. Do not let His Majesty's Government
> believe – I am sure they do not believe – that all that Germany is
> asking for is equal status. I believe the refined term now is equal
> qualitative status by indefinitely deferred stages. That is not what
> Germany is seeking.
>
> All these bands of sturdy Teutonic youths, marching through the
> streets and roads of Germany, with the light of desire in their eyes to
> suffer for their Fatherland, are not looking for status. They are
> looking for weapons, and, when they have the weapons, believe me
> they will then ask for the return of lost territories and lost colonies,
> and when that demand is made it cannot fail to shake and possibly
> shatter to their foundations of every one of the countries I have
> mentioned, and some other countries I have not mentioned.
>
> [· · ·]
>
> The removal of the just grievances of the vanquished ought to
> precede the disarmament of the victors. To bring about anything like
> equality of armaments if it were in our power to do so, which it
> happily is not, while those grievances remain unredressed, would be
> almost to appoint the day for another European war – to fix it as if it
> were a prize-fight.
>
> It would be far safer to reopen questions like those of the Danzig

Corridor and Transylvania, with all their delicacy and difficulty, in cold blood and in a calm atmosphere and while the victor nations still have ample superiority, than to wait and drift on, inch by inch and stage by stage, until once again vast combinations, equally matched, confront each other face to face.

[···]

As far as this island is concerned, the responsibility of Ministers to guarantee the safety of the country from day to day and from hour to hour is direct and inalienable.

'WIIEN WE READ ABOUT GERMANY'

In 1932 and 1933, the British Government – a National Government established in 1931, headed by the former Labour Prime Minister, Ramsay MacDonald, and with a predominantly Conservative House of Commons – was active at the League of Nations in supporting the search for world disarmament. Churchill addressed this issue, and also the nature of Nazi rule in Germany – where Hitler had become Chancellor on 30 January 1933 – when he spoke in the House of Commons on 23 March 1933:

We all desire to see peace and goodwill established among the nations, old scores forgotten, old wounds healed, the peoples of Christendom united to rebuild their portion of the world, to solve the problem of their toiling masses, to give a higher standard of life to the harassed populations. We can all expatiate upon that. The differences which arise are those of method. They arise when our sentiments come into contact with baffling and extremely obstinate concrete obstacles.

Our first supreme object is not to go to war. To that end we must do our best to prevent others from going to war. But we must be very careful that, in so doing, we do not increase the risk to ourselves of being involved in a war if, unfortunately, our well-meant efforts fail to prevent a quarrel between other Powers. It is by this test that I wish to examine the foreign policy of the Prime Minister. During the whole of the last four years he has directed, and not only directed, but dominated, our foreign policy, and no one can pretend that the results are satisfactory. On the contrary, the state of Europe, the condition of the Far East, our relations with Japan, the authority and prestige of the League of Nations, the security of this island – all have in various degrees sensibly deteriorated. It may be that events have been too strong for the Prime Minister. There are tasks beyond the power of mortal man. It may well be so, and his friends will naturally like to adopt that view, but others may think that the course that he has adopted, from the highest motives, has actually aggravated the position.

The staple of the policy of the right hon. Gentleman has been disarmament. Of course, it is true that in that respect he was only following the policy to which all Parties were committed and many nations committed by treaty. Nevertheless, the undue insistence upon disarmament, the prolonged attempts at Geneva of one nation to disarm another, and latterly of each nation to put some other nation in the wrong before public opinion – this prolonged process, which began before the Prime Minister was responsible for our affairs, but which he has impelled with all the resources at his disposal, has not had good results – in fact, it has in some respects worsened the relations between the Great Powers. I have held this view for some years, and I see it continually confirmed by events. I am very doubtful whether there is any use in pressing national disarmament to a point where nations think their safety is compromised, while the quarrels which divide them and which lead to their armaments and their fears are still unadjusted.

The elaborate process of measuring swords around the table at Geneva, which has gone on for so many years, stirs all the deepest suspicions and anxieties of the various Powers, and forces all the statesmen to consider many hypothetical contingencies which but for this prolonged process perhaps would not have crossed their minds and would only have remained buried in the archives of some General Staff.

I have always hoped and believed that the continuance of a long peace and the pressure of taxation would lead to a gradual, progressive neglect of armaments in all countries, as was the case after the conclusion of the great Napoleonic wars. I say nothing against private interchanges in secret diplomacy between the Foreign Offices of the different countries of a friendly character – 'If you will not do this, we shall not have to do that,' 'If your program did not start so early, ours would begin even later,' and so on such as have always gone on, and may perfectly legitimately go on. I believe a greater advance and progress towards a diminution of expenditure on armaments might have been achieved by these methods than by the conferences and schemes of disarmament which have been put forward at Geneva. It is in this mood that I look at the Prime Minister's latest plan.

Taking a layman's view of these facts and figures, I cannot say that they are injurious to our own defensive interests, but I doubt very much indeed the wisdom of pressing this plan upon France at the present time. I do not think it is at all likely that the French will agree. They must be greatly concerned at what is taking place in Germany, as well as at the attitude of some others of their neighbours. I dare say that during this anxious month – we seem to have passed through a very anxious month – there are a good many people who have said to themselves, as I have been saying for several years, 'Thank God for the French Army'.

When we read about Germany, when we watch with surprise and distress the tumultuous insurgency of ferocity and war spirit, the pitiless ill-treatment of minorities, the denial of the normal protections of civilized society to large numbers of individuals solely on the ground of race – when we see that occurring in one of the most gifted, learned, scientific and formidable nations in the world, one cannot help feeling glad that the fierce passions that are now raging in Germany have not found, as yet, any other outlet but upon Germans.

At a moment like this, to ask France to halve her army while Germany doubles hers – that is the scale of figures – to ask France to halve her air force while the German air force remains whatever it is – I am aware that there is no military air force permitted to remain – such a proposal, it seems to me, is likely to be considered by the French Government, at present at any rate, as somewhat unreasonable.

[···]

I warn the Government if we press France to disarm and encourage Germany to rearm to a point where dangerous conditions are created. If you press a country to reduce its defences beyond its better judgment, and it takes your advice, every obligation you have contracted, however carefully it has been expressed, will be multiplied in force, and you will find your position complicated by fresh obligations of comradeship, honour and compassion which will be brought very prominently to the front when a country which has taken your advice falls into grave jeopardy, perhaps as a result of what you have pressed upon it.

[···]

As long as France is strong and Germany is but inadequately armed there is no chance of France being attacked with success, and therefore no obligation will arise under Locarno for us to go to the aid of France. I am very sure, on the other hand, that France, which is the most pacific nation in Europe at the present time, as she is, fortunately, the most efficiently armed, would never attempt any violation of the Treaty or commit an overt act against Germany without the sanctions of the Treaty, without reference to the Treaty, and, least of all, in opposition to the country with which she is in such amicable relations – Great Britain.

'THE MONSTROSITY OF THE TOTALITARIAN STATE'

Churchill watched carefully and with deep concern as Hitler imposed the Nazi dictatorship on Germany. In June 1934 he set out his thoughts in an article published in *Pearson's Magazine*, entitled 'Are Parliaments Obsolete?' in which he wrote, about the Germans:

This mighty people, the most powerful and most dangerous in the Western world, have reverted to the conditions of the Middle Ages with all the modern facilities and aggravations. We are confronted with the monstrosity of the Totalitarian State. All are to think alike. No one is to disagree. To point out an obvious mistake or miscalculation is to be convicted of heresy and treason. Every link with the past, even with the most glorious traditions, has been severed. A despotism has been erected only less frightful than the Russian nightmare. Its aims are different, its forms are opposite, but its methods are the same.

Kingship and the glorious memories of bygone days are brushed aside in the interests of the newcomers who usurp all the loyalties due to the slowly woven fabric of the race. Religion must be read from the drill book. Jews must be baited for being born Jews. Little Jewish children must be insulted by regulation and routine on particular days of the week or of the month, and made to feel the ignominy of the state of life to which the Creator has called them.

Venerable pastors, upright magistrates, world famous scientists and philosophers, capable statesmen, independent minded manly citizens, frail poor old women of unfashionable opinions, are invaded, bullied and brutalised by gangs of armed hooligans to resist whom is a capital offence. To be thought disloyal or even unenthusiastic to the regime which only yesterday was unknown, warrants indefinite bondage in an internment camp under persecutions which though they may crush the victim, abase also the dignity of man. What a fate for Europe's strongest, most industrious and most learned sons!

Is there anything in all this which should lead us, the English-speaking world, to repudiate the famous chain of events which has made us what we are? – to cast away our Parliament, our habeas corpus, our rights and many freedoms, our tolerances, our decencies? On the contrary, ought we not betimes to buttress and fortify our ancient constitution, and to make sure that it is not ignorantly or lightly deranged? What a lamentable result it would be if the British and American democracies when enfranchised squandered in a few short years or even between some night and morning all the long-stored hard-won treasures of our island civilisation. It must not be.

'I WAS UNDER HIS SPELL'

In 1921, Churchill had appointed Colonel T. E. Lawrence ('Lawrence of Arabia') as his Arab Affairs Adviser at the Colonial Office. For two years the two men worked closely together on the evolution of Britain's Palestine Mandate and the creation of the Kingdom of Transjordan. In the late 1920s and early 1930s, Lawrence was an infrequent but welcome visitor to Chartwell, Churchill's country home in Kent. Lawrence died in May 1935, killed in a motorcycle accident. Two years later, Churchill wrote an essay published in *T. E. Lawrence by his Friends* (edited by Lawrence's brother, A. W. Lawrence):

When Clemenceau came back from India in his old age the reporters asked him, 'What will you do now?' He replied, 'I am going to live till I die'. This was the case of Lawrence. For twelve years he served as an air mechanic. The gallant Service, the decent fellows, good-hearted British comrades, the mechanism of aeroplane engines, the design of flying boats – he held on to these. On one of the very rare occasions when I saw him I taxed him with hiding his talent in a napkin while the Empire needed its best. He rejoined that he was setting an example, and that there was nothing in life better than to be a good aircraftman. He was certainly that. But how much more besides!

His grip upon the imagination of the modern world was due to his indifference to all the delights which nature offers to her multitudes of children. He could feel her pangs to the full. Her prizes did not stir him. Home, money, comfort, fame, power itself – meant little or nothing to him. The modern world had no means of exerting the slightest pull upon him. Solitary, austere, inexorable, he moved upon a plane apart from and above our common lot. Existence was no more than a duty, yet a duty faithfully to be discharged.

It was only at long intervals that we talked together. But I was under his spell, and deemed myself his friend. Sometimes he would stop on his motor bicycle at my house, and I would make haste to kill the fatted calf. Sometimes he would stop, and then hurry away for fear of intruding – where he was ever welcome.

The last time he came was a few weeks before his death. He was riding only a 'push-bike'! He could not afford such luxuries. I reminded him that he had the purse of Fortunatus. He had but to lift his hand. But he tossed his head disdainfully. Such a thing as a motorcycle was beyond his means. Alas, he did not stick to this opinion!

I deem him one of the greatest beings alive in our time. I do not see his like elsewhere. I fear whatever our need we shall never see his like again. King George V wrote to his brother, 'His name will live in history'. That is true. It will live in English letters; it will live in the annals of war; it will live in the traditions of the Royal Air Force, and in the legends of Arabia.

'HAUNTING FEARS AND SUSPICIONS'

In speech after speech, in the House of Commons and in the country, Churchill sought to warn of the dangers of allowing Germany to steal a march on Britain in military and air preparations. He hoped that his warnings would gain him a place in the predominantly Conservative National Government, formed at a time of grave economic crisis in 1931, and headed for nearly four years by the former Labour Prime Minister Ramsay MacDonald. The Conservative leader, Stanley Baldwin, succeeded the ailing MacDonald as Prime Minister on 7 June 1935. That same day, Churchill told the House of Commons:

It is only in the twentieth century that this hateful conception of inducing nations to surrender by terrorising the helpless civil population, by massacring the women and children, has gained acceptance and countenance among men. This is not the cause of any one nation. Every country would feel safer if once it were found that the bombing aeroplane was at the mercy of appliances directed from the earth, and the haunting fears and suspicions which are leading nations nearer and nearer to another catastrophe would be abated.

We have not only to fear attacks upon our civil population in our great cities, in respect of which we are more vulnerable than any other country in the world, but also attacks upon the dockyards and other technical establishments without which our Fleet, still an essential factor in our defence, might be paralysed or even destroyed.

Therefore it is not only for the sake of a world effort to eliminate one of the worst causes of suspicion and of war, but as a means of restoring to us here in Great Britain the old security of our Island, that this matter should receive and command the most vigorous thought of the greatest men in our country and our Government, and should be pressed forward by every resource that the science of Britain can apply and the wealth of the country can liberate.

'DO YOU NOT TREMBLE FOR YOUR CHILDREN?'

On 1 September 1935, as Mussolini was threatening to invade Ethiopia – which he did that October – Churchill left England to spend three weeks in the South of France, at the villa of his mother's friend Maxine Elliott. Among the other guests at the villa was the American author Vincent Sheean, who, in his book *Between the Thunder and the Sun*, published two years later, recorded Churchill's deep concern for international order:

> He had a distinction which he tried to bring out in every talk about Ethiopia just then: it seemed to him very important. 'It's not the <u>thing</u> we object to,' he would say, 'it's the <u>kind</u> of thing.' I had not then succumbed as much to his genial charm as I did later, and I could not quite accept this. I mentioned the Red Sea, the route to India, the importance of Aden. Mr Churchill brushed all that aside: 'We don't need to worry about the Italians,' he said. 'It isn't that at all. It isn't the thing. It's the <u>kind</u> of thing . . .'
>
> Mr Churchill was pinned down firmly one day by an elegant lady, Mme Lepelletier, who said that an objection to the <u>thing</u> might be practical and necessary, but that England had no historical right to object to the <u>kind</u> of thing. England had too often profited by 'the kind of thing'.
>
> 'Ah, but you see, all that belongs to the unregenerate past, is locked away in the limbo of the old, the wicked days,' Mr Churchill said,

smiling benevolently upon her across the luncheon table. 'The world progresses. We have endeavoured, by means of the League of Nations and the whole fabric of international law, to make it impossible for nations nowadays to infringe upon each other's rights. In trying to upset the empire of Ethiopia, Mussolini is making a most dangerous and foolhardy attack upon the whole established structure, and the results of such an attack are quite incalculable. Who is to say what will come of it in a year, or two, or three? With Germany arming at break-neck speed, England lost in a pacifist dream, France corrupt and torn by dissension, America remote and indifferent – Madame, my dear lady, do you not tremble for your children?'

'SOMEBODY HAS TO STATE THE TRUTH'

One of Churchill's main fears during the 1930s was that the British Government was not putting sufficient resources into anti-aircraft defence. When the inventor of radar, Robert Watson Watt, came to see him to ask for help in obtaining greater government funding for his work, Churchill interceded with the relevant government Minister. Risking their careers, senior civil servants from across Whitehall, including the Air Ministry, Foreign Office, and the Secret Intelligence Service, brought Churchill evidence of the neglect of Britain's defences and of the true scale of German rearmament. On 26 September 1935, he spoke at the City Carlton Club in London:

So far from being half as strong again as Germany, so far from making up leeway, we are already greatly inferior in number and falling further and further behind every month.

[···]

No doubt it is not popular to say these things, but I am accustomed to abuse and I expect to have a great deal more of it before I have finished. Somebody has to state the truth. There ought to be a few members of the House of Commons who are in a sufficiently independent position to confront both Ministers and electors with unpalatable truths. We do not wish our ancient freedom and the decent tolerant civilisation we have preserved in this island to hang upon a rotten thread.

'EVERY KIND OF PERSECUTION'

Churchill read Hitler's book *Mein Kampf* ('My Struggle') and took seriously Hitler's threats towards the Jews. In November 1935 he published an article, 'The Truth about Hitler', in the *Strand* magazine:

The Jews, supposed to have contributed, by a disloyal and pacifist influence, to the collapse of Germany at the end of the Great War, were also deemed to be the main prop of communism and the authors of defeatist doctrines in every form. Therefore, the Jews of Germany, a community numbered by many hundreds of thousands, were to be stripped of all power, driven from every position in public and social life, expelled from the professions, silenced in the Press, and declared a foul and odious race.

The Twentieth Century has witnessed with surprise, not merely the promulgation of these ferocious doctrines, but their enforcement with brutal vigour by the Government and by the populace. No past services, no proved patriotism, even wounds sustained in war, could procure immunity for persons whose only crime was that their parents had brought them into the world. Every kind of persecution, grave or petty, upon the world-famous scientists, writers, and composers at the top down to the wretched little Jewish children in the national schools, was practised, was glorified, and is still being practised and glorified.

A similar proscription fell upon socialists and communists of every hue. The Trade Unionists and liberal intelligentsia are equally smitten. The slightest criticism is an offence against the State. The courts of justice, though allowed to function in ordinary cases, are superseded for every form of political offence by so-called people's courts composed of ardent Nazis.

Side by side with the training grounds of the new armies and the great aerodromes, the concentration camps pockmark the German soil. In these thousands of Germans are coerced and cowed into submission to the irresistible power of the Totalitarian State.

'DECIDED ONLY TO BE UNDECIDED'

Churchill's warnings about the neglect of Britain's defences were continuous and emphatic. On 12 November 1936 he told the House of Commons:

> The First Lord of the Admiralty in his speech the other night [. . .] said, 'We are always reviewing the position.' Everything, he assured us, is entirely fluid. I am sure that that is true. Anyone can see what the position is. The Government simply cannot make up their minds, or they cannot get the Prime Minister to make up his mind. So they go on in strange paradox, decided only to be undecided, resolved to be irresolute, adamant for drift, solid for fluidity, all-powerful to be impotent.
>
> So we go on preparing more months and years – precious, perhaps vital to the greatness of Britain – for the locusts to eat. They will say to me, 'A Minister of Supply is not necessary, for all is going well.' I deny it. 'The position is satisfactory.' It is not true. 'All is proceeding according to plan.' We know what that means.

'WE ARE WITH EUROPE
BUT NOT OF IT'

On 29 May 1938 the *News of the World* published an article by Churchill entitled 'Why Not "The United States of Europe"?' In it he urged a unified European community, based on those States 'with a tradition of liberty'. His article ended:

But we have our own dream and our own task. We are with Europe, but not of it. We are linked, but not comprised. We are interested and associated, but not absorbed. And should European statesmen address us in the words which were used of old – 'Shall I speak for thee to the King or the Captain of the host?' – we should reply with the Shunamite woman: 'Nay, Sir, for we dwell among our own people.'

The conception of a 'United States of Europe' is right. Every step taken to that end which appeases the obsolete hatreds and vanished oppressions, which makes easier the traffic and reciprocal services of Europe, which encourages its nations to lay aside their threatening arms or precautionary panoply, is good in itself, is good for them and good for all.

It is, however, imperative that as Europe advances towards higher internal unity there shall be a proportionate growth of solidarity throughout the British Empire, and also a deepening self-knowledge and mutual recognition among the English-speaking peoples. Then without misgiving and without detachment we can watch and aid the assuagement of the European tragedy, and without envy survey their sure and sound approach to mass-wealth; being very conscious that every stride towards European cohesion which is beneficial to the general welfare will make us a partner in their good fortune.

'THE ABANDONMENT AND RUIN OF CZECHOSLOVAKIA'

At the Munich Conference at the end of September 1938, Britain and France agreed to put pressure on Czechoslovakia to cede its large German-speaking region – the Sudetenland – to Germany. Before 1914, the Sudetenland had been a part of the Austro-Hungarian Empire, not of Germany. Hitler, who in March 1938 had annexed Austria, was triumphant. With the Sudetenland, he acquired territory rich in minerals and industry without firing a shot. Returning to Britain from Munich, the British Prime Minister, Neville

Chamberlain, who had succeeded Stanley Baldwin in May 1937, declared that he brought back with him 'peace in our time'. In the House of Commons, Churchill emerged as a leading critic of the Munich Agreement, addressing Members on 5 October 1938 in one of the most anguished speeches he had delivered during his almost nine years out of office and out of power. It was a speech that, as several of the supporters of appeasement who heard it later commented, left them in trepidation for the future:

> All is over. Silent, mournful, abandoned, broken, Czechoslovakia recedes into the darkness. She has suffered in every respect by her association with the Western democracies and with the League of Nations, of which she has always been an obedient servant.
>
> I venture to think that in future the Czechoslovak State cannot be maintained as an independent entity. You will find that in a period of time which may be measured by years, but may be measured only by months, Czechoslovakia will be engulfed in the Nazi regime. Perhaps they may join it in despair or in revenge. At any rate, that story is over and told. But we cannot consider the abandonment and ruin of Czechoslovakia in the light of what happened only last month. It is the most grievous consequence which we have yet experienced of what we have done and of what we have left undone in the last five years – five years of futile good intention, five years of eager search for the line of least resistance, five years of uninterrupted retreat of British power, five years of neglect of our air defences.
>
> Those are the features which I stand here to declare and which marked an improvident stewardship for which Great Britain and France have dearly to pay.
>
> So far as this country is concerned the responsibility must rest with those who have the undisputed control of our political affairs. They neither prevented Germany from rearming, nor did they rearm ourselves in time. They quarrelled with Italy without saving Ethiopia. They exploited and discredited the vast institution of the League of Nations and they neglected to make alliances and combinations which might have repaired previous errors, and thus they left us in the hour of trial without adequate national defence or effective international security.

[· · ·]

We are in the presence of a disaster of the first magnitude which has befallen Great Britain and France. Do not let us blind ourselves to that. It must now be accepted that all the countries of Central and Eastern Europe will make the best terms they can with the triumphant Nazi Power.

The system of alliances in Central Europe upon which France has relied for her safety has been swept away, and I can see no means by which it can be reconstituted. The road down the Danube Valley to the Black Sea, the resources of corn and oil, the road which leads as far as Turkey, has been opened.

[· · ·]

You will see, day after day, week after week, the entire alienation of those regions. Many of those countries, in fear of the rise of the Nazi Power, have already got politicians, Ministers, Governments, who were pro-German, but there was always an enormous popular movement in Poland, Rumania, Bulgaria and Yugoslavia which looked to the Western democracies and loathed the idea of having this arbitrary rule of the totalitarian system thrust upon them, and hoped that a stand would be made. All that has gone by the board. We are talking about countries which are a long way off and of which, as the Prime Minister might say, we know nothing.

[· · ·]

Many people, no doubt, honestly believe that they are only giving away the interests of Czechoslovakia, whereas I fear we shall find that we have deeply compromised, and perhaps fatally endangered, the safety and even the independence of Great Britain and France.

This is not merely a question of giving up the German Colonies, as I am sure we shall be asked to do. Nor is it a question only of losing influence in Europe. It goes far deeper than that. You have to consider the character of the Nazi movement and the rule which it implies.

The Prime Minister desires to see cordial relations between this country and Germany. There is no difficulty at all in having cordial relations with the German people. Our hearts go out to them. But they have no power.

You must have diplomatic and correct relations, but there can never be friendship between the British democracy and the Nazi Power, that Power which spurns Christian ethics, which cheers its onward course by a barbarous paganism, which vaunts the spirit of aggression and conquest, which derives strength and perverted pleasure from persecution, and uses, as we have seen, with pitiless brutality the threat of murderous force. That Power cannot ever be the trusted friend of the British democracy.

What I find unendurable is the sense of our country falling into the power, into the orbit and influence of Nazi Germany and of our existence becoming dependent upon their good will or pleasure. It is to prevent that that I have tried my best to urge the maintenance of every bulwark of defence – first the timely creation of an Air Force superior to anything within striking distance of our shores; secondly the gathering together of the collective strength of many nations; and thirdly, the making of alliances and military conventions, all within the Covenant, in order to gather together forces at any rate to restrain the onward movement of this Power. It has all been in vain. Every position has been successively undermined and abandoned on specious and plausible excuses.

I have been casting about to see how measures can be taken to protect us from this advance of the Nazi Power, and to secure those forms of life which are so dear to us. What is the sole method that is open? The sole method that is open is for us to regain our old island independence by acquiring that supremacy in the air which we were promised, that security in our air defences which we were assured we had, and thus to make ourselves an island once again.

That, in all this grim outlook, shines out as the overwhelming fact. An effort at rearmament the like of which has not been seen ought to be made forthwith, and all the resources of this country and all its united strength should be bent to that task. I was very glad to see that Lord Baldwin yesterday in the House of Lords said that he would mobilise industry to-morrow. But I think it would have been much better if Lord Baldwin had said that 2½ years ago, when everyone demanded a Ministry of Supply. I will venture to say to hon.

Gentlemen sitting here behind the Government Bench, hon. Friends of mine, whom I thank for the patience with which they have listened to what I have to say, that they have some responsibility for all this too, because, if they had given one tithe of the cheers they have lavished upon this transaction of Czechoslovakia to the small band of Members who were endeavouring to get timely rearmament set in motion, we should not now be in the position in which we are. Hon. Gentlemen opposite, and hon. Members on the Liberal benches, are not entitled to throw these stones.

I remember for two years having to face, not only the Government's deprecation, but their stern disapproval. Lord Baldwin has now given the signal, tardy though it may be; let us at least obey it. After all, there are no secrets now about what happened in the air and in the mobilisation of our anti-aircraft defences. These matters have been, as my hon. and gallant Friend the Member for the Abbey Division said, seen by thousands of people. They can form their own opinions of the character of the statements which have been persistently made to us by Ministers on this subject. Who pretends now that there is air parity with Germany? Who pretends now that our anti-aircraft defences were adequately manned or armed? We know that the German General Staff are well informed upon these subjects, but the House of Commons has hitherto not taken seriously its duty of requiring to assure itself on these matters.

The Home Secretary said the other night that he would welcome investigation. Many things have been done which reflect the greatest credit upon the administration. But the vital matters are what we want to know about. I have asked again and again during these three years for a secret Session where these matters could be thrashed out, or for an investigation by a Select Committee of the House, or for some other method. I ask now that, when we meet again in the autumn, that should be a matter on which the Government should take the House into its confidence, because we have a right to know where we stand and what measures are being taken to secure our position.

I do not grudge our loyal, brave people, who were ready to do their duty no matter what the cost, who never flinched under the strain of last week – I do not grudge them the natural, spontaneous outburst of joy and relief when they learned that the hard ordeal would no longer be required of them at the moment; but they should know the truth. They should know that there has been gross neglect and deficiency in our defences; they should know that we have sustained a defeat without a war the consequences of which will travel far with us along our road; they should know that we have passed an awful milestone in our history, when the whole equilibrium of Europe has been deranged, and that the terrible words have for the time being been pronounced against the Western democracies:

'Thou art weighed in the balance and found wanting.'

And do not suppose that this is the end. This is only the beginning of the reckoning. This is only the first sip, the first foretaste of a bitter cup which will be proffered to us year by year unless by a supreme recovery of moral health and martial vigour, we arise again and take our stand for freedom as in the olden time.

'ONE HEALTHY GROWL'

Churchill's fears that Britain would not be properly prepared if war came were accentuated by Neville Chamberlain's refusal to create a Ministry of Supply. On 17 November 1938, Churchill told the House of Commons, during a debate on the need for such a Ministry:

I confess that I find some difficulty in making another speech in favour of a Ministry of Supply. I have used all the arguments of urgency and I have endeavoured to explain many of the processes of detail, three years ago, two years ago, and, finally, only six months ago. I have pleaded this cause in good time, I have pleaded when it was already late; and perhaps my right hon. Friend may remember I have even adjured him not to be deterred from doing right because it was impressed on him by the devil. But neither reason nor persuasion nor coaxing has had the slightest effect against the massive obstinacy of the powers that be, the powers that have led us to where we are now.

This Debate, however, differs from others we have had on the same subject. It is possible to vote tonight upon a perfectly clear issue. We are indebted to the Liberal Party for having brought the House of Commons squarely up to the fence. The House must jump that fence or swerve ignominiously away from it and, in the result, as I believe, lose a race upon which the stakes not only comprise the safety of our country, but also affect great causes of world significance.

I am going to address myself particularly to hon. Friends of mine above the Gangway who sit behind the Ministers. I cannot believe that many of them do not share the anxieties which are pressing upon the thinking majority of their fellow-countrymen. I appeal, therefore, to these gentlemen, but I do not appeal in suppliant terms; indeed, if at all, it is in minatory and comminatory terms. I say they have a grave responsibility for our present plight.

The history of England is still to be written and unfolded. History will disentangle individual responsibility and will lay the blame on the shoulders where blame should be, but hon. Gentlemen above the Gangway – pledged, loyal, faithful supporters on all occasions of His Majesty's Government – must not imagine that they can throw their burden wholly on the Ministers of the Crown. Much power has rested with them. One healthy growl from those benches three years ago – and how different today would be the whole lay-out of our armaments production! Alas, that service was not forthcoming.

We have drifted on in general good-natured acquiescence for three whole years – not for three whole years of ignorance or unawareness, but for three whole years with the facts glaring us full in the face.

We have drifted on and we have drifted down, and the question to-night is sharply, brutally even, whether we shall go on drifting or make a renewed effort to rise abreast of the level of events.

I put it as bluntly as I possibly can. If only 50 Members of the Conservative Party went into the Lobby to-night to vote for this Amendment, it would not affect the life of the Government, but it would make them act. It would make a forward movement of real power, of real energy. We should get our Ministry of Supply no doubt, but much more than that: we should get a feeling of renewed strength and a prestige outside this country which would be of real service and

value. I think it right to put these points at the outset of my observations. They are not meant in any spirit but that of one who shares
with hon. Gentlemen the perils of the country in which we are all
involved. This is no Party question. It has nothing to do with Party. It
is entirely an issue affecting the broad safety of the nation.

'WHERE I FAILED, FOR ALL MY BRILLIANT GIFTS'

When the division was taken in the Ministry of Supply debate on
17 November 1938, only two Conservatives followed Churchill into
the Lobby: Brendan Bracken and Harold Macmillan. Neville
Chamberlain's comment during the debate that, for all his brilliant
gifts, Churchill lacked the faculty of judgement had made its mark –
and stung Churchill to the quick. On December 9, he took up the
challenge, at Chingford in his Epping constituency:

The Prime Minister said in the House of Commons the other day that
where I failed, for all my brilliant gifts, was in the faculty of judging.
I will gladly submit my judgment about foreign affairs and national
defence during the last five years, in comparison with his own.

In February the Prime Minister said that tension in Europe had
greatly relaxed. A few weeks later Nazi Germany seized Austria. I
predicted that he would repeat this statement as soon as the shock of
the rape of Austria passed away. He did so in the very same words at
the end of July. By the middle of August Germany was mobilising for
those bogus manoeuvres which, after bringing us all to the verge of a
world war, ended in the complete destruction and absorption of the
Republic of Czechoslovakia.

At the Lord Mayor's banquet in November at the Guildhall, he told
us that Europe was settling down to a more peaceful state. The words
were hardly out of his mouth before the Nazi atrocities on the Jewish
population resounded throughout the civilised world.

Churchill then spoke of Chamberlain's predecessor:

> In 1934 I warned Mr Baldwin that the Germans had a secret Air Force and were rapidly overhauling ours. I gave definite figures and forecasts. Of course, it was all denied with all the weight of official authority. I was depicted a scaremonger. Less than six months after, Mr Baldwin had to come down to the House and admit he was wrong and he said, 'We are all to blame' and everybody said, 'How very honest of him to admit his mistake.'
>
> He got more applause for making this mistake, which may prove fatal to the British Empire and to British freedom, than ordinary people would do after they rendered some great service which added to its security and power. Well, Mr Chamberlain was, next to Mr Baldwin, the most powerful Member of that Government. He was Chancellor of the Exchequer. He knew all the facts. His judgment failed just like that of Mr Baldwin and we are suffering from the consequences of it today.

Churchill next referred to Lord Samuel, his colleague in the Liberal Government before the First World War:

> Four years ago, when I asked that the Air Force should be doubled and redoubled – more than that is being done now – Lord Samuel thought my judgment so defective that he likened me to a Malay running amok. It would have been well for him and his persecuted race if my advice had been taken. They would not be where they are now and we should not be where we are now.
>
> [...]

It is on the background of these proved errors of judgment in the past that I draw your attention to some of the judgments which have been passed upon the future, the results of which have not yet been proved.

'ANOTHER CONFRONTATION AND TRIAL OF STRENGTH'

In the months following the Munich Agreement, Churchill looked for any sign that Neville Chamberlain's Government was taking steps to stand up to any future German aggression. On 9 February 1939 he wrote, in one of his fortnightly newspaper articles for the *Daily Telegraph* and *Morning Post* (later reprinted in his collection of speeches *Step by Step*):

> The momentous declaration made by Mr. Chamberlain in the House of Commons on Monday that an act of aggression against France from any quarter would be equally resisted by Great Britain shows that the two Western democracies are resolved to act as one and stand together. Few can escape the feeling that the next few months will witness another confrontation and trial of strength and willpower between the rival forces in Europe.
>
> When Herr Hitler expressed his belief that a long period of peace lay ahead, it was no doubt in the expectation that matters would, after a time of tension, be adjusted to the satisfaction of the two Dictatorial Powers. Whether this will be so or not no man can predict. The assurances which Signor Mussolini has renewed that Italy seeks no territorial gains at the expense of Spain do not touch the military issue. The victory of General Franco may be followed by arrangements which, without altering sovereignty, give the effective use of all Spanish bases, both naval and air, to the two countries who have helped him so much. Such arrangements would, to all intents and purposes, be as detrimental to British and French interests as an actual transference of territory.
>
> It would not, however, be right only to look upon the darker side. The remarkable action of President Roosevelt, undoubtedly sustained by the government and people of the United States, in letting it be widely known that not only American moral support but also practical aid in munitions and supplies will be accorded to the Western democracies should they become the victims of unprovoked aggression, is a potent stabilising force. It may well be that the

preservation of European peace will be secured through his far-sighted and courageous policy. The spirit of resistance to Nazi encroachment has not been extinguished in Eastern and South-eastern Europe. Countries which before Munich were under the impression that they were being asked to confer favours on France and Great Britain, have now realised forcibly that it is their own lives which are endangered.

Here at home in England there has been a reconsolidation of national union. The attitude of the Government has stiffened, and some past differences are fading into history. Above all, there is a sense of gathering strength. The power and condition of the Royal Navy relative to its possible tasks is unprecedented. The long-delayed flow of aircraft and munitions is now arriving.

If redoubled exertions are made, a far greater measure of security may be procured for the civil population against air raids. While only astrologers and other merchants of superstition can declare the future, the day may yet come when the peaceful, law-respecting British nation may once again be able to pursue its journey without having to wait and listen on the wireless from week to week to the dictatorial orations of countries they defeated or succoured in the past.

'A SCALE IMMENSELY GREATER'

Churchill's worries that the Government had not fully grasped the extent to which its war preparations needed to be accelerated were reflected in his constant pressure for the establishment of a Ministry of Supply. Raising this topic yet again, and referring to the failure of the ideals and hopes invested in the appeasement policy of Neville Chamberlain and his parliamentary supporters, Churchill told the House of Commons on 21 February 1939:

We may all deplore the unhappy and turbulent events which have swept much before us, but I hope my right hon. Friend will realise the very great share that he and all who sit with him have had in presenting these ideals to the country and in gaining the support for them of great numbers in the country who are absolutely loyal in their desire to support policies which he puts forward, and I hope he will make it clear that it was in no spirit of airy satisfaction that he referred to the undoubted downfall of so many hopes and ideals which the Government had encouraged.

However, I did not come to chide, because my first desire is to congratulate the right hon. Gentleman the Chancellor of the Exchequer [Sir John Simon] upon the way in which he is handling the immense task which has descended upon him. This is no time for financial pedantry. The period through which we are passing is not an ordinary period of peace. It is a period of what we may call bloodless war. We all hope and pray that this war will remain bloodless, and that, after an interval as short as possible, real peace will emerge. But in this present midway condition, quite unparalleled in our history, it is essential to the realisation of our hopes that the full strength of Britain, actual and potential, should be used to the highest advantage; and the Chancellor of the Exchequer is, therefore, quite right to use the powerful heavy weapon of British credit, which has hitherto been so carefully kept bright and clean, as far as he can without blunting or breaking it. Of the extent to which he can use it, I must say that he and the Treasury, with their many varied sources of information and the great apparatus at their disposal, are certainly the best judges.

Moreover, the Government have no incentive, no unworthy incentive, to take more from loan than from credit, to trespass unduly upon borrowing powers, because it is perfectly well known that whatever new additional taxation they think necessary will be supported by an overwhelming majority in the House, and will be paid punctually by the taxpayers in the country.

[···]

Whenever we speak of 'bloodless war' it must not be supposed that it is not attended in every country in this anxious, melancholy time by strain, by loss, and, in some countries, by a very severe degree of privation and suffering among the mass of the population. Moreover, the bloodless war is becoming intensified. There is hardly a day when the papers do not show that it is becoming intensified. The strains resulting from it will in this year, still more if it is prolonged, test not only the financial and economic strength of nations but the health of their institutions and the social structure of their civilisation.

It is certainly not an hour in which we should indulge in any vainglorious boastings. Nevertheless, it is right to say, as the Chancellor of the Exchequer indicated, with proper modesty but undoubted truth, that probably we can stand this strain, which may be prolonged, better than any other community in the world. That is from every point of view, not merely because of the financial and economic strength of the country but from the association of the whole people, through Parliament, in the processes of government.

It is a great comfort and source of additional security that both the Opposition parties, in spite of many grievous differences which exist, and in spite of the many searching criticisms which they may make, and which ought to be made, are nevertheless not in any way challenging the principle of these exceptional measures which the Government feel it their duty to propose. On the contrary, the only political risk which Ministers run is if they are thought to have proposed too little, or if they are reproached with not having proposed it soon enough.

[···]

It seems to me that the production of munitions for an army should long ago have been undertaken upon a scale immensely greater than anything which the War Office have been allowed hitherto to contemplate, and it is another reason for the immediate appointment of a Minister of Supply. It is not a question of allowing plant and factories to come to full fruition; there is a need to provide, quite definitely, for the supply of munitions for very large forces which will be pressing themselves upon us should this hateful evil of war ever come upon us.

Moreover – to continue dealing with unpopular and unpalatable topics – we ought surely to have available in the first few months of war military forces larger than anything of which we have yet heard.

'A DEVOTED VANGUARD OF THE BRITISH NATION'

Despite the determined opposition of the Labour and Liberal Parties, Churchill pressed the Government to announce the introduction of military conscription. On 24 April 1939 he spoke outside the Mansion House in London, at a lunchtime meeting on behalf of voluntary Territorial recruiting, and in support of the London Division recruiting campaign. During the course of his remarks to a large gathering outside the Mansion House, he said:

I am told that all the units have reached their strength, and the formation of the second series of units has not only begun but has made good progress. These are remarkable results, considering the cumbrous way in which the schedule of reserved occupations has been framed, which seems to rate military service at less than its proper importance and which rules out so many people on this score. Nevertheless, the results obtained have been so good that these recruiting meetings are a cause of satisfaction to all who have the responsible task to perform.

The first and highest form of national service is service in arms and with the fighting units. Nothing can compare with that in value or in honour, and until the ranks are full up to the limit thought necessary nothing can be put in the way of that service being rendered. Our weakness is that with national approval we have guaranteed to many countries in Europe that we will make common cause with them against further aggression, and that we have not so far taken any adequate steps, or attempted steps, to provide ourselves with a sufficient army with which to back our words.

That is a position morally indefensible; moreover, it is a position which lessens the chances of peace. It lessens those chances in two ways. First of all, military weakness in this country encourages potential enemies, and military weakness in this country discourages our allies, or possible allies, and prevents, or at any rate retards, the weaving together of that great association of peace-loving countries whose collective armed strength is the greatest guarantee of the maintenance of peace. All Parties have agreed to join in the giving of those guarantees to other countries, and all parties are bound to make sure that we can honourably and faithfully execute them.

It is a splendid quality in the British national character that the more severe and more onerous the duty, the more near and grievous the danger, the more our men would come forward to volunteer in the face of that danger.

I do not want it to be thought that those volunteers are going to be left to bear the whole burden themselves. That would not be right. That would not be fair. Moreover, there would be far too few for the task. Anyone can see public opinion is growing in favour of compulsory national service in all its forms, and especially in the highest form. It is increasingly probable that we shall have compulsory national service before long. (Cheers.)

It is certain that we should have compulsory national service should war unhappily break out. Therefore those who now come forward voluntarily to bear the brunt, and sustain, if necessary, the first shock, may be sure their countrymen will be inspired by their example to go to their aid and insist that this burden of national defence and self-preservation shall be equally and justly shared without respect to class or fortune. Those, therefore, who volunteer today must not think of themselves as the lonely champions of British strength and honour but as a devoted vanguard of the British nation now arming reluctantly but resolvingly in the defence of the freedom and progress of mankind.

'THE AMBASSADOR SHOULD NOT HAVE SPOKEN SO'

During the summer of 1939, Churchill became increasingly worried about the sense of defeatism and despair that he began to feel around him. At a dinner on June 14, he found himself sitting next to the American columnist Walter Lippmann. He was shocked to learn from

Lippmann that the United States Ambassador to Britain, Joseph Kennedy, was telling his friends that when war came Britain, facing defeat, would negotiate with Hitler. The National Labour MP Harold Nicolson, who was present at the dinner, noted in his diary that, the moment Churchill heard the word 'defeat', he turned to Lippmann with the words:

> No, the Ambassador should not have spoken so, Mr Lippmann; he should not have said that dreadful word. Yet supposing (as I do not for one moment suppose) that Mr Kennedy were correct in his tragic utterance, then I for one would willingly lay down my life in combat, rather than, in fear of defeat, surrender to the menaces of these most sinister men. It will then be for you, for the Americans, to preserve and to maintain the great heritage of the English-speaking peoples.

In his own diary, Walter Lippmann noted down the chief points of Churchill's argument:

> German army can't pierce French carapace; Spain negligible; British territorials can hold Spanish army and blockade of Spain would ruin her. Would rather Turks than Italians as allies. Italy a prey, Turkey a falcon. Would cut losses in Far East; no dispersal of the fleet; settle with Japan after the war.
>
> Central Europe mobilised as a unit in 1914. Then Germany had ten divisions from Czechoslovakia; now they need six divisions to hold it. Hungary, Yugoslavia, Rumania, dangerous and unreliable. Poland, a new force, and behind it, the Russian pad. No use to say to Germany they are not being encircled. Better to overwhelm them with righteous indignation.
>
> Only argument that counts is force. No use shaping policy in accordance with Goebbels' propaganda. Take your own line and make them follow. In event of German mobilisation, mobilise fleet; at first provocative action, cut German railway communications with Europe and defy them to do anything about it.
>
> As for negotiated peace, there never can be peace in Europe while eight million Czechs are in bondage.

'A MOST FORMIDABLE EXPRESSION OF THE BRITISH NATIONAL WILL'

On 2 August 1939 the Government proposed to adjourn Parliament until October 3. On August 2, in the House of Commons, Churchill led a growing number of MPs who were uneasy at ending the session while Europe was in such a state of crisis. His appeal was not successful:

> I must say I regret the terms of the Government's Motion, and, although not altogether for the same reasons, I find myself endorsing the pleas which have been advanced from both the Opposition Parties in the House. But I still hope that the Prime Minister has not said his last word on this subject. It is in that hope that I venture to offer a few reasons for my opposition to the Motion.
>
> This House is sometimes disparaged in this country, but abroad it counts. Abroad, the House of Commons is counted, and especially in Dictator countries, as a most formidable expression of the British national will and an instrument of that will in resistance to aggression. Surely that is a fact which must be admitted. The Dictators themselves have not been slow to notice that minority opinion in this House has seemed in one way to influence the course of Government action. It is in accordance with minority opinion in this House that we have come together upon a foreign policy upon which all are now agreed, a foreign policy which the two Dictator States deeply deprecate. Therefore, I say that we count largely in their thoughts.
>
> If you wish to check this by examination, see how oddly they have timed various strokes which have been made in the recent past for occasions when the House has risen and the Members are on their holidays. Take the latest of all, the Albanian outrage at Easter. It was nicely timed for the moment when it was known that Parliament was scattered, when the Ministers were scattered – and when the Mediterranean Fleet, unfortunately, was scattered, too. They timed it for that purpose. Then look at last year, when we parted in similar circumstances to the present. Until then there were no suspicious

troop movements in Germany. It was only then that there began all these movements for the pretended peaceful purposes of a local manoeuvre.

It may sound rather a vain thing for a Member of Parliament to say, but it seems to me that this House is a recognized addition to the defences of Great Britain, that we are safer when the House is sitting, and that the power and will of this House count very much, and, properly commanded, will reinforce the power of His Majesty's Government. Therefore, it seems to me that it would be regrettable if we were to go out of action just at a time when the situation is becoming most acute.

I would not press this argument so far as to suggest that if the House goes on sitting night and day there will be no crisis. That would, indeed, be exaggerating the argument, but I have the feeling that things are in a great balance, and that even minor matters of a favourable character cannot be neglected if they can be thrown in on the right side of the scale. Therefore, I should regret it very much if we were now to pass a Resolution scattering ourselves to the winds till October.

This is an odd moment for the House to declare that it will go on a two months' holiday. It is only an accident that our summer holidays coincide with the danger months in Europe, when the harvests have been gathered, and when the powers of evil are at their strongest. The situation in Europe is graver than it was at this time last year. The German Government have already 2,000,000 men under arms actually incorporated in their Army. When the new class joins before the end of August more than 500,000 will be added to this number automatically.

All along the Polish frontier from Danzig to Cracow there are heavy massings of troops, and every preparation is being made for a speedy advance. There are five German divisions in a high state of mobility around Breslau alone. The roads, as the Leader of the Liberal Party mentioned, towards Poland through Czechoslovakia are being raised to the highest condition. Quarries are being opened for material, by enforced Czechoslovak labour.

I have been told – I may be wrong, but I have not always been wrong – that many of the public buildings and of the schools in large parts of Czechoslovakia, Bohemia certainly, have been cleared and prepared for the accommodation of wounded. But that is not the only place. There is a definite movement of supplies and troops through Austria towards the east.

[· · ·]

On our side, too, and among our Allies, are great preparations. The Fleet is largely mobilized. We congratulate the Government on the timely step they have taken, and we support them in it. As many men as can possibly be accommodated in camps are in training, and the anti-aircraft gunners are at their stations. Is this, then, the moment that we should separate and declare that we separate until the 3rd October? Who can doubt that there is going to be a supreme trial of will power, if not indeed a supreme trial of arms?

At this moment in its long history, it would be disastrous, it would be pathetic, it would be shameful for the House of Commons to write itself off as an effective and potent factor in the situation, or reduce whatever strength it can offer to the firm front which the nation will make against aggression.

Then, of course, it is asked, 'Do you trust the Prime Minister?' The Leaders of both Oppositions made it perfectly clear that they did not trust him, but that is not the position of some of those who are anxious that an arrangement should be reached by which Parliament will not pass entirely out of being for so long a time; that is not the position which we on this side of the House adopt. I, personally, accept what the Prime Minister says, and when he makes solemn public declarations I believe that he will do his best to carry them out. I trust his good faith in every respect, but that does not really dispose of the whole issue. It might be that his good faith was in no way in question, either about the rising of the House or other matters at all, but there might be a difference of judgment. I use the word 'judgment' with some temerity, because my right hon. Friend twitted me some time ago about that notorious defect which I have in my composition.

I have not looked up all his own declarations in any captious spirit, and I will not pursue that this afternoon, but it is quite clear that the judgment which the Prime Minister might form upon the facts as they unfolded would be a legitimate and natural topic upon which differences of opinion would arise between us.

Take, for instance, a very late example, this question of Danzig. The Leader of the Labour Party [Clement Attlee] stated how grievous the situation was in Danzig, and my right hon. Friend [Neville Chamberlain] said that the situation was exaggerated. That was only two days ago, but now we read in *The Times* that the official *Gazette of Poland* has made a statement of the facts in Danzig which goes much further than the statement put forward by the Leaders of the Labour Party which my right hon. Friend the Prime Minister thought was exaggerated. So there may be differences, quite honest differences, upon the emphasis and upon the facts; and it is in respect of these differences which arise when men are working on the same policy that an interchange of opinion in the House of Commons would be from time to time most desirable.

It is a very hard thing, and I hope it will not be said, for the Government to say to the House, 'Begone! Run off and play. Take your gas masks with you. Do not worry about public affairs. Leave them to the gifted and experienced Ministers' – who, after all, so far as our defences are concerned, landed us where we were landed in September last year, and who, after all – I make all allowances for the many difficulties – have brought us in foreign policy at this moment to the point where we have guaranteed Poland and Rumania, after having lost Czechoslovakia, and not having gained Russia.

This is, indeed, a hard, an unreasonable and unnatural proposal, especially when the House is agreed upon the basis of policy, and when if it has a difference with the Government, it is because it desires to urge them more vigorously forward and not to hinder them in the policy which they have declared.

I did hope that my right hon. Friend would have taken exactly the opposite point of view, and that the roles would be reversed. I should have expected to see him come down to the House, and, at that Box, assume an air of exceptional gravity, and say that he regretted that he had to make a demand on the good will and patience of the House, and upon its public spirit; but that the circumstances were such that he could not bear the whole responsibility for months at a time without recourse to the sense of the Commons and that, therefore, he must ask the House to come back on frequent occasions during the interval. Then it would have been for the Opposition to say, 'Of course it is very serious, but if the Prime Minister demands it on a policy on which we are agreed, it will be our duty to comply with his request.'

How would it be if we came back in three weeks' time, just before the end of August, so that we could all be in complete agreement? I should think it would be a pretty safe thing to adjourn for a fortnight or three weeks now. Surely we are not going to ask either that we should stay here night and day, or that we should never come back. That is far too narrow a dilemma. Lord Balfour used to say that this was a singularly ill-contrived world, but that it was not so ill-contrived as that. I would like to endorse the argument that it will not be so easy to recall Parliament once it has been dispersed. The reason is that events move on from day to day, and it is very difficult to say at what point a situation is being created which requires the recall of Parliament. Moreover, the recall of Parliament in the present circumstances will denote a situation of the gravest emergency, because the Fleet is already mobilized. The recall of Parliament will mean in all probability that something has occurred which brings us right up against the supreme decision.

I should have thought that it would be a matter of foresight and prudent convenience to have had a day at the end of August up your sleeve. If the date were the 22nd or 25th August, or whatever it might be, then, if all is well, very few people need come. The Ministers need not attend. After all, we are all in the same boat. I noticed a sort of spirit on these benches to try and run this matter through on ordinary Party loyalty, but we are not going to get through these troubles on the basis of Party loyalty and calling everyone who differs unpatriotic. If that sort of atmosphere were created I am sure that it would be absolutely swept away by the country.

I am very sensitive to the atmosphere of the House, and I think that the effort ought to be to try to bring us as much together as possible, and not to imagine that people will be deterred from saying what they intend to say at any time because it causes unpopularity, or because there is a sort of organized scowl directed at them. I think it would be a very wise and prudent step from the point of view of national administration to have this date which you could put your hand on if needed and, if not, it would pass off as nothing but a needless formality. I suggest and hope that that may be weighed and considered by my right hon. Friend.

There is only one thing more that I wish to say, and it is in the nature of an appeal to my right hon. Friend. He wrote a letter in a recent election, Monmouthshire, I think, appealing for national unity. What does national unity mean? It surely means that reasonable sacrifices of Party opinions, personal opinion, and Party interest should be made by all in order to contribute to the national security.

Here is an opportunity for my right hon. Friend to take a quite important step to put himself in a better relation with those forces in the country who lie outside the ranks of his numerous and faithful adherents. This is not an occasion when the House should part with reproaches and with difference of opinion. On the contrary, we ought to part as friends who are facing common problems and resolved to aid each other as far as it is possible. I hope, indeed, that my right hon. Friend will even at this moment not refuse to take into consideration the opinion of the House as a whole, including minorities in the House, and, if they want to meet again at the end of the month, endeavour to meet them upon that point. If he were to do so now, I tell him here that he would render a great service to his country, because this country cannot be guided through its present difficulties except by the Leader of the Conservative Party, and the Leader of the Conservative Party will never be chosen from any quarter except by that Party itself. It is, therefore, necessary for him to do his utmost to conciliate other opinion, now so widely estranged, and make himself the true leader of the nation as a whole.

'THE RESURGENCE OF THE ONE-MAN POWER'

Churchill was an early pioneer of radio broadcasting, making the annual Appeal for the Blind on the BBC in 1930. But for many years, the BBC would not let him make a political broadcast. On 8 August

1939 – less than a month before the outbreak of the Second World War – as German pressure on Poland intensified, Churchill broadcast to the United States, using an American broadcast network:

The Nazis say that they are being encircled. They have encircled themselves with a ring of neighbours who have to keep on guessing who will be struck down next. This kind of guesswork is a very tiring game. Countries, especially small countries, have long ceased to find it amusing. Can you wonder that the neighbours of Germany, both great and small, have begun to think of stopping the game, by simply saying to the Nazis on the principle of the Covenant of the League of Nations: 'He who attacks any, attacks all. He who attacks the weakest will find he has attacked the strongest.' That is how we are spending our holiday over here, in poor weather, in a lot of clouds. We hope it is better with you.

One thing that has struck me as very strange, and that is the resurgence of the one-man power after all these centuries of experience and progress. It is curious how the English-speaking peoples have always had this horror of one-man power. They are quite ready to follow a leader for a time, as long as he is serviceable to them, but the idea of handing themselves over, lock, stock and barrel, body and soul, to one man, and worshipping him as if he were an idol; that has always been odious to the whole theme and nature of our civilisation. The architects of the American Constitution were as careful as those who shaped the British Constitution, to guard against the whole life and fortunes, and all the laws and freedom of the nation, being placed in the hands of a tyrant.

Checks and counter-checks in the body politic, large devolutions of State government, instruments and processes of free debate, frequent recurrence to first principles, the right of opposition to the most powerful governments, and above all ceaseless vigilance, have preserved, and will preserve, the broad characteristics of British and American institutions. But in Germany, on a mountain peak, there sits one man, who in a single day can release the world from the fear which now oppresses it; or, in a single day can plunge all that we have and are into a volcano of smoke and flame.

If Herr Hitler does not make war, there will be no war. No one else is going to make war. Britain and France are determined to shed no blood except in self-defence or in defence of their Allies. No one has ever dreamed of attacking Germany. If Germany desires to be reassured against attack by her neighbours, she has only to say the word and we will give her the fullest guarantees in accordance with the principles of the Covenant of the League. We have said repeatedly we ask nothing for ourselves in the way of security that we are not willing freely to share with the German people. Therefore if war should come there can be no doubt upon whose head the blood-guiltiness will fall. Thus lies the great issue at this moment, and none can tell how it will be settled.

It is not, believe me, my American friends, from any ignoble shrinking from pain and death that the British and French peoples pray for peace. It is not because we have any doubts how a struggle between Nazi Germany and the civilised world would ultimately end, that we pray tonight and every night for peace. But whether it be peace or war; peace with its broadening and brightening prosperity, now within our reach; or war with its measureless carnage and destruction, we must strive to frame some system of human relations in the future, which will bring to an end this prolonged hideous uncertainty, which will let the working and creative forces of the world get on with their job, and which will no longer leave the whole of life of mankind dependent upon the virtues, the caprice, or the wickedness of a single man.

'A WAR TO ESTABLISH AND REVIVE THE STATURE OF MAN'

On 1 September 1939, Germany invaded Poland. Two days later, Britain and France, honouring their treaties with Poland, declared war on Germany. That same day, September 3, the Prime Minister, Neville Chamberlain, brought Churchill back into the Cabinet as First Lord of the Admiralty, the position he had held from 1911 to 1915. In his short speech in the House of Commons that afternoon, Churchill declared:

In this solemn hour it is a consolation to recall and to dwell upon our repeated efforts for peace. All have been ill-starred, but all have been faithful and sincere. This is of the highest moral value – and not only moral value, but practical value – at the present time, because the wholehearted concurrence of scores of millions of men and women, whose co-operation is indispensable and whose comradeship and brotherhood are indispensable, is the only foundation upon which the trial and tribulation of modern war can be endured and surmounted.

This moral conviction alone affords that ever-fresh resilience which renews the strength and energy of people in long, doubtful and dark days. Outside, the storms of war may blow and the lands may be lashed with the fury of its gales, but in our own hearts this Sunday morning there is peace. Our hands may be active, but our consciences are at rest.

We must not underrate the gravity of the task which lies before us or the temerity of the ordeal, to which we shall not be found unequal. We must expect many disappointments, and many unpleasant surprises, but we may be sure that the task which we have freely accepted is one not beyond the compass and the strength of the British Empire and the French Republic. The Prime Minister said it was a sad day, and that is indeed true, but at the present time there is another note which may be present, and that is a feeling of thankfulness that, if these great trials were to come upon our Island, there is a generation of Britons here now ready to prove itself not unworthy of the days of yore and not unworthy of those great men, the fathers of our land, who laid the foundations of our laws and shaped the greatness of our country.

This is not a question of fighting for Danzig or fighting for Poland. We are fighting to save the whole world from the pestilence of Nazi tyranny and in defence of all that is most sacred to man. This is no war of domination or imperial aggrandizement or material gain; no war to shut any country out of its sunlight and means of progress. It is a war, viewed in its inherent quality, to establish, on impregnable rocks, the rights of the individual, and it is a war to establish and revive the stature of man. Perhaps it might seem a paradox that a war undertaken in the name of liberty and right should require, as a necessary part of its processes, the surrender for the time being of so many of the dearly valued liberties and rights.

In these last few days the House of Commons has been voting dozens of Bills which hand over to the executive our most dearly valued traditional liberties. We are sure that these liberties will be in hands which will not abuse them, which will use them for no class or party interests, which will cherish and guard them, and we look forward to the day, surely and confidently we look forward to the day, when our liberties and rights will be restored to us, and when we shall be able to share them with the peoples to whom such blessings are unknown.

'WE MUST EXPECT FURTHER LOSSES'

On the evening of 3 September 1939, less than eight hours after Britain's declaration of war on Germany, the unarmed passenger liner *Athenia*, on its way from Liverpool to Montreal with 1,418 passengers on board, was torpedoed by a German submarine, the *U-30*; ninety-eight passengers and nineteen crewmen were killed. On 15 September 1939, the aircraft carrier *Ark Royal* was attacked by a German U-boat, but managed to avoid the torpedoes. On September 18, the aircraft carrier *Courageous* was torpedoed and sunk in the Bristol Channel; of her crew of 1,260, more than 500 were lost. There was unease in Britain about the vulnerability of British seaborne vessels, both warships and merchant ships. On September 26, Churchill gave the House of Commons his first survey of the war at sea. The Leader of the Labour Opposition, Clement Attlee, complimented him on his 'robust, vigorous statement'. Churchill had spoken for twenty minutes. The National Labour MP Harold Nicolson noted in his diary that evening: 'In those 20 minutes Churchill brought himself nearer the post of Prime Minister than he has ever been before. In the lobbies afterwards even Chamberlainites were saying "we have now found our leader". Old Parliamentary hands have confessed that never in their experience had they seen a single speech so change the temper of the House.' Churchill told the House of Commons:

The war at sea opened with some intensity. All our ships were going about the world in the ordinary way, when they were set upon by lurking U-boats, carefully posted beforehand. In the first week our losses in tonnage were half the weekly losses of the month of April, 1917, which was the peak year of U-boat attack in the late War. That was a very serious proportion. We immediately replied in three ways. First, we set in motion the convoy system. This could be very quickly done for all outgoing ships, but it took a fortnight to organise from the other end the convoys of homeward-bound ships.

This system is now in full operation – in full operation both ways. Meanwhile, however, large numbers of ships which had started independently, under the ordinary conditions of peace, had day after day to run the gauntlet of the waiting U-boats without being either armed or escorted, and in consequence a serious, though, I am glad to say, diminishing, toll was exacted.

The convoy system is a good and well-tried defence against U-boat attack, but no one can pretend that it is a complete defence. Some degree of risk and a steady proportion of losses must be expected. There are also other forms of attack besides U-boats, attacks from surface craft and from the air, against which we must be on our guard.

I can assure the House that every preparation is being made to cope with such attacks, but I must again warn the House that we cannot guarantee immunity and that we must expect further losses.

Our second reply to the U-boat attack is to arm all our merchant vessels and fast liners with defensive armament against both the U-boat and the aeroplane. For a fortnight past armed ships have been continually leaving the harbours of this island in large numbers. Some go in convoy, some go independently. This applies not only to the United Kingdom, but to our ports all over the world. Thus in a short time the immense Mercantile Marine of the British Empire will be armed. As we usually have 2,000 ships on salt water every day, this is a considerable operation. However, all the guns and equipment are ready at the various arming stations, together with a proportion of trained gunners to man them and to instruct the ordinary seamen. Let me pay my tribute to the care of my predecessors at the Admiralty, who have provided so well for this contingency.

Our third reply is, of course, the British attack upon the U-boats. This is being delivered with the utmost vigour and intensity. It is a strange experience to me to sit at the Admiralty again, after a quarter of a century, and to find myself moving over the same course, against the same enemy, and in the same months of the year – the sort of thing that one would hardly expect to happen. But it gives me an opportunity of making comparisons which, perhaps, no one else could make, and I see how much greater are the advantages which we possess to-day in coping with the U-boat than we did in the first U-boat campaign 25 years ago. In those days there were moments when the problem seemed well-nigh insoluble. Very often to hunt down a U-boat it was necessary to use a flotilla of 15 or 20 vessels working together for a whole day on the vaguest indications. Now two destroyers or even one can maintain prolonged and relentless pursuit. A very large number of attacks have been made by our flotillas and hunting craft [. . .] it is no exaggeration to say that the attacks upon the German U-boats have been five or six times as numerous as in any equal period in the Great War, in which, after all, they did not beat us.

My right hon. Friend the Prime Minister mentioned last week the figure of six or seven U-boats destroyed. That was, as he said, probably an understatement. Since then we have had some fruitful and hopeful days; but even taking six or seven as a safe figure, that is one-tenth of the total enemy submarine fleet as it existed at the declaration of war destroyed during the first fortnight of the war, and it is probably one-quarter, or perhaps even one-third, of all the U-boats which are being employed actively. All these vessels, those that have been sunk and those that have escaped, have subjected themselves to what is said to be one of the most trying ordeals which men can undergo in wartime. A large proportion never return home, and those who do have grim tales to tell. But the British attack upon the U-boat is only just beginning. Our hunting force is getting stronger every day. By the end of October we expect to have three times the hunting force which was operating at the beginning of the war, while at the same time the number of targets open to U-boats upon the vast expanses of the seas and oceans will be greatly reduced by the use of convoys, and, at the same time, the U-boat means of attacking them will be heavily clogged and fettered.

In all this very keen and stern warfare the Royal Air Force and the Fleet Air Arm, as the Prime Minister has already mentioned this afternoon, have played an important part both in directing the hunting destroyers upon their quarry and in actually attacking it themselves. It was to bridge the gap between what we had ready at the beginning and what we have ready now that the Admiralty decided to use the aircraft carriers with some freedom in order to bring in the unarmed, unorganised and uncovered traffic which was then approaching our shores in large numbers. Risks have to be run all the time in naval war, and sometimes grievous forfeit is exacted. The *Courageous* was attended by four destroyers, but two had to go to hunt a U-boat attacking a merchant ship towards evening. When the *Courageous* turned into the wind at the dusk in order to enable her own aircraft to alight upon her landing deck, she happened, by what may have been a hundred to one chance or more, to meet a U-boat in her unpredictable course.

[Mr. Bellenger]: But only two destroyers?

[Mr. Churchill]: But that is the great problem for us – to find destroyers for our many needs, many needs which I cannot mention to the House, which make great demands upon us. This hard stroke of war in no way diminishes our confidence in the methods now at our disposal. On the contrary, our confidence in them has grown with every day they have been employed, and I believe that their potency will become more apparent in proportion as the great numbers of new vessels come into action, and in proportion as our hunting officers get the knack of using depth charges by frequent practice.

Therefore, I cannot feel at the end of the first three weeks of the naval war that the judgment formed by the Admiralty before the war which I myself, after having been afforded full opportunity of seeing it at work, endorsed as a private Member, was at fault or stands in any need of revision, except perhaps in a favourable sense. In the first week our losses by U-boat sinkings amounted to 65,000 tons; in the second week, they were 46,000 tons: and in the third week they were 21,000 tons. In the last six days we have lost only 9,000 tons. One must not dwell upon these reassuring figures too much, for war is full of unpleasant surprises, but certainly I am entitled to say that so far as they go these figures do not need to cause any undue despondency or alarm.

Meanwhile, the whole vast business of our worldwide trade continues without interruption and without appreciable diminution. Great convoys of troops are escorted to their various destinations. The enemy's ships and commerce have been swept from the seas. Over 2,000,000 tons of German shipping is now sheltering in German, or interned in neutral, harbours. Our system of contraband control, to which my right hon. Friend has just alluded, is being perfected, and so far as the first fortnight of the war is concerned, for which alone I have the figures, we have actually arrested, seized and converted to our own use 67,000 tons more German merchandise than has been sunk in ships of our own. Even in oil—

[Mr. Benjamin Smith]: But you have lost the ships.

[Mr. Churchill]: —where we were unlucky in losing some tankers, we have lost 60,000 tons in the first fortnight and gained 50,000 tons from the enemy, apart from the enormous additional stores we have brought safely in the ordinary way. Again, I reiterate my caution against over-sanguine deductions. We have, however, in fact got more supplies in this country this afternoon than we should have had had no war been declared and no U-boat had come into action. It is not going beyond the limits of prudent statement if I say that at that rate it will take a long time to starve us out.

I will now deal a little with the character of this warfare. From time to time the German U-boat commanders have tried their best to behave with humanity. We have seen them give good warning and also endeavour to help the crews to find their way to port. One German captain signalled to me personally the position of a British ship which he had just sunk, and urged that rescue should be sent. He signed his message, 'German submarine'. I was in some doubt at the time as to what address I should direct a reply. However, he is now in our hands, and is treated with all consideration.

But many cruel and ruthless acts have been done. There was the *Athenia*, then later the *Royal Sceptre*, whose crew of 32 were left in open boats hundreds of miles from land and are assumed to have perished. Then there was the *Hazelside* – only the day before yesterday –12 of whose sailors were killed by surprise gunfire, in an ordinary merchant ship, and whose captain died in so gallant a fashion, going down with his vessel.

We cannot at all recognise this type of warfare as other than contrary to all the long acquired and accepted traditions of the sea. We cannot recognise it as other than a violation of the laws of war, to which the Germans themselves have in recent years so lustily subscribed. But it is a measure of the success of our attack upon the U-boats in the last few days that they seem, as the Prime Minister has told us, to prefer neutral shipping or humble fishing boats to our regular merchant ships. Finnish, Dutch, Swedish, Greek, Norwegian and Belgian ships have been sunk on the high seas, in an in-discriminate manner, and with loss of life. In all the far-reaching control, becoming increasingly more effective, which we ourselves are exercising upon the movements of contraband no neutral ship has ever been put in danger, and no law recognised among civilised nations has been contravened. Even when German ships have deliberately sunk themselves to avoid the formalities of the Prize Court we have so far succeeded in rescuing their crews.

Such is the U-boat war – hard, widespread and bitter, a war of groping and drowning, a war of ambuscade and stratagem, a war of science and seamanship. All the more must we all respect the resolute spirit of the officers and men of the Mercantile Marine who put to sea with alacrity, sure that they are discharging a duty indispensable to the life of their island home.

What of the future? In the last war the first U-boat attack in the winter of 1914 was beaten off by such primitive measures as we could devise, and thereafter there was a long pause. Then came a terrible change. A much larger number of U-boats were built and launched upon the seas in the summer and autumn of 1917; but by that time we also had great counter-preparations ready. We have made great progress in these counter-preparations at the present time, and if we must expect a renewed and more severe attack at a later stage we have every reason to believe that our arrangements will be adequate to meet it. Let it be noted that in the late War one-third of the damage done to British and neutral commerce, one-third of the whole vast catalogue of damage from U-boat attack, was due to 25 experienced professional U-boat captains belonging to the old submarine service of Germany. It would seem from this that it will be much easier for our enemies, who seek our destruction, to build more U-boats than it will be to replace the highly-skilled limited class of professional officers and crews who are now being captured or destroyed.

Moreover, if we are losing tonnage we are also taking steps to replace it on a far larger scale. Old ships which were laid up are being refitted and prepared for sea. An enormous building programme of new ships of a simple character, capable of being very rapidly built, is already in full career, in fulfilment of the action taken and of the plans made before the war by my right hon. Friend the President of the Board of Trade. We therefore hope to have a much larger margin in the future to meet new forms of attack or new scales of attack.

The House will observe that I have confined myself this afternoon entirely to this topic of U-boat warfare. I am not attempting now to deal with any of the other widespread activities of the Royal Navy, or with any other of those grave problems which require vigilance and merit description. As occasion serves, as events suggest, I shall seek other opportunities of making statements to the House. But, after all, the U-boat attack upon British ocean-wide commerce was one of the most heart-shaking hazards of the last war. It seemed during the early months of 1917 that it might compass our total ruin. Only those who lived through it at the summit know what it was like. I was not at that time in office, but my right hon. Friend the Prime Minister of those days, the right hon. Member for Carnarvon Boroughs (Mr. Lloyd George), kept me closely informed, and I watched with a fear that I never felt at any other moment in that struggle the deadly upward movement of the curve of sinkings over the arrival of new construction. That was, in my opinion, the gravest peril which we faced in all the ups and downs of that war.

We have no reason, upon the information and experience which are now available, to suppose that such a situation will recur. And if this surmise – and it cannot be more than that – should prove correct, what does it mean? It means that one primary danger is falling into its proper confines, and that amid all our anxieties we can feel a certain steady measure of assurance that, so far as the submarine is concerned, the British Empire and all its friends in every quarter of the globe will be able to develop their immeasurable latent force and that the whole strength, wealth, resources and man-power of these many communities can be concentrated in every growing intensity upon the task we have in hand, in which task we have only to persevere to conquer.

'ROUGH TIMES LIE AHEAD'

Churchill made his first wartime radio broadcast on 1 October 1939. He spoke both of the events of the previous few weeks and of lessons to be learnt from history. That night, Neville Chamberlain's Junior Private Secretary, John Colville – who had not been a fan of Churchill – wrote in his diary, having heard him speak: 'He certainly gives one confidence and will, I suspect, be Prime Minister before the war is over.' In the course of his broadcast, Churchill said:

Poland has been again overrun by two of the great Powers which held her in bondage for 150 years, but were unable to quench the spirit of the Polish nation. The heroic defence of Warsaw shows that the soul of Poland is indestructible, and that she will rise again like a rock, which may for a spell be submerged by a tidal wave, but which remains a rock.

What is the second event of this first month? It is, of course, the assertion of the power of Russia. Russia has pursued a cold policy of self-interest. We could have wished that the Russian armies should be standing on their present line as the friends and allies of Poland instead of as invaders. But that the Russian armies should stand on this line, was clearly necessary for the safety of Russia against the Nazi menace. At any rate, the line is there, and an Eastern Front has been created which Nazi Germany does not dare assail. When Herr von Ribbentrop was summoned to Moscow last week, it was to learn the fact, and to accept the fact, that the Nazi designs upon the Baltic States and upon the Ukraine must come to a dead stop.

I cannot forecast to you the action of Russia. It is a riddle wrapped in a mystery inside an enigma: but perhaps there is a key. That key is Russian national interest.

[···]

Here I am in the same post as I was twenty-five years ago. Rough times lie ahead; but how different is the scene from that of October 1914! Then the French front, with the British army fighting in the line, seemed to be about to break under the terrible impact of German Imperialism. Then Russia had been laid low at Tannenberg; then the whole might of the Austro-Hungarian Empire was in battle against us; then the brave, warlike Turks were about to join our enemies. Then we had to be ready night and day to fight a decisive sea battle with a formidable German fleet almost, in many respects, the equal of our own. We faced those adverse conditions then; we have nothing worse to face tonight.

In those days of 1914 also, Italy was neutral; but we did not know the reason for her neutrality. It was only later on that we learned that by a secret clause in the original Treaty of the Triple Alliance, Italy had expressly reserved to herself the right to stand aside from any war which brought her into conflict with Great Britain. Much has happened since then. Misunderstandings and disputes have arisen, but all the more do we appreciate in England the reason why this great and friendly nation of Italy, with whom we have never been at war, has not seen fit to enter the struggle.

I do not underrate what lies before us, but I must say this: I cannot doubt we have the strength to carry a good cause forward, and to break down the barriers which stand between the wage-earning masses of every land and that free and more abundant daily life which science is ready to afford. That is my conviction, and I look back upon the history of the past to find many sources of encouragement.

Of all the wars that men have fought in their hard pilgrimage, none was more noble than the great Civil War in America nearly eighty years ago. Both sides fought with high conviction, and the war was long and hard. All the heroism of the South could not redeem their cause from the stain of slavery, just as all the courage and skill which the Germans always show in war will not free them from the reproach of Naziism, with its intolerance and its brutality. We may take good heart from what happened in America in those famous days of the nineteenth century. We may be sure that the world will roll forward into broader destinies.

'THE STORM WILL NOT PASS. IT WILL RAGE AND IT WILL ROAR'

As First Lord of the Admiralty, Churchill bore a heavy burden, as German warships and U-boats continued to attack British warships and merchant shipping. On 20 January 1940, he gave the House of Commons a survey of the war at sea and the equally dangerous war on land, where Poland had been partitioned between Germany and the Soviet Union, and Soviet forces had invaded Finland:

Here we are, after nearly five months of all they can do against us on the sea, with the first U-boat campaign for the first time being utterly broken, with the mining menace in good control, with our shipping virtually undiminished, and with all the oceans of the world free from surface raiders. It is true that the *Deutschland* escaped the clutches of our cruisers by the skin of her teeth, but the *Spee* still sticks up in the harbour of Montevideo as a grisly monument and as a measure of the fate in store for any Nazi warship which dabbles in piracy on the broad waters.

As you know, I have always – after some long and hard experience – spoken with the utmost restraint and caution about the war at sea; and I am quite sure that there are many losses and misfortunes which lie ahead of us there, but in all humility and self-questioning I feel able to declare that at the Admiralty, as, I have no doubt, at the French Ministry of Marine, things are not going so badly after all. Indeed, they have never gone so well in any naval war. We look forward as the months go by to establishing such a degree of safe sailings as will enable the commerce of all the nations whose ships accept our

22 Churchill speaks to the crew of HMS *Exeter* after its return from the Battle of the River Plate, Portsmouth, 15 February 1940.

23 **Above** The Anglo-
French Supreme War
Council meets in Paris
on 31 May 1940. Next
to Churchill: General
Sir John Dill, Chief of the
Imperial General Staff.
With dark moustache:
Clement Attlee, the Lord
Privy Seal and member of
the War Cabinet. Next to
Attlee, with buttoned
jacket: the French Prime
Minister, Paul Reynaud.
The British officer just
behind Reynaud is
Brigadier General
Edward Louis Spears.

24 **Left** Churchill's appeal
'to maintain a spirit of alert
and confident energy',
4 July 1940.

10, DOWNING STREET,

WHITEHALL.

ON what may be the eve of an attempted invasion or battle
for our native land, the Prime Minister desires to impress
upon all persons holding responsible positions in the
Government, in the Fighting Services, or in the Civil
Departments, their duty to maintain a spirit of alert and
confident energy. While every precaution must be taken that
time and means afford, there are no grounds for supposing
that more German troops can be landed in this country, either
from the air or across the sea, than can be destroyed or captured
by the strong forces at present under arms. The Royal Air
Force is in excellent order and at the highest strength it has
yet attained. The German Navy was never so weak, nor the
British Army at home so strong as now. The Prime Minister
expects all His Majesty's servants in high places to set an
example of steadiness and resolution. They should check and
rebuke expressions of loose and ill-digested opinion in their
circles, or by their subordinates. They should not hesitate to
report, or if necessary remove, any officers or officials who are
found to be consciously exercising a disturbing or depressing
influence, and whose talk is calculated to spread alarm and
despondency. Thus alone will they be worthy of the fighting
men, who in the air, on the sea, and on land, have already met
the enemy without any sense of being out-matched in martial
qualities.

Winston S. Churchill

4th July, 1940.

25 Above Churchill inspects bomb damage in London during the early stages of the Blitz, 10 September 1940.

26 Below Churchill and his wife inspect the ruins of the London Guildhall, 31 December 1940.

27, 28 Above, left and right Churchill addresses both Houses of Congress, Washington DC, 26 December 1941.

29 Below Churchill addresses the Canadian Parliament, Ottawa, 30 December 1941.

30 Above Churchill sets foot on Soviet soil for the first time in his life, at an airport near Moscow, 13 August 1942. This picture is a still from a film, taken while Churchill was listening to a Russian band playing the Soviet and British national anthems.

31 Below Churchill, Stalin and Averell Harriman (Roosevelt's emissary) at the Kremlin, August 1942.

32 Above Churchill addressing British and Commonwealth troops, Tripoli, 3 February 1943.

33 Below Churchill about to address British and Commonwealth troops in the Roman amphitheatre, Carthage, 1 June 1943. With him is Lieutenant-General Kenneth Anderson, Officer Commanding the British 1st Army (and behind them in the dark hat, Anthony Eden)

34 Above Churchill at Harvard, addressing American naval and army cadets then in training at Harvard University, 6 September 1943.

35 Below Normandy, 22 July 1944: Churchill speaks to some of the British troops who took part in the Normandy Landings of 6 June 1944. Behind him, General Sir Bernard Montgomery, Commander of the 21st Army Group, in command of all Allied ground troops at Normandy.

36 Above Churchill leaving Westminster Abbey after the memorial service to David Lloyd George, 28 March 1945. To his left, the Deputy Prime Minister Clement Attlee. To his right, the Foreign Secretary Anthony Eden and (in military uniform) Field Marshal Smuts. Later that day, Churchill delivered a tribute to Lloyd George in the House of Commons.

37 Below Churchill broadcasts to the nation at three in the afternoon of 8 May 1945: Victory-in-Europe Day.

guidance, not only to live but to thrive. This part – this sea affair – at least, of the Nazi attack upon freedom is not going to bar the path of justice or of retribution.

Very different is the lot of the unfortunate neutrals. Whether on sea or on land, they are the victims upon whom Hitler's hate and spite descend. Look at the group of small but ancient and historic States which lie in the North; or look again at that other group of anxious peoples in the Balkans or in the Danube Basin behind whom stands the resolute Turk. Every one of them is wondering which will be the next victim on whom the criminal adventurers of Berlin will cast their rending stroke.

A German major makes a forced landing in Belgium with plans for the invasion of that country whose neutrality Germany has so recently promised to respect. In Rumania there is deep fear lest by some deal between Moscow and Berlin they may become the next object of aggression. German intrigues are seeking to undermine the newly strengthened solidarity of the Southern Slavs. The hardy Swiss arm and man their mountain passes. The Dutch – whose services to European freedom will be remembered long after the smear of Hitler has been wiped from the human path – stand along their dykes, as they did against the tyrants of bygone days. All Scandinavia dwells brooding under Nazi and Bolshevik threats.

Only Finland – superb, nay, sublime – in the jaws of peril – Finland shows what free men can do. The service rendered by Finland to mankind is magnificent. They have exposed, for all the world to see, the military incapacity of the Red Army and of the Red Air Force. Many illusions about Soviet Russia have been dispelled in these few fierce weeks of fighting in the Arctic Circle. Everyone can see how Communism rots the soul of a nation; how it makes it abject and hungry in peace, and proves it base and abominable in war. We cannot tell what the fate of Finland may be, but no more mournful spectacle could be presented to what is left to civilised mankind than that this splendid Northern race should be at last worn down and reduced to servitude worse than death by the dull brutish force of overwhelming numbers.

If the light of freedom which still burns so brightly in the frozen North should be finally quenched, it might well herald a return to the

Dark Ages, when every vestige of human progress during two thousand years would be engulfed.

But what would happen if all these neutral nations I have mentioned – and some others I have not mentioned – were with one spontaneous impulse to do their duty in accordance with the Covenant of the League, and were to stand together with the British and French Empires against aggression and wrong? At present their plight is lamentable; and it will become much worse. They bow humbly and in fear to German threats of violence, comforting themselves meanwhile with the thought that the Allies will win, that Britain and France will strictly observe all the laws and conventions, and that breaches of these laws are only to be expected from the German side.

Each one hopes that if he feeds the crocodile enough, the crocodile will eat him last. All of them hope that the storm will pass before their turn comes to be devoured. But I fear – I fear greatly – the storm will not pass. It will rage and it will roar, ever more loudly, ever more widely. It will spread to the South; it will spread to the North. There is no chance of a speedy end except through united action; and if at any time Britain and France, wearying of the struggle, were to make a shameful peace, nothing would remain for the smaller States of Europe, with their shipping and their possessions, but to be divided between the opposite, though similar, barbarisms of Nazidom and Bolshevism.

The one thing that will be most helpful in determining the action of neutrals is their increasing sense of the power and resolution of the Western Allies. These small States are alarmed by the fact that the German armies are more numerous, and that their Air Force is still more numerous, and also that both are nearer to them than the forces of Great Britain and France. Certainly it is true that we are facing numerical odds; but that is no new thing in our history.

Very few wars have been won by mere numbers alone. Quality, will-power, geographical advantages, natural and financial resources, the command of the sea, and, above all, a cause which rouses the spontaneous surgings of the human spirit in millions of hearts – these have proved to be the decisive factors in the human story. If it were otherwise, how would the race of men have risen above the apes; how otherwise would they have conquered and extirpated dragons and monsters; how would they have ever evolved the moral theme; how would they have marched forward across the centuries to broad conceptions of compassion, of freedom, and of right? How would they ever have discerned those beacon lights which summon and guide us across the rough dark waters, and presently will guide us across the flaming lines of battle towards better days which lie beyond?

'CEASELESS TRIAL AND VIGILANCE ON COLD, DARK, STORMY SEAS'

In the South Atlantic, throughout October, November and early December 1939, the German pocket battleship *Graf Spee* had been sinking merchant ships without respite. On December 13 she was tracked down by three British cruisers, hit more than thirty times, and forced to seek refuge in the Uruguayan territorial waters of the River Plate. Four days later, she sailed out to sea and blew herself up. When HMS *Exeter*, one of the British cruisers that had pursued her, reached Plymouth on 15 February 1940, Churchill went on board and addressed the crew. On February 23, in London, he welcomed them and the crew of HMS *Ajax* to the Guildhall:

My colleagues of the Board of Admiralty and of the War Cabinet are grateful to you for inviting us here today to share the hospitality which the City of London has extended to the victors of the River Plate. It is an occasion at once joyous, memorable, and unique. It is the highest compliment your ancient Corporation could give to the Officers and Men of the *Exeter* and *Ajax* and through them to the whole of our Navy, upon whom under Providence our lives and State depend from hour to hour.

I do not suppose that the bonds which unite the British Navy to the British nation – and they have taken a long time to form – or those which join the Navy and the Mercantile Marine were ever so strong as they are to-day. The brunt of the war so far has fallen upon the sailormen, and their comrades in the Coastal Air Force, and we have already lost nearly 3,000 lives in a hard, unrelenting struggle which goes on night and day and is going on now without a moment's respite.

The brilliant sea fight which Admiral Harwood conceived, and which those who are here executed, takes its place in our naval annals, and I might add that in a dark, cold winter it warmed the cockles of the British heart. But it is not only in those few glittering, deadly hours of action, which rivet all eyes, that the strain falls upon the Navy. Far more does it fall in the weeks and months of ceaseless trial and vigilance on cold, dark, stormy seas from whose waves at any moment death and destruction may leap, with sullen roar. There is the task which these men were discharging and which their comrades are discharging. There was the task from which, in a sense, the fierce action was almost a relief.

Here let me say a word for the naval members of the Board of Admiralty and especially for the First Sea Lord, Sir Dudley Pound, and his Deputy Chief of Naval Staff (the newly promoted Vice-Admiral Phillips), for the skilful combination for which they have been responsible. You must remember that for one stroke that goes home, for one clutch that grips the raider, there are many that miss their mark on the broad oceans; for every success there are many disappointments. You must never forget that the dangers that are seen are only a small part of those that are warded off by care and fore-sight, and therefore pass unnoticed.

The Admiralty and the Fleet are learning together the special conditions of this hard and novel war, and although mistakes and accidents will certainly occur, and sorrow will fall from time to time upon us, we hope that from Whitehall the sense of resolution and design at the centre will impart itself to all afloat, and will lighten the burden of their task and concert the vigour of their action. It is not, for instance, a mere coincidence that has brought the *Achilles* out of the vast Pacific Ocean to the shores of far-off New Zealand, in order to receive in the Antipodes the same warm-hearted welcome as her sisters the *Ajax* and the *Exeter* are receiving now in dear old London.

The spirit of all our forces serving on salt water has never been more strong and high than now. The warrior heroes of the past may look down, as Nelson's monument looks down upon us now, without any feeling that the island race has lost its daring or that the examples they set in bygone centuries have faded as the generations have succeeded one another. It was not for nothing that Admiral Harwood, as he instantly at full speed attacked an enemy which might have sunk any one of his ships by a single successful salvo from its far heavier guns, flew Nelson's immortal signal, of which neither the new occasion, nor the conduct of all ranks and ratings, nor the final result were found unworthy.

To the glorious tale of the action off the Plate, there has recently been added an epilogue – the rescue last week by the *Cossack* and her flotilla, under the nose of the enemy and amid the tangles of one-sided neutrality, of the British captives taken from the sunken German raider. Their rescue at the very moment when these unhappy men were about to be delivered over to German bondage, proves that the long arm of British sea power can be stretched out, not only for foes but also for faithful friends.

And to Nelson's signal of 135 years ago, 'England expects that every man will do his duty', there may now be added last week's not less proud reply: 'The Navy is here!'

'I FELT AS IF I WERE WALKING WITH DESTINY'

On 10 May 1940, Neville Chamberlain resigned as Prime Minister and Churchill succeeded him. He was sixty-five years old. He at once set about forming an all-Party coalition government, the first in Britain since Lloyd George's First World War coalition had broken up in 1922. At Buckingham Palace, having been told by King George VI: 'I want to ask you to form a Government', he gave the King the names of four senior Labour Party politicians whom he wanted in his administration. By midnight the main appointments had been made. As Churchill later wrote in *The Second World War*:

Thus, then, on the night of the 10th of May, at the outset of this mighty battle, I acquired the chief power in the State, which henceforth I wielded in ever-growing measure for five years and three months of world war, at the end of which time, all our enemies having surrendered unconditionally or being about to do so, I was immediately dismissed by the British electorate from all further conduct of their affairs.

During these last crowded days of the political crisis my pulse had not quickened at any moment: I took it all as it came. But I cannot conceal from the reader of this truthful account that as I went to bed at about 3 a.m. I was conscious of a profound sense of relief. At last I had the authority to give directions over the whole scene.

I felt as if I were walking with destiny, and that all my past life had been but a preparation for this hour and for this trial. Ten years in the political wilderness had freed me from ordinary party antagonisms. My warnings over the last six years had been so numerous, so detailed, and were now so terribly vindicated, that no one could gainsay me. I could not be reproached either for making the war or with want of preparation for it. I thought I knew a good deal about it all, and I was sure I should not fail. Therefore, although impatient for the morning, I slept soundly and had no need for cheering dreams. Facts are better than dreams.

'NUMBER ONE'

In 1900, during the war in South Africa, a 47-year-old naval gunnery officer, Captain Percy Scott, then Military Commandant of Durban, wrote to the 25-year-old Churchill: 'I am certain that I shall some day shake hands with you as Prime Minister of England, you possess the two necessary qualifications, genius and plod. Combined, I believe nothing can keep them back.' Forty years were to pass before Scott's prediction was fulfilled, but fulfilled it was. Scott, alas, had died in 1924. On 12 May 1940, Churchill's son Randolph wrote to his father from his army camp: 'At last you have the power and authority out of which the caucus have cheated you and England for nine long years! I cannot tell you how proud and happy I am. I only hope that it is not too late.' In *The Second World War*, Churchill reflected on what his power as Prime Minister meant:

In my long political experience I had held most of the great offices of State, but I readily admit that the post which had now fallen to me was the one I liked the best. Power, for the sake of lording it over fellow-creatures, or adding to personal pomp, is rightly judged base. But power in a national crisis, when a man believes he knows what orders should be given, is a blessing. In my sphere of action there can be no comparison between the positions of number one and numbers two, three, or four.

The duties and the problems of all persons other than number one are quite different and in many ways more difficult. It is always a misfortune when number two or three has to initiate a dominant plan or policy. He has to consider not only the merits of the policy, but the mind of his chief; not only what to advise, but what it is proper for him in his situation to advise; not only what to do, but how to get it agreed, and how to get it done. Moreover, number two or three will have to reckon with numbers four, five and six, or maybe some bright outsider, number twenty.

Ambition, not so much for vulgar ends, but for fame, glints in every mind. There are always several points of view which may be right, and many which are plausible. I was ruined for the time being in 1915 over the Dardanelles, and a supreme enterprise was cast away, through my trying to carry out a major and cardinal operation of war from a subordinate position. Men are ill advised to try such ventures. This lesson had sunk into my nature.

At the top there are great simplifications. An accepted leader has only to be sure of what it is best to do, or at least to have made up his mind about it. The loyalties which centre upon number one are enormous. If he trips he must be sustained. If he makes mistakes they must be covered. If he sleeps he must not be wantonly disturbed. If he is no good he must be pole-axed. But this last extreme process cannot be carried out every day; and certainly not in the days just after he has been chosen.

'BLOOD, TOIL, TEARS AND SWEAT'

Throughout 11 and 12 May 1940, Churchill was forming his new administration. He called it the Grand Coalition. During May 13, most of the senior positions were filled. When Churchill summoned the new Ministers to Admiralty House that afternoon, he told them: 'I have nothing to offer but blood, toil, tears and sweat.' A few hours later he repeated that phrase in the House of Commons, when he spoke there for the first time as Prime Minister:

Mr. Speaker, on Friday evening last I received His Majesty's commission to form a new Administration. It was the evident wish and will of Parliament and the nation that this should be conceived on the broadest possible basis and that it should include all parties, both those who supported the late Government and also the parties of the Opposition. I have completed the most important part of this task. A War Cabinet has been formed of five Members, representing, with the Liberal Opposition, the unity of the nation. The three party Leaders have agreed to serve, either in the War Cabinet or in high executive office. The three Fighting Services have been filled.

It was necessary that this should be done in one single day, on account of the extreme urgency and rigour of events. A number of other key positions were filled yesterday, and I am submitting a further list to His Majesty tonight. I hope to complete the appointment of the principal Ministers during tomorrow. The appointment of the other Ministers usually takes a little longer, but I trust that when Parliament meets again, this part of my task will be completed, and that the administration will be complete in all respects.

Sir, I considered it in the public interest to suggest that the House should be summoned to meet today. Mr. Speaker agreed, and took the necessary steps, in accordance with the powers conferred upon him by the Resolution of the House. At the end of the proceedings today, the Adjournment of the House will be proposed until Tuesday, the 21st of May, with, of course, provision for earlier meeting, if need be. The business to be considered during that week will be notified to Members at the earliest opportunity. I now invite the House, by the Resolution which stands in my name, to record its approval of the steps taken and to declare its confidence in the new Government.

Sir, to form an Administration of this scale and complexity is a serious undertaking in itself, but it must be remembered that we are in the preliminary stage of one of the greatest battles in history, that we are in action at many points in Norway and in Holland, that we have to be prepared in the Mediterranean, that the air battle is continuous and that many preparations have to be made here at home.

In this crisis I hope I may be pardoned if I do not address the House at any length today. I hope that any of my friends and colleagues, or former colleagues, who are affected by the political reconstruction, will make allowance, all allowance, for any lack of ceremony with which it has been necessary to act. I would say to the House, as I said to those who have joined this Government: 'I have nothing to offer but blood, toil, tears and sweat.'

We have before us an ordeal of the most grievous kind. We have before us many, many long months of struggle and of suffering. You ask, what is our policy? I will say: It is to wage war, by sea, land and air, with all our might and with all the strength that God can give us; to wage war against a monstrous tyranny, never surpassed in the dark and lamentable catalogue of human crime. That is our policy.

You ask, what is our aim? I can answer in one word: it is victory, victory at all costs, victory in spite of all terror, victory, however long and hard the road may be; for without victory, there is no survival. Let that be realized; no survival for the British Empire, no survival for all that the British Empire has stood for, no survival for the urge and impulse of the ages, that mankind will move forward towards its goal.

But I take up my task with buoyancy and hope. I feel sure that our cause will not be suffered to fail among men. At this time I feel entitled to claim the aid of all, and I say, 'Come then, let us go forward together with our united strength.'

'I SANG MY USUAL SONG'

As German forces overran Belgium and Holland, and pressed towards Paris, 198,229 British and 139,997 French troops trapped at Dunkirk were evacuated to Britain, leaving almost all their ammunition and armoured vehicles on the beachhead. On 31 May 1940, Churchill flew to Paris for a meeting of the Anglo-French War Council. With him were the senior Labour Party member of his administration, Clement Attlee, and Brigadier-General Edward Louis Spears, one of Churchill's oldest friends, whom he had met in the trenches in 1916. Spears was bilingual in French and English, and could, Churchill wrote, 'say things to the high French personnel with an ease and force which I have never seen equalled'. Basing himself on the then-secret records of the meeting, Churchill wrote in *The Second World War*:

> Attlee and I found Reynaud and Marshal Pétain opposite to us as the only French Ministers. This was the first appearance of Pétain, now Vice-President of the Council, at any of our meetings. He wore plain clothes.
>
> [···]
>
> The first question was the position in Norway. I said that the British Government was of the considered opinion that the Narvik area should be evacuated at once. Our troops there, the destroyers involved, and a hundred anti-aircraft guns were badly wanted elsewhere. We therefore proposed an evacuation beginning on June 2. The British Navy would transport and repatriate the French forces, the King of Norway, and any Norwegian troops who wished to come. Reynaud said that the French Government agreed with this policy. The destroyers would be urgently required in the Mediterranean in the event of war with Italy. The 16,000 men would be very valuable on the line of the Aisne and the Somme. This matter was therefore settled.
>
> I then turned to Dunkirk. The French seemed to have no more idea of what was happening to the Northern Armies than we had about the main French front. When I told them that 165,000 men, of

whom 15,000 were French, had been taken off they were astonished. They naturally drew attention to the marked British preponderance. I explained that this was due largely to the fact that there had been many British administrative units in the back area who had been able to embark before fighting troops could be spared from the front. Moreover, the French up to the present had had no orders to evacuate. One of the chief reasons why I had come to Paris was to make sure that the same orders were given to the French troops as to the British. The three British divisions now holding the centre would cover the evacuation of all the Allied forces. That, and the sea transport, would be the British contribution to offset the heavy Allied losses which must now be faced. His Majesty's Government had felt it necessary in the dire circumstances to order Lord Gort to take off fighting men and leave the wounded behind. If present hopes were confirmed, 200,000 able-bodied troops might be got away. This would be almost a miracle. Four days ago I would not have wagered on more than 50,000 as a maximum. I dwelt upon our terrible losses in equipment. Reynaud paid a handsome tribute to the work of the British Navy and Air Force, for which I thanked him. We then spoke at some length upon what could be done to rebuild the British forces in France.

Meanwhile Admiral Darlan had drafted a telegram to Admiral Abrial at Dunkirk:

(1) A bridgehead shall be held round Dunkirk with the divisions under your command and those under British command.
(2) As soon as you are convinced that no troops outside the bridgehead can make their way to the points of embarkation the troops holding the bridgehead shall withdraw and embark, the British forces embarking first.

I intervened at once to say that the British would not embark first, but that the evacuation should proceed on equal terms between the British and the French – '*Bras dessus bras dessous.*' The British would form the rearguard. This was agreed.

[···]

I was absolutely convinced we had only to carry on the fight to conquer. Even if one of us should be struck down, the other must not abandon the struggle. The British Government were prepared to wage war from the New World, if through some disaster England herself were laid waste. If Germany defeated either ally or both, she would give no mercy; we should be reduced to the status of vassals and slaves for ever. It would be better far that the civilisation of Western Europe with all its achievements should come to a tragic but splendid end than that the two great democracies should linger on, stripped of all that made life worth living.

Mr. Attlee then said that he entirely agreed with my view. 'The British people now realise the danger with which they are faced, and know that in the event of a German victory everything they have built up will be destroyed. The Germans kill not only men, but ideas. Our people are resolved as never before in their history.'

Reynaud thanked us for what we had said. He was sure that the morale of the German people was not up to the level of the momentary triumph of their Army. If France could hold the Somme with the help of Britain and if American industry came in to make good the disparity in arms, then we could be sure of victory. He was most grateful, he said, for my renewed assurance that if one country went under the other would not abandon the struggle.

The formal meeting then ended.

After we rose from the table some of the principals talked together in the bay window in a somewhat different atmosphere. Chief among these was Marshal Pétain. Spears was with me, helping me out with my French and speaking himself. The young Frenchman, Captain de Margerie, had already spoken about fighting it out in Africa. But Marshal Pétain's attitude, detached and sombre, gave me the feeling that he would face a separate peace. The influence of his personality, his reputation, his serene acceptance of the march of adverse events, apart from any words he used, was almost overpowering to those under his spell. One of the Frenchmen, I cannot remember who, said in their polished way that a continuance of military reverses might in certain eventualities enforce a modification of foreign policy upon France. Here Spears rose to the occasion, and, addressing himself particularly to Marshal

Pétain, said in perfect French: 'I suppose you understand, M. le Maréchal, that that would mean blockade?' Someone else said: 'That would perhaps be inevitable.' But then Spears to Pétain's face: 'That would not only mean blockade, but bombardment of all French ports in German hands.' I was glad to have this said. I sang my usual song: we would fight on whatever happened or whoever fell out.

'WE SHALL NOT FLAG OR FAIL. WE SHALL GO ON TO THE END.'

Following the evacuation from Dunkirk, the possibility of an imminent German invasion of Britain could not be ruled out. On June 4, the last day of the Dunkirk evacuation, and only twenty-five days after becoming Prime Minister, Churchill – echoing the words he had twice heard Clemenceau utter in Paris in March 1918 – set out his thoughts on invasion in the House of Commons, to anxious parliamentarians, and to an anxious British people:

I would observe that there has never been a period in all these long centuries of which we boast when an absolute guarantee against invasion, still less against serious raids, could have been given to our people. In the days of Napoleon the same wind which would have carried his transports across the Channel might have driven away the blockading fleet. There was always the chance, and it is that chance which has excited and befooled the imaginations of many Continental tyrants.

Many are the tales that are told. We are assured that novel methods will be adopted, and when we see the originality of malice, the ingenuity of aggression, which our enemy displays, we may certainly prepare ourselves for every kind of novel stratagem and every kind of brutal and treacherous manoeuvre. I think that no idea is so outlandish that it should not be considered and viewed with a searching, but at the same time, I hope, with a steady eye. We must never forget the solid assurances of sea power and those which belong to air power if it can be locally exercised.

I have, myself, full confidence that if all do their duty, if nothing is neglected, and if the best arrangements are made, as they are being made, we shall prove ourselves once again able to defend our island home, to ride out the storm of war, and to outlive the menace of tyranny, if necessary for years, if necessary alone. At any rate, that is what we are going to try to do. That is the resolve of His Majesty's Government – every man of them. That is the will of Parliament and the nation.

The British Empire and the French Republic, linked together in their cause and in their need, will defend to the death their native soil, aiding each other like good comrades to the utmost of their strength.

Even though large tracts of Europe and many old and famous States have fallen or may fall into the grip of the Gestapo and all the odious apparatus of Nazi rule, we shall not flag or fail. We shall go on to the end, we shall fight in France, we shall fight on the seas and oceans, we shall fight with growing confidence and growing strength in the air, we shall defend our island, whatever the cost may be, we shall fight on the beaches, we shall fight on the landing grounds, we shall fight in the fields and in the streets, we shall fight in the hills; we shall never surrender, and even if, which I do not for a moment believe, this island or a large part of it were subjugated and starving, then our Empire beyond the seas, armed and guarded by the British Fleet, would carry on the struggle, until, in God's good time, the new world, with all its power and might, steps forth to the rescue and the liberation of the old.

'WE SHALL FIGHT ON UNCONQUERABLE'

Four times between 16 May and 13 June 1940, Churchill flew to France to urge the French Government not to surrender. Meanwhile, as German troops thrust deeper and deeper into France, a further 111,000 British troops were evacuated from Western France, and

16,000 more taken prisoner before they could embark. On 16 June 1940, as German troops swept southward through France, a crisis meeting of the French Government was held at Bordeaux. Paul Reynaud, the French Prime Minister, pleaded in vain for the fight to continue. The Minister of War, the venerable Marshal Pétain – hero of the defence of Verdun in 1916 – prevailed: France must seek an armistice with Germany. Learning this on June 17, Churchill made a short public statement to the British people:

> The news from France is very bad and I grieve for the gallant French people who have fallen into this terrible misfortune. Nothing will alter our feelings towards them or our faith that the genius of France will rise again. What has happened in France makes no difference to our actions and purpose.
>
> We have become the sole champions now in arms to defend the world cause. We shall do our best to be worthy of this high honour. We shall defend our island home and with the British Empire we shall fight on unconquerable until the curse of Hitler is lifted from the brows of mankind.
>
> We are sure that in the end all will come right.

'WE HAVE TO THINK OF THE FUTURE AND NOT OF THE PAST'

There was bitterness in France that Britain had not been able to do more to help halt the German advance, but the weight of German armour and air power was formidable. There was also bitterness in Britain against the pre-war Ministers who had failed to put Britain in a stronger position militarily and in the air. On 18 June 1940, Churchill told the House of Commons:

> Our Army and 120,000 French troops were indeed rescued by the British Navy from Dunkirk but only with the loss of their cannon, vehicles and modern equipment. This loss inevitably took some

weeks to repair, and in the first two of those weeks the battle in France has been lost.

When we consider the heroic resistance made by the French Army against heavy odds in this battle, the enormous losses inflicted upon the enemy and the evident exhaustion of the enemy, it may well be thought that these 25 divisions of the best-trained and best-equipped troops might have turned the scale. However, General Weygand had to fight without them. Only three British divisions or their equivalent were able to stand in the line with their French comrades. They have suffered severely, but they have fought well. We sent every man we could to France as fast as we could re-equip and transport their formations.

I am not reciting these facts for the purpose of recrimination. That, I judge to be utterly futile and even harmful. We cannot afford it. I recite them in order to explain why it was we did not have, as we could have had, between 12 and 14 British divisions fighting in the line in this great battle instead of only three. Now I put all this aside. I put it on the shelf, from which the historians, when they have time, will select their documents to tell their stories.

We have to think of the future and not of the past. This also applies in a small way to our own affairs at home. There are many who would hold an inquest in the House of Commons on the conduct of the Governments – and of Parliaments, for they are in it, too – during the years which led up to this catastrophe. They seek to indict those who were responsible for the guidance of our affairs. This also would be a foolish and pernicious process. There are too many in it. Let each man search his conscience and search his speeches. I frequently search mine.

Of this I am quite sure, that if we open a quarrel between the past and the present, we shall find that we have lost the future. Therefore, I cannot accept the drawing of any distinctions between Members of the present Government. It was formed at a moment of crisis in order to unite all the parties and all sections of opinion. It has received the almost unanimous support of both Houses of Parliament. Its Members are going to stand together, and, subject to the authority of the House of Commons, we are going to govern the country and fight the war.

It is absolutely necessary at a time like this that every Minister who tries each day to do his duty shall be respected, and their subordinates must know that their chiefs are not threatened men, men who are here to-day and gone to-morrow, but that their directions must be punctually and faithfully obeyed. Without this concentrated power we cannot face what lies before us.

'IF HITLER FAILS TO INVADE'

On 20 June 1940, in a speech to a Secret Session in the House of Commons, from which all journalists and members of the public were excluded, Churchill gave Members of Parliament a sense of his own confidence in the course of the war. No text of the speech was recorded in *Hansard*, but Churchill's notes, from which he spoke, survive. This page from them gives the central part of his message, in the form in which the notes were typed out by his secretary:

If Hitler fails to invade
    or destroy Britain
        he has lost the war.

I do not consider only the severities
    of the winter in Europe.

I look to superiority in Air power
    in the future.

Transatlantic reinforcements.

If get through next 3 months
    get through next 3 years.

It may well be our fine Armies
    have not said goodbye to the Continent
        of Europe.

If enemy coastline extends from the Arctic
    to the Mediterranean

    and we retain sea-power
        and a growing Air power

    it is evident that Hitler
        master of a starving, agonized and
            surging Europe;

    will have his dangers as well as we.

'THE SUPREME HOUR'

France signed an armistice with Germany on 25 June 1940. The terms included the transfer of the French Fleet to German control. On 3 July 1940, when the French warships at the French military port of Mers el-Kebir, in French North Africa, refused a British demand to hand themselves over to Britain, or to transfer to a neutral port, Churchill ordered an immediate British naval bombardment to prevent the ships sailing to German-controlled Toulon. In that bombardment, 1,297 French sailors were killed. On the following day Churchill told the House of Commons:

It is with sincere sorrow that I must now announce to the House the measures which we have felt bound to take in order to prevent the French Fleet from falling into German hands. When two nations are fighting together under long and solemn alliance against a common foe, one of them may be stricken down and overwhelmed, and may be forced to ask its Ally to release it from its obligations. But the least that could be expected was that the French Government, in abandoning the conflict and leaving its whole weight to fall upon Great Britain and the British Empire, would have been careful not to inflict needless injury upon their faithful comrade, in whose final victory the sole chance of French freedom lay, and lies.

As the House will remember, we offered to give full release to the French from their Treaty obligations, although these were designed for precisely the case which arose, on one condition, namely, that the French Fleet should be sailed for British harbours before the separate armistice negotiations with the enemy were completed. This was not done, but on the contrary, in spite of every kind of private and personal promise and assurance given by Admiral Darlan to the First Lord and to his Naval colleague the First Sea Lord of the British Admiralty, an armistice was signed which was bound to place the French Fleet as effectively in the power of Germany and its Italian following, as that portion of the French Fleet was placed in our power when many of them, being unable to reach African ports, came into the harbours of Portsmouth and Plymouth about ten days ago.

Thus I must place on record that what might have been a mortal injury was done to us by the Bordeaux Government with full knowledge of the consequences and of our dangers, and after rejecting all our appeals at the moment when they were abandoning the Alliance, and breaking the engagements which fortified it.

There was another example of this callous and perhaps even malevolent treatment which we received, not indeed from the French nation, who have never been and apparently never are to be consulted upon these transactions, but from the Bordeaux Government. This is the instance. There were over four hundred German air pilots who were prisoners in France, many of them, perhaps most of them, shot down by the Royal Air Force. I obtained from M. Reynaud a personal promise that these pilots should be sent for safe keeping to England, and orders were given by him to that effect; but when M. Reynaud fell, these pilots were delivered over to Germany in order, no doubt, to win favour for the Bordeaux Government with their German masters, and to win it without regard to the injury done to us.

The German Air Force already feels acutely the shortage of high grade pilots, and it seemed to me particularly odious, if I may use the word, that these four hundred skilled men should be handed over with the sure knowledge that they would be used to bomb this country, and thus force our airmen to shoot them down for the second time over. Such wrongful deeds I am sure will not be condoned by history, and I firmly believe that a generation of

Frenchmen will arise who will clear their national honour from all countenance of them.

I said last week that we must now look with particular attention to our own salvation. I have never in my experience seen so grim and sombre a question as what we were to do about the French Fleet discussed in a Cabinet. It shows how strong were the reasons for the course which we thought it our duty to take, that every Member of the Cabinet had the same conviction about what should be done and there was not the slightest hesitation or divergence among them, and that the three Service Ministers, as well as men like the Minister of Information and the Secretary of State for the Colonies, particularly noted for their long friendship with France, when they were consulted were equally convinced that no other decision than that which we took was possible.

We took that decision, and it was a decision to which, with aching hearts but with clear vision, we unitedly came. Accordingly early yesterday morning, 3rd July, after all preparations had been made, we took the greater part of the French Fleet under our control, or else called upon them, with adequate force, to comply with our requirements. Two battleships, two light cruisers, some submarines, including a very large one, the *Surcouf*, eight destroyers and approximately 200 smaller but extremely useful minesweeping and anti-submarine craft, which lay for the most part at Portsmouth and Plymouth, though there were some at Sheerness, were boarded by superior forces, after brief notice had been given wherever possible to their captains.

This operation was successfully carried out without resistance or bloodshed except in one instance. A scuffle arose through a misunderstanding in the submarine *Surcouf*, in which one British leading seaman was killed and two British officers and one rating wounded and one French officer killed and one wounded.

For the rest, the French sailors in the main cheerfully accepted the end of a period of uncertainty. A considerable number, 800 or 900, have expressed an ardent desire to continue the war, and some have asked for British nationality. This we are ready to grant without prejudice to the other Frenchmen, numbered by thousands, who prefer to fight on with us as Frenchmen. All the rest of those crews will be immediately repatriated to French ports, if the French Government are able to make arrangements for their reception by permission of their German rulers.

We are also repatriating all French troops who were in this country, excepting those who, of their own free will, have volunteered to follow General de Gaulle in the French forces of liberation of whom he is chief. Several French submarines have also joined us independently, and we have accepted their services.

Now I turn to the Mediterranean. At Alexandria, where a strong British battle fleet is lying, there are, besides a French battleship, four French cruisers, three of them modern 8-inch gun vessels, and a number of smaller ships. These have been informed that they cannot be permitted to leave harbour and thus fall within the power of the German conquerors of France. Negotiations and discussions, with the details of which I need not trouble the House, have necessarily been taking place, and measures have now been taken to ensure that those ships, which are commanded by a very gallant Admiral, shall be sunk or otherwise made to comply with our wishes.

The anguish which this process has, naturally, caused to the British and French naval officers concerned may be readily imagined, when I tell the House that only this morning, in the air raid upon Alexandria by Italian aircraft, some of the French ships fired heavily and effectively with us against the common enemy. We shall, of course, offer the fullest facilities to all French officers and men at Alexandria who wish to continue the war, and will provide for them and maintain them during the conflict. We have also promised to repatriate all the rest, and every care in our power will be taken, if they allow it, for their safety and their comfort. So much for Alexandria.

But the most serious part of the story remains. Two of the finest vessels of the French Fleet, the *Dunkerque* and the *Strasbourg*, modern battle cruisers much superior to *Scharnhorst* and *Gneisenau* – and built for the purpose of being superior to them – lay with two battleships, several light cruisers and a number of destroyers and submarines and other vessels at Oran and at its adjacent military port of Mers-El-Kebir on the Northern African shore . . . Yesterday morning, a carefully chosen British officer, Captain

Holland, lately Naval Attaché in Paris, was sent on in a destroyer and waited upon the French Admiral Gensoul. After being refused an interview, he presented the following document, which I will read to the House. The first two paragraphs of the document deal with the general question of the Armistice, which I have already explained in my own words. The fourth paragraph begins as follows:

This is the operative paragraph: 'It is impossible for us, your comrades up to now, to allow your fine ships to fall into the power of the German or Italian enemy. We are determined to fight on to the end, and if we win, as we think we shall, we shall never forget that France was our Ally, that our interests are the same as hers and that our common enemy is Germany. Should we conquer, we solemnly declare that we shall restore the greatness and territory of France. For this purpose, we must make sure that the best ships of the French Navy are not used against us by the common foe. In these circumstances, His Majesty's Government have instructed me' – that is, the British Admiral – 'to demand that the French Fleet now at Mers-El-Kebir and Oran shall act in accordance with one of the following alternatives:

'(a) Sail with us and continue to fight for victory against the Germans and Italians. (b) Sail with reduced crews under our control to a British port. The reduced crews will be repatriated at the earliest moment. If either of these courses is adopted by you, we will restore your ships to France at the conclusion of the war or pay full compensation, if they are damaged meanwhile. (c) Alternatively, if you feel bound to stipulate that your ships should not be used against the Germans or Italians unless these break the Armistice, then sail them with us with reduced crews, to some French port in the West Indies, Martinique, for instance, where they can be demilitarised to our satisfaction or be perhaps entrusted to the United States and remain safe until the end of the war, the crews being repatriated. If you refuse these fair offers, I must, with profound regret, require you to sink your ships within six hours. Finally, failing the above, I have the orders of His Majesty's Government to use whatever force may be necessary to prevent your ships from falling into German or Italian hands.'

We had hoped that one or other of the alternatives which we

presented would have been accepted, without the necessity of using the terrible force of a British battle squadron. Such a squadron arrived before Oran two hours after Captain Holland and his destroyer. This battle squadron was commanded by Vice-Admiral Somerville, an officer who distinguished himself lately in the bringing-off of over 100,000 Frenchmen during the evacuation from Dunkirk. Admiral Somerville was further provided, besides his battleships, with a cruiser force and strong flotillas.

All day the parleys continued, and we hoped until the afternoon that our terms would be accepted without bloodshed. However, no doubt in obedience to the orders dictated by the Germans from Wiesbaden, where the Franco-German Armistice Commission is in session, Admiral Gensoul refused to comply and announced his intention of fighting. Admiral Somerville was therefore ordered to complete his mission before darkness fell, and at 5.53 p.m. he opened fire upon this powerful French Fleet, which was also protected by its shore batteries. At 6 p.m. he reported that he was heavily engaged. The action lasted for some 10 minutes and was followed by heavy attacks from our naval aircraft, carried in the *Ark Royal*. At 7.20 p.m. Admiral Somerville forwarded a further report, which stated that a battle cruiser of the Strasbourg class was damaged and ashore; that a battleship of the Bretagne class had been sunk, that another of the same class had been heavily damaged, and that two French destroyers and a seaplane carrier, *Commandant Teste*, were also sunk or burned.

While this melancholy action was being fought, either the battle cruiser *Strasbourg* or the *Dunkerque*, one or the other, managed to slip out of harbour in a gallant effort to reach Toulon or a North African port and place herself under German control, in accordance with the Armistice terms of the Bordeaux Government.

[···]

I need hardly say that the French ships were fought, albeit in this unnatural cause, with the characteristic courage of the French Navy, and every allowance must be made for Admiral Gensoul and his officers who felt themselves obliged to obey the orders they received from their Government and could not look behind that Government to see the German dictation.

I fear the loss of life among the French and in the harbour must have been heavy, as we were compelled to use a severe measure of force and several immense explosions were heard. None of the British ships taking part in the action was in any way affected in gun-power or mobility by the heavy fire directed upon them. I have not yet received any reports of our casualties, but Admiral Somerville's Fleet is, in all military respects, intact and ready for further action.

The Italian Navy, for whose reception we had also made arrangements and which is, of course, considerably stronger numerically than the Fleet we used at Oran, kept prudently out of the way. However, we trust that their turn will come during the operations which we shall pursue to secure the effectual command of the Mediterranean.

A large proportion of the French Fleet has, therefore, passed into our hands or has been put out of action or otherwise withheld from Germany by yesterday's events. The House will not expect me to say anything about other French ships which are at large except that it is our inflexible resolve to do everything that is possible in order to prevent them falling into the German grip.

I leave the judgment of our action, with confidence, to Parliament. I leave it to the nation, and I leave it to the United States. I leave it to the world and to history.

Now I turn to the immediate future. We must, of course, expect to be attacked, or even invaded, if that proves to be possible – it has not been proved yet – in our own island before very long. We are making every preparation in our power to repel the assaults of the enemy, whether they be directed upon Great Britain, or upon Ireland, which all Irishmen, without distinction of creed or party, should realise is in imminent danger. These again are matters upon which we have clear views. These preparations are constantly occupying our toil from morn till night, and far into the night. But, although we have clear views, it would not, I think, be profitable for us to discuss them in public, or even, so far as the Government are concerned, except under very considerable reserve, in a private session. I call upon all subjects of His Majesty, and upon our Allies, and well-wishers – and they are not a few – all over the world, on both sides of the Atlantic, to give us their utmost aid. In the fullest harmony with our

Dominions, we are moving through a period of extreme danger and of splendid hope, when every virtue of our race will be tested, and all that we have and are will be freely staked. This is no time for doubt or weakness. It is the supreme hour to which we have been called.

'WE SHALL NOT FAIL IN OUR DUTY, HOWEVER PAINFUL'

On 4 July 1940, faced with reports of defeatist talk at many levels of his administration, Churchill sent a message to every senior civil servant in all government departments. At the end of his speech on the bombardment of the French Fleet at Mers el-Kebir, he told the assembled Members of Parliament:

I will venture to read to the House a message which I have caused to be sent to all who are serving in positions of importance under the Crown, and if the House should view it with sympathy, I should be very glad to send a copy of it to every Member for his own use, not that such exhortations are needed. This is the message:

'On what may be the eve of an attempted invasion or battle for our native land, the Prime Minister desires to impress upon all persons holding responsible positions in the Government, in the Fighting Services, or in the Civil Departments, their duty to maintain a spirit of alert and confident energy. While every precaution must be taken that time and means afford, there are no grounds for supposing that more German troops can be landed in this country, either from the air or across the sea, than can be destroyed or captured by the strong forces at present under arms. The Royal Air Force is in excellent order and at the highest strength it has yet attained. The German Navy was never so weak, nor the British Army at home so strong as now.

'The Prime Minister expects all His Majesty's servants in high places to set an example of steadiness and resolution. They should check and rebuke expressions of loose and ill-digested opinion in their circles, or by their subordinates. They should not hesitate to report, or if necessary remove, any officers or officials who are found to be consciously exercising a disturbing or depressing influence, and whose talk is calculated to spread alarm and despondency. Thus alone will they be worthy of the fighting men, who, in the air, on the sea, and on land, have already met the enemy without any sense of being outmatched in martial qualities.'

I feel that we are entitled to the confidence of the House and that we shall not fail in our duty, however painful. The action we have already taken should be, in itself, sufficient to dispose once and for all of the lies and rumours which have been so industriously spread by German propaganda and Fifth Column activities that we have the slightest intention of entering into negotiations in any form and through any channel with the German and Italian Governments. We shall, on the contrary, prosecute the war with the utmost vigour by all the means that are open to us until the righteous purposes for which we entered upon it have been fulfilled.

'A WAR OF THE UNKNOWN WARRIORS'

Throughout the first two weeks of July 1940, as Britain awaited a German invasion, Churchill held emergency meetings with those who would have to organize the defence of Britain's beaches. As German warplanes bombed the Channel ports, Churchill inspected the troops and fortifications of the South Coast defences. Rifles and ammunition were arriving by sea from the United States. On July 14, Churchill broadcast a message of optimism and defiance to the British people:

We must prepare not only for the summer, but for the winter; not only for 1941, but for 1942; when the War will, I trust, take a different form from the defensive, in which it has hitherto been bound. I dwell on these elements in our strength – on these resources which we have mobilised and control – I dwell on it and them because it is right to show that the good cause can command the means of survival; and that while we toil through the dark valley we can see the sunlight on the uplands beyond.

I stand at the head of a Government representing all parties in the State – all creeds, all classes, every recognisable section of opinion. We are ranged beneath the Crown of our ancient monarchy. We are supported by a free Parliament and a free Press; but there is one bond which unites us all and sustains us in the public regard – namely (as is increasingly becoming known), that we are prepared to proceed to all extremities, to endure them and to enforce them; <u>that</u> is our bond of union in His Majesty's Government to-night. Thus only, in times like these, can nations preserve their freedom; and thus only can they uphold the cause entrusted to their care.

But all depends now upon the whole life-strength of the British race in every part of the world and of all our associated peoples and of all our well-wishers in every land, doing their utmost night and day, giving all, daring all, enduring all – to the utmost – to the end.

This is no war of chieftains or of princes, of dynasties or national ambition; it is a war of peoples and of causes. There are vast numbers not only in this island but in every land, who will render faithful service in this War, but whose names will never be known, whose deeds will never be recorded.

This is a War of the Unknown Warriors; but let all strive without failing in faith or in duty; and the dark curse of Hitler will be lifted from our age.

'NEVER IN THE FIELD OF HUMAN CONFLICT'

On 14 August 1940, Churchill learned that 526 British pilots had been killed in action in the skies above Britain and the English Channel in June and July. On August 15, he informed Roosevelt of 'the severe air fighting' of the previous week. On August 16, he went to RAF Uxbridge, to visit the Operations Room of No. 11 Group RAF at the height of that day's air battle. As he drove away, he remarked to General Sir Hastings Ismay, the head of his Defence Secretariat, who was sitting in front of him: 'Don't speak to me; I have never been so moved.' Then, after about five minutes of silence, Churchill leant forward and said: 'Never in the field of human conflict has so much been owed by so many to so few.' Ismay later recalled: 'The words burned into my brain and I repeated them to my wife when I got home. Churchill too had evidently photographed them in his mind.' The phrase 'The Few' soon came to describe the Allied aircrew of RAF Fighter Command, whose desperate struggle in August and September 1940 prevented the German Air Force from destroying Britain's fighter air defences. With those defences still in place, a German invasion of Britain would have been extremely difficult. On 20 August 1940, four days after his visit to RAF Uxbridge, Churchill told the House of Commons:

> Rather more than a quarter of a year has passed since the new Government came into power in this country. What a cataract of disaster has poured out upon us since then! . . . Meanwhile, we have not only fortified our hearts but our Island. We have rearmed and rebuilt our armies in a degree which would have been deemed impossible a few months ago . . . The whole Island bristles against invaders, from the sea or from the air.
>
> [· · ·]
>
> The stronger our Army at home, the larger must the invading expedition be, and the larger the invading expedition, the less difficult will be the task of the Navy in detecting its assembly and in intercepting and destroying it in passage; and the greater also would be the difficulty of feeding and supplying the invaders if ever they landed . . . Our Navy is far stronger than it was at the beginning of the war. The great flow of new construction set on foot at the outbreak is now beginning to come in.
>
> [· · ·]
>
> Why do I say all this? Not, assuredly, to boast; not, assuredly, to give the slightest countenance to complacency. The dangers we face are still enormous, but so are our advantages and resources. I recount them because the people have a right to know that there are solid grounds for

the confidence which we feel, and that we have good reason to believe ourselves capable, as I said in a very dark hour two months ago, of continuing the war 'if necessary alone, if necessary for years'.

[· · ·]

The great air battle which has been in progress over this Island for the last few weeks has recently attained a high intensity. It is too soon to attempt to assign limits either to its scale or to its duration. We must certainly expect that greater efforts will be made by the enemy than any he has so far put forth.

[· · ·]

It is quite plain that Herr Hitler could not admit defeat in his air attack on Great Britain without sustaining most serious injury. If after all his boastings and bloodcurdling threats and lurid accounts trumpeted round the world of the damage he has inflicted, of the vast numbers of our Air Force he has shot down, so he says, with so little loss to himself [. . .] if after all this his whole air onslaught were forced after a while tamely to peter out, the Fuhrer's reputation for veracity of statement might be seriously impugned. We may be sure, therefore, that he will continue as long as he has the strength to do so.

[· · ·]

It must also be remembered that all the enemy machines and pilots which are shot down over our Island, or over the seas which surround it, are either destroyed or captured; whereas a considerable proportion of our machines, and also of our pilots, are saved, and soon again in many cases come into action.

[· · ·]

We believe that we shall be able to continue the air struggle indefinitely and as long as the enemy pleases, and the longer it continues the more rapid will be our approach, first towards that parity, and then into that superiority, in the air upon which in a large measure the decision of the war depends.

[· · ·]

The gratitude of every home in our Island, in our Empire, and indeed throughout the world, except in the abodes of the guilty, goes out to the British airmen who, undaunted by odds, unwearied in their constant challenge and mortal danger, are turning the tide of the World War by their prowess and by their devotion. Never in the field of human conflict was so much owed by so many to so few.

All hearts go out to the fighter pilots, whose brilliant actions we see with our own eyes day after day, but we must never forget that all the time, night after night, month after month, our bomber squadrons travel far into Germany, find their targets in the darkness by the highest navigational skill, aim their attacks, often under the heaviest fire, often with serious loss, with deliberate, careful discrimination, and inflict shattering blows upon the whole of the technical and war-making structure of the Nazi power. On no part of the Royal Air Force does the weight of the war fall more heavily than on the daylight bombers who will play an invaluable part in the case of invasion and whose unflinching zeal it has been necessary in the meanwhile on numerous occasions to restrain.

[···]

A good many people have written to me to ask me to make on this occasion a fuller statement of our war aims, and of the kind of peace we wish to make after the war, than is contained in the very considerable declaration which was made early in the autumn [...] I do not think it would be wise at this moment, while the battle rages and the war is still perhaps only in its earlier stage, to embark upon elaborate speculations about the future shape which should be given to Europe [...] But before we can undertake the task of rebuilding we have not only to be convinced ourselves, but we have to convince all other countries that the Nazi tyranny is going to be finally broken. The right to guide the course of world history is the noblest prize of victory. We are still toiling up the hill; we have not yet reached the crest-line of it; we cannot survey the landscape or even imagine what its condition will be when that longed-for morning comes. The task which lies before us immediately is at once more practical, more simple and more stern.

[· · ·]

For the rest, we have to gain the victory. That is our task.

[· · ·]

Some months ago we came to the conclusion that the interests of the United States and of the British Empire both required that the United States should have facilities for the naval and air defence of the Western Hemisphere against the attack of a Nazi power [. . .] We had therefore decided spontaneously, and without being asked or offered any inducement, to inform the Government of the United States that we would be glad to place such defence facilities at their disposal by leasing suitable sites in our Transatlantic possessions for their greater security against the unmeasured dangers of the future [. . .]

His Majesty's Government are entirely willing to accord defence facilities to the United States on a 99 years' leasehold basis [. . .]

Undoubtedly this process means that these two great organisations of the English-speaking democracies, the British Empire and the United States, will have to be somewhat mixed up together in some of their affairs for mutual and general advantage. For my own part, looking out upon the future, I do not view the process with any misgivings. I could not stop it if I wished; no one can stop it. Like the Mississippi, it just keeps rolling along. Let it roll. Let it roll on full flood, inexorable, irresistible, benignant, to broader lands and better days.

'LET GOD DEFEND THE RIGHT'

During August 1940, German preparations for invasion were continuous, with invasion barges in the Channel and North Sea ports of France, Belgium and Holland being made ready to transport troops to the beaches of South East England. In the air, German bombers sought to destroy British airfields and fighter defences. That August, more than five thousand civilians were killed during German air raids, the majority in London. On 11 September 1940, as the bombing intensified, it was announced that 1,211 civilians had been killed in the previous week, 976 of them in London. That day Churchill broadcast again to the British people:

If this invasion is going to be tried at all, it does not seem that it can be long delayed. The weather may break at any time. Besides this, it is difficult for the enemy to keep these gatherings of ships waiting about indefinitely, while they are bombed every night by our bombers, and very often shelled by our warships which are waiting for them outside.

Therefore, we must regard the next week or so as a very important period in our history. It ranks with the days when the Spanish Armada was approaching the Channel, and Drake was finishing his game of bowls; or when Nelson stood between us and Napoleon's Grand Army at Boulogne. We have read all about this in the history books; but what is happening now is on a far greater scale and of far more consequence to the life and future of the world and its civilization than these brave old days of the past.

Every man and woman will therefore prepare himself to do his duty, whatever it may be, with special pride and care. Our fleets and flotillas are very powerful and numerous; our Air Force is at the highest strength it has ever reached, and it is conscious of its proved superiority, not indeed in numbers, but in men and machines. Our shores are well fortified and strongly manned, and behind them, ready to attack the invaders, we have a far larger and better equipped mobile Army than we have ever had before.

Besides this, we have more than a million and a half men of the Home Guard, who are just as much soldiers of the Regular Army as the Grenadier Guards, and who are determined to fight for every inch of the ground in every village and in every street.

It is with devout but sure confidence that I say: Let God defend the Right.

These cruel, wanton, indiscriminate bombings of London are, of course, a part of Hitler's invasion plans. He hopes, by killing large numbers of civilians, and women and children, that he will terrorize and cow the people of this mighty imperial city, and make them a burden and an anxiety to the Government and thus distract our attention unduly from the ferocious onslaught he is preparing. Little does he know the spirit of the British nation, or the tough fibre of the Londoners, whose forebears played a leading part in the establishment of Parliamentary institutions and who have been bred to value freedom far above their lives.

This wicked man, the repository and embodiment of many forms of soul-destroying hatred, this monstrous product of former wrongs and shame, has now resolved to try to break our famous Island race by a process of indiscriminate slaughter and destruction. What he has done is to kindle a fire in British hearts, here and all over the world, which will glow long after all traces of the conflagration he has caused in London have been removed. He has lighted a fire which will burn with a steady and consuming flame until the last vestiges of Nazi tyranny have been burnt out of Europe, and until the Old World and the New can join hands to rebuild the temples of man's freedom and man's honour, upon foundations which will not soon or easily be overthrown.

[···]

All the world that is still free marvels at the composure and fortitude with which the citizens of London are facing and surmounting the great ordeal to which they are subjected, the end of which or the severity of which cannot yet be foreseen. It is a message of good cheer to our fighting Forces on the seas, in the air, and in our waiting Armies in all their posts and stations, that we send them from this capital city. They know that they have behind them a people who will not flinch or weary of the struggle – hard and protracted though it will be; but that we shall rather draw from the heart of suffering itself the means of inspiration and survival, and of a victory won not only for ourselves but for all – a victory won not only for our own time, but for the long and better days that are to come.

[···]

Whenever the weather is favourable waves of German bombers, protected by fighters, often three or four hundred at a time, surge over this Island, especially the promontory of Kent, in the hope of attacking military and other objectives by daylight. However, they are met by our fighter squadrons and nearly always broken up, and their losses average three to one in machines and six to one in pilots.

This effort of the Germans to secure daylight mastery of the air over England is of course the crux of the whole war. So far it has failed conspicuously. It has cost them very dear, and we have felt stronger, and actually are relatively a good deal stronger, than when the hard fighting began in July. There is no doubt that Herr Hitler is using up his fighter force at a very high rate, and that if he goes on for many more weeks he will wear down and ruin this vital part of his Air Force. That will give us a great advantage.

On the other hand, for him to try to invade this country without having secured mastery in the air would be a very hazardous under-taking. Nevertheless, all his preparations for invasion on a great scale are steadily going forward. Several hundreds of self-propelled barges are moving down the coasts of Europe, from the German and Dutch harbours to the ports of Northern France, from Dunkirk to Brest, and beyond Brest to the French harbours in the Bay of Biscay.

Besides this, convoys of merchant ships in tens and dozens are being moved through the Straits of Dover into the Channel, dodging along from port to port under the protection of the new batteries which the Germans have built on the French shore. There are now considerable gatherings of shipping in the German, Dutch, Belgian and French harbours, all the way from Hamburg to Brest. Finally, there are some preparations made of ships to carry an invading force from Norwegian waters.

Behind these clusters of ships or barges there stand large numbers of German troops, awaiting the order to go on board and set out on their very dangerous and uncertain voyage across the seas. We cannot tell when they will try to come; we cannot be sure that in fact they will try at all; but no-one should blind himself to the fact that a heavy full-scale invasion of this Island is being prepared with all the usual German thoroughness and method, and that it may be launched now – upon England, upon Scotland, or upon Ireland, or upon all three.

'THESE NEXT FEW WEEKS ARE GRAVE AND ANXIOUS'

In the first two weeks of September, two thousand British civilians had been killed and eight thousand wounded, four-fifths in London, by German air bombardment. At the same time, Churchill knew from the most secret sources of British intelligence that the German Air Force had been alerted to prepare for providing cover for the invasion barges then awaiting the troops who would be landing on British soil. He also knew that the increasing number of foggy days in the English Channel and North Sea would be a further protection for those barges. What he did not know was that Hitler was about to change his mind, and to set the invasion of the Soviet Union as his priority. On 17 September 1940, Churchill told the House of Commons, in a Secret Session from which all visitors and journalists were barred:

These next few weeks are grave and anxious. I said just now in the Public Session that the deployment of the enemy's invasion preparations and the assembly of his ships and barges is steadily proceeding, and that at any moment a major assault may be launched upon this Island. I now say in secret that upwards of 1,700 self-propelled barges and more than 200 sea-going ships, some very large ships, are already gathered at the many invasion ports in German occupation.

If this is all a pretence and stratagem to pin us down here, it has been executed with surprising thoroughness and on a gigantic scale. Some of these ships and barges, when struck by our bombing counter-attack and preventive attack, have blown up with tremendous explosions, showing that they are fully loaded with all the munitions needed for the invading armies and to beat us down and subjugate us utterly.

The shipping available and now assembled is sufficient to carry in one voyage nearly half a million men. We should, of course, expect to drown a great many on the way over, and to destroy a large proportion of their vessels. But when you reflect upon the many points from which they could start, and upon the fact that even the most likely sector of invasion, i.e., the sector in which enemy fighter support is available for their bombers and dive-bombers, extending from the Wash to the Isle of Wight, is nearly as long as the whole front in France from the Alps to the sea, and also upon the dangers of fog or artificial fog, one must expect many lodgments or attempted lodgments to be made on our Island simultaneously. These we shall hope to deal with as they occur, and also to cut off the supply across the sea by which the enemy will seek to nourish his lodgments.

The difficulties of the invader are not ended when he sets foot on shore. A new chapter of perils opens upon him. I am confident that we shall succeed in defeating and largely destroying this most tremendous onslaught by which we are now threatened, and anyhow, whatever happens, we will all go down fighting to the end. I feel as sure as the sun will rise tomorrow that we shall be victorious.

'MAN'S INSTINCTIVE DEFIANCE OF TYRANNY'

The last day of September 1940 marked the second anniversary of the Munich Agreement, whereby Hitler – having assured Neville Chamberlain that he did not wish to have any more Czechs under German rule – obtained Britain's and France's agreement to his demand for the annexation of the mineral-rich and predominantly German-speaking Sudetenland border regions of Czechoslovakia. On that day, September 30, Churchill broadcast over the BBC to the people of Czechoslovakia, all of whom had been living under the harsh severity of Nazi rule since the German occupation of Prague in March 1939:

To-day is the second anniversary of the Munich Agreement, a date which the world will always remember for the tragic sacrifice made by the Czechoslovak people in the interest of European peace. The hopes which this agreement stirred in the heart of civilized mankind have been frustrated. Within six months the solemn pledges given by the unscrupulous men who control the destiny of Germany were broken and the agreement destroyed with a ruthlessness which unmasked the true nature of their reckless ambitions to the whole world.

The protection which Hitler forced upon you has been a sham and a cloak for the incorporation of your once flourishing country in the so-called Greater Reich. Instead of protection he has brought you nothing but moral and material devastation, and to-day the followers of that great and tolerant humanitarian, President Masaryk, are being persecuted with a deliberate cruelty which has few parallels in modern history.

In this hour of your martyrdom I send you this message: The battle which we in Britain are fighting today is not only our battle. It is also your battle, and, indeed, the battle of all nations who prefer liberty to a soulless serfdom. It is the struggle of civilized nations for the right to live their own life in the manner of their own choosing. It represents man's instinctive defiance of tyranny and of an impersonal universe.

Throughout history no European nation has shown a greater will to survive than yours, and today again your people have given count-less proofs of their courage in adversity. Here in Britain we have welcomed with pride and gratitude your soldiers and airmen who have come by daring escape to take part with ever-increasing success in that battle for Britain which is also the battle for Czechoslovakia. And no less sincere is our admiration of those Czechs and Slovaks who on the home front are risking death, and worse than death, in order to foster resistance against a cruel and heartless oppressor.

It is because we both are fighting for the fundamental decencies of human life that we are determined that neither our struggle nor your struggle shall be in vain. It is for this reason that we have refused to recognize any of the brutal conquests of Germany in Central Europe and elsewhere, that we have welcomed a Czechoslovak Provisional Government in this country, and that we have made the restoration of Czechoslovak liberties one of our principal war aims. With firm-ness and resolution, two qualities which our nations share in equal measure, these aims will be achieved.

Be of good cheer. The hour of your deliverance will come. The soul of freedom is deathless; it cannot, and will not, perish.

'SLEEP TO GATHER STRENGTH
FOR THE MORNING'

Churchill anguished over the plight of France under German occupation and control, just as he had anguished over the order to bombard the French warships at Mers el-Kebir. On 22 July 1940 he had created the Special Operations Executive (SOE), charged with setting up resistance groups inside France, and elsewhere in German-occupied Europe, that could in due course carry out anti-German sabotage. His instruction to its members was: 'Set Europe ablaze!' On October 21 he broadcast, first in English and then in French, an appeal to all Frenchmen and women:

> Remember we shall never stop, never weary, and never give in, and that our whole people and Empire have vowed themselves to the task of cleansing Europe from the Nazi pestilence and saving the world from the new Dark Ages. Do not imagine, as the German-controlled wireless tells you, that we English seek to take your ships and colonies. We seek to beat the life and soul out of Hitler and Hitlerism. That alone, that all the time, that to the end.
>
> We do not covet anything from any nation except their respect. Those Frenchmen who are in the French Empire, and those who are in so-called unoccupied France, may see their way from time to time to useful action. I will not go into details. Hostile ears are listening. As for those, to whom English hearts go out in full, because they see them under the sharp discipline, oppression, and spying of the Hun – as to those Frenchmen in the occupied regions, to them I say, when they think of the future let them remember the words which Gambetta, that great Frenchman, uttered after 1870 about the future of France and what was to come: 'Think of it always: speak of it never.'
>
> Goodnight then: sleep to gather strength for the morning. For the morning will come. Brightly will it shine on the brave and true, kindly upon all who suffer for the cause, glorious upon the tombs of heroes. Thus will shine the dawn. Vive la France! Long live also the forward march of the common people in all the lands towards their just and true inheritance, and towards the broader and fuller age.

'THE ONLY GUIDE TO A MAN IS HIS CONSCIENCE'

Neville Chamberlain died on 9 November 1940. For the two peacetime years of his premiership, he had been Churchill's main political adversary, keeping Churchill out of office and publicly belittling his judgement. In September 1939 he had brought Churchill into his War Cabinet, and in April 1940 he had increased Churchill's powers within it. On becoming Prime Minister on 10 May 1940, Churchill had made Chamberlain a member of his own War Cabinet; and it fell to him as Prime Minister to speak in the House of Commons on November 12 about his predecessor:

> Since we last met, the House has suffered a very grievous loss in the death of one of its most distinguished Members and of a statesman and public servant who, during the best part of three memorable years, was first Minister of the Crown.
>
> The fierce and bitter controversies which hung around him in recent times were hushed by the news of his illness and are silenced by his death. In paying a tribute of respect and of regard to an eminent man who has been taken from us, no one is obliged to alter the opinions which he has formed or expressed upon issues which have become a part of history; but at the Lychgate we may all pass our own conduct and our own judgments under a searching review.
>
> It is not given to human beings, happily for them, for otherwise life would be intolerable, to foresee or to predict to any large extent the unfolding course of events. In one phase men seem to have been right, in another they seem to have been wrong. Then again, a few years later, when the perspective of time has lengthened, all stands in a different setting. There is a new proportion. There is another scale of values. History with its flickering lamp stumbles along the trail of the past, trying to reconstruct its scenes, to revive its echoes, and kindle with pale gleams the passion of former days.
>
> What is the worth of all this? The only guide to a man is his conscience; the only shield to his memory is the rectitude and sincerity of his actions. It is very imprudent to walk through life

without this shield, because we are so often mocked by the failure of our hopes and the upsetting of our calculations; but with this shield, however the fates may play, we march always in the ranks of honour.

It fell to Neville Chamberlain in one of the supreme crises of the world to be contradicted by events, to be disappointed in his hopes, and to be deceived and cheated by a wicked man. But what were these hopes in which he was disappointed? What were these wishes in which he was frustrated? What was that faith that was abused? They were surely among the most noble and benevolent instincts of the human heart – the love of peace, the toil for peace, the strife for peace, the pursuit of peace, even at great peril and certainly to the utter disdain of popularity or clamour.

Whatever else history may or may not say about these terrible, tremendous years, we can be sure that Neville Chamberlain acted with perfect sincerity according to his lights and strove to the utmost of his capacity and authority, which were powerful, to save the world from the awful, devastating struggle in which we are now engaged. This alone will stand him in good stead as far as what is called the verdict of history is concerned.

But it is also a help to our country and to our whole Empire, and to our decent faithful way of living that, however long the struggle may last, or however dark may be the clouds which overhang our path, no future generation of English-speaking folks – for that is the tribunal to which we appeal – will doubt that, even at a great cost to ourselves in technical preparation, we were guiltless of the bloodshed, terror and misery which have engulfed so many lands and peoples, and yet seek new victims still. Herr Hitler protests with frantic words and gestures that he has only desired peace. What do these ravings and outpourings count before the silence of Neville Chamberlain's tomb? Long and hard, hazardous years lie before us, but at least we entered upon them united and with clean hearts.

I do not propose to give an appreciation of Neville Chamberlain's life and character, but there were certain qualities, always admired in these Islands, which he possessed in an altogether exceptional degree. He had a physical and moral toughness of fibre which enabled him all through his varied career to endure misfortune and disappointment without being unduly discouraged or wearied. He had a precision of mind and an aptitude for business which raised him far above the ordinary levels of our generation. He had a firmness of spirit which was not often elated by success, seldom downcast by failure and never swayed by panic.

When, contrary to all his hopes, beliefs and exertions, the war came upon him, and when, as he himself said, all that he had worked for was shattered, there was no man more resolved to pursue the unsought quarrel to the death. The same qualities which made him one of the last to enter the war, made him one of the last who would quit it until the full victory of a righteous cause was won. I had the singular experience of passing in a day from being one of his most prominent opponents and critics to being one of his principal lieutenants, and on another day of passing from serving under him to become the head of a Government of which, with perfect loyalty, he was content to be a member. Such relationships are unusual in our public life.

I have before told the House how, on the morrow of the Debate which in the early days of May challenged his position, he declared to me and a few other friends that only a National Government could face the storm about to break upon us, and that if he were an obstacle to the formation of such a Government, he would instantly retire. Thereafter, he acted with that singleness of purpose and simplicity of conduct which at all times, and especially in great times, ought to be a model for us all. When he returned to duty a few weeks after a most severe operation, the bombardment of London and of the seat of Government had begun. I was a witness during that fortnight of his fortitude under the most grievous and painful bodily afflictions, and I can testify that, although physically only the wreck of a man, his nerve was unshaken and his remarkable mental faculties unimpaired.

After he left the Government he refused all honours. He would die like his father, plain Mr. Chamberlain. I sought the permission of the King however to have him supplied with the Cabinet papers, and until a few days of his death he followed our affairs with keenness, interest and tenacity. He met the approach of death with a steady eye. If he grieved at all, it was that he could not be a spectator of our victory, but I think he died with the comfort of knowing that his country had, at least, turned the corner concerned.

At this time our thoughts must pass to the gracious and charming lady who shared his days of triumph and adversity with a courage and quality the equal of his own. He was, like his father and his brother, Austen, before him, a famous Member of the House of Commons, and we here assembled this morning, Members of all parties, without a single exception, feel that we do ourselves and our country honour in saluting the memory of one whom Disraeli would have called an 'English worthy'.

'GIVE US THE TOOLS, AND WE WILL FINISH THE JOB'

Notwithstanding the heroic efforts of the Royal Air Force in repelling the German air assault throughout the summer and autumn of 1940, the British public, after the fierce battering of the Blitz, remained deeply anxious lest Hitler, having subjugated Denmark and Norway, Belgium, Luxembourg, Holland and France to Nazi rule, would invade Britain in the spring of 1941. In a broadcast on 9 February 1941, Churchill spoke with confidence and conviction:

You will have seen that Sir John Dill, our principal military adviser, the Chief of the Imperial General Staff, has warned us all that Hitler may be forced by the strategic, economic and political stresses in Europe, to try to invade these islands in the near future. That is a warning which no one should disregard.

Naturally, we are working night and day to have everything ready. Of course, we are far stronger than we ever were before, incomparably stronger than we were in July, August and September. Our Navy is more powerful, our flotillas are more numerous; we are far stronger, actually and relatively, in the air above these islands, than we were when our Fighter Command beat off and beat down the Nazi attack last autumn. Our Army is more numerous, more mobile and far better equipped and trained than in September, and still more than in July.

I have the greatest confidence in our Commander-in-Chief, General Brooke, and in the generals of proved ability who, under him, guard the different quarters of our land. But most of all I put my faith in the simple unaffected resolve to conquer or die which will animate and inspire nearly four million Britons with serviceable weapons in their hands. It is not an easy military operation to invade an island like Great Britain, without the command of the sea and without the command of the air, and then to face what will be waiting for the invader here.

But I must drop one word of caution; for next to cowardice and treachery, over-confidence, leading to neglect or slothfulness, is the worst of martial crimes. Therefore, I drop one word of caution. A Nazi invasion of Great Britain last autumn would have been a more or less improvised affair. Hitler took it for granted that when France gave in we should give in; but we did not give in. And he had to think again. An invasion now will be supported by a much more carefully prepared tackle and equipment of landing-craft and other apparatus, all of which will have been planned and manufactured in the winter months. We must all be prepared to meet gas attacks, parachute attacks, and glider attacks, with constancy, forethought and practised skill.

I must again emphasize what General Dill has said, and what I pointed out myself last year. In order to win the war Hitler must destroy Great Britain. He may carry havoc into the Balkan States; he may tear great provinces out of Russia; he may march to the Caspian; he may march to the gates of India. All this will avail him nothing. It may spread his curse more widely throughout Europe and Asia, but it will not avert his doom. With every month that passes the many proud and once happy countries he is now holding down by brute force and vile intrigue are learning to hate the Prussian yoke and the Nazi name as nothing has ever been hated so fiercely and so widely among men before. And all the time, masters of the sea and air, the British Empire – nay, in a certain sense, the whole English-speaking world – will be on his track, bearing with them the swords of justice.

The other day, President Roosevelt gave his opponent in the late

Presidential Election a letter of introduction to me, and in it he wrote out a verse, in his own handwriting, from Longfellow, which he said, 'applies to you people as it does to us'. Here is the verse:

> . . . Sail on, O Ship of State!
> Sail on, O Union, strong and great!
> Humanity with all its fears,
> With all the hopes of future years,
> Is hanging breathless on thy fate!

What is the answer that I shall give, in your name, to this great man, the thrice-chosen head of a nation of a hundred and thirty millions? Here is the answer which I will give to President Roosevelt: Put your confidence in us. Give us your faith and your blessing, and, under Providence, all will be well.

We shall not fail or falter; we shall not weaken or tire. Neither the sudden shock of battle, nor the long-drawn trials of vigilance and exertion, will wear us down. Give us the tools, and we will finish the job.

'WONDERFUL EXERTIONS HAVE BEEN MADE'

On 11 March 1941, President Roosevelt signed the Lend–Lease Act, whereby Britain was able to purchase all the war supplies she needed, to be paid for only after the war. But America remained neutral; Roosevelt had promised in the November 1940 presidential election campaign that no American troops would be sent overseas to fight. He kept his promise, while in mid-April 1941 agreeing that an American fleet would patrol the western Atlantic and would warn all merchant ships of the presence of German and Italian submarines. On 27 April 1941, with German troops, having attacked and conquered Yugoslavia, about to overrun Greece, Churchill broadcast to the United States:

Wonderful exertions have been made by our Navy and Air Force; by the hundreds of mine-sweeping vessels which with their marvellous appliances keep our ports clear in spite of all the enemy can do; by the men who build and repair our immense fleets of merchant ships; by the men who load and unload them; and need I say by the officers and men of the Merchant Navy who go out in all weathers and in the teeth of all dangers to fight for the life of their native land and for a cause they comprehend and serve.

Still, when you think how easy it is to sink ships at sea and how hard it is to build them and protect them, and when you remember that we have never less than two thousand ships afloat and three or four hundred in the danger zone; when you think of the great armies we are maintaining and reinforcing in the East, and of the world-wide traffic we have to carry on – when you remember all this, can you wonder that it is the Battle of the Atlantic which holds the first place in the thoughts of those upon whom rests the responsibility for procuring the victory?

It was therefore with indescribable relief that I learned of the tremendous decisions lately taken by the President and people of the United States. The American Fleet and flying boats have been ordered to patrol the wide waters of the Western Hemisphere, and to warn the peaceful shipping of all nations outside the combat zone of the presence of lurking U-boats or raiding cruisers belonging to the two aggressor nations. We British shall therefore be able to concentrate our protecting forces far more upon the routes nearer home, and to take a far heavier toll of the U-boats there. I have felt for some time that something like this was bound to happen.

The President and Congress of the United States, having newly fortified themselves by contact with their electors, have solemnly pledged their aid to Britain in this war because they deem our cause just, and because they know their own interests and safety would be endangered if we were destroyed. They are taxing themselves heavily. They have passed great legislation. They have turned a large part of their gigantic industry to making the munitions which we need. They have even given us or lent us valuable weapons of their own. I could not believe that they would allow the high purposes to which they have set themselves to be frustrated and the products of their skill and labour sunk to the bottom of the sea.

U-boat warfare as conducted by Germany is entirely contrary to international agreements freely subscribed to by Germany only a few years ago. There is no effective blockade, but only a merciless murder and marauding over wide, indiscriminate areas utterly beyond the control of the German sea power.

When I said ten weeks ago: 'Give us the tools and we will finish the job', I meant, give them to us: put them within our reach – and that is what it now seems the Americans are going to do. And that is why I feel a very strong conviction that though the Battle of the Atlantic will be long and hard, and its issue is by no means yet determined, it has entered upon a more grim but at the same time a far more favourable phase. When you come to think of it, the United States are very closely bound up with us now, and have engaged themselves deeply in giving us moral, material, and, within the limits I have mentioned, naval support.

It is worthwhile therefore to take a look on both sides of the ocean at the forces which are facing each other in this awful struggle, from which there can be no drawing back. No prudent and far-seeing man can doubt that the eventual and total defeat of Hitler and Mussolini is certain, in view of the respective declared resolves of the British and American democracies. There are less than seventy million malignant Huns – some of whom are curable and others killable – many of whom are already engaged in holding down Austrians, Czechs, Poles, French, and the many other ancient races they now bully and pillage.

The peoples of the British Empire and of the United States number nearly two hundred millions in their homelands and in the British Dominions alone. They possess the unchallengeable command of the oceans, and will soon obtain decisive superiority in the air. They have more wealth, more technical resources, and they make more steel, than the whole of the rest of the world put together. They are determined that the cause of freedom shall not be trampled down, nor the tide of world progress turned backwards, by the criminal Dictators.

While therefore we naturally view with sorrow and anxiety much that is happening in Europe and in Africa, and may happen in Asia, we must not lose our sense of proportion and thus become discouraged or alarmed. When we face with a steady eye the difficulties which lie before us, we may derive new confidence from remembering those we have already overcome. Nothing that is happening now is comparable in gravity with the dangers through which we passed last year. Nothing that can happen in the East is comparable with what is happening in the West.

Last time I spoke to you I quoted the lines of Longfellow which President Roosevelt had written out for me in his own hand. I have some other lines which are less well known but which seem apt and appropriate to our fortunes to-night, and I believe they will be so judged wherever the English language is spoken or the flag of freedom flies:

> For while the tired waves, vainly breaking,
> Seem here no painful inch to gain,
> Far back, through creeks and inlets making,
> Comes silent, flooding in, the main.
>
> And not by eastern windows only,
> When daylight comes, comes in the light;
> In front the sun climbs slow, how slowly!
> But westward, look, the land is bright.

'OUR PULSES THROB AND BEAT AS ONE'

On 16 June 1941, Churchill broadcast from the Central War Room in London to the United States: it was his acceptance speech for an honorary degree that he had been awarded by the University of Rochester in New York State. Churchill's mother had lived in Rochester as a child, but had not – as he said in his speech – been born there; she had in fact been born in Brooklyn. Churchill used the opportunity to make a powerful appeal to the Americans. The words and phrases that Churchill changed before reading the speech are shown in square brackets.

I am grateful, President Valentine, for the honour which you have conferred upon me in making me a Doctor of Laws of Rochester University in the State of New York. I am extremely complimented by the expressions of praise and commendation in which you have addressed me, not because I am or ever can be worthy of them, but because they are an expression of American confidence and affection which I shall ever strive to deserve.

But what touches me most in this ceremony is that sense of kinship and of unity which I feel exists between us this afternoon. As I speak from Downing Street to Rochester University and through you to the people of the United States, I almost feel I have the right to do so, because my mother, as you have stated, was born in your city, and here my grandfather, Leonard Jerome, lived for so many years, conducting as a prominent and rising citizen a newspaper with the excellent eighteenth-century title of the *Plain Dealer*.

The great Burke has truly said, 'People will not look forward to posterity who never look backward to their ancestors', and I feel it most agreeable to recall to you that the Jeromes were rooted for many generations in American soil, and fought in Washington's armies for the independence of the American Colonies and the foundation of the United States. I expect I was on both sides then. And I must say I feel on both sides of the Atlantic Ocean now.

At intervals during the last forty years I have addressed scores of great American audiences in almost every part of the Union. I have learnt to admire the courtesy of these audiences; their sense of fair play; their sovereign sense of humour, never minding the joke that is turned against themselves; their earnest, voracious desire to come to the root of the matter and to be well and truly informed on Old World affairs.

And now, in this time of world storm, when I have been called upon by King and Parliament and with the support of all Parties in the State to bear the chief responsibility in Great Britain, and when I have had the supreme honour of speaking for the British nation in its most deadly danger and in its finest hour, it has given me comfort and inspiration to feel that I think as you do, that our hands are joined across the oceans, and that our pulses throb and beat as one. Indeed I will make so bold as to say that here at least, in my mother's birth city of Rochester, I hold a latchkey to American hearts.

Strong tides of emotion, fierce surges of passion, sweep the broad expanses of the Union in this year of fate. In that prodigious travail there are many elemental forces, there is much heart-searching and self-questioning; some pangs, some sorrow, some conflict of voices, but no fear. The world is witnessing the birth throes of a sublime resolve. I shall presume to confess to you that I have no doubts what that resolve will be.

The [fate] destiny of mankind is not decided by material computation. When great causes are on the move in the world, stirring all men's souls, drawing them from their [hearths and homes] firesides, casting [away] aside comfort, wealth and the pursuit of happiness [for something quite out of the ordinary] in response to impulses at once [awful] awestriking and [sublime] irresistible, we learn that we are spirits, not animals, and that something is going on in space and time, and beyond space and time, which, whether we like it or not, spells duty.

A wonderful story is unfolding before our eyes. How it will end we are not allowed to know. But on both sides of the Atlantic we all feel, I repeat, all, that we are a part of it, that our future and that of many generations is at stake. We are sure that the character of human society will be shaped by the resolves we take and the deeds we do. We need not bewail the fact that we have been called upon to face such solemn responsibilities. We may be proud, and even rejoice amid our tribulations, that we have been born at this cardinal time for so great an age and so splendid an opportunity of service here below.

Wickedness, enormous, panoplied, embattled, seemingly triumphant, casts its shadow over Europe and Asia. Laws [and position], customs and traditions are broken up. Justice is cast from her seat. The rights of the weak are trampled down. The grand freedoms of which the President of the United States has spoken so movingly are spurned and chained. The whole stature of man, his genius, his [better nature] initiative and his nobility, is ground down under systems of mechanical barbarism and of organized and scheduled terror.

For more than a year we British have stood alone, uplifted by your sympathy and respect and sustained by our own unconquerable will power and by the increasing growth and hopes of your massive aid. In these [small] British Islands that look so small upon the map we stand, the faithful guardians of the rights and dearest hopes of a dozen States and nations now gripped and tormented in a base and cruel servitude. Whatever happens we shall endure to the end.

But what is the explanation of the enslavement of Europe by the German Nazi regime? How did they do it? It is but a few years ago since one united gesture by the peoples, great and small, who are now broken in the dust, would have [stood between] warded off from mankind [and] the fearful ordeal it has had to undergo. But there was no unity. There was no vision. The nations were pulled down one by one while the others gaped and chattered. One by one, each in his turn, they let themselves be caught. One after another they were felled by brutal violence or poisoned from within by subtle intrigue.

And now the old lion [and] with her lion cubs at her side stands alone against hunters who are armed with [their] deadly weapons and [held] impelled by desperate and destructive rage. Is the tragedy to repeat itself once more? Ah no. This is not the end of the tale. The stars in their courses proclaim the deliverance of mankind. Not so easily shall the onward progress of [the nations] the peoples be barred. Not so easily shall the lights of freedom die.

But time is short. Every [day] month that passes adds to the [difficulty] length & to the perils of the journey that will have to be made. United we stand. Divided we fall. [United] Divided, the dark ages return. United, [we can save mankind] we can save & guide the world.

'WE SHALL GIVE WHATEVER HELP WE CAN TO RUSSIA'

On 22 June 1941, within a week of Churchill's broadcast to the United States, Germany invaded the Soviet Union. Since August 1939, Hitler's Germany and Stalin's Soviet Union had been allies. In

October 1939 they had jointly overrun and partitioned Poland, for whose independence Britain had gone to war. With the sudden and ferocious German attack on June 22, Churchill had to decide whether or not Britain would consider the Soviet Union an ally, and give whatever aid Britain could to try to prevent a German victory. He gave his answer in a radio broadcast that night to the British people:

> The Nazi regime is indistinguishable from the worst features of Communism. It is devoid of all theme and principle except appetite and racial domination. It excels all forms of human wickedness in the efficiency of its cruelty and ferocious aggression. No one has been a more consistent opponent of Communism than I have for the last twenty-five years. I will unsay no word that I have spoken about it. But all this fades away before the spectacle which is now unfolding. The past with its crimes, its follies and its tragedies, flashes away.
>
> [···]
>
> We have but one aim and one single, irrevocable purpose. We are resolved to destroy Hitler and every vestige of the Nazi regime. From this nothing will turn us – nothing.
>
> That is our policy and that is our declaration. It follows, therefore, that we shall give whatever help we can to Russia and to the Russian people. We shall appeal to all our friends and allies in every part of the world to take the same course and pursue it, as we shall, faithfully and steadfastly to the end. We will never parley, we will never negotiate with Hitler or any of his gang. We shall fight him by land, we shall fight him by sea, we shall fight him in the air, until with God's help we have rid the earth of his shadow and liberated its peoples from his yoke.
>
> Any man or State who fights on against Nazidom will have our aid. Any man or state who marches with Hitler is our foe. This applies not only to organized states but to all representatives of that vile race of quislings who make themselves the tools and agents of the Nazi regime against their fellow-countrymen and the lands of their birth. They – these quislings – like the Nazi leaders themselves, if not disposed of by their fellow-countrymen, which would save trouble,

will be delivered by us on the morrow of victory to the justice of the Allied tribunals.

We have offered the Government of Soviet Russia any technical or economic assistance which is in our power, and which is likely to be of service to them. We shall bomb Germany by day as well as by night in ever-increasing measure, casting upon them month by month a heavier discharge of bombs, and making the German people taste and gulp each month a sharper dose of the miseries they have showered upon mankind. It is noteworthy that only yesterday the Royal Air Force, fighting inland over French territory, cut down with very small loss to themselves twenty-eight of the Hun fighting machines in the air above the French soil they have invaded, defiled and profess to hold. But this is only a beginning. From now forward the main expansion of our Air Force proceeds with gathering speed. In another six months the weight of the help we are receiving from the United States in war materials of all kinds, and especially in heavy bombers, will begin to tell.

This is no class war, but a war in which the whole British Empire and Commonwealth of Nations is engaged without distinction of race, creed or party. It is not for me to speak of the action of the United States, but this I will say: if Hitler imagines that his attack on Soviet Russia will cause the slightest division of aims or slackening of effort in the great Democracies who are resolved upon his doom, he is woefully mistaken. On the contrary, we shall be fortified and encouraged in our efforts to rescue mankind from his tyranny. We shall be strengthened and not weakened in determination and in resources.

This is no time to moralize on the follies of countries and governments which have allowed themselves to be struck down one by one, when by united action they could have saved themselves and saved the world from this catastrophe. But when I spoke a few minutes ago of Hitler's blood lust and the hateful appetites which have impelled or lured him on his Russian adventure, I said there was one deeper motive behind his outrage. He wishes to destroy the Russian power because he hopes that if he succeeds in this, he will be able to bring back the main strength of his army and air force from the East and hurl it upon this Island, which he knows he must conquer or suffer the penalty of his crimes.

His invasion of Russia is no more than a prelude to an attempted invasion of the British Isles. He hopes, no doubt, that all this may be accomplished before the winter comes, and that he can overwhelm Great Britain before the fleet and air power of the United States may intervene. He hopes that he may once again repeat, upon a greater scale than ever before, that process of destroying his enemies one by one, by which he has so long thrived and prospered, and that then the scene will be clear for the final act, without which all his conquests would be in vain – namely, the subjugation of the Western Hemisphere to his will and to his system.

The Russian danger is therefore our danger, and the danger of the United States, just as the cause of any Russian fighting for his hearth and home is the cause of free men and free peoples in every quarter of the globe. Let us learn the lessons already taught by such cruel experience. Let us redouble our exertions, and strike with united strength while life and power remain.

'NEVER GIVE IN'

When Churchill visited Harrow School on 29 October 1941, for the second time in a year, to hear the traditional songs, he learnt that an additional verse had been added to one of them, which included the lines: 'Not less we praise in darker days / The leader of our nation / And Churchill's name shall win acclaim / From each new generation.' Churchill told the boys:

Almost a year has passed since I came down here at your Head Master's kind invitation in order to cheer myself and cheer the hearts of a few of my friends by singing some of our own songs. The ten months that have passed have seen very terrible catastrophic events in the world – ups and downs, misfortunes – but can anyone sitting here this afternoon, this October afternoon, not feel deeply thankful for what has happened in the time that has passed and for the very great improvement in the position of our country and of our home?

Why, when I was here last time we were quite alone, desperately alone, and we had been so for five or six months. We were poorly armed. We are not so poorly armed today; but then we were very poorly armed. We had the unmeasured menace of the enemy and their air attack still beating upon us, and you yourselves had had experience of this attack; and I expect you are beginning to feel impatient that there has been this long lull with nothing particular turning up!

But we must learn to be equally good at what is short and sharp and what is long and tough. It is generally said that the British are often better at the last. They do not expect to move from crisis to crisis; they do not always expect that each day will bring up some noble chance of war; but when they very slowly make up their minds that the thing has to be done and the job put through and finished, then, even if it takes months, if it takes years, they do it.

Another lesson I think we may take, just throwing our minds back to our meeting here ten months ago, and know, is that appearances are often very deceptive, and as Kipling well says, we must

> . . . meet with Triumph and Disaster
> And treat those two impostors just the same.

You cannot tell from appearances how things will go. Sometimes imagination makes things out far worse than they are; yet without imagination not much can be done. Those people who are imaginative see many more dangers than perhaps exist, certainly many more than will happen: but then they must also pray to be given that extra courage to carry this far-reaching imagination. But for everyone, surely, what we have gone through in this period – I am addressing myself to the School – surely from this period of ten months this is the lesson:

Never give in. Never give in. Never, never, never – in nothing, great or small, large or petty – never give in, except to convictions of honour and good sense. Never yield to force; never yield to the apparently overwhelming might of the enemy.

We stood all alone a year ago, and to many countries it seemed that our account was closed, we were finished. All this tradition of ours, our songs, our School history, this part of the history of this country, were gone and finished and liquidated.

Very different is the mood today. Britain, other nations thought, had drawn a sponge across her slate. But instead our country stood in the gap. There was no flinching and no thought of giving in; and by what seemed almost a miracle to those outside these Islands, though we ourselves never doubted it. We now find ourselves in a position where I say that we can be sure that we have only to persevere to conquer.

You sang here a verse of a School Song; you sang that extra verse written in my honour, which I was very greatly complimented by and which you have repeated today. But there is one word in it I want to alter. I wanted to do so last year, but I did not venture to. It is the line: 'Not less we praise in darker days.' I have obtained the Head Master's permission to alter 'darker' to 'sterner': 'Not less we praise in sterner days.'

Do not let us speak of darker days; let us speak rather of sterner days. These are not dark days: these are great days – the greatest days our country has ever lived; and we must all thank God that we have been allowed, each of us according to our stations, to play a part in making these days memorable in the history of our race.

'WE HAD WON THE WAR'

On 7 December 1941, Japan attacked the United States naval base at Pearl Harbor, and moved with its naval and air forces against American possessions in the Pacific Ocean (Guam, Midway, Wake Island and the Philippines). Japanese forces also attacked British possessions in South East Asia (Hong Kong and Malaya) and the Netherlands East Indies. Looking back at this fateful moment, Churchill wrote in *The Second World War*:

No American will think it wrong of me if I proclaim that to have the United States at our side was to me the greatest joy. I could not fore- tell the course of events. I do not pretend to have measured accurately the martial might of Japan, but now at this very moment I knew the United States was in the war, up to the neck and in to the death. So we had won after all! Yes, after Dunkirk, after the fall of France; after the horrible episode of Oran; after the threat of invasion, when, apart from the Air and the Navy, we were an almost unarmed people; after the deadly struggle of the U-boat war – the first Battle of the Atlantic, gained by a hand's-breadth; after seventeen months of lonely fighting and nineteen months of my responsibility in dire stress.

We had won the war. England would live; Britain would live; the Commonwealth of Nations and the Empire would live. How long the war would last or in what fashion it would end no man could tell, nor did I at this moment care. Once again in our long Island history we should emerge, however mauled or mutilated, safe and victorious. We should not be wiped out. Our history would not come to an end. We might not even have to die as individuals.

Hitler's fate was sealed. Mussolini's fate was sealed. As for the Japanese, they would be ground to powder. All the rest was merely the proper application of overwhelming force. The British Empire, the Soviet Union, and now the United States, bound together with every scrap of their life and strength, were, according to my lights, twice or even thrice the force of their antagonists. No doubt it would take a long time. I expected terrible forfeits in the East; but all this would be merely a passing phase. United we could subdue everybody else in the world. Many disasters, immeasurable cost and tribulation lay ahead, but there was no more doubt about the end.

Silly people, and there were many, not only in enemy countries, might discount the force of the United States. Some said they were soft, others that they would never be united. They would fool around at a distance. They would never come to grips. They would never stand bloodletting. Their democracy and system of recurrent elections would paralyse their war effort. They would be just a vague blur on the horizon to friend or foe. Now we should see the weakness of this numerous but remote, wealthy, and talkative people.

But I had studied the American Civil War, fought out to the last desperate inch. American blood flowed in my veins. I thought of a remark which Edward Grey had made to me more than thirty years before – that the United States is like 'a gigantic boiler. Once the fire is lighted under it there is no limit to the power it can generate'. Being saturated and satiated with emotion and sensation, I went to bed and slept the sleep of the saved and thankful.

'A STRANGE CHRISTMAS EVE'

Germany declared war on the United States on 11 December 1941, four days after the Japanese attack on Pearl Harbor. Churchill, concerned that the United States might nevertheless focus its main energies on the war in the Pacific, left Britain by ship on December 13 for Washington, where, starting on December 22, he spent a total of fourteen days in talks with President Roosevelt, who agreed that the war in Europe and the Mediterranean would take priority over the defeat of Japan. On 24 December 1941, from Washington, he broadcast to the American people:

I spend this anniversary and festival far from my country, far from my family, yet I cannot truthfully say that I feel far from home. Whether it be the ties of blood on my mother's side, or the friendships I have developed here over many years of active life, or the commanding sentiment of comradeship in the common cause of great peoples who speak the same language, who kneel at the same altars and, to a very large extent, pursue the same ideals, I cannot feel myself a stranger here in the centre and at the summit of the United States. I feel a sense of unity and fraternal association which, added to the kindliness of your welcome, convinces me that I have a right to sit at your fireside and share your Christmas joys.

This is a strange Christmas Eve. Almost the whole world is locked in deadly struggle, and, with the most terrible weapons which science can devise, the nations advance upon each other. Ill would it be for us this Christmastide if we were not sure that no greed for the land or wealth of any other people, no vulgar ambition, no morbid lust for material gain at the expense of others, had led us to the field. Here, in the midst of war, raging and roaring over all the lands and seas, creeping nearer to our hearts and homes, here, amid all the tumult, we have tonight the peace of the spirit in each cottage home and in every generous heart. Therefore we may cast aside for this night at least the cares and dangers which beset us, and make for the children an evening of happiness in a world of storm. Here, then, for one night only, each home throughout the English-speaking world should be a brightly lighted island of happiness and peace.

Let the children have their night of fun and laughter. Let the gifts of Father Christmas delight their play. Let us grown-ups share to the full in their unstinted pleasures before we turn again to the stern task and the formidable years that lie before us, resolved that, by our sacrifice and daring, these same children shall not be robbed of their inheritance or denied their right to live in a free and decent world.

And so, in God's mercy, a happy Christmas to you all.

'PRODIGIOUS HAMMER-STROKES HAVE BEEN NEEDED'

On 26 December 1941, Churchill went to Capitol Hill, where he addressed the United States Senate and House of Representatives:

I feel greatly honoured that you should have invited me to enter the United States Senate Chamber and address the representatives of both branches of Congress. The fact that my American forebears have for so many generations played their part in the life of the United States, and that here I am, an Englishman, welcomed in your midst, makes this experience one of the most moving and thrilling in my life, which is already long and has not been entirely uneventful. I wish indeed that my mother, whose memory I cherish across the vale of years, could have been here to see.

By the way, I cannot help reflecting that if my father had been American and my mother British, instead of the other way round, I might have got here on my own. In that case, this would not have been the first time you would have heard my voice. In that case I should not have needed any invitation, but if I had, it is hardly likely it would have been unanimous. So perhaps things are better as they are. I may confess, however, that I do not feel quite like a fish out of water in a legislative assembly where English is spoken.

I am a child of the House of Commons. I was brought up in my father's house to believe in democracy. 'Trust the people' – that was his message. I used to see him cheered at meetings and in the streets by crowds of working men way back in those aristocratic Victorian days when, as Disraeli said, the world was for the few, and for the very few. Therefore I have been in full harmony all my life with the tides which have flowed on both sides of the Atlantic against privilege and monopoly, and I have steered confidently towards the Gettysburg ideal of 'government of the people by the people for the people'. I owe my advancement entirely to the House of Commons, whose servant I am. In my country, as in yours, public men are proud to be the servants of the State and would be ashamed to be its masters. On any day, if they thought the people wanted it, the House of Commons could by a simple vote remove me from my office. But I am not worrying about it at all. As a matter of fact, I am sure they will approve very highly of my journey here, for which I obtained the King's permission in order to meet the President of the United States and to arrange with him all that mapping-out of our military plans, and for all those intimate meetings of the high officers of the armed services of both countries, which are indispensable to the successful prosecution of the war.

[···]

When we consider the resources of the United States and the British Empire compared to those of Japan, when we remember those of China, which has so long and valiantly withstood invasion and when also we observe the Russian menace which hangs over Japan, it becomes still more difficult to reconcile Japanese action with prudence or even with sanity. What kind of a people do they think we are? Is it possible they do not realize that we shall never cease to persevere against them until they have been taught a lesson which they and the world will never forget?

Members of the Senate and members of the House of Representatives, I turn for one moment more from the turmoil and convulsions of the present to the broader basis of the future. Here we are together facing a group of mighty foes who seek our ruin; here we are together defending all that to free men is dear. Twice in a single generation the catastrophe of world war has fallen upon us; twice in our lifetime has the long arm of fate reached across the ocean to bring the United States into the forefront of the battle. If we had kept together after the last War, if we had taken common measures for our safety, this renewal of the curse need never have fallen upon us.

Do we not owe it to ourselves, to our children, to mankind tormented, to make sure that these catastrophes shall not engulf us for the third time? It has been proved that pestilences may break out in the Old World, which carry their destructive ravages into the New World, from which, once they are afoot, the New World cannot by any means escape. Duty and prudence alike command first that the germ-centres of hatred and revenge should be constantly and vigilantly surveyed and treated in good time, and, secondly, that an adequate organization should be set up to make sure that the pestilence can be controlled at its earliest beginnings before it spreads and rages throughout the entire earth.

Five or six years ago it would have been easy, without shedding a drop of blood, for the United States and Great Britain to have insisted on fulfilment of the disarmament clauses of the treaties which Germany signed after the Great War; that also would have been the opportunity for assuring to Germany those raw materials which we declared in the Atlantic Charter should not be denied to any nation, victor or vanquished. That chance has passed. It is gone. Prodigious hammer-strokes have been needed to bring us together again, or if you will allow me to use other language, I will say that he must indeed have a blind soul who cannot see that some great purpose and design is being worked out here below, of which we have the honour to be the faithful servants.

It is not given to us to peer into the mysteries of the future. Still, I avow my hope and faith, sure and inviolate, that in the days to come the British and American peoples will for their own safety and for the good of all walk together side by side in majesty, in justice, and in peace.

'SOME CHICKEN! SOME NECK!'

Churchill broke off his talks in Washington to travel by train to the Canadian capital, Ottawa, where he addressed the Canadian Parliament on 30 December 1941. He had first visited Canada on his North American lecture tour of 1900, and had returned in 1929 for a holiday, travelling from coast to coast. This was his third visit:

It is with feelings of pride and encouragement that I find myself here in the House of Commons of Canada, invited to address the Parliament of the senior Dominion of the Crown.

I bring you the assurance of good will and affection from every one in the Motherland. We are most grateful for all you have done in the common cause, and we know that you are resolved to do whatever more is possible as the need arises and as opportunity serves. Canada occupies a unique position in the British Empire because of its unbreakable ties with Britain and its ever-growing friendship and intimate association with the United States. Canada is a potent magnet, drawing together those in the new world and in the old whose fortunes are now united in a deadly struggle for life and honour against the common foe. The contribution of Canada to the Imperial war effort in troops, in ships, in aircraft, in food, and in finance has been magnificent.

[· · ·]

We did not make this war, we did not seek it. We did all we could to avoid it. We did too much to avoid it. We went so far at times in trying to avoid it as to be almost destroyed by it when it broke upon us. But that dangerous corner has been turned, and with every month and every year that passes we shall confront the evil-doers with weapons as plentiful, as sharp, and as destructive as those with which they have sought to establish their hateful domination.

I should like to point out to you that we have not at any time asked for any mitigation in the fury or malice of the enemy. The peoples of the British Empire may love peace. They do not seek the lands or wealth of any country, but they are a tough and hardy lot. We have not journeyed all this way across the centuries, oceans, across the mountains, across the prairies, because we are made of sugar candy.

Look at the Londoners, the Cockneys: look at what they have stood up to. Grim and gay with their cry 'We can take it,' and their war-time mood of 'What is good enough for anybody is good enough for us.' We have not asked that the rules of the game should be modified. We shall never descend to the German and Japanese level, but if anybody likes to play rough we can play rough too. Hitler and his Nazi gang have sown the wind; let them reap the whirlwind. Neither the length of the struggle nor any form of severity which it may assume shall make us weary or shall make us quit.

I have been all this week with the President of the United States, that great man whom destiny has marked for this climax of human fortune. We have been concerting the united pacts and resolves of more than thirty States and nations to fight on in unity together and in fidelity one to another, without any thought except the total and final extirpation of the Hitler tyranny, the Japanese frenzy, and the Mussolini flop.

There shall be no halting, or half measures, there shall be no compromise, or parley. These gangs of bandits have sought to darken the light of the world; have sought to stand between the common people of all the lands and their march forward into their inheritance. They shall themselves be cast into the pit of death and shame, and only when the earth has been cleansed and purged of their crimes and their villainy shall we turn from the task which they have forced upon us; a task which we were reluctant to undertake, but which we shall now most faithfully and punctiliously discharge.

According to my sense of proportion, this is no time to speak of the hopes of the future, or the broader world which lies beyond our struggles and our victory. We have to win that world for our children. We have to win it by our sacrifices. We have not won it yet. The crisis is upon us. The power of the enemy is immense. If we were in any way to underrate the strength, the resources or the ruthless savagery of that enemy, we should jeopardize, not only our lives, for they will be offered freely, but the cause of human freedom and progress to which we have vowed ourselves and all we have. We cannot for a moment afford to relax. On the contrary we must drive ourselves forward with unrelenting zeal. In this strange, terrible world war there is a place for everyone, man and woman, old and young, hale and halt; service in a thousand forms is open.

There is no room now for the dilettante, the weakling, for the shirker, or the sluggard. The mine, the factory, the dockyard, the salt sea waves, the fields to till, the home, the hospital, the chair of the scientist, the pulpit of the preacher – from the highest to the humblest tasks, all are of equal honour; all have their part to play.

The enemies ranged against us – coalesced and combined against us – have asked for total war. Let us make sure they get it.

[···]

We plunged into this war all unprepared because we had pledged our word to stand by the side of Poland, which Hitler had feloniously invaded, and in spite of a gallant resistance had soon struck down. There followed those astonishing seven months which were called on this side of the Atlantic the 'phony' war. Suddenly the explosion of pent-up German strength and preparation burst upon Norway, Denmark, Holland and Belgium. All these absolutely blameless neutrals, to most of whom Germany up to the last moment was giving every kind of guarantee and assurance, were overrun and trampled down.

On top of all this came the great French catastrophe. The French Army collapsed, and the French nation was dashed into utter and, as it has so far proved, irretrievable confusion. The French Government had at their own suggestion solemnly bound themselves with us not to make a separate peace. It was their duty and it was also their interest to go to North Africa, where they would have been at the head of the French Empire. In Africa, with our aid, they would have had overwhelming sea power. They would have had the recognition of the United States, and the use of all the gold they had lodged beyond the seas. If they had done this Italy might have been driven out of the war before the end of 1940, and France would have held her place as a nation in the counsels of the Allies and at the conference table of the victors. But their generals misled them. When I warned them that Britain would fight on alone whatever they did, their generals told their Prime Minister and his divided Cabinet, 'In three weeks England will have her neck wrung like a chicken.' Some chicken! Some neck!

[· · ·]

What a contrast has been the behaviour of the valiant, stout-hearted Dutch, who still stand forth as a strong living partner in the struggle! Their venerated Queen and their Government are in England, their Princess and her children have found asylum and protection here in your midst. But the Dutch nation are defending their Empire with dogged courage and tenacity by land and sea and in the air. Their submarines are inflicting a heavy daily toll upon the Japanese robbers who have come across the seas to steal the wealth of the East Indies, and to ravage and exploit its fertility and its civilization. The British Empire and the United States are going to the aid of the Dutch. We are going to fight out this new war against Japan together. We have suffered together and we shall conquer together.

But the men of Bordeaux, the men of Vichy, they would do nothing like this. They lay prostrate at the foot of the conqueror. They fawned upon him. What have they got out of it? The fragment of France which was left to them is just as powerless, just as hungry as, and even more miserable, because more divided, than the occupied regions themselves. Hitler plays from day to day a cat-and-mouse game with these tormented men. One day he will charge them a little less for holding their countrymen down. Another day he will let out a few thousand broken prisoners of war from the one-and-a-half or one-and-three-quarter millions he has collected. Or again he will shoot a hundred French hostages to give them a taste of the lash. On these blows and favours the Vichy Government have been content to live from day to day. But even this will not go on indefinitely. At any moment it may suit Hitler's plans to brush them away. Their only guarantee is Hitler's good faith, which, as everyone knows, biteth like the adder and stingeth like the asp.

But some Frenchmen there were who would not bow their knees and who under General de Gaulle have continued the fight on the side of the Allies. They have been condemned to death by the men of Vichy, but their names will be held and are being held in increasing respect by nine Frenchmen out of every ten throughout the once happy, smiling land of France. But now strong forces are at hand. The tide has turned against the Hun. Britain, which the men of Bordeaux thought and then hoped would soon be finished, Britain with her Empire around her carried the weight of the war alone for a whole long year through the darkest part of the valley. She is growing stronger every day. You can see it here in Canada. Anyone who has the slightest knowledge of our affairs is aware that very soon we shall be superior in every form of equipment to those who have taken us at the disadvantage of being but half-armed.

[···]

As I speak this afternoon an important battle is being fought around Jedabia. We must not attempt to prophesy its result, but I have good confidence. All this fighting in Libya proves that when our men have equal weapons in their hands and proper support from the air they are more than a match for the Nazi hordes. In Libya, as in Russia, events of great importance and of most hopeful import have taken place. But greatest of all, the mighty Republic of the United States has entered the conflict, and entered it in a manner which shows that for her there can be no withdrawal except by death or victory.

Churchill then spoke in French:

[Translation:] And everywhere in France, occupied and unoccupied, for their fate is identical, these honest folk, this great people, the French nation, are rising again. Hope is springing up again in the hearts of a warrior race even though disarmed, cradle of revolutionary liberty and terrible to slavish conquerors. And everywhere dawn is breaking and light spreading, reddish yet, but clear. We shall never lose confidence that France will play the role of free men again and, by hard paths, will once again attain her place in the great company of freedom-bringing and victorious nations. Here in Canada, where the French language is honoured and spoken, we are armed and ready to help and to hail this national resurrection.

Now that the whole of the North American continent is becoming one gigantic arsenal, and armed camp; now that the immense reserve power of Russia is gradually becoming apparent; now that long-suffering, unconquerable China sees help approaching; now that the outraged and subjugated nations can see daylight ahead, it is permissible to take a broad forward view of the war.

[···]

Churchill's speech continued in English:

I feel it is right at this moment to make it clear that, while an ever-increasing bombing offensive against Germany will remain one of the principal methods by which we hope to bring the war to an end, it is by no means the only method which our growing strength now enables us to take into account.

Evidently the most strenuous exertions must be made by all. As to the form which those exertions take, that is for each partner in the grand alliance to judge for himself in consultation with others and in harmony with the general scheme. Let us then address ourselves to our task, not in any way underrating its tremendous difficulties and perils, but in good heart and sober confidence, resolved that, whatever the cost, whatever the suffering, we shall stand by one another, true and faithful comrades, and do our duty God helping us, to the end.

'HAVOC CONTINUED TO REIGN'

The British ability to read top-secret German signals had led, in 1941, to a dramatic drop in German U-boat sinkings. But at the beginning of 1942, the German Navy's top-secret signalling system changed, and for the rest of that year there was no way in which the Allies could know in advance where the U-boats would be ordered to strike. While not able to reveal this fact in *The Second World War* – or to explain how the German Navy's codes were again broken for good at the beginning of 1943 – Churchill was able to convey in his memoirs the seriousness of the situation in the Atlantic throughout 1942:

We had greeted the entry of the United States into the war with relief and an uprising of spirit. Henceforth our load would be shared by a partner of almost unlimited resources and we might hope that in the war at sea the U-boats would soon be brought under control. With American help our Atlantic lifeline would become secure, although losses must be expected until the full power of our Ally was engaged. Thus preserved, we could prosecute the war against Hitler in Europe and in the Middle East. The Far East would for the time be the darkest scene.

But the year 1942 was to provide many rude shocks and prove in the Atlantic the toughest of the whole war. By the end of 1941 the U-boat fleet had grown to nearly two hundred and fifty, of which Admiral Doenitz could report nearly a hundred operational, with a monthly addition of fifteen. At first our joint defences, although much stronger than when we stood alone, proved unequal to the new assault upon what had now become a much larger target. For six or seven months the U-boats ravaged American waters almost un-controlled, and in fact almost brought us to the disaster of an indefinite prolongation of the war. Had we been forced to suspend, or even seriously to restrict for a time, the movement of shipping in the Atlantic all our joint plans would have been arrested.

[···]

In the Caribbean Sea, amid a wealth of targets, the U-boats chose to prey chiefly on the tankers. Neutrals of all kinds were assailed equally with Allied ships. Week by week the scale of this massacre grew. In February the U-boat losses in the Atlantic rose to seventy-one ships, of 384,000 tons, all but two of which were sunk in the American zone. This was the highest rate of loss which we had so far suffered throughout the war. It was soon to be surpassed.

All this destruction, far exceeding anything known in this war, though not reaching the catastrophic figures of the worst period of 1917, was caused by no more than twelve to fifteen boats working in the area at one time. The protection afforded by the United States Navy was for several months hopelessly inadequate. It is surprising indeed that during two years of the advance of total war towards the American continent more provision had not been made against this deadly onslaught. Under the President's policy of 'all aid to Britain short of war' much had been done for us. We had acquired the fifty old destroyers and the ten American Revenue cutters. In exchange we had given the invaluable West Indian bases. But the vessels were now sadly missed by our Ally. After Pearl Harbor the Pacific pressed heavily on the United States Navy. Still, with all the information they had about the protective measures we had adopted, both before and during the struggle, it is remarkable that no plans had been made for coastal convoys and for multiplying small craft.

[···]

Meanwhile havoc continued to reign along the Atlantic coast of the United States. A U-boat commander reported to Doenitz that ten times as many U-boats could find ample targets. Resting on the bottom during daylight, the U-boats used their high surface speed at night to select the richest prey. Nearly every torpedo they carried claimed its victim, and when torpedoes were expended the gun was almost equally effective. The towns of the Atlantic shore, where for a while the waterfronts remained fully lighted, heard nightly the sounds of battle near the coast, saw the burning, sinking ships off-shore, and rescued the survivors and wounded. There was bitter anger against the Administration, which was much embarrassed. It is however easier to infuriate Americans than to cow them.

[···]

On February 10 we offered unasked twenty-four of our best-equipped anti-submarine trawlers and ten corvettes with their trained crews to the American Navy. These were welcomed by our Ally, and the first arrived in New York early in March. It was little enough, but the utmost we could spare. "Twas all she gave – 'twas all she had to give.' Coastal convoys could not begin until the necessary organisation had been built up and the essential minimum escorts gathered. The available fighting ships and aircraft were at first used only to patrol threatened areas. The enemy, easily evading the patrols, pursued their defenceless prey elsewhere. On February 16 a U-boat appeared off the great oil port of Aruba, in the Dutch West Indies, and, after sinking one small tanker and damaging another, shelled the installations ashore from outside the harbour, without causing serious damage. An attempt to torpedo a large tanker lying alongside also failed. The same day other U-boats sank three more tankers at sea in the same area. Soon afterwards another U-boat entered the British harbour of Trinidad, sank two ships at anchor, and withdrew unharmed. This latter incident forced us to divert the liners transporting troops to the Far East, which frequently refuelled there. By good fortune neither the *Queen Mary* nor any other of these great ships was attacked in this area.

In March the main stress fell in the area between Charleston and New York, while single U-boats prowled over all the Caribbean and the Gulf of Mexico, with a freedom and insolence which were hard to bear. During this month the sinkings were nearly half a million tons, of which three-quarters was sunk within three hundred miles of the American coast, and nearly half was in tanker tonnage. Against this could only be set the loss of two U-boats in American waters sunk by American aircraft on ocean convoy escort off Newfoundland in March.

[···]

In August the U-boats turned their attention to the area around Trinidad and the north coast of Brazil, where the ships carrying bauxite to the United States for the aircraft industry and the stream of outward-bound ships with supplies for the Middle East offered the most attractive targets. Other roving U-boats were at work near Freetown; some ranged as far south as the Cape of Good Hope, and a few even penetrated into the Indian Ocean. For a time the South Atlantic caused us anxiety. Here in September and October five large homeward-bound liners sailing independently were sunk, but all our troop transports outward-bound for the Middle East in convoy came through unscathed. Among the big ships lost was the *Laconia*, of nearly 20,000 tons, carrying two thousand Italian prisoners of war to England. Many were drowned.

The main battle was by now once more joined along the great convoy routes in the North Atlantic. The U-boats had already learned to respect the power of the air, and in their new assault they worked almost entirely in the central section, beyond the reach of aircraft based on Iceland and Newfoundland. Two convoys were severely mauled in August, one of them losing eleven ships, and during this month U-boats sank 108 ships, amounting to over half a million tons. In September and October the Germans reverted to the earlier practice of submerged attack by day. With the larger numbers now working in the 'wolf packs', and with our limited resources, serious losses in convoy could not be prevented.

[···]

So menacing were the conditions in the outer waters beyond the range of air cover that on November 4, I personally convened a new Anti-U-boat Committee to deal specially with this aspect. The power of this body to take far-reaching decisions played no small part in the conflict. In a great effort to lengthen the range of our Radar-carrying Liberator aircraft, we decided to withdraw them from action for the time needed to make the necessary improvements. As part of this policy the President at my request sent all suitable American aircraft, fitted with the latest type of Radar, to work from the United Kingdom. Thus we were presently able to resume operations in the Bay of Biscay in greater strength and with far better equipment. This decision, and other measures taken in November 1942, were to reap their reward in 1943.

[···]

The Battle of the Atlantic was the dominating factor all through the war. Never for one moment could we forget that everything happening elsewhere, on land, at sea, or in the air, depended ultimately on its outcome, and amid all other cares we viewed its changing fortunes day by day with hope or apprehension. The tale of hard and unremitting toil, often under conditions of acute discomfort and frustration and always in the presence of unseen danger, is lighted by incident and drama. But for the individual sailor or airman in the U-boat war there were few moments of exhilarating action to break the monotony of an endless succession of anxious, uneventful days. Vigilance could never be relaxed. Dire crisis might at any moment flash upon the scene with brilliant fortune or glare with mortal tragedy. Many gallant actions and incredible feats of endurance are recorded, but the deeds of those who perished will never be known. Our merchant seamen displayed their highest qualities, and the brotherhood of the sea was never more strikingly shown than in their determination to defeat the U-boat.

'TONIGHT THE JAPANESE
ARE TRIUMPHANT'

On 15 February 1942, General Percival, commanding the British and Dominion troops in Singapore, surrendered unconditionally to the Japanese. This devastating blow for Britain took place only four days after three German battle cruisers, *Scharnhorst, Gneisenau* and *Prinz Eugen*, had managed to sail in daylight from the Atlantic coast port of Brest through the English Channel to their German home ports. There was considerable public unease in Britain at this turn of events. On the night of the fall of Singapore, Churchill broadcast to the British people, and to the world, giving a comprehensive survey of the war thus far, culminating in the fall of Singapore:

Nearly six months have passed since at the end of August, I made a broadcast directly to my fellow-countrymen; it is therefore worthwhile looking back over this half-year of struggle for life, for that is what it has been, and what it is, to see what has happened to our fortunes and to our prospects.

At that time in August, I had the pleasure of meeting the President of the United States and drawing up with him the declaration of British and American policy which has become known to the world as the Atlantic Charter. We also settled a number of other things about the war, some of which have had an important influence upon its course. In those days we met on the terms of a hard-pressed combatant seeking assistance from a great friend who was, however, only a benevolent neutral.

In those days the Germans seemed to be tearing the Russian armies to pieces and striding on with growing momentum to Leningrad, to Moscow, to Rostov, and even farther into the heart of Russia. It was thought a very daring assertion when the President declared that the Russian armies would hold out till the winter. You may say that the military men of all countries – friend, foe, and neutral alike – were very doubtful whether this would come true.

As for us, our British resources were stretched to the utmost. We had already been for more than a whole year absolutely alone in the struggle with Hitler and Mussolini. We had to be ready to meet a German invasion of our own Island; we had to defend Egypt, the Nile Valley and the Suez Canal. Above all we had to bring in across the Atlantic in the teeth of the German and Italian U-boats and aircraft the food, raw materials and finished munitions without which we could not live, without which we could not wage war. We have to do all this still.

It seemed our duty in those August days to do everything in our power to help the Russian people to meet the prodigious onslaught which had been launched against them. It is little enough we have done for Russia, considering all she has done to beat Hitler and for the common cause. In these circumstances, we British had no means whatever of providing effectively against a new war with Japan. Such was the outlook when I talked with President Roosevelt in the middle of August on board the good ship *Prince of Wales*, now, alas, sunk beneath the waves. It is true that our position in August 1941 seemed vastly better than it had been a year earlier in 1940, when France had just been beaten into the awful prostration in which she now lies, when we were almost entirely unarmed in our own Island, and when it looked as if Egypt and all the Middle East would be conquered by the Italians who still held Abyssinia and had newly driven us out of British Somaliland.

Compared with those days of 1940, when all the world except ourselves thought we were down and out for ever, the situation the President and I surveyed in August 1941 was an enormous improvement. Still, when you looked at it bluntly and squarely – with the United States neutral and fiercely divided, with the Russian armies falling back with grievous losses, with the German military power triumphant and unscathed, with the Japanese menace assuming an uglier shape each day – it certainly seemed a very bleak and anxious scene.

How do matters stand now? Taking it all in all, are our chances of survival better or are they worse than in August 1941? How is it with the British Empire or Commonwealth of Nations? Are we up or down? What has happened to the principles of freedom and decent civilisation for which we are fighting? Are they making headway, or are they in greater peril?

Let us take the rough with the smooth, let us put the good and bad side by side, and let us try to see exactly where we are. The first and greatest of events is that the United States is now unitedly and whole-heartedly in the war with us. The other day, I crossed the Atlantic again to see President Roosevelt. This time we met not only as friends, but as comrades standing side by side and shoulder to shoulder in a battle for dear life and dearer honour in the common cause and against a common foe.

When I survey and compute the power of the United States and its vast resources and feel that they are now in it with us, with the British Commonwealth of Nations all together, however long it lasts, till death or victory, I cannot believe there is any other fact in the whole world which can compare with that. That is what I have dreamed of, aimed at and worked for, and now it has come to pass. But there is another fact, in some ways more immediately effective. The Russian armies have not been defeated, they have not been torn to pieces.

The Russian people have not been conquered or destroyed. Leningrad and Moscow have not been taken. The Russian armies are in the field. They are not holding the line of the Urals or the line of the Volga. They are advancing victoriously, driving the foul invader from that native soil they have guarded so bravely and loved so well. More than that: for the first time they have broken the Hitler legend. Instead of the easy victories and abundant booty which he and his hordes had gathered in the West, he has found in Russia so far only disaster, failure, the shame of unspeakable crimes, the slaughter or loss of vast numbers of German soldiers, and the icy wind that blows across the Russian snow.

Here, then, are two tremendous fundamental facts which will in the end dominate the world situation and make victory possible in a form never possible before. But there is another heavy and terrible side to the account, and this must be set in the balance against these inestimable gains. Japan has plunged into the war, and is ravaging the beautiful, fertile, prosperous, and densely populated lands of the Far East. It would never have been in the power of Great Britain while fighting Germany and Italy – the nations long hardened and prepared for war – while fighting in the North Sea, in the Mediterranean and in the Atlantic – it would never have been in our power to defend the

Pacific and the Far East single-handed against the onslaught of Japan.

We have only just been able to keep our heads above water at home; only by a narrow margin have we brought in the food and the supplies; only by so little have we held our own in the Nile Valley and the Middle East. The Mediterranean is closed, and all our transports have to go round the Cape of Good Hope, each ship making only three voyages in the year.

Not a ship, not an aeroplane, not a tank, not an anti-tank gun or an anti-aircraft gun has stood idle. Everything we have has been deployed either against the enemy or awaiting his attack. We are struggling hard in the Libyan Desert, where perhaps another serious battle will soon be fought. We have to provide for the safety and order of liberated Abyssinia, of conquered Eritrea, of Palestine, of liberated Syria, and redeemed Iraq, and of our new ally, Persia. A ceaseless stream of ships, men, and materials has flowed from this country for a year and a half, in order to build up and sustain our armies in the Middle East, which guard those vast regions on either side of the Nile Valley.

We had to do our best to give substantial aid to Russia. We gave it her in her darkest hour, and we must not fail in our undertaking now. How then in this posture, gripped and held and battered as we were, could we have provided for the safety of the Far East against such an avalanche of fire and steel as has been hurled upon us by Japan? Always, my friends, this thought overhung our minds.

There was, however, one hope and one hope only – namely that if Japan entered the war with her allies, Germany and Italy, the United States would come in on our side, thus far more than repairing the balance. For this reason, I have been most careful, all these many months, not to give any provocation to Japan, and to put up with Japanese encroachments, dangerous though they were, so that if possible, whatever happened, we should not find ourselves forced to face this new enemy alone. I could not be sure that we should succeed in this policy, but it has come to pass. Japan has struck her felon blow, and a new, far greater champion has drawn the sword of implacable vengeance against her and on our side.

I shall frankly state to you that I did not believe it was in the interests of Japan to burst into war both upon the British Empire and the United States. I thought it would be a very irrational act. Indeed, when you remember that they did not attack us after Dunkirk when we were so much weaker, when our hopes of United States help were of the most slender character, and when we were all alone, I could hardly believe that they would commit what seemed to be a mad act. Tonight the Japanese are triumphant. They shout their exultation round the world. We suffer. We are taken aback. We are hard pressed. But I am sure even in this dark hour that 'criminal madness' will be the verdict which history will pronounce upon the authors of Japanese aggression, after the events of 1942 and 1943 have been inscribed upon its sombre pages.

The immediate deterrent which the United States exercised upon Japan – apart of course from the measureless resources of the American Union – was the dominant American battle fleet in the Pacific, which, with the naval forces we could spare, confronted Japanese aggression with the shield of superior sea-power. But, my friends, by an act of sudden violent surprise, long-calculated, balanced and prepared, and delivered under the crafty cloak of nego-tiation, the shield of sea-power which protected the fair lands and islands of the Pacific Ocean was for the time being, and only for the time being, dashed to the ground. Into the gap thus opened rushed the invading armies of Japan. We were exposed to the assault of a warrior race of nearly eighty millions, with a large outfit of modern weapons, whose war lords had been planning and scheming for this day, and looking forward to it perhaps for twenty years while all the time our good people on both sides of the Atlantic were prating about perpetual peace, and cutting down each other's navies in order to set a good example. The overthrow, for a while, of British and United States sea-power in the Pacific was like the breaking of some mighty dam; the long-gathered pent-up waters rushed down the peaceful valley, carrying ruin and devastation forward on their foam, and spreading their inundations far and wide.

No one must underrate any more the gravity and efficiency of the Japanese war machine. Whether in the air or upon the sea, or man to man on land, they have already proved themselves to be formidable, deadly, and, I am sorry to say, barbarous antagonists. This proves a hundred times over that there never was the slightest chance, even though we had been much better prepared in many ways than we were, of our standing up to them alone while we had Nazi Germany at our throat and Fascist Italy at our belly.

It proves something else. And this should be a comfort and a reassurance. We can now measure the wonderful strength of the Chinese people who under Generalissimo Chiang Kai-shek have single-handed fought this hideous Japanese aggressor for four and a half years and left him baffled and dismayed. This they have done, although they were a people whose whole philosophy for many ages was opposed to war and warlike arts, and who in their agony were caught ill-armed, ill-supplied with munitions, and hopelessly outmatched in the air.

We must not underrate the power and malice of our latest foe, but neither must we undervalue the gigantic, overwhelming forces which now stand in the line with us in this world-struggle for freedom, and which, once they have developed their full natural inherent power, whatever has happened in the meanwhile, will be found fully capable of squaring all accounts and setting all things right for a good long time to come.

You know I have never prophesied to you or promised smooth and easy things, and now all I have to offer is hard adverse war for many months ahead. I must warn you, as I warned the House of Commons before they gave me their generous vote of confidence a fortnight ago, that many misfortunes, severe torturing losses, remorseless and gnawing anxieties lie before us. To our British folk these may seem even harder to bear when they are at a great distance than when the savage Hun was shattering our cities and we all felt in the midst of the battle ourselves. But the same qualities which brought us through the awful jeopardy of the summer of 1940 and its long autumn and winter bombardment from the air, will bring us through this other new ordeal, though it may be more costly and will certainly be longer.

One fault, one crime, and one crime only, can rob the United Nations and the British people, upon whose constancy this grand alliance came into being, of the victory upon which their lives and honour depend. A weakening in our purpose and therefore in our unity – that is the mortal crime. Whoever is guilty of that crime, or of bringing it about in others, of him let it be said that it were better for him that a millstone were hanged about his neck and he were cast into the sea.

Last autumn, when Russia was in her most dire peril, when vast numbers of her soldiers had been killed or taken prisoner, when one-third of her whole munitions capacity lay, as it still lies, in Nazi German hands, when Kiev fell, and the foreign Ambassadors were ordered out of Moscow, the Russian people did not fall to bickering among themselves. They just stood together and worked and fought all the harder. They did not lose trust in their leaders; they did not try to break up their Government. Hitler had hoped to find quislings and fifth columnists in the wide regions he overran, and among the unhappy masses who fell into his power. He looked for them. He searched for them. But he found none.

The system upon which the Soviet Government is founded is very different from ours or from that of the United States. However that may be, the fact remains that Russia received blows which her friends feared and her foes believed were mortal, and through preserving national unity and persevering undaunted, Russia has had the marvellous comeback for which we thank God now. In the English-speaking world we rejoice in free institutions. We have free parliaments and a free press. This is the way of life we have been used to. This is the way of life we are fighting to defend. But it is the duty of all who take part in those free institutions to make sure, as the House of Commons and the House of Lords have done, and will I doubt not do, that the National Executive Government in time of war have a solid foundation on which to stand and on which to act; that the misfortuncs and mistakes of war are not exploited against them; that while they are kept up to the mark by helpful and judicious criticism or advice, they are not deprived of the persisting power to run through a period of bad times and many cruel vexations and come out on the other side and get to the top of the hill.

Tonight I speak to you at home; I speak to you in Australia and New Zealand, for whose safety we will strain every nerve; to our loyal friends in India and Burma: to our gallant Allies, the Dutch and Chinese; and to our kith and kin in the United States. I speak to you all under the shadow of a heavy and far-reaching military defeat. It is a British and Imperial defeat.

Singapore has fallen. All the Malay Peninsula has been overrun. Other dangers gather about us out there, and none of the dangers which we have hitherto successfully withstood at home and in the East are in any way diminished. This, therefore, is one of those moments when the British race and nation can show their quality and their genius. This is one of those moments when it can draw from the heart of misfortune the vital impulses of victory. Here is the moment to display that calm and poise combined with grim determination which not so long ago brought us out of the very jaws of death. Here is another occasion to show as so often in our long story that we can meet reverses with dignity and with renewed accessions of strength. We must remember that we are no longer alone.

We are in the midst of a great company. Three-quarters of the human race are now moving with us. The whole future of mankind may depend upon our action and upon our conduct. So far we have not failed. We shall not fail now. Let us move forward steadfastly together into the storm and through the storm.

'TESTING, TRYING, ADVERSE, PAINFUL TIMES LIE AHEAD'

On 23 April 1942, Churchill addressed an anxious House of Commons in Secret Session. No journalists or members of the public were allowed in the Chamber. Having outlined the recent course of the war on land, at sea and in the air, in both Europe and the Far East, he continued, looking to the future:

Everything goes to show that perhaps even before the end of May Hitler will hurl a renewed offensive upon Russia, and there are no indications which contradict the general impression that his main thrust will be towards the Caspian and the Caucasus. We do not know what reserves the Russians have gathered. Everybody has always underrated the Russians. They keep their own secrets alike from foe and friends. The renewed German onslaught will start this year perhaps somewhat earlier and certainly a good deal farther east than last year. But this time there will be no surprise on the Russian side.

Terrible injuries have been inflicted during the winter by the Russian armies, not only upon the German military power, but biting and searing deep into the whole life of the Nazi regime. With all its power and organization, it is a haggard Germany that Hitler leads into this new, ferocious, and sanguinary campaign against Russia. Behind lies a Europe writhing with hatred and thirsting for revolt.

What can we do to help Russia? There is nothing that we would not do. If the sacrifice of thousands of British lives would turn the scale, our fellow countrymen would not flinch. But at this present time there are two important contributions we can make. The first is the supply of munitions to the utmost extent which our shipping can carry. We have hitherto not failed in any way in the immense under-takings which we made to Stalin.

It is not, however, only a question of giving up what we need ourselves, but of carrying it there safely and punctually. Our northern convoys are a task of enormous difficulty and hazard. For the next few weeks the ice drifts lower and lower, and the channel between the ice floes and the North Cape becomes narrower. We convoy not only our own contribution but that of the United States, which to a large extent is taken from what the United States would otherwise have given us. Our ships and their escorts, the heaviest we have ever used, are pressed by the ice ever nearer to the shores of Norway, and large numbers of German U-boats and powerful air forces can strike continually at the merchant ships and their guardians.

There is a further serious complication – the *Tirpitz*, the *Scheer* and the *Hipper* lie in Trondheim fiord. Every British–American convoy to Russia is liable to attack by swift, heavy, modern German surface ships. Battleship escort has to be provided on every occasion. The enemy has great opportunities, by threatening attack upon the convoys and laying traps of U-boats, of inflicting vital losses upon our fleet. Serious risks are run by our great ships – so few, so precious – only one where in the last war there was a squadron of eight – every time they go north on this perilous duty; at any time the Admiralty or even the Minister of Defence may have to account to you for some loss which would take five years to replace.

I cannot speak of our naval dispositions further than to say that the United States are with us on this. It is a grim and bitter effort amid fearful gales and ceaseless perils, but if it be in human power we will carry our tanks, our aircraft, and all the other essential supplies to our heroic ally in his sublime struggle.

There is another immediate way in which we can help. While the German armies will be bleeding copiously upon a two-thousand-mile front in the East we shall be on their backs in the German homeland. The British bombing offensive upon Germany has begun. Half a dozen German cities have already received the full measure that they meted out to Coventry. Another thirty or more are on the list. We have improved methods of finding the targets and built-up areas by night. The wastage of bombs has been reduced, perhaps by half.

Daylight thrusts far into the heart of Germany, striking with deadly precision at the most sensitive industrial spots – such as the immortal feat of arms on Friday last – will be launched upon the enemy. Presently – indeed, quite soon – heavy United States formations will be established here in England and will work at our side. This summer and autumn, aye, and winter, too, Germany will experience scientific and accurate bombing of a weight and upon a scale and frequency which none of the nations they have maltreated has ever endured. We must not let false guides divert our minds from these major and terrible strokes of war, or tempt us to fritter away the solid mass of our endeavour.

[···]

When I went to the United States in December last, I proposed to the President the preparation of a combined British and American invasion of German-occupied Europe for the liberation of its enslaved peoples and for the ultimate destruction of Hitlerism. The war cannot be ended by driving Japan back to her own bounds and defeating her overseas forces. The war can only be ended through the defeat in Europe of the German armies, or through internal convulsions in Germany produced by the unfavourable course of the war, economic privations, and the Allied bombing offensive.

As the strength of the United States, Great Britain, and Russia develops and begins to be realized by the Germans, an internal collapse is always possible, but we must not count upon this. Our plans must proceed upon the assumption that the resistance of the German Army and Air Force will continue at its present level and that their U-boat warfare will be conducted by increasingly numerous flotillas.

We have, therefore, to prepare for the liberation of the captive countries of western and southern Europe by the landing at suitable points, successively or simultaneously, of British and American armies strong enough to enable the conquered populations to revolt. By themselves they will never be able to revolt, owing to the ruthless countermeasures that will be employed: but if adequate and suitably equipped forces were landed in several of the following countries, namely, Norway, Denmark, Holland, Belgium, and the French Channel coasts and the French Atlantic coasts, as well as Italy and possibly the Balkans, the German garrisons would prove insufficient to cope both with the strength of the liberating forces and the fury of the revolting peoples.

It is impossible for the Germans, while we retain the sea power necessary to choose the place or places of attack, to have sufficient troops in each of these countries for effective resistance. In particular, they cannot move their armour about laterally from north to south or west to east: either they must divide it between the various conquered countries – in which case it would become hopelessly dispersed – or they must hold it back in a central position in Germany, in which case it will not arrive until large and important lodgments have been made by us from overseas.

We had expected to find United States attention concentrated upon the war with Japan, and we prepared ourselves to argue that the defeat of Japan would not spell the defeat of Hitler, but that the defeat of Hitler left the finishing off of Japan merely a matter of time and trouble. We were relieved to find that these simple but classical conceptions of war, although vehemently opposed by the powerful isolationalist faction, were earnestly and spontaneously shared by the government and dominant forces in the United States. The visit of General Marshall and Mr. Hopkins was to concert with us the largest and the swiftest measures of this offensive character.

It will no doubt become common knowledge that the liberation of the Continent by equal numbers of British and American troops is the main war plan of our two nations. The timing, the scale, the method, the direction of this supreme undertaking must remain unknown and unknowable till the hour strikes and the blows fall. More than that I cannot say – except that in the early hours of this morning, I received a message from the President of which, since we are in Secret Session, I will read the material part:

'I am delighted with the agreement which was reached between you and your military advisers and Marshall and Hopkins. They have reported to me of the unanimity of opinion relative to the proposal which they carried with them and I appreciate ever so much your personal message confirming this. I believe that this move will be very disheartening to Hitler and may well be the wedge by which his down-fall will be accomplished. I am very heartened at the prospect and you can be sure that our army will approach the matter with great enthusiasm and vigour. While our mutual difficulties are many, I am frank to say that I feel better about the war than at any time in the past two years.'

Testing, trying, adverse, painful times lie ahead of us. We must all strive to do our duty to the utmost of our strength. As the war rises remorselessly to its climax, the House of Commons, which is the foundation of the British life struggle – this House of Commons which has especial responsibilities – will have the opportunity once again of proving to the world that the firmness of spirit, sense of proportion, steadfastness of purpose which have gained it renown in former days, will now once again carry great peoples and a greater cause to a victorious deliverance.

'CARRYING A LARGE LUMP OF ICE TO THE NORTH POLE'

As German forces battled deep inside the Soviet Union, Josef Stalin called for a 'Second Front' – an Anglo-American landing in North-West Europe, to take pressure off the Eastern Front. But Britain and America did not have the resources for such a landing (codenamed 'Sledgehammer' for 1942 and 'Round-up' for 1943). Instead, they planned an amphibious landing against French Morocco (Operation 'Torch'), with the aim of driving the Germans from North Africa. In addition, Britain and the United States would bomb Germany on a 24-hour rota, the United States by day, Britain by night. In August 1942, Churchill flew to Moscow to explain this to Stalin. Later he recalled in *The Second World War* his thoughts during the ten-hour flight from Teheran on August 12, and his meetings with Stalin:

> I pondered on my mission to this sullen, sinister Bolshevik State I had once tried so hard to strangle at its birth, and which, until Hitler appeared, I had regarded as the mortal foe of civilised freedom. What was it my duty to say to them now? General Wavell, who had literary inclinations, summed it all up in a poem. There were several verses, and the last line of each was, 'No Second Front in nineteen forty-two'. It was like carrying a large lump of ice to the North Pole. Still, I was sure it was my duty to tell them the facts personally and have it all out face to face with Stalin, rather than trust to telegrams and inter-mediaries. At least it showed that one cared for their fortunes and understood what their struggle meant to the general war.
>
> We had always hated their wicked regime, and, till the German flail beat upon them, they would have watched us being swept out of existence with indifference and gleefully divided with Hitler our Empire in the East.
>
> [···]
>
> The first two hours were bleak and sombre. I began at once with the question of the Second Front, saying that I wished to speak frankly and would like to invite complete frankness from Stalin. I would not have come to Moscow unless he had felt sure that he would be able to discuss realities. When M. Molotov had come to London I had told him that we were trying to make plans for a diversion in France. I had also made it clear to M. Molotov that I could make no promises about 1942, and had given M. Molotov a memorandum to this effect. Since then an exhaustive Anglo-American examination of the problem had been carried out. The British and American Governments did not feel themselves able to undertake a major operation in September, which was the latest month in which the weather was to be counted

upon. But, as M. Stalin knew, they were preparing for a very great operation in 1943. For this purpose a million American troops were now scheduled to reach the United Kingdom at their point of assembly in the spring of 1943, making an expeditionary force of 27 divisions, to which the British Government were prepared to add 21 divisions. Nearly half of this force would be armoured. So far only two and a half American divisions had reached the United Kingdom, but the big transportation would take place in October, November and December.

I told Stalin that I was well aware that this plan offered no help to Russia in 1942, but thought it possible that when the 1943 plan was ready it might well be that the Germans would have a stronger army in the West than they now had. At this point Stalin's face crumpled up into a frown, but he did not interrupt. I then said I had good reasons against an attack on the French coast in 1942. We had only enough landing craft for an assault landing on a fortified coast – enough to throw ashore six divisions and maintain them. If it were successful, more divisions might be sent, but the limiting factor was landing craft, which were now being built in very large numbers in the United Kingdom, and especially in the United States. For one division which could be carried this year it would be possible next year to carry eight or ten times as many.

Stalin, who had begun to look very glum, seemed unconvinced by my argument, and asked if it was impossible to attack any part of the French coast. I showed him a map which indicated the difficulties of making an air umbrella anywhere except actually across the Straits. He did not seem to understand, and asked some questions about the range of fighter planes. Could they not, for instance, come and go all the time? I explained that they could indeed come and go, but at this range they would have no time to fight, and I added that an air umbrella to be of any use had to be kept open. He then said that there was not a single German division in France of any value, a statement which I contested. There were in France twenty-five German divisions, nine of which were of the first line. He shook his head. I said that I had brought the Chief of the Imperial General Staff and General Sir Archibald Wavell with me in order that such points might be examined in detail with the Russian General Staff. There was a point beyond which statesmen could not carry discussions of this kind.

Stalin, whose glumness had by now much increased, said that, as he understood it, we were unable to create a second front with any large force and unwilling even to land six divisions. I said that this was so. We could land six divisions, but the landing of them would be more harmful than helpful, for it would greatly injure the big operation planned for next year. War was war but not folly, and it would be folly to invite a disaster which would help nobody. I said I feared the news I brought was not good news. If by throwing in 150,000 to 200,000 men we could render him aid by drawing away from the Russian front appreciable German forces, we would not shrink from this course on the grounds of loss. But if it drew no men away and spoiled the prospects for 1943 it would be a great error.

Stalin, who had become restless, said that his view about war was different. A man who was not prepared to take risks could not win a war. Why were we so afraid of the Germans? He could not understand. His experience showed that troops must be blooded in battle. If you did not blood your troops you had no idea what their value was. I inquired whether he had ever asked himself why Hitler did not come to England in 1940, when he was at the height of his power and we had only 20,000 trained troops, 200 guns, and 50 tanks. He did not come. The fact was that Hitler was afraid of the operation. It is not so easy to cross the Channel. Stalin replied that this was no analogy. The landing of Hitler in England would have been resisted by the people, whereas in the case of a British landing in France the people would be on the side of the British. I pointed out that it was all the more important therefore not to expose the people of France by a withdrawal to the vengeance of Hitler and to waste them when they would be needed in the big operation in 1943.

There was an oppressive silence. Stalin at length said that if we could not make a landing in France this year he was not entitled to demand it or to insist upon it, but he was bound to say that he did not agree with my arguments.

I then unfolded a map of Southern Europe, the Mediterranean, and North Africa. What was a 'Second Front'? Was it only a landing on a fortified coast opposite England? Or could it take the form of some other great enterprise which might be useful to the common cause? I thought it better to bring him southward by steps. If, for instance, we could hold the enemy in the Pas de Calais by our concentrations in Britain, and at the same time attack elsewhere – for instance, in the Loire, the Gironde, or alternatively the Scheldt – this was full of promise. There indeed was a general picture of next year's big operation. Stalin feared that it was not practicable. I said that it would indeed be difficult to land a million men, but that we should have to persevere and try.

We then passed on to the bombing of Germany, which gave general satisfaction. M. Stalin emphasised the importance of striking at the morale of the German population. He said he attached the greatest importance to bombing, and that he knew our raids were having a tremendous effect in Germany.

After this interlude, which relieved the tension, Stalin observed that from our long talk it seemed that all we were going to do was no 'Sledgehammer', no 'Round-up', and pay our way by bombing Germany. I decided to get the worst over first and to create a suitable background for the project I had come to unfold. I did not therefore try at once to relieve the gloom. Indeed, I asked specially that there should be the plainest speaking between friends and comrades in peril. However, courtesy and dignity prevailed.

The moment had now come to bring 'Torch' into action. I said that I wanted to revert to the question of a Second Front in 1942, which was what I had come for. I did not think France was the only place for such an operation. There were other places, and we and the Americans had decided upon another plan, which I was authorised by the American President to impart to Stalin secretly. I would now proceed to do so. I emphasised the vital need of secrecy. At this Stalin sat up and grinned and said that he hoped that nothing about it would appear in the British Press.

I then explained precisely Operation 'Torch'. As I told the whole story Stalin became intensely interested. His first question was what would happen in Spain and Vichy France. A little later on he remarked that the operation was militarily right, but he had political doubts about the effect on France. He asked particularly about the timing, and I said not later than October 30, but the President and all of us were trying to pull it forward to October 7. This seemed a great relief to the three Russians.

I then described the military advantages of freeing the Mediterranean, whence still another front could be opened. In September we must win in Egypt, and in October in North Africa, all the time holding the enemy in Northern France. If we could end the year in possession of North Africa we could threaten the belly of Hitler's Europe, and this operation should be considered in conjunction with the 1943 operation. That was what we and the Americans had decided to do.

To illustrate my point I had meanwhile drawn a picture of a crocodile, and explained to Stalin with the help of this picture how it was our intention to attack the soft belly of the crocodile as we attacked his hard snout. And Stalin, whose interest was now at a high pitch, said, 'May God prosper this undertaking'.

[· · ·]

At this point Stalin seemed suddenly to grasp the strategic advantages of 'Torch'. He recounted four main reasons for it: first, it would hit Rommel in the back; second, it would overawe Spain; third, it would produce fighting between Germans and Frenchmen in France; and, fourth, it would expose Italy to the whole brunt of the war.

I was deeply impressed with this remarkable statement. It showed the Russian Dictator's swift and complete mastery of a problem hitherto novel to him. Very few people alive could have comprehended in so few minutes the reasons which we had all so long been wrestling with for months. He saw it all in a flash.

[· · ·]

We then gathered round a large globe, and I explained to Stalin the immense advantages of clearing the enemy out of the Mediterranean. I told Stalin I should be available should he wish to see me again. He replied that the Russian custom was that the visitor should state his wishes and that he was ready to receive me at any time. He now knew the worst, and yet we parted in an atmosphere of goodwill.

The meeting had now lasted nearly four hours. It took half an hour or more to reach State Villa No. 7. Tired as I was, I dictated my telegram to the War Cabinet and the President after midnight, and then, with the feeling that at least the ice was broken and a human contact established, I slept soundly and long.

'THESE VILE CRIMES'

In the autumn of 1942, information smuggled out of Germany to neutral Switzerland was published in the British newspapers. It revealed the extent of the German slaughter of Jews in German-occupied Russia and Poland, and the deportation of Jews from France, Belgium and Holland to an 'unknown destination' in the East. On 29 October 1942, a protest meeting was held at the Albert Hall. For the meeting, Churchill sent a message to be read out by the Archbishop of Canterbury, William Temple:

> I cannot refrain from sending, through you, to the audience which is assembling under your Chairmanship at the Albert Hall today to protest against Nazi atrocities inflicted on the Jews, the assurance of my warm sympathy with the objects of the meeting.
>
> The systematic cruelties to which the Jewish people – men, women, and children – have been exposed under the Nazi regime are amongst the most terrible events of history, and place an indelible stain upon all who perpetrate and instigate them.
>
> Free men and women denounce these vile crimes, and when this world struggle ends with the enthronement of human rights, racial persecution will be ended.

'I CANNOT FEEL THAT DE GAULLE IS FRANCE'

Churchill shared President Roosevelt's reluctance to recognise the Free French leader General de Gaulle as the sole representative of the French nation. In a Secret Session of the House of Commons on

10 December 1942 – in a passage that he decided to omit when the Secret Session speeches were published after the war – he explained why:

I must now say a word about General de Gaulle.

On behalf of His Majesty's Government I exchanged letters with him in 1940 recognising him as the Leader of all Free Frenchmen wherever they might be, who should rally to him, in support of the Allied cause. We have most scrupulously kept our engagements with him and have done everything in our power to help him. We finance his Movement. We have helped his operations. But we have never recognized him as representing France. We have never agreed that he and those associated with him, because they were right and brave at the moment of French surrender, have a monopoly on the future of France.

I have lived myself for the last 35 years or more in a mental relationship and to a large extent in sympathy with an abstraction called France. I still do not think it is an illusion. I cannot feel that de Gaulle is France, still less that Darlan and Vichy are France. France is something greater, more complex, more formidable than any of these sectional manifestations.

I have tried to work as far as possible with General de Gaulle, making allowances for his many difficulties, for his temperament and for the limitations of his outlook. In order to sustain his Movement at the moment of the American occupation of French North Africa and to console him and his friends for their exclusion from the enterprise we agreed to his nominee, General Legentilhomme, being proclaimed as High Commissioner for Madagascar, although this adds somewhat to our difficulties in pacifying that large Island, which oddly as it seems to us would much prefer Darlan. We are at the present time endeavouring to rally Jibuti to the Free French Movement. Therefore I consider that we have been in every respect faithful in the discharge of our obligations to de Gaulle, and we shall so continue to the end.

However, now we are in Secret Session the House must not be led to believe that General de Gaulle is an unfaltering friend of Britain. On the contrary, I think he is one of those good Frenchmen who have a traditional antagonism engrained in French hearts by centuries of war against the English. On his way back from Syria in the summer of 1941 through the French Central and West African Colonies he left a trail of Anglophobia behind him. On August 25, 1941, he gave an interview to the correspondent of the *Chicago Daily News* at Brazzaville in which he suggested that England coveted the African colonies of France, and said: 'England is afraid of the French Fleet. What in effect England is carrying out is a war-time deal with Hitler in which Vichy serves as a go-between.' He explained that Vichy served Germany by keeping the French people in subjection and England by keeping the fleet out of German hands.

All this and much more was very ungrateful talk, but we have allowed no complaint of ours to appear in public.

Again this year in July, General de Gaulle wished to visit Syria. He promised me before I agreed to facilitate his journey, which I was very well able to stop, that he would behave in a helpful and friendly manner, but no sooner did he get to Cairo than he adopted a most hectoring attitude and in Syria his whole object seemed to be to foment ill-will between the British military and Free French civil administrations and state the French claims to rule Syria at the highest, although it had been agreed that after the war, and as much as possible even during the war, the Syrians are to enjoy their independence.

I continue to maintain friendly personal relations with General de Gaulle and I help him as much as I possibly can. I feel bound to do this because he stood up against the Men of Bordeaux and their base surrender at a time when all resisting willpower had quitted France. All the same, I could not recommend you to base all your hopes and confidence upon him, and still less to assume at this stage that it is our duty to place, so far as we have the power, the destiny of France in his hands. Like the President in the telegram I have read, we seek to base ourselves on the will of the entire French nation rather than any sectional manifestations, even the most worthy.

'YOUR FEATS WILL GLEAM AND GLOW'

On 3 February 1943, Churchill flew from Cairo to Tripoli, where he went to Eighth Army Headquarters. It was his second visit to the British and Commonwealth troops in North Africa in five months. Their great victory over the combined German and Italian forces, commanded by General Rommel, had come on 4 November 1942, after twelve days of heavy fighting at Alamein. Of this battle Churchill later wrote: 'Before Alamein we never had a victory, after Alamein we never had a defeat.' In an army camp, he spoke to the assembled soldiers, sailors and airmen. Churchill's doctor, Sir Charles Wilson (later Lord Moran), who was with him, noted: 'PM was in his element when he addressed the troops. No one can do this sort of thing so well.' Churchill told the men, gathered on a hillside:

> The last time I saw this army was in the closing days of August on those sandy and rocky bluffs near Alamein and the Ruweisat Ridge, when it was apparent from all the signs that Rommel was about to make his final thrust on Alexandria and Cairo. Then all was to be won or lost. Now I come to you a long way from Alamein, and I find this army and its famous commander [General Montgomery] with a record of victory behind it which has undoubtedly played a decisive part in altering the whole character of the war.
>
> The fierce and well-fought battle of Alamein, the blasting through of the enemy's seaward flank, and the thunderbolt of the armoured attack, irretrievably broke the army which Rommel had boasted would conquer Egypt, and upon which the German and Italian peoples had set their hopes. Thereafter and ever since, in these remorseless three months, you have chased this hostile army and driven it from pillar to post over a distance of more than 1,400 miles – in fact, as far as from London to Moscow. You have altered the face of the war in a most remarkable way.
>
> What it has meant in the skill and organisation of movement and manoeuvres, what it has meant in the tireless endurance and self-denial of the troops and in the fearless leadership displayed in action, can be appreciated only by those who were actually on the spot. But I must tell you that the fame of the Desert Army has spread throughout the world.

After the surrender of Tobruk, there was a dark period when many people, not knowing us, not knowing the British and the nations of the British Empire, were ready to take a disparaging view. But now everywhere your work is spoken of with respect and admiration. When I was with the Chief of the Imperial General Staff [General Brooke] at Casablanca and with the President of the United States, the arrival of the Desert Army in Tripoli was a new factor which influenced the course of our discussions and opened up hopeful vistas for the future. You are entitled to know these things, and to dwell upon them with that satisfaction which men in all modesty feel when a great work has been finally done. You have rendered a high service to your country and the common cause.

It must have been a tremendous experience driving forward day after day over this desert which it has taken me this morning more than six hours to fly at 200 miles an hour. You were pursuing a broken enemy, dragging on behind you this ever-lengthening line of communications, carrying the whole art of desert warfare to perfection. In the words of the old hymn, you have 'nightly pitched your moving tents a day's march nearer home.' Yes, not only in the march of the army but in the progress of the war you have brought home nearer. I am here to thank you on behalf of His Majesty's Government of the British Isles and of all our friends the world over.

Hard struggles lie ahead. Rommel, the fugitive of Egypt, Cyrenaica, and Tripolitania, in a non-stop race of 1,400 miles, is now trying to present himself as the deliverer of Tunisia. Along the Eastern coast of Tunisia are large numbers of German and Italian troops, not yet equipped to their previous standard, but growing stronger. On the other side, another great operation, planned in conjunction with your advance, has carried the First British Army, our American comrades, and the French armies to within 30 or 40 miles of Bizerta and Tunis. Therefore a military situation arises which everyone can understand.

The days of your victories are by no means at an end, and with forces which march from different quarters we may hope to achieve the final destruction or expulsion from the shores of Africa of every armed German or Italian. You must have felt relief when, after those many a hundred miles of desert, you came once more into a green land with trees and grass, and I do not think you will lose that advantage.

As you go forward on further missions that will fall to your lot, you will fight in countries which will present undoubtedly serious tactical difficulties, but which none the less will not have that grim character of desert war which you have known how to endure and how to overcome.

Let me then assure you, soldiers and airmen, that your fellow countrymen regard your joint work with admiration and gratitude, and that after the war when a man is asked what he did it will be quite sufficient for him to say, 'I marched and fought with the Desert Army.' And when history is written and all the facts are known, your feats will gleam and glow and will be a source of song and story long after we who are gathered here have passed away.

'THE HEART OF AUSTRIA'

On 18 February 1943, Churchill spoke outside 10 Downing Street when Sir George Franckenstein, the former Austrian Minister in London, presented a trailer canteen to the Women's Voluntary Service (WVS) on behalf of Austrians in Britain:

It is not without deep emotion that I attend this simple ceremony. Here we see the heart of Austria, although trampled down under the Nazi and Prussian yoke. We can never forget here in this island that Austria was the first victim of Nazi aggression. We know that happy life which might have been led by scores of millions in central Europe. We remember the charm, beauty, and historic splendour of Vienna, the grace of life, the dignity of the individual; all the links of past generations which are associated in our minds with Austria and with Vienna.

Sir George Franckenstein, you are here as a link with us between the dark past, the haggard present, and what I still believe will be the glorious future.

We shall struggle on and fight on. The people of Britain will never desert the cause of the freeing of Austria from the Prussian yoke. We shall go forward. Many long miles have to be marched and many leagues at sea to be covered by ships; many millions of miles of aeroplane flights be accomplished; great heart and effort will be needed from large masses of human beings, but we have three-quarters of the human race upon our side.

Only our own follies can deprive us of victory; and in the victory of the Allies, Free Austria shall find her honoured place.

'THE ENEMY IS STILL PROUD AND POWERFUL'

Churchill made five voyages across the Atlantic to the United States between December 1941 and September 1944. During each of those visits, he used all his powers of persuasion with President Roosevelt to co-ordinate the war strategies of the two countries to defeat Germany and Japan. He also understood the importance of Congressional support. In what was his second address to Congress, on 19 May 1943, he set out the heavy tasks that faced Britain and the United States:

If we wish to abridge the slaughter and ruin which this war is spreading to so many lands and to which we must ourselves contribute so grievous a measure of suffering and sacrifice, we cannot afford to relax a single fibre of our being or to tolerate the slightest abatement of our efforts. The enemy is still proud and powerful. He is hard to get at. He still possesses enormous armies, vast resources, and invaluable strategic territories.

War is full of mysteries and surprises. A false step, a wrong direction, an error in strategy, discord or lassitude among the Allies, might soon give the common enemy power to confront us with new and hideous facts. We have surmounted many serious dangers, but there is one grave danger which will go along with us till the end; that danger is the undue prolongation of the war. No one can tell what new complications and perils might arise in four or five more years of war. And it is in the dragging-out of the war at enormous expense, until the democracies are tired or bored or split, that the main hopes of Germany and Japan must now reside.

We must destroy this hope as we have destroyed so many others, and for that purpose we must beware of every topic however attractive and every tendency however natural which turns our minds and energies from this supreme objective of the general victory of the United Nations. By singleness of purpose, by steadfastness of conduct, by tenacity and endurance such as we have so far displayed – by these, and only by these, can we discharge our duty to the future of the world and to the destiny of man.

'I HAVE NO IDEA WHAT I SAID'

On 1 June 1943, when Churchill was in Tunis, he spoke to a vast concourse of British troops in the Roman amphitheatre in Carthage. That evening, he told his guests at dinner, including the Chief of the Imperial General Staff, General Alan Brooke: 'Yes, I was speaking from where the cries of Christian virgins rent the air whilst roaring lions devoured them – and yet – I am no lion and certainly not a virgin.' Of his appearance in the amphitheatre, he wrote in *The Second World War*:

The sense of victory was in the air. The whole of North Africa was cleared of the enemy. A quarter of a million prisoners were cooped in our cages. Everyone was very proud and delighted. There is no doubt that people like winning very much. I addressed many thousand soldiers at Carthage in the ruins of an immense amphitheatre. Certainly the hour and setting lent themselves to oratory. I have no idea what I said, but the whole audience clapped and cheered as doubtless their predecessors of two thousand years ago had done as they watched gladiatorial combats.

'TYRANNY IS OUR FOE'

On 6 September 1943, during his fourth wartime visit to the United States, Churchill visited Harvard University, where he received an honorary degree. Elizabeth Layton, one of the secretaries to whom he had dictated his speech during the night train journey from Washington, wrote to her parents: 'It was one of his very best deliveries – one felt he was completely master of everything he said and that even a bomb wouldn't have shaken him.' During the course of his speech Churchill said:

> Even elderly Parliamentarians like myself are forced to acquire a high degree of mobility. But to the youth of America, as to the youth of Britain, I say 'You cannot stop.' There is no halting-place at this point. We have now reached a stage in the journey where there can be no pause. We must go on. It must be world anarchy or world order. Throughout all this ordeal and struggle which is characteristic of our age, you will find in the British Commonwealth and Empire good comrades to whom you are united by other ties besides those of State policy and public need. To a large extent, they are the ties of blood and history. Naturally I, a child of both worlds, am conscious of these.
>
> Law, language, literature – these are considerable factors. Common conceptions of what is right and decent, a marked regard for fair play, especially to the weak and poor, a stern sentiment of impartial justice, and above all the love of personal freedom, or as Kipling put it: 'Leave to live by no man's leave underneath the law' – these are common conceptions on both sides of the ocean among the English-speaking peoples. We hold to these conceptions as strongly as you do.
>
> We do not war primarily with races as such. Tyranny is our foe, whatever trappings or disguise it wears, whatever language it speaks, be it external or internal, we must for ever be on our guard, ever mobilized, ever vigilant, always ready to spring at its throat. In all this, we march together. Not only do we march and strive shoulder to shoulder at this moment under the fire of the enemy on the fields of war or in the air, but also in those realms of thought which are conse-crated to the rights and the dignity of man.

[···]

The great Bismarck – for there were once great men in Germany – is said to have observed towards the close of his life that the most potent factor in human society at the end of the nineteenth century was the fact that the British and American peoples spoke the same language. That was a pregnant saying. Certainly it has enabled us to wage war together with an intimacy and harmony never before achieved among allies.

This gift of a common tongue is a priceless inheritance, and it may well some day become the foundation of a common citizenship. I like to think of British and Americans moving about freely over each other's wide estates with hardly a sense of being foreigners to one another. But I do not see why we should not try to spread our common language even more widely throughout the globe and, without seeking selfish advantage over any, possess ourselves of this invaluable amenity and birthright.

'I ADMIRED THE ADMIRAL'S SPORTING SPIRIT'

On 6 June 1944, British, Canadian and United States forces carried out the long-awaited landings on the Channel Coast of France: the Normandy Landings. Churchill, who had been closely involved in the planning for the previous six months, made several visits to the beaches, the first on June 12. In *The Second World War*, he recalled his meetings on that first visit with General Montgomery, at his headquarters some five miles inland, and with Admiral Vian on board the Admiral's Barge:

We lunched in a tent looking towards the enemy. The General was in the highest spirits. I asked him how far away was the actual front. He said about three miles. I asked him if he had a continuous line. He said 'No.'

'What is there then to prevent an incursion of German armour breaking up our luncheon?' He said he did not think they would come.

The staff told me the chateau had been heavily bombed the night before, and certainly there were a good many craters around it. I told him he was taking too much of a risk if he made a habit of such proceedings. Anything can be done once or for a short time, but custom, repetition, prolongation, is always to be avoided when possible in war. He did in fact move two days later, though not till he and his staff had had another dose.

It continued fine, and apart from occasional air alarms and anti-aircraft fire there seemed to be no fighting. We made a considerable inspection of our limited bridgehead.

[···]

Churchill then went on board the Admiral's Barge:

The bombardment was leisurely and continuous, but there was no reply from the enemy. As we were about to turn I said to Vian, 'Since we are so near, why shouldn't we have a plug at them ourselves before we go home?'

He said, 'Certainly,' and in a minute or two all our guns fired on the silent coast. We were of course well within the range of their artillery, and the moment we had fired Vian made the destroyer turn about and depart at the highest speed. We were soon out of danger and passed through the cruiser and battleship lines.

This is the only time I have ever been on board a naval vessel when she fired 'in anger' – if it can be so called. I admired the Admiral's sporting spirit.

'AN IMPRESSIVE PERFORMANCE'

Churchill's second visit to the Normandy beachhead began on 20 July 1944, eight days after the first. On this visit he spent some time observing the landing of men and machinery, including the delivery of supplies by DUKWs – the amphibious trucks commonly known as 'Ducks'. He recalled in *The Second World War*:

On the 20th I flew direct in an American Army Dakota to their landing-ground on the Cherbourg peninsula, and was taken all round the harbour by the United States commander. Here I saw for the first time a flying bomb launching-point. It was a very elaborate affair. I was shocked at the damage the Germans had done to the town, and shared the staff disappointment at the inevitable delay in getting the port to work. The basins of the harbour were thickly sown with contact mines. A handful of devoted British divers were at work day and night disconnecting these at their mortal peril. Warm tributes were paid to them by their American comrades.

After a long and dangerous drive to the United States beachhead known as Utah Beach, I went aboard a British motor torpedo-boat, and thence had a rough passage to Arromanches. As one gets older seasickness retreats. I did not succumb, but slept soundly till we were in the calm waters of our synthetic lagoon. I went aboard the cruiser *Enterprise*, where I remained for three days, making myself thoroughly acquainted with the whole working of the harbour, on which all the armies now almost entirely depended, and at the same time transacting my London business.

The nights were very noisy, there being repeated raids by single aircraft, and more numerous alarms. By day I studied the whole process of the landing of supplies and troops, both at the piers, in which I had so long been interested, and on the beaches. On one occasion six tank landing craft came to the beach in line. When their prows grounded their drawbridges fell forward and out came the tanks, three or four from each, and splashed ashore. In less than eight minutes by my stopwatch the tanks stood in column of route on the highroad ready to move into action. This was an impressive performance, and typical of the rate of discharge which had now been achieved.

I was fascinated to see the DUKWs swimming through the harbour, waddling ashore, and then hurrying up the hill to the great dump where the lorries were waiting to take their supplies to the various units. Upon the wonderful efficiency of this system, now yielding results far greater than we had ever planned, depended the hopes of a speedy and victorious action.

On the first night when I visited the wardroom the officers were singing songs. At the end they sang the chorus of 'Rule, Britannia'. I asked them what were the words. Nobody knew them. So I recited some of Thomson's noble lines myself, and for the benefit and the instruction of the reader (if he needs any) I reprint them here:

> The nations not so blest as thee
> Must in their turn to tyrants fall:
> While thou shalt flourish great and free,
> The dread and envy of them all.
>
> The Muses still, with freedom found,
> Shall to thy happy coasts repair;
> Blest isle, with matchless beauty crowned,
> And manly hearts to guard the fair.

On my last day at Arromanches I visited Montgomery's headquarters, a few miles inland. The Commander-in-Chief was in the best of spirits on the eve of his largest operation, which he explained to me in all detail. He took me into the ruins of Caen and across the river, and we also visited other parts of the British front. Then he placed at my disposal his captured Storch aeroplane, and the Air Commander himself piloted me all over the British positions. This aircraft could land at a pinch almost anywhere, and consequently one could fly at a few hundred feet from the ground, gaining a far better view and knowledge of the scene than by any other method. I also visited several of the air stations, and said a few words to gatherings of officers and men.

Finally I went to the field hospital, where, though it was a quiet day, a trickle of casualties was coming in. One poor man was to have a serious operation, and was actually on the table about to take the anaesthetic. I was slipping away when he said he wanted me. He smiled warily and kissed my hand. I was deeply moved, and very glad to learn later on that the operation had been entirely successful.

'THE SOUL OF FRANCE DID NOT DIE'

President Roosevelt was reluctant to see the Free French accorded the position of an Allied Power, which would involve giving them, after Germany's defeat, a Zone of Occupation in Germany. He was also openly critical of General de Gaulle. Despite his earlier reservations about the Free French leader, on this occasion Churchill did not share Roosevelt's view, as he explained to the House of Commons on 2 August 1944:

> In these last four years I have had many differences with General de Gaulle, but I have never forgotten, and can never forget, that he stood forth as the first eminent Frenchman to face the common foe in what seemed to be the hour of ruin of his country, and possibly of ours, and it is only fair and becoming that he should stand first and foremost in the days when France shall again be raised, and raise herself, to her rightful place among the great Powers of Europe and of the world.
>
> For forty years I have been a consistent friend of France and her brave Army; all my life I have been grateful for the contribution France has made to the culture and glory of Europe, and above all for the sense of personal liberty and the rights of man which has radiated from the soul of France. But these are not matters of sentiment or personal feeling. It is one of the main interests of Great Britain that a friendly France should regain and hold her place among the major Powers of Europe and the world. Show me a moment when I swerved from this conception, and you will show me a moment when I have been wrong.
>
> I must confess that I never liked Trotsky, but there is one thing he said at the time of the brutal German Treaty of Brest-Litovsk which stuck in my mind. He said to the German bullies: 'The destiny of a great nation has never yet been settled by the temporary condition of its technical apparatus.' So it will be with France, struck down in a few weeks of agony, and deprived thereafter of the power of self-expression and almost of the right of existence. But the soul of France did not die. It burned here and there with exceptional brightness. It burned over wider areas with a dim but unquenchable flame.

Our landing in Normandy, the course of the war, the whole tide of events, show quite clearly that we shall presently once again have to deal with the problem of France and Germany along the Rhine, and from that discussion France can by no means be excluded. It is evident from what I have said that I look forward to the closest association of the British Empire, the United States and the Russian and French representatives in the settlement of these important European problems.

We are an alliance of united, peace-loving nations who have been forced to take up arms to defend our fundamental rights, and we must not fail in the hour of victory to make the arrangements necessary to perpetuate the peace that we shall have so dearly bought.

'HAVE THE PEOPLE THE RIGHT TO TURN OUT A GOVERNMENT?'

On 8 September 1943, Italy surrendered, and a new Italian Government came into being, determined to turn its back on Italian Fascism, and to fight alongside the Western Allies as they battled with the German forces who had swiftly occupied all but southern Italy. On a visit to Italy in August 1944, Churchill was asked about the principles on which the new Italian democracy should be based. On August 28, he set out seven questions for all would-be democracies, which he later published in *The Second World War*:

Is there the right to free expression of opinion and of opposition and criticism of the Government of the day?

Have the people the right to turn out a Government of which they disapprove, and are constitutional means provided by which they can make their will apparent?

Are their courts of justice free from violence by the Executive and from threats of mob violence, and free of all association with particular political parties?

Will these courts administer open and well-established laws which are associated in the human mind with the broad principles of decency and justice?

Will there be fair play for poor as well as for rich, for private persons as well as Government officials?

Will the rights of the individual, subject to his duties to the State, be maintained and asserted and exalted?

Is the ordinary peasant or workman who is earning a living by daily toil and striving to bring up a family free from the fear that some grim police organisation under the control of a single party, like the Gestapo, started by the Nazi and Fascist parties, will tap him on the shoulder and pack him off without fair or open trial to bondage or ill-treatment?

These simple, practical tests are some of the title deeds on which a new Italy could be founded.

'THE FOUNDATION OF ALL DEMOCRACY'

In the late summer of 1944, there were calls at Westminster for an early General Election. The previous General Election had been nine years earlier, in 1935, when the National Government was re-elected by a large majority, with the Conservative Party winning 386 seats, the Labour Party 154 seats, and the Liberal Party 21 seats. After four years as partners in Churchill's All-Party Grand Coalition, the Labour leaders wanted a chance to reverse their earlier electoral fortunes, and form a government of their own. On 31 October 1944, Churchill gave the House of Commons his views on the issue:

I am very clearly of opinion that the coalition of Parties ought not to be broken before Nazidom is broken. This was the purpose for which we came together in the present Government, and it is still the supreme purpose which affects the safety of the nation and the Empire. As I said the other day, any attempt to estimate the date when the war with Germany can be officially declared over could be no more than a guess. A political convulsion in Germany might bring it to a speedy end at any time, but against that must be set the iron control of German life in all its forms, including the Army, which has been established by Hitler's storm troops and secret police. This exceeds anything previously known among men. Therefore, we cannot count upon any of the normal reactions of public opinion. From every quarter it seems that the civil population are plunged in a dull apathy, and certainly anyone who stirred against the police would instantly be shot or decapitated. Therefore I simply cannot place any dependence upon political uprisings in Germany.

On military grounds it seems difficult to believe that the war could be ended before Christmas, or even before Easter, although, as I have said, many high military authorities with every means to form a correct judgment have expressed themselves more hopefully, and although every effort is being made, and will be made, against the enemy. The German troops are fighting with the utmost tenacity, although cut off in many places, and in defence of positions evidently forlorn. They have been counter-attacking with vigour, though as yet without success, in Holland and on the Moselle. A great deal of work has still to be done to improve the ports and build up supplies and concentrate forward the ever-growing Allied Army. In Italy the fighting is also of the most obstinate character, and the weather has broken. The Eastern Front has shown its main activity on the north and south flanks. Immense successes have rewarded strenuous Russian military efforts and skilful Russian and Allied diplomacy. The distances are however very large, and many hostile defence positions have to be stormed or turned. In all these circumstances I certainly could not predict, still less guarantee, the end of the German war before the end of the spring, or even before we reach the early summer. It may come earlier, and no one will rejoice more than I if it should.

Anyhow, I have no hesitation in declaring that it would be a wrongful act, unworthy of our country's fame, to break up the present governing instrument before we know where we are with Hitler's Germany. Those who forced such a disaster, even thoughtlessly, would take on themselves a measureless responsibility, and their action would be fiercely resented by the nation at large. I am thankful to say that there are no signs of any such desire in any responsible quarter.

Let us assume, however, that the German war ends in March, April or May, and that some or all the other parties in the Coalition recall their Ministers out of the Government, or wish to bring it to an end from such dates. That would be a matter of regret, both on public and on personal grounds, to a great many people, but it would not be a matter of reproach or bitterness between us in this Government or in this House once Germany has been defeated.

We are told there must on no account be what is called a coupon election. By that I presume is meant an agreement between the official parties not to oppose each other in most of the seats, and to form a solid front against those who criticize or oppose us. In other words, it would mean that the present Coalition should go to the country and obtain from it a renewal of confidence. I have no doubt they would get it, but there would be some who would say it was too easy. But one must admit that many people would think this would hardly be a fair way of testing opinion in the country, and in fact it would be quite impossible to obtain party agreement to such a course. Many people feel that it would impede the electorate in expressing their free choice. Neither would it be seemly, or indeed practicable, once a dissolution had been announced, for Ministers to go all over the country expressing the utmost distaste for each other's views and records, and yet be together in Cabinet discussing as colleagues all the gravest matters of the hour. Nor again would it be proper for the Ministers who are also in some cases leaders, and whose knowledge is needed to guide the country, to remain silent and apparently indifferent to the fortunes of their parties or of their candidates. I do not find it easy to escape from the weight and force of these arguments.

The announcement of the dissolution would therefore necessarily mark the close of the present Administration. The Conservative Party have a majority of more than one hundred above all parties and independents in the present House, and it would therefore fall to us to make arrangements for the inevitable General Election. I cannot conceive that anyone would wish that election to be held in a violent hurry or while we were all rejoicing together and rendering thanks to

God for our deliverance. There must be an interval. Moreover, we have above all things to be careful that practically everybody entitled to vote has a fair chance to do so. This applies above all to the soldiers, many of whom are serving at great distances from this country.

Nothing would be more shameful or more dishonourable than to deny the great mass of the soldiers, and the Service men of the Air Force and of the Navy, a full opportunity of recording their votes. In my opinion they have more right to vote than anyone else in the country, and we should all be ashamed if anything were done which prevented these men, to whom we owe almost everything, from taking their full part in deciding the immediate future of their country. That is not to say that every single man in the most remote station can be certain of being able to vote, but everything in human power will be done to give the fullest possible opportunities for the exercise of the franchise to all in the fighting Services.

It is, however, in fact not legally possible, after the new electoral arrangements have come into force, as they do on the 1st December this year, for polling to take place in less than eight weeks from the issue of the writs. A minimum of six weeks must in fact elapse between the issue of the writs and the nomination of candidates alone. All this has been concerted with a general measure of assent by the House, and with the sole view of obtaining the fullest and fairest expression of the national opinion. Besides all this, the partial re-distribution authorized by the recent Act has to be carried through. A start will be made immediately, not waiting for the end of the German war, but the process will certainly take several months.

It may therefore be taken as certain that from the moment the King gives his consent to a dissolution a period of between two and three months would be required. This also would be fair to the political parties and candidates, who have to set about one another in the usual lusty manner [. . .] It follows therefore that if events should take the course I have indicated, it would seem that, roughly speaking, there is no likelihood of a General Election for from seven to nine months from now. Finally, it is contrary to precedent for Governments to hold on to office until the last moment of their legal tenure, or legally extended tenure, and it would be very unwholesome for any practice of that kind to be introduced. For these reasons we have decided not to accept any proposals or suggestions such as I have seen bruited about to reduce the period in the Bill from twelve months to six months, and I ask to-day, in introducing it, for a twelve months' prolongation of the life of the present Parliament.

We think that we have given good reasons to the House to show that the twelve months' period would be a sensible and proper provision to make at the present time. On the other hand, we must assume that the Japanese war will have to be carried on for an indefinite period after the destruction of the Nazi power. Here again there may be the possibilities of some political upheaval in Japan inducing a sudden surrender, but it would be very foolish to count upon this in a race of men of this desperate and barbarous character, whose whole constitution is dominated by the military and naval hierarchies who dragged them into their mad aggression. When the whole of the Japanese problem is examined, on military grounds alone it would certainly not be prudent to assume that a shorter period than eighteen months after the destruction of Hitler would be required for the final destruction of the Japanese will or capacity to fight, and this period must be continually revised every few months by the combined Chiefs of Staffs.

The prolongation of the life of the existing Parliament by another two or three years would be a very serious constitutional lapse. Even now, no one under thirty has ever cast a vote at a General Election, or even at a by-election, since the registers fell out of action at the beginning of the war. Therefore, it seems to me that, unless all political parties resolve to maintain the present Coalition until the Japanese are defeated, we must look to the termination of the war against Nazism as a pointer which will fix the date of the General Election. I should regret the break-up of the present highly efficient Government, which has waged war with unsurpassed success and has shaped or carried out within the last two years a programme of reform and social progress which might well have occupied a whole Parliament under the ordinary conditions of peace for five or six years. In fact, I may say – and I will indeed be quite candid on this point – that having served for 42 years in this House I have never seen any Government to which I have been able to give a more loyal, confident and consistent support.

But while I should regret and deplore the break-up of these forces, so knit together by personal goodwill, by the comradeship of fighting a great cause, and by the sense of growing success arising from that comradeship, yet I could not blame anyone who claimed that there should be an appeal to the people once the German peril is removed. Indeed, I have myself a clear view that it would be wrong to continue this Parliament beyond the period of the German war.

The foundation of all democracy is that the people have the right to vote. To deprive them of that right is to make a mockery of all the high-sounding phrases which are so often used. At the bottom of all the tributes paid to democracy is the little man, walking into the little booth, with a little pencil, making a little cross on a little bit of paper – no amount of rhetoric or voluminous discussion can possibly diminish the overwhelming importance of that point.

The people have the right to choose representatives in accordance with their wishes and feelings, and I cannot think of anything more odious than for a Prime Minister to attempt to carry on with a Parliament so aged, and to try to grapple with the perplexing and tremendous problems of war and peace, and of the transition from war to peace, without being refreshed by contact with the people.

'HE STOOD, WHEN AT HIS ZENITH, WITHOUT A RIVAL'

Churchill's friend and former Prime Minister, David Lloyd George, died on 26 March 1945. He was eighty-two years old. Two days later, on March 28, Churchill paid tribute to his friend and colleague in the House of Commons:

There was no man so gifted, so eloquent, so forceful, who knew the life of the people so well. His warm heart was stirred by the many perils which beset the cottage homes: the health of the bread-winner, the fate of his widow, the nourishment and upbringing of his children, the meagre and haphazard provision of medical treatment and sanatoria, and the lack of any organized accessible medical service of a kind worthy of the age, from which the mass of the wage earners and the poor suffered. All this excited his wrath. Pity and compassion lent their powerful wings. He knew the terror with which old age threatened the toiler – that after a life of exertion he could be no more than a burden at the fireside and in the family of a struggling son.

When I first became Lloyd George's friend and active associate, now more than 40 years ago, this deep love of the people, the profound knowledge of their lives and of the undue and needless pressures under which they lived, impressed itself indelibly upon my mind.

Although unacquainted with the military arts, although by public repute a pugnacious pacifist, when the life of our country was in peril he rallied to the war effort and cast aside all other thoughts or aims. He was the first to discern the fearful shortages of ammunition and artillery and all the other appliances of war which would so soon affect, and in the case of Imperial Russia mortally affect, the warring nations on both sides. He saw it before anyone.

Lloyd George left the Exchequer, when the Coalition Government was formed, for the Ministry of Munitions. Here he hurled himself into the mobilisation of British industry. In 1915 he was building great war factories that could not come into operation for two years. There was the usual talk about the war being over in a few months, but he did not hesitate to plan on a vast scale for two years ahead. It was my fortune to inherit the output of those factories in 1917 – the vast, overflowing output which came from them. Presently Lloyd George seized the main power in the State and the headship of the Government.

[HON. MEMBERS: 'Seized?']

Seized. I think it was Carlyle who said of Oliver Cromwell: 'He coveted the place; perhaps the place was his.' He imparted immediately a new surge of strength, of impulse, far stronger than anything that had been known up to that time, and extending over the whole field of wartime Government, every part of which was of equal interest to him.

I have already written about him at this time, when I watched him so closely and enjoyed his confidence and admired him so much, and I have recorded two characteristics of his which seemed to me invaluable in those days: first, his power to live in the present yet without taking short views; and secondly, his power of drawing from misfortune itself the means of future success.

All this was illustrated by the successful development of the war; by the adoption of the convoy system, which he enforced upon the Admiralty and by which the U-boats were defeated; by the unified command on the Western Front which gave Marshal Foch the power to lead us all to victory; and in many other matters which form a part of the story of those sombre and tremendous years, the memory of which for ever abides with me, and to which I have often recurred in thought during our present second heavy struggle against German aggression, now drawing towards its victorious close.

Thus the statesman and guide whose gentle passing in the fullness of his years we mourn today served our country, our Island and our age, both faithfully and well in peace and in war. His long life was, from almost the beginning to almost the end, spent in political strife and controversy. He aroused intense and sometimes needless antagonisms. He had fierce and bitter quarrels at various times with all the parties. He faced undismayed the storms of criticism and hostility. In spite of all obstacles, including those he raised himself, he achieved his main purposes. As a man of action, resource and creative energy he stood, when at his zenith, without a rival.

Much of his work abides, some of it will grow greatly in the future, and those who come after us will find the pillars of his life's toil upstanding, massive and indestructible, and we ourselves, gathered here today, may indeed be thankful that he voyaged with us through storm and tumult with so much help and guidance to bestow.

'VICTORY HAD CAST ITS SURE AND STEADY BEAM UPON HIM'

As Churchill worked at his desk after midnight on 12 April 1945, he was brought the news that Franklin Roosevelt had died. 'I am much weakened in every way by his loss', he told Captain Richard Pim, the head of his Map Room, early the following morning. On April 17, having attended the national memorial service for Roosevelt at St Paul's Cathedral, Churchill went to the House of Commons to pay tribute to his – and Britain's – friend:

I conceived an admiration for him as a statesman, a man of affairs, and a war leader. I felt the utmost confidence in his upright, inspiring character and outlook, and a personal regard – affection I must say – for him beyond my power to express today. His love of his own country, his respect for its constitution, his power of gauging the tides and currents of its mobile public opinion, were always evident, but added to these were the beatings of that generous heart which was always stirred to anger and to action by spectacles of aggression and oppression by the strong against the weak.

It is, indeed, a loss, a bitter loss to humanity that those heart beats are stilled for ever.

[· · ·]

He devised the extraordinary measure of assistance called Lend–Lease, which will stand forth as the most unselfish and un-sordid financial act of any country in all history. The effect of this was greatly to increase British fighting power, and for all the purpose of the war effort to make us, as it were, a much more numerous community. In that autumn I met the President for the first time during the war at Argentia in Newfoundland, and together we drew up the declaration which has since been called the Atlantic Charter, and which will, I trust, long remain a guide for both our peoples and for other people of the world.

All this time in deep and dark and deadly secrecy, the Japanese were preparing their act of treachery and greed. When next we met in Washington, Japan, Germany and Italy had declared war upon the United States, and both our countries were in arms, shoulder to shoulder. Since then we have advanced over the land and over the sea through many difficulties and disappointments, but always with a broadening measure of success. I need not dwell upon the series of great operations which have taken place in the Western Hemisphere, to say nothing of that other immense war proceeding on the other side of the world. Nor need I speak of the plans which we made with our great ally, Russia, at Teheran, for these have now been carried out for all the world to see.

But at Yalta I noticed that the President was ailing. His captivating smile, his gay and charming manner, had not deserted him, but his face had a transparency, an air of purification, and often there was a faraway look in his eyes. When I took my leave of him in Alexandria harbour I must confess that I had an indefinable sense of fear that his health and his strength were on the ebb. But nothing altered his inflexible sense of duty. To the end he faced his innumerable tasks unflinching. One of the tasks of the President is to sign maybe a hundred or two State papers with his own hand every day, commissions and so forth. All this he continued to carry out with the utmost strictness.

When death came suddenly upon him 'he had finished his mail'. That portion of his day's work was done. As the saying goes, he died in harness, and we may well say in battle harness, like his soldiers, sailors, and airmen, who side by side with ours are carrying on their task to the end all over the world. What an enviable death was his. He had brought his country through the worst of its perils and the heaviest of its toils. Victory had cast its sure and steady beam upon him.

In President Roosevelt, there died the greatest American friend we have ever known, and the greatest champion of freedom who has ever brought help and comfort from the new world to the old.

'THE GERMAN WAR IS THEREFORE AT AN END'

Germany surrendered unconditionally on 7 May 1945. The war against Japan continued. In Britain, the Commonwealth and the United States, May 8 was declared Victory-in-Europe Day. That evening, shortly before speaking in the House of Commons, Churchill broadcast to the British people:

Yesterday morning at 2.41 a.m. at Headquarters, General Jodl, the representative of the German High Command, and Grand Admiral Doenitz, the designated head of the German State, signed the act of unconditional surrender of all German land, sea, and air forces in Europe to the Allied Expeditionary Force, and simultaneously to the Soviet High Command.

General Bedell Smith, Chief of Staff of the Allied Expeditionary Force, and General François Sevez signed the document on behalf of the Supreme Commander of the Allied Expeditionary Force, and General Susloparov signed on behalf of the Russian High Command.

Today this agreement will be ratified and confirmed at Berlin where Air Chief Marshal Tedder, Deputy Supreme Commander of the Allied Expeditionary Force, and General de Lattre de Tassigny will sign on behalf of General Eisenhower. Marshal Zhukov will sign on behalf of the Soviet High Command. The German representatives will be Field Marshal Keitel, Chief of the High Command, and the commanders-in-chief of the German Army, Navy, and Air Force.

Hostilities will end officially at one minute after midnight tonight, but in the interests of saving lives the 'Cease fire' began yesterday to be sounded all along the front, and our dear Channel Islands are also to be freed today.

The Germans are still in places resisting the Russian troops, but should they continue to do so after midnight they will, of course, deprive themselves of the protection of the laws of war, and will be attacked from all quarters by the Allied troops. It is not surprising that on such long fronts and in the existing disorder of the enemy the orders of the German High Command should not in every case be obeyed immediately. This does not, in our opinion, with the best military advice at our disposal, constitute any reason for withholding from the nation the facts communicated to us by General Eisenhower of the unconditional surrender already signed at Rheims, nor should it prevent us from celebrating today and tomorrow as Victory-in-Europe days.

Today, perhaps we shall think mostly of ourselves. Tomorrow we shall pay a particular tribute to our Russian comrades, whose prowess in the field has been one of the grand contributions to the general victory.

The German war is therefore at an end. After years of intense preparation, Germany hurled herself on Poland at the beginning of September 1939; and, in pursuance of our guarantee to Poland and in agreement with the French Republic, Great Britain, the British Empire and Commonwealth of Nations, declared war upon this foul aggression. After gallant France had been struck down we, from this island and from our united Empire, maintained the struggle single-handed for a whole year until we were joined by the military might of Soviet Russia, and later by the overwhelming power and resources of the United States of America.

Finally almost the whole world was combined against the evil-doers, who are now prostrate before us. Our gratitude to our splendid allies goes forth from all our hearts in this island and throughout the British Empire.

We may allow ourselves a brief period of rejoicing; but let us not forget for a moment the toil and efforts that lie ahead. Japan, with all her treachery and greed, remains unsubdued. The injury she has inflicted on Great Britain, the United States, and other countries, and her detestable cruelties, call for justice and retribution. We must now devote all our strength and resources to the completion of our task, both at home and abroad. Advance, Britannia. Long live the cause of freedom. God save the King.

After making this broadcast announcement of Germany's unconditional surrender, the Prime Minister read the same statement to the House of Commons a few minutes later, and added:

That is the message which I have been instructed to deliver to the British nation and Commonwealth. I have only two or three sentences to add. They will convey to the House my deep gratitude to this House of Commons, which has proved itself the strongest foundation for waging war that has ever been seen in the whole of our long history. We have all of us made our mistakes, but the strength of the Parliamentary institution has been shown to enable it at the same moment to preserve all the title deeds of democracy while waging war in the most stern and protracted form.

I wish to give my hearty thanks to men of all parties, to everyone in every part of the House where they sit, for the way in which the liveliness of Parliamentary institutions has been maintained under the fire of the enemy, and for the way in which we have been able to persevere – and we could have persevered much longer if need had been – till all the objectives which we set before us for the procuring of the unlimited and unconditional surrender of the enemy had been achieved.

I recollect well at the end of the last war, more than a quarter of a century ago, that the House, when it heard the long list of the surrender terms, the armistice terms, which had been imposed upon the Germans, did not feel inclined for debate or business, but desired to offer thanks to Almighty God, to the Great Power which seems to shape and design the fortunes of nations and the destiny of man; and I therefore beg, Sir, with your permission to move:

'That this House do now attend at the Church of St Margaret, Westminster, to give humble and reverent thanks to Almighty God for our deliverance from the threat of German domination.'

This is the identical Motion which was moved in former times.

'YOU NEVER FLINCHED OR WAVERED'

On 9 May 1945, with Britain celebrating for a second day the victory over Germany, Churchill went out onto the balcony of the Ministry of Health and addressed a vast crowd gathered in Whitehall:

My dear friends, I hope you have had two happy days. Happy days are what we have worked for, but happy days are not easily worked for. By discipline, by morale, by industry, by good laws, by fair institutions – by those ways we have won through to happy days for millions and millions of people.

You have been attacked by a monstrous enemy – but you never flinched or wavered. Your soldiers were everywhere in the field, your airmen in the skies – and never let us forget our grand Navy. They dared and they did all those feats of adventure and audacity which have ever enabled brave men to wrest victory from obstinate and bestial circumstances.

And you people at home have taken all you had to take – which was enough, when all is said and done. You never let the men at the front down. No one ever asked for peace because London was suffering. London, like a great rhinoceros, a great hippopotamus, saying: 'Let them do their worst. London can take it.' London could take anything. My heart goes out to the Cockneys. Any visitors we may happen to have here today – and many great nations are represented here, by all those who have borne arms with us in the struggle – they echo what I say when I say 'Good Old London!'

In every capital of the victorious world there are rejoicings tonight, but in none is there any lack of respect for the part which London has played. I return my hearty thanks to you for never having failed in the long, monotonous days and in the long nights black as hell.

God bless you all. May you long remain as citizens of a great and splendid city. May you long remain as the heart of the British Empire.

'IT IS THE VICTORS WHO MUST SEARCH THEIR HEARTS'

Following Victory-in-Europe Day, 8 May 1945, the war against Japan continued. The Burmese capital, Rangoon, was liberated on May 9, but much fierce fighting was yet to come. On May 10, fifteen Polish political leaders who Stalin had promised Churchill and Roosevelt at Yalta could take part in free and open post-war elections were arrested just outside the Polish capital Warsaw, flown to Moscow, and incarcerated in the Lubianka Prison. On May 12, Churchill telegraphed to the new American President, Harry S. Truman, about the 'Muscovite advance' and presence in the centre of Europe: 'An iron curtain is drawn down upon their front.' On May 13, Churchill broadcast from 10 Downing Street, beginning on a personal note, followed by a survey of Britain at war, and an appeal for the future:

It was five years ago on Thursday last that His Majesty the King commissioned me to form a National Government of all parties to carry on our affairs. Five years is a long time in human life, especially when there is no remission for good conduct. However, this National Government was sustained by Parliament and by the entire British nation at home and by all our fighting men abroad, and by the unswerving co-operation of the Dominions far across the oceans and of our Empire in every quarter of the globe. After various episodes had occurred it became clear last week that so far things have worked out pretty well, and that the British Commonwealth and Empire stands more united and more effectively powerful than at any time in its long romantic history. Certainly we are – this is what may well, I think, be admitted by any fair-minded person – in a far better state to cope with the problems and perils of the future than we were five years ago.

For a while our prime enemy, our mighty enemy, Germany, overran almost all Europe. France, who bore such a frightful strain in the last great war, was beaten to the ground and took some time to recover. The Low Countries, fighting to the best of their strength, were subjugated. Norway was overrun. Mussolini's Italy stabbed us in the back when we were, as he thought, at our last gasp. But for ourselves – our lot, I mean – the British Commonwealth and Empire, we were absolutely alone.

In July, August and September 1940, forty or fifty squadrons of British fighter aircraft in the Battle of Britain broke the teeth of the German air fleet at odds of seven or eight to one. May I repeat again the words I used at that momentous hour: 'Never in the field of human conflict was so much owed by so many to so few.'

[· · ·]

Then began the blitz, when Hitler said he would 'rub out our cities'. That's what he said, 'rub out our cities'. This blitz was borne without a word of complaint or the slightest sign of flinching, while a very large number of people – honour to them all – proved that London could 'take it', and so could our other ravaged centres. But the dawn of 1941 revealed us still in jeopardy. The hostile craft could fly across the approaches to our Island, where forty-six millions of people had to import half their daily bread and all the materials they needed for peace or war: these hostile aircraft could fly across the approaches from Brest to Norway and back again in a single flight. They could observe all the movements of our shipping in and out of the Clyde and Mersey, and could direct upon our convoys the large and increasing numbers of U-boats with which the enemy bespattered the Atlantic – the survivors or successors of which U-boats are now being collected in British harbours.

The sense of envelopment, which might at any moment turn to strangulation, lay heavy upon us. We had only the North-Western approach between Ulster and Scotland through which to bring in the means of life and to send out the forces of war. Owing to the action of Mr. de Valera, so much at variance with the temper and instinct of thousands of Southern Irishmen who hastened to the battle-front to prove their ancient valour, the approaches which the Southern Irish ports and airfields could so easily have guarded were closed by the hostile aircraft and U-boats. This was indeed a deadly moment in our life, and if it had not been for the loyalty and friendship of Northern Ireland we should have been forced to come to close quarters with Mr. de Valera or perish for ever from the earth.

However, with a restraint and poise to which, I say, history will find few parallels, His Majesty's Government never laid a violent hand upon them, though at times it would have been quite easy and quite natural, and we left the de Valera government to frolic with the Germans and later with the Japanese representatives to their heart's content.

When I think of these days I think also of other episodes and personalities. I think of Lieutenant-Commander Esmonde, VC, of Lance-Corporal Kenneally, VC, and Captain Fegen, VC and other Irish heroes that I could easily recite, and then I must confess that bitterness by Britain against the Irish race dies in my heart. I can only pray that in years which I shall not see the shame will be forgotten and the glories will endure, and that the peoples of the British Isles as of the British Commonwealth of Nations will walk together in mutual comprehension and forgiveness.

My friends, when our minds turn to the North-Western approaches, we will not forget the devotion of our merchant seamen, and our minesweepers out every night, and so rarely mentioned in the headlines. Nor will we forget the vast, inventive, adaptive, all-embracing and, in the end, all-controlling power of the Royal Navy, with its ever more potent new ally, the air. These have kept the lifeline open. We were able to breathe; we were able to live; we were able to strike.

Dire deeds we had to do. We had to destroy or capture the French fleet which, had it ever passed undamaged into German hands, would, together with the Italian fleet, have perhaps enabled the German Navy to face us on the high seas. This we did. We had to make the dispatch to General Wavell all round the Cape, at our darkest hour, of the tanks – practically all we had in the Island – and this enabled us as far back as November, 1940, to defend Egypt against invasion and hurl back with the loss of a quarter of a million captives and with heavy slaughter the Italian armies at whose tail Mussolini had already planned to ride into Cairo or Alexandria.

Great anxiety was felt by President Roosevelt, and indeed by thinking men throughout the United States, about what would happen to us in the early part of 1941. The President felt to the depths of his being that the destruction of Britain would not only be an event fearful in itself, but that it would expose to mortal danger the vast and as yet largely unarmed potentialities and the future destiny of the United States. He feared greatly that we should be invaded in that spring of 1941.

[···]

We were, however, in a fairly tough condition by the early months of 1941, and felt very much better about ourselves than in those months immediately after the collapse of France. Our Dunkirk army and field force troops in Britain, almost a million strong, were nearly all equipped or re-equipped. We had ferried over the Atlantic a million rifles and a thousand cannon from the United States, with all their ammunition, since the previous June. In our munition works, which were becoming very powerful, men and women had worked at their machines till they dropped senseless from fatigue.

Nearly one million of men, growing to two millions at the peak, although working all day, had been formed into the Home Guard.

They were armed at least with rifles, and armed also with the spirit 'Conquer or Die'.

Later in 1941, when we were still alone, we sacrificed unwillingly, to some extent unwittingly, our conquests of the winter in Cyrenaica and Libya in order to stand by Greece; and Greece will never forget how much we gave, albeit unavailingly, of the little we had. We did this for honour.

We repressed the German-instigated rising in Iraq. We defended Palestine. With the assistance of General de Gaulle's indomitable Free French we cleared Syria and the Lebanon of Vichyites and of German aviators and intriguers.

And then, in June 1941, another tremendous world event occurred. You have no doubt noticed in your reading of British history – and I hope you will take pains to read it, for it is only from the past that one can judge the future, and it is only from reading the story of the British nation, of the British Empire, that you can feel a well-grounded sense of pride to dwell in these islands – you have sometimes noticed in your reading of British history that we have had to hold out from time to time all alone, or to be the mainspring of coalitions, against a Continental tyrant or dictator, and we have had to hold out for quite a long time: against the Spanish Armada, against the might of Louis XIV, when we led Europe for nearly twenty-five years under William III and Marlborough, and a hundred and fifty years ago, when Nelson, Pitt and Wellington broke Napoleon, not without assistance from the heroic Russians of 1812. In all these world wars our Island kept the lead of Europe or else held out alone.

And if you hold out alone long enough, there always comes a time when the tyrant makes some ghastly mistake which alters the whole balance of the struggle. On June 22, 1941, Hitler, master as he thought himself of all Europe – nay, indeed, soon to be master of the world, so he thought – treacherously, without warning, without the slightest provocation, hurled himself on Russia and came face to face with Marshal Stalin and the numberless millions of the Russian people.

And then at the end of the year Japan struck a felon blow at the United States at Pearl Harbor, and at the same time attacked us in Malaya and Singapore. Thereupon Hitler and Mussolini declared war on the Republic of the United States.

Years have passed since then. Indeed every year seems to me almost a decade. But never since the United States entered the war have I had the slightest doubt but that we should be saved, and that we only had to do our duty in order to win. We have played our part in all this process by which the evil-doers have been overthrown, and I hope I do not speak vain or boastful words, but from Alamein in October 1942, through the Anglo-American invasion of North Africa, of Sicily, of Italy, with the capture of Rome, we marched many miles and never knew defeat.

And then last year, after two years' patient preparation and marvellous devices of amphibious warfare – and mark you, our scientists are not surpassed in any nation in the world, especially when their thought is applied to naval matters – last year on June 6 we seized a carefully selected little toe of German-occupied France and poured millions in from this Island and from across the Atlantic, until the Seine, the Somme, and the Rhine all fell behind the advancing Anglo-American spearheads.

France was liberated. She produced a fine army of gallant men to aid her own liberation. Germany lay open.

Now from the other side the mighty military achievements of the Russian people, always holding many more German troops on their front than we could do, rolled forward to meet us in the heart and centre of Germany. At the same time, in Italy, Field Marshal Alexander's army of so many nations, the largest part of which was British or British Empire, struck their final blow and compelled more than a million enemy troops to surrender. This Fifteenth Army Group, as we call it, British and Americans joined together in almost equal numbers, are now deep in Austria, joining their right hand with the Russians and their left with the United States armies of General Eisenhower's command.

It happened, as you may remember – but memories are short – that in the space of three days we received the news of the un-lamented departures of Mussolini and Hitler, and in three days also surrenders were made to Field Marshal Alexander and Field Marshal Montgomery of over two million five hundred thousand soldiers of this terrible warlike German army.

I shall make it clear at this moment that we never failed to recognize the immense superiority of the power used by the United States in the rescue of France and the defeat of Germany. For our part, British and Canadians, we have had about one-third as many men over there as the Americans, but we have taken our full share of the fighting, as the scale of our losses shows. Our Navy has borne incomparably the heaviest burden in the Atlantic Ocean, in the narrow seas and the Arctic convoys to Russia, while the United States Navy has had to use its immense strength mainly against Japan. We made a fair division of the labour, and we can each report that our work is either done or going to be done.

It is right and natural that we should extol the virtues and glorious services of our own most famous commanders, Alexander and Montgomery, neither of whom was ever defeated since they began together at Alamein. Both of them have conducted in Africa, in Italy, in Normandy and in Germany, battles of the first magnitude and of decisive consequence. At the same time we know how great is our debt to the combining and unifying command and high strategic direction of General Eisenhower.

[···]

It may well be said that our strategy was conducted so that the best combinations, the closest concerts, were imparted into the operations by the combined staffs of Britain and the United States, with whom, from Teheran onwards, the war leaders of Russia were joined. And it may also be said that never have the forces of two nations fought side-by-side and intermingled in the lines of battle with so much unity, comradeship and brotherhood as in the great Anglo-American Armies.

Some people say: Well, what would you expect, if both nations speak the same language, have the same laws, have a great part of their history in common, and have very much the same outlook upon life with all its hope and glory? Isn't it just the sort of thing that would happen? And others may say: It would be an ill day for all the world and for the pair of them if they did not go on working together and marching together and sailing together and flying together, whenever something has to be done for the sake of freedom and fair play all over the world. That is the great hope of the future.

There was one final danger from which the collapse of Germany has saved us. In London and the South-Eastern counties we have suffered for a year from various forms of flying-bombs – perhaps you have heard about this – and rockets, and our Air Force and our back-pack batteries have done wonders against them. In particular the Air Force, turned on in good time on what then seemed very slight and doubtful evidence, hampered and vastly delayed all German prepar-ations. But it was only when our Armies cleaned up the coast and overran all the points of discharge, and when the Americans captured vast stores of rockets of all kinds near Leipzig, which only the other day added to the information we had, and when all the preparations being made on the coasts of France and Holland could be examined in detail, in scientific detail, that we knew how grave had been the peril, not only from rockets and flying bombs but from multiple long-range artillery which was being prepared against London. Only just in time did the Allied armies blast the viper in his nest. Otherwise the autumn of 1944, to say nothing of 1945, might well have seen London as shattered as Berlin.

For the same period the Germans had prepared a new U-boat fleet and novel tactics which, though we should have eventually destroyed them, might well have carried anti-U-boat warfare back to the high peak days of 1942. Therefore we must rejoice and give thanks, not only for our preservation when we were all alone, but for our timely deliverance from new suffering, new perils not easily to be measured.

I wish I could tell you tonight that all our toils and troubles were over. Then indeed I could end my five years' service happily, and if you thought that you had had enough of me and that I ought to be put out to grass, I tell you I would take it with the best of grace. But, on the contrary, I must warn you, as I did when I began this five years' task – and no one knew then that it would last so long – that there is still a lot to do, and that you must be prepared for further efforts of mind and body and further sacrifices to great causes if you are not to fall back into the rut of inertia, the confusion of aim, and the craven fear of being great.

You must not weaken in any way in your alert and vigilant frame of mind. Though holiday rejoicing is necessary to the human spirit, yet it must add to the strength and resilience with which every man and woman turns again to the work they have to do, and also to the outlook and watch they have to keep on public affairs.

On the continent of Europe we have yet to make sure that the simple and honourable purposes for which we entered the war are not brushed aside or over-looked in the months following our success, and that the words 'freedom', 'democracy' and 'liberation' are not distorted from their true meaning as we have understood them. There would be little use in punishing the Hitlerites for their crimes if law and justice did not rule, and if totalitarian or police governments were to take the place of the German invaders.

We seek nothing for ourselves. But we must make sure that those causes which we fought for find recognition at the peace table in facts as well as words, and above all we must labour that the world organization which the United Nations are creating at San Francisco does not become an idle name, does not become a shield for the strong and a mockery for the weak. It is the victors who must search their hearts in their glowing hours, and be worthy by their nobility of the immense forces that they wield.

We must never forget that beyond all lurks Japan, harassed and failing but still a people of a hundred millions, for whose warriors death has few terrors. I cannot tell you tonight how much time or what exertions will be required to compel the Japanese to make amends for their odious treachery and cruelty. We – like China, so long undaunted – have received horrible injuries from them ourselves, and we are bound by the ties of honour and fraternal loyalty to the United States to fight this great war at the other end of the world at their side without flagging or failing. We must remember that Australia and New Zealand and Canada were and are all directly menaced by this evil Power. They came to our aid in our dark times, and we must not leave unfinished any task which concerns their safety and their future.

I told you hard things at the beginning of these last five years; you did not shrink, and I should be unworthy of your confidence and generosity if I did not still cry: Forward, unflinching, unswerving, indomitable, till the whole task is done and the whole world is safe and clean.

'ENORMOUS PROBLEMS LIE BEFORE US'

Churchill hoped that his Grand Coalition would continue in power until the defeat of Japan. But the Labour Party was determined to have a General Election as soon as possible, and to seek a popular mandate. On 21 May 1945, Clement Attlee, Leader of the Labour Party, and Churchill's deputy in the War Cabinet, telephoned him with the message: 'My colleagues and I do not believe that it would be possible to lay aside political controversy now that the expectation of an election has engaged the attention of the country.' His hopes thus rebuffed, on May 23 Churchill tendered his resignation to King George VI. The Grand Coalition was at an end. A General Election would take place in July. Until then, Churchill would remain Prime Minister at the head of a predominantly Conservative 'Caretaker Government'. The Labour Party would go into opposition, and an electoral struggle would begin. On 26 May 1945, Churchill broadcast to the nation whose war leader he had been for the previous five years and sixteen days:

The great victory in Europe has been won. Enormous problems lie before us. A shattered continent is torn by passions and hatred such as have rarely been known in history. We have to carry on with the strong lines of policy to which we have pledged ourselves in the course of the war, and which I shall expound to you as the time offers during the next six weeks.

You are told that this is a rush election. Most of the elections we have fought have been seventy days, but this one has to be rushed through in forty, and we must not use all our powder and shot in the early stages of battle. We must work up to the highest point, which will be reached on polling day.

It has been – I do not conceal it – a matter of grief to me that many Labour and trade union friends and the Liberals have thought it their duty to their parties to leave the National Administration which has just come to an end. While I am well aware of the difficulties which they felt, it is my duty to carry on, and I have called upon those of good will of all Parties and no Parties to join in the Administration. I consider it is one which is capable of discharging the heavy tasks that lie before it and that it will bear comparison with almost any Administration of recent times for ability and single mindedness of purpose.

They call us the 'Caretakers'. No doubt they chose that, and we adopt it, because it means that we shall take very good care of everything that affects the welfare of Britain and of all classes in Britain.

'SOME FORM OF GESTAPO'

In his first party political broadcast, on 4 June 1945, on behalf of the Conservative Party, Churchill sought to influence the voters in favour of the Conservative Party by stressing what he feared were the dictatorial traits of Socialism. His daughter Mary has recalled how his wife Clementine 'begged him to delete the odious and invidious reference to the Gestapo. But he would not heed her.' In his broadcast, Churchill declared:

Socialism is, in its essence, an attack not only upon British enterprise, but upon the right of the ordinary man or woman to breathe freely without having a harsh, clumsy, tyrannical hand clapped across their mouths and nostrils. A Free Parliament – look at that – a Free Parliament is odious to the Socialist doctrinaire.

[···]

No Socialist Government conducting the entire life and industry of the country could afford to allow free, sharp, or violently-worded expressions of public discontent. They would have to fall back on some form of Gestapo, no doubt very humanely directed in the first instance. And this would nip opinion in the bud; it would stop criticism as it reared its head, and it would gather all the power to the supreme party and the party leaders, rising like stately pinnacles above their vast bureaucracies of Civil Servants, no longer servants and no longer civil. And where would the ordinary simple folk – the common people, as they like to call them in America – where would they be, once this mighty organism had got them in its grip?

[···]

My friends, I must tell you that a Socialist policy is abhorrent to the British ideas of freedom. Although it is now put forward in the main by people who have a good grounding in the Liberalism and Radicalism of the early part of this century, there can be no doubt that Socialism is inseparably interwoven with Totalitarianism and the abject worship of the State. It is not alone that property, in all its forms, is struck at, but that liberty, in all its forms, is challenged by the fundamental conceptions of Socialism.

[···]

How is an ordinary citizen or subject of the King to stand up against this formidable machine, which, once it is in power, will prescribe for every one of them where they are to work; what they are to work at; where they may go and what they may say; what views they are to hold and within what limits they may express them; where their wives are to go to queue up for the State ration; and what education their children are to receive to mould their views of human liberty and conduct in the future?

[···]

My sincere hope was that we could have held together until the war against Japan was finished. On the other hand, there was a high duty to consult the people after all these years. I could only be relieved of that duty by the full agreement of the three parties, further fortified, perhaps, by a kind of official Gallup Poll, which I am sure would have resulted in an overwhelming request that we should go on to the end and finish the job. That would have enabled me to say at once, 'There will be no election for a year', or words to that effect.

I know that many of my Labour colleagues would have been glad to carry on. On the other hand, the Socialist Party as a whole had been for some time eager to set out upon the political warpath, and when large numbers of people feel like that it is not good for their health to deny them the fight they want. We will therefore give it to them to the best of our ability.

[···]

Party, my friends, has always played a great part in our affairs. Party ties have been considered honourable bonds, and no one could doubt that when the German war was over and the immediate danger to this country, which had led to the Coalition, had ceased, conflicting loyalties would arise. Our Socialist and Liberal friends felt themselves forced, therefore, to put party before country. They have departed, and we have been left to carry the nation's burden.

'NOTHING IS EASIER THAN TO PREVENT FREE SPEECH'

On 3 July 1945, as the election campaign drew to a close, Churchill spoke in the Stadium at Walthamstow to a crowd of more than twenty thousand people, some of whom were vehemently hostile. At times, his voice was drowned out by booing and uproar. He was in a pugnacious electioneering mood:

This is a peculiar gathering in which both sides are taking part. (Laughter.) I think I will begin by testing the microphone. I would like to know whether my voice reaches you or not. Can you hear me? (There were cries of 'Yes' and when he continued 'Are we down-hearted?' there was a thunderous 'No' from the crowd.)

I should like to ask for the help of all members of the audience. Of course, in a free country like ours which has fought for freedom all over the world, and gained it for many countries that never knew it; in a free country every one has a perfect right to cheer or boo as much as he likes. (Cheers and boos.) The winners cheer and the beaten boo.

But it is a serious question if interruptions are made with the opportunity and intention of stopping free speech. Nothing is easier than to prevent free speech, but the only result of doing that is to reduce ourselves to those totalitarian States that were established by Hitler and Mussolini, and anyone who interrupts in an organized manner a great public gathering is guilty of those very crimes which our soldiers have swept away across Europe with fire and sword.

38 Above Victory-in-Europe, Day Two, 9 May 1945. Churchill on the balcony of the Ministry of Health, Whitehall. To his right, Ernest Bevin, Minister of Labour and National Service, and Oliver Lyttelton, Minister of Production.

39 Below On the Ministry of Health balcony, 9 May 1945. Bevin is on Churchill's right and Sir John Anderson, Chancellor of the Exchequer, on his left.

40 Churchill, standing in an open car, makes his way through the crowd in Whitehall, 9 May 1945.

41 **Above** Churchill in his constituency, electioneering with his wife, 26 May 1945.

42 **Below** Churchill electioneering in his constituency, 4 July 1945.

43 Above Churchill and President Truman, accompanied by two G-Men, on their way to Westminster College, where Churchill was to deliver his Fulton speech, 5 March 1946.

44 Below Churchill delivering his Fulton speech. Truman is sitting below him, wearing a mortar board. In front of Churchill is the 'Seal of the President of the United States'.

45 Above On 8 March 1946, three days after his Fulton speech, Churchill reaches Richmond, Virginia, where he was to speak. With him is General Eisenhower. Behind them are Clementine Churchill and Mamie Eisenhower.

46 Below Churchill is overwhelmed as he is accorded a standing ovation after his speech at the Congress of Europe, The Hague, 7 May 1948. Left to right behind him, applauding, are four of the leaders of the European Movement: Pieter Adriaan Kerstens (Holland), Paul Ramadier (France), Joseph Retinger (Secretary General of the Congress) and Denis de Rougement (Switzerland).

47 Above Churchill arrives at Harrow School, 7 November 1952, for the annual school songs.

48, 49 Below, left and right Churchill speaking at the Conservative Party conference, Margate, 10 October 1953.

50 Churchill's 80th birthday tribute in Westminster Hall, 30 November 1954. The Graham Sutherland portrait is behind him. Clement Attlee is sitting on the far right.

51 Churchill working on the proofs of his last book, the four-volume *A History of the English-Speaking Peoples*, at Villa La Pausa, Roquebrune, South of France. This photograph was taken by his host at La Pausa and literary agent, Emery Reves.

I have come in the first place to say something to you which is not at all of a controversial character. So both cheerers and boo-ers can take a moment off. I want to congratulate London, as it is the first great speech I have made, the first important gathering I have addressed, in London – upon her wonderful record in the war. Would you like to boo that?

The triumphs which this great city has gained by her conduct in the war – Greater London – are without parallel in the whole world. If you take Greater London as a whole, the people who were living here before the war began, and you look at them now, one in every 130 has been killed either by going abroad from this area to fight or by remaining here to receive the full blast of the bombs. And in this part of the world they have fallen more heavily than in any other part of London, especially Walthamstow, Ilford, Woodford, and those areas around there.

I offer you my sincere thanks and congratulations for the composure and steady attention to duty with which you have succeeded in enduring this exceptionally severe strain, the consequences of which have been to give our country an effective power to maintain unperturbed and unwearied the long and vehement impulse of war.

There was a time when we were all alone, all alone for a year, but by holding firm we not only came through ourselves but we enabled great nations like Soviet Russia (cheers and interruptions) – Well, surely no one is going to boo Soviet Russia? I thought it was common ground between us that they had fought a valiant fight in defence of their hearths and homes – and the United States, these two great nations were able to come together and be fully armed. Thus we obtained great superiority over the enemy, which led to the present victory in Europe.

Now, in Europe we own complete control but much remains to be done. Very grave problems have to be settled – the conquered enemy and the destroyed countries which have fallen into our control – in a manner which will best conduce to the healing of the wounds, to the curing of the horrible destruction and ruin which has fallen upon Europe, and to enable the continent to rise again in the same united form with her old glories and all the hopes of future progress which lie within us.

There has been a gentleman on my left who keeps on hollering about policy. I will answer his inquiry. Our policy is in the first place to beat Japan (loud cheers), that greedy and treacherous Power which attacked the United States at Pearl Harbor and also attacked us.

The war against Japan must be conducted at the other end of the world, and therefore only a small portion of the great armies we have used in Europe can go there; but it is our duty to fight with our utmost strength.

The United States sent men over here in millions to help us and to break the power of Hitler, and we must stand by them in another fight at the other end of the world which is also in an important degree our battle too.

That is the first element in our policy. The next is to bring the armies home. (Loud cheering.) At the same time as we are bringing the great majority of the armies home we are reorganizing and redeploying other armies to go and fight against Japan. Thus we have that as our first practical business.

Then we have to build up the homes and houses that have been shattered by the enemy's bombardment, and also to make up for the loss of six years' building which the war had entailed. When the war had broken out, in the year before the war we had built 350,000 houses in one year. Look out. Hold on to your chairs. This is one you will not like – two-thirds of those houses were built by private enterprise. (Loud cheers.) Have a good boo about that; have a good boo – private enterprise.

Well, six years of 350,000 houses a year is very near two millions, and we are short all those, apart from all the houses that the enemy blew down, or broke in pieces. Why have we not repaired and rebuilt those houses? Well, you can ask Mr. Attlee and Mr. Bevin and that great London hero Mr. Herbert Morrison, because if we are to blame, they are to blame too. But some of the Socialists and Labour's friends will be relieved to hear that I do not think they were to blame, nor are we.

But all the builders were at the war. We could have had a lot more houses here if we had recalled the builders a year ago, if we had brought them from the front and brought them from the munitions works, but then we would not have ended the war. We might have had the houses but the war would have been going on, dragging on from the summer to the winter. (Loud cheers.)

That is the excuse I offer on behalf of Mr. Attlee, Mr. Bevin, and Mr. Morrison – (interruptions) – and of myself. (Cheers and counter-cheers.)

Well, the first thing we have to do is to build the houses, and I am here to tell you that we will do everything in human power to get them built. Nothing shall stand in the way. We will use our powers as if it was a military operation, and I hope and trust – though I cannot guarantee – there will not be a long period of shortage. I hope and trust unexpected progress will be made, more than anything we were able to promise in the days of the famous Coalition, when all the booers could cheer as well as boo. (Cheers and boos followed this statement.)

We have a four years' plan. In this have figured largely the Socialist leaders. Then we have the great insurance scheme which covers everybody from the cradle to the grave, and which certainly Sir William Beveridge, who does not belong to the Labour Party, had a great deal to do with. We have also a large development of the health services, and we have to put in operation the Education Bill.

A lot of silly loud-mouthed people make (cheers and boos) – all sorts of comments at these great measures in which the Socialist Party have had a great part, and for which they deserve better credit from their supporters than this senseless booing. All that is in the policy. In addition we have to get our trade started. We have a good chance of getting it started here at home because everybody is short of everything. Pots and pans, clothes, blankets, furniture, everything has been neglected in the last six years. On the other hand, consider-able war savings have been accumulated, and there should be a perfectly good demand in the island for what can be produced in it.

[···]

I would say that when we are asked what is our policy I can only tell you of the enormous amount of work that lies before you, but I believe we are quite capable of achieving that task providing we are not thrown into foolish faction fights about idiotic ideologies and philosophical dreams of absurd Utopias – worlds which will be seen only by a great improvement of the human heart and improvement of human heads [interruption].

I am sorry that one hurts, I cannot help it. I did not mean it to hurt, but I repeat – improvement of human hearts and human heads before we can achieve the glorious Utopia that the Socialist wool-gatherers place before us.

Now where is the boo party? I shall call them henceforward in my speech the booing party. Everyone have a good boo.

Churchill then turned from the hostile side of the stadium and, looking at the other side, said:

Any help from this side? (Cheering broke out.)

Where I think the booing party are making such a mistake is dragging all this stuff across the practical tasks we have to fulfil. They are spoiling the tasks that have to be done in order to carry out their nightmares. They have no chance of carrying them out. They are going to be defeated at this election in a most decisive manner. (Cheers.) Their exhibition here shows very clearly the sort of ideas they have of free speech. (Cheers.)

That should be a great warning to the British people as a whole to make no error on Thursday next and vote against men who to mental confusion would not hesitate to add civic disorder in such a way as to prevent the exercise of the British right of free speech which has always been adopted.

I am not going to speak any more to the booers, but I am going to urge all those, who wish to see the great victory which our country has won carried into conclusion in the years after the war is over, to see that great victory herald in a time of peaceful progress.

I am anxious that they should help in the establishment of a great world organisation to prevent future wars, that we should ourselves preserve a unity among ourselves, so as to take our part in the van of the great nations, and so that at the end when all the story is told, whether you look at the picture of our deeds abroad in the war, or to the use we made of the victory after it was won, people will be able to say in future times they did a fine job of work. (Prolonged cheers mixed with booing.)

'DEAR DESERT RATS'

On 15 July 1945, Churchill flew to Berlin for the Potsdam Conference with the new American President, Harry S. Truman, and Marshal Stalin. On July 21, after six days of intense negotiations, he was driven into Berlin to take the salute at a Victory Parade of British troops. After the parade, he spoke at the opening of the 'Winston Club' for British servicemen and women in Berlin:

I am delighted to be able to open this club. I shall always consider it an honour to have it named after me.

This morning's parade brings back to my mind a great many moving incidents of these last long, fierce years. Now you are here in Berlin, and I find you established in this great centre which, as a volcano, erupted smoke and fire all over Europe. Twice in our generation as in bygone times the German fury has been unleashed on her neighbours.

Now it is we who take our place in the occupation of this country. I think I may go so far as to ask Field Marshal Montgomery to signalize the happy event of this great victory parade today by giving all the troops in Berlin a whole-day holiday. I hope, Field Marshal, you can accommodate this operation.

I have only one more word to say to the Desert Rats. You were the first to begin. The 11th Hussars were in action in the Desert in 1940, and ever since you have kept marching steadily forward on the long road to Victory: through so many countries and changing scenes you have marched and fought your way.

I am unable to speak without emotion. Dear Desert Rats, may your glory ever shine. May your laurels never fade. May the memory of this glorious pilgrimage which you have made from Alamein to the Baltic and Berlin never die. A march – as far as my reading of history leads me to believe – unsurpassed in the whole story of war.

May fathers long tell their children the tale. May you all feel that through following your great ancestors you have accomplished something which has done good to the whole world, which has raised the honour of your country and of which every man has the right to feel proud.

'MY PROFOUND GRATITUDE'

Churchill returned to Britain from Potsdam while the conference was still in session to learn the General Election result, which was announced on 26 July 1945. The Conservative Party, which had effectively ruled Britain for eight years before the war, was defeated, and a Labour Government, pledged to carry out radical social reform, came into office. The Labour Ministers, many of whom had for five years been an integral part of Churchill's wartime coalition, acquired, by democratic means and a free and fair election, the authority to govern the nation. That day, Churchill resigned the premiership he had held since May 1940, and issued a public statement:

> The decision of the British people has been recorded in the votes counted today. I have therefore laid down the charge which was placed upon me in darker times. I regret that I have not been permitted to finish the work against Japan. For this however all plans and preparations have been made, and the results may come much quicker than we have hitherto been entitled to expect.
>
> Immense responsibilities abroad and at home fall upon the new Government, and we must all hope that they will be successful in bearing them.
>
> It only remains for me to express to the British people, for whom I have acted in these perilous years, my profound gratitude for the unflinching, unswerving support which they have given me during my task, and for the many expressions of kindness which they have shown towards their servant.

'NO BOY OR GIRL SHOULD EVER BE DISHEARTENED'

Following the defeat of the Conservative Party at the 1945 General Election, Clementine Churchill remarked to her husband that it was 'a blessing in disguise' – to which he replied: 'Very heavily disguised.'

To a friend, he commented: 'I don't pretend not to be vexed. Defeat, however explained, consoled or discounted, is odious.' On 7 January 1946, he and Clementine set sail from England for an extended visit to the United States and Cuba. Reaching New York on January 14, they took the train to Miami. On February 26 he was awarded an honorary degree at the University of Miami. Although he had never been to university, he already had several dozen honorary degrees. In his acceptance speech – part of which is reproduced here in his standard 'speech form' or 'psalm form' notes from which he delivered it – he told a crowd of 17,500 in the Burdine Stadium:

> I am surprised that in my later life
>   I should have become so experienced
>   In taking degrees,
> When, as a school-boy,
>   I was so bad at passing examinations.
> In fact one might almost say
>   that no one ever passed so few examinations
>   and received so many degrees.
> From this a superficial thinker might argue
>   that the way to get the most degrees
>   is to fail in the most examinations.
> This would however, ladies and gentlemen, be a conclusion
>   unedifying in the academic atmosphere
>   in which I now preen myself,
> and I therefore hasten to draw another moral
>   with which I am sure we shall all be in accord:
> namely, that no boy or girl
>   should ever be disheartened
>   by lack of success in their youth
> but should diligently and faithfully
>   continue to persevere
>   and make up for lost time.

'AN IRON CURTAIN HAS DESCENDED'

In the immediate aftermath of the war, Churchill contemplated with alarm a Europe divided between East and West, by what he called an 'Iron Curtain'. The dominance of the Soviet Union and of Communism in Eastern Europe was his overriding concern in the international sphere. He expressed his fears, and also his hopes, when he spoke, at the request of President Harry S. Truman, at Westminster College, Fulton, Missouri, on 5 March 1946. He gave his speech the title 'The Sinews of Peace':

A shadow has fallen upon the scenes so lately lighted by the Allied victory. Nobody knows what Soviet Russia and its Communist inter- national organisation intends to do in the immediate future, or what are the limits, if any, to their expansive and proselytising tendencies. I have a strong admiration and regard for the valiant Russian people and for my wartime comrade, Marshal Stalin. There is deep sympathy and goodwill in Britain – and I doubt not here also – towards the peoples of all the Russias and a resolve to persevere through many differences and rebuffs in establishing lasting friendships. We under- stand the Russian need to be secure on her western frontiers by the removal of all possibility of German aggression. We welcome Russia to her rightful place among the leading nations of the world. We welcome her flag upon the seas. Above all, we welcome constant, frequent and growing contacts between the Russian people and our own people on both sides of the Atlantic. It is my duty however, for I am sure you would wish me to state the facts as I see them to you, to place before you certain facts about the present position in Europe.

From Stettin in the Baltic to Trieste in the Adriatic, an iron curtain has descended across the Continent. Behind that line lie all the capitals of the ancient states of Central and Eastern Europe. Warsaw, Berlin, Prague, Vienna, Budapest, Belgrade, Bucharest and Sofia, all these famous cities and the populations around them lie in what I must call the Soviet sphere, and all are subject in one form or another, not only to Soviet influence but to a very high and, in many cases, increasing measure of control from Moscow. Athens alone – Greece with its immortal glories – is free to decide its future at an election under British, American and French observation. The Russian-dominated Polish Government has been encouraged to make enormous and wrongful inroads upon Germany, and mass expulsions of millions of Germans on a scale grievous and undreamed-of are now taking place. The Communist parties, which were very small in all these Eastern States of Europe, have been raised to pre-eminence and power far beyond their numbers and are seeking everywhere to obtain totalitarian control. Police governments are prevailing in nearly every case and so far, except in Czechoslovakia, there is no true democracy.

[···]

If now the Soviet Government tries, by separate action, to build up a pro-Communist Germany in their areas, this will cause new serious difficulties in the British and American zones, and will give the defeated Germans the power of putting themselves up to auction between the Soviets and the Western Democracies. Whatever conclusions may be drawn from these facts – and facts they are – this is certainly not the Liberated Europe we fought to build up. Nor is it one which contains the essentials of permanent peace.

The safety of the world requires a new unity in Europe, from which no nation should be permanently outcast. It is from the quarrels of the strong parent races in Europe that the world wars we have witnessed, or which occurred in former times, have sprung. Twice in our own lifetime we have seen the United States, against their wishes and their traditions, against arguments, the force of which it is impossible not to comprehend, drawn by irresistible forces, into these wars in time to secure the victory of the good cause, but only after frightful slaughter and devastation had occurred. Twice the United States has had to send several millions of its young men across the Atlantic to find the war; but now war can find any nation, wherever it may dwell between dusk and dawn. Surely we should work with conscious purpose for a grand pacification of Europe, within the structure of the United Nations and in accordance with its Charter. That I feel is an open cause of policy of very great importance.

In front of the iron curtain which lies across Europe are other causes for anxiety. In Italy the Communist Party is seriously hampered by having to support the Communist-trained Marshal Tito's claims to former Italian territory at the head of the Adriatic. Nevertheless the future of Italy hangs in the balance. Again one cannot imagine a regenerated Europe without a strong France. All my public life I have worked for a strong France and I never lost faith in her destiny, even in the darkest hours. I will not lose faith now. However, in a great number of countries, far from the Russian frontiers and throughout the world, Communist fifth columns are established and work in complete unity and absolute obedience to the directions they receive from the Communist centre. Except in the British Commonwealth and in the United States where Communism is in its infancy, the Communist parties or fifth columns constitute a growing challenge and peril to Christian civilisation. These are sombre facts for anyone to have to recite on the morrow of a victory gained by so much splendid comradeship in arms and in the cause of freedom and democracy; but we should be most unwise not to face them squarely while time remains.

[...]

I have felt bound to portray the shadow which, alike in the West and in the East, falls upon the world. I was a high minister at the time of the Versailles Treaty and a close friend of Mr Lloyd George, who was the head of the British delegation at Versailles. I did not myself agree with many things that were done, but I have a very strong impression in my mind of that situation, and I find it painful to contrast it with that which prevails now. In those days there were high hopes and unbounded confidence that the wars were over, and that the League of Nations would become all-powerful. I do not see or feel that same confidence or even the same hopes in the haggard world at the present time.

On the other hand I repulse the idea that a new war is inevitable; still more that it is imminent. It is because I am sure that our fortunes are still in our own hands and that we hold the power to save the future, that I feel the duty to speak out now that I have the occasion and the opportunity to do so. I do not believe that Soviet Russia desires war. What they desire is the fruits of war and the indefinite expansion of their power and doctrines. But what we have to consider here today while time remains, is the permanent prevention of war and the establishment of conditions of freedom and democracy as rapidly as possible in all countries.

Our difficulties and dangers will not be removed by closing our eyes to them. They will not be removed by mere waiting to see what happens; nor will they be removed by a policy of appeasement. What is needed is a settlement, and the longer this is delayed, the more difficult it will be and the greater our dangers will become.

From what I have seen of our Russian friends and Allies during the war, I am convinced that there is nothing they admire so much as strength, and there is nothing for which they have less respect than for weakness, especially military weakness. For that reason the old doctrine of a balance of power is unsound. We cannot afford, if we can help it, to work on narrow margins, offering temptations to a trial of strength. If the Western Democracies stand together in strict adherence to the principles of the United Nations Charter, their influence for furthering those principles will be immense and no one is likely to molest them. If however they become divided or falter in their duty and if these all-important years are allowed to slip away then indeed catastrophe may overwhelm us all.

Last time I saw it all coming and cried aloud to my own fellow-countrymen and to the world, but no one paid any attention. Up till the year 1933 or even 1935, Germany might have been saved from the awful fate which has overtaken her and we might all have been spared the miseries Hitler let loose upon mankind.

There never was a war in all history easier to prevent by timely action than the one which has just desolated such great areas of the globe. It could have been prevented in my belief without the firing of a single shot, and Germany might be powerful, prosperous and honoured to-day; but no one would listen and one by one we were all sucked into the awful whirlpool. We surely must not let that happen again. This can only be achieved by reaching now a good under-standing on all points with Russia under the general authority of the United Nations Organisation and by the maintenance of that good understanding through many peaceful years, by the world instru-ment, supported by the whole strength of the English-speaking world and all its connections. There is the solution which I respectfully offer to you in this Address to which I have given the title 'The Sinews of Peace'.

Let no man underrate the abiding power of the British Empire and Commonwealth. Because you see the 46 millions in our island harassed about their food supply, of which they only grow one half, even in war-time, or because we have difficulty in restarting our industries and export trade after six years of passionate war effort, do not suppose that we shall not come through these dark years of privation as we have come through the glorious years of agony, or that half a century from now, you will not see 70 or 80 millions of Britons spread about the world and united in defence of our traditions, our way of life, and of the world causes which you and we espouse.

If the population of the English-speaking Commonwealths be added to that of the United States with all that such co-operation implies in the air, on the sea, all over the globe and in science and in industry, and in moral force, there will be no quivering, precarious balance of power to offer its temptation to ambition or adventure. On the contrary, there will be an overwhelming assurance of security. If we adhere faithfully to the Charter of the United Nations and walk forward in sedate and sober strength seeking no one's land or treasure, seeking to lay no arbitrary control upon the thoughts of men; if all British moral and material forces and convictions are joined with your own in fraternal association, the high-roads of the future will be clear, not only for us but for all, not only for our time, but for a century to come.

'GREATHEART MUST HAVE HIS SWORD AND ARMOUR'

Speaking to the General Assembly of Virginia, at Richmond, Virginia, on 8 March 1946, in the presence of General Eisenhower, Churchill stressed that Britain and the United States must be united if democracy was to be preserved:

It has been said that the dominant lesson of history is that mankind is unteachable. You will remember how my dear friend, the late President Roosevelt, had to argue only a few years ago, that Americans were not what is called 'soft' and how he asserted that this was 'The land of unending challenge', and I myself have read in secret documents German reports which spoke before they met them of 'these ridiculous American troops'.

Surely these European countries should not have forgotten or ignored so soon the example of tenacity, willpower and self-devotion which shines through all the records of the great war between the American States. We, too, in our British islands and in our great self-governing Empire spread about the world, have proved that our race when stirred to its depth has qualities deserving of respect. In fact, in proportion to our numbers, our efforts, our sacrifices and our losses have not been surpassed. Moreover, it fell to us to have the honour of standing alone for a whole year against the main strength of the mighty Axis and the time for preparation which was thus gained was, as I am sure General Eisenhower will agree, a vital service to the United States and to the common cause.

But it is upon the future rather than upon the past that I wish to rest this morning. In these last years of my life there is a message of which I conceive myself to be a bearer. It is a very simple message which can be well understood by the people of both our countries. It is that we should stand together. We should stand together in malice to none, in greed for nothing but in defence of those causes which we hold dear not only for our own benefit, but because we believe they mean the honour and the happiness of long generations of men.

We ought, as I said to the Congress of the United States in a dark hour in 1941, to walk together in majesty and peace. That I am sure is the wish of the overwhelming majority of the 200 million Britons and Americans who are spread about the globe. That this is our destiny, or, as most of us would put it, the Will of God, seems sure and certain. How it is to be expressed, in what way and in what hour it is to be achieved I cannot tell.

I read the other day that an English nobleman, whose name is new to me, has stated that England would have to become the 49th state of the American Union. I read yesterday that an able American editor had written that the United States ought not to be asked to re-enter the British Empire. It seems to me and I dare say it seems to you, that the path of wisdom lies somewhere between these scarecrow extremes. We must find the means and the method of working together not only in times of war and mortal anguish but in times of peace with all its bewilderments and clamour and clatter of tongues.

It is in the years of peace that wars are prevented and that those foundations are laid upon which the noble structures of the future can be built. But peace will not be preserved without the virtues that make victory possible in war. Peace will not be preserved by pious sentiments expressed in terms of platitudes or by official grimaces and diplomatic correctitude, however desirable this may be from time to time. It will not be preserved by casting aside in dangerous years the panoply of warlike strength.

There must be earnest thought. There must also be faithful perseverance and foresight. Greatheart must have his sword and armour to guard the pilgrims on their way. Above all, among the English-speaking peoples, there must be the union of hearts based upon conviction and common ideals. This is what I offer. That is what I seek.

'LET GERMANY LIVE'

Churchill had visited Berlin in July 1945 and had seen for himself the devastation caused by the war to the German capital. In his memoirs he wrote: 'My hate ended with their surrender.' There were those in Britain and beyond who wanted the whole German people to be punished. Churchill rejected this, and in a speech in the House of Commons on 5 June 1946 explained why:

Indescribable crimes have been committed by Germany under the Nazi rule. Justice must take its course, the guilty must be punished, but once that is over and I trust it will soon be over – I fall back on the declaration of Edmund Burke, 'I cannot frame an indictment against an entire people.'

We cannot plan or even dream of a new world or a new Europe which contains pariah nations, that is to say, nations permanently or for prolonged periods outcast from the human family. Our ultimate hopes must be founded – can only be founded – on the harmony of the human family.

So far as it remains in the power of this island people to influence the course of events, we must strive over a period of years to redeem and to reincorporate the German and the Japanese peoples in a world system of free and civilised democracy. The idea of keeping scores of millions of people hanging about in a sub-human state between earth and hell, until they are worn down to a slave condition or embrace Communism, or die off from hunger, will only, if it is pursued, breed at least a moral pestilence and probably an actual war.

[···]

It is better to have a world united than a world divided; but it is also better to have a world divided, than a world destroyed. Nor does it follow that even in a world divided there should not be equilibrium from which a further advance to unity might be attempted as the years pass by. Anything is better than this ceaseless degeneration of the heart of Europe. Europe will die of that.

[···]

Europe is far worse off in every respect than she was at the end of the last war. Her miseries, confusion and hatreds far exceed anything that was known in those bygone days.

[···]

Let us proclaim them fearlessly. Let Germany live. Let Austria and Hungary be freed. Let Italy resume her place in the European system. Let Europe arise again in glory, and by her strength and unity ensure the peace of the world.

'OUR TWO COUNTRIES HAVE STRUGGLED ALONG TOGETHER'

Post-war Europe saw a much weakened France, divided internally between those who had collaborated with the Germans and those who had refused to do so, even resisting as best they could under the harsh rigours of occupation. On 14 July 1946, Bastille Day, while in the French city of Metz, Churchill made a powerful appeal to France:

Many memories are stirred in my mind by this visit to Metz and your joyous welcome. Sixty-three years ago my father took me on my first visit to France. It was in the summer of 1883. We drove along together through the Place de la Concorde. Being an observant child I noticed that one of the monuments was covered with wreaths and crêpe and I at once asked him why. He replied, 'These are monuments of the Provinces of France. Two of them, Alsace and Lorraine, have been taken from France by the Germans in the last war. The French are very unhappy about it and hope some day to get them back.'

I remember quite distinctly thinking to myself, 'I hope they will get them back'. This hope at least has not been disappointed.

Many years passed before I attended the manoeuvres of the French Army in 1907. The Entente Cordiale had been established between Great Britain and France. I was already a youthful Minister of the Crown. In those days the soldiers wore blue tunics and red trousers and many of the movements were still in close order. When I saw, at the climax of the manoeuvres, the great masses of French infantry storming the position, while the bands played the Marseillaise, I felt that by those valiant bayonets the rights of man had been gained and that by them these rights and also the liberties of Europe would be faithfully guarded.

That was nearly 40 years ago, but from that moment I have always worked with you not only out of friendship for France but because of the great causes for which our two countries have suffered so much and risked all. The road has been long and terrible. I am astonished to find myself here at the end of it. In all that ordeal of two generations our two countries have marched and struggled side by side and

I, your guest here today, have never neglected anything that could preserve and fortify our united action. Therefore I speak to you not only as a friend but as a lifelong comrade. In all the frightful experiences we have undergone in our resistance to German aggression and tyranny our two countries have struggled along together to keep the flag of freedom flying and at an awful and hideous cost we have accomplished our duty. Never let us part.

[···]

There can be no revival of Europe with its culture, its charm, its tradition and its mighty power, without a strong France. Many nations in the past have wished and tried to be strong. But never before has there been such a clear need for one country to be strong as there is now for France. When I think of the young Frenchmen growing into manhood in this shattered and bewildered world, I cannot recall any generation in any country before in whose eyes duty is written more plainly or in more gleaming characters.

Two hundred years ago in England the Elder and the greater Pitt addressed this invocation to his fellow-countrymen, torn, divided and confused by faction as they then were: 'Be one people'. That was his famous invocation. And in our island, for all its fogs and muddles, we are one people today, and dangers if they threaten will only bind us more firmly together.

Using my privilege as your old and faithful friend, I do not hesitate to urge upon all Frenchmen, worn or worried though they may be, to unite in the task of leading Europe back in peace and freedom to broader and better days. By saving yourselves you will save Europe and by saving Europe you will save yourselves.

'THE UNITED STATES OF EUROPE'

During 1946, Churchill developed his theme of a United States of Europe. He wanted France and Germany to come together, and even envisaged a time when the Soviet Union, a member of the United Nations Organisation (UNO), would be part of a single European entity. He explained his ideas in a speech at Zurich University on 19 September 1946:

I am now going to say something that will astonish you. The first step in the re-creation of the European family must be a partnership between France and Germany. In this way only can France recover the moral leadership of Europe. There can be no revival of Europe without a spiritually great France and a spiritually great Germany. The structure of the United States of Europe, if well and truly built, will be such as to make the material strength of a single state less important. Small nations will count as much as large ones and gain their honour by their contribution to the common cause.

The ancient states and principalities of Germany, freely joined together for mutual convenience in a federal system, might each take their individual place among the United States of Europe. I shall not try to make a detailed programme for hundreds of millions of people who want to be happy and free, prosperous and safe, who wish to enjoy the four freedoms of which the great President Roosevelt spoke, and live in accordance with the principles embodied in the Atlantic Charter. If this is their wish, they have only to say so, and means can certainly be found, and machinery erected, to carry that wish into full fruition.

[···]

Time may be short. At present there is a breathing space. The cannon have ceased firing. The fighting has stopped; but the dangers have not stopped. If we are to form the United States of Europe or whatever name or form it may take, we must begin now.

In these present days we dwell strangely and precariously under the shield and protection of the atomic bomb. The atomic bomb is still only in the hands of a State and nation which we know will never use it except in the cause of right and freedom. But it may well be that in a few years this awful agency of destruction will be widespread and the catastrophe following from its use by several warring nations will not only bring to an end all that we call civilisation, but may possibly disintegrate the globe itself.

I must now sum up the propositions which are before you. Our constant aim must be to build and fortify the strength of UNO. Under and within that world concept we must re-create the European family in a regional structure called, it may be, the United States of Europe. The first step is to form a Council of Europe. If at first all the States of Europe are not willing or able to join the Union, we must nevertheless proceed to assemble and combine those who will and those who can.

The salvation of the common people of every race and of every land from war or servitude must be established on solid foundations and must be guarded by the readiness of all men and women to die rather than submit to tyranny. In all this urgent work, France and Germany must take the lead together. Great Britain, the British Commonwealth of Nations, mighty America, and I trust Soviet Russia – for then indeed all would be well – must be the friends and sponsors of the new Europe and must champion its right to live and shine.

'WHEN DID PUNISHMENT BEGIN?'

Churchill did not believe in vengeance. He had seen it carried out by British troops in the Sudan in 1898, and it had repelled him. On 12 November 1946 he told the House of Commons:

I am told that Germany must be punished. I ask: When did punishment begin? It certainly seems to have been going on for a long time. It began in 1943, and continued during 1944 and 1945, when the most frightful air bombardments were cast upon German cities, and when the general exhaustion of their life under the cruel Nazi regime had drained the last ounces of strength from the German race and nation.

The Nuremberg trials are over, and the guilty leaders of the Nazi regime have been hanged by the conquerors. We are told that thousands yet remain to be tried, and that vast categories of Germans are classed as potentially guilty because of their association with the Nazi regime. After all, in a country which is handled as Germany was, the ordinary people have very little choice about what to do.

I think some consideration should always be given to ordinary people. Everyone is not a Pastor Niemöller or a martyr, and when ordinary people are hurled this way and that, when the cruel hands of tyrants are laid upon them and vile systems of regimentation are imposed and enforced by espionage and other forms of cruelty, there are great numbers of people who will succumb.

I thank God that in this island home of ours, we have never been put to the test which many of the peoples of Europe have had to undergo. It is my hope that we shall presently reach the end of the executions, penalties, and punishments, and that without forgetting the hard lessons of the past, we shall turn our faces resolutely towards the future.

'NO TWO RACES HAVE SET SUCH A MARK UPON THE WORLD'

While writing *The Second World War*, Churchill reflected on two peoples – the Greeks and the Jews. During the war, he had tried to help both. In 1942 he had powerfully denounced the Nazi crimes against the Jews. In 1944 he had flown to Athens over Christmas to help avert a Greek civil war. But the murder in Cairo in 1944 of one of his closest friends, Lord Moyne, by Jewish terrorists, had shaken his belief in the victory of Jewish moderation. Even while he was writing his memoirs, he had been shocked by the renewed terrorist activities of a small minority of Jews in British Mandate Palestine, and had welcomed the outspoken denunciation of that violence by the leaders of the Jewish community there. These events led to a poignant reflection in his memoirs:

The Greeks rival the Jews in being the most politically minded race in the world. No matter how forlorn their circumstances or how grave the peril to their country, they are always divided into many parties, with many leaders who fight among themselves with desperate vigour. It has been well said that wherever there are three Jews it will be found that there are two Prime Ministers and one leader of the Opposition. The same is true of this other famous ancient race, whose stormy and endless struggle for life stretches back to the fountain springs of human thought.

No two races have set such a mark upon the world. Both have shown a capacity for survival, in spite of unending perils and sufferings from external oppressors, matched only by their own ceaseless feuds, quarrels, and convulsions. The passage of several thousand years sees no change in their characteristics and no diminution of their trials or their vitality. They have survived in spite of all that the world could do against them, and all they could do against themselves, and each of them from angles so different have left us the inheritance of their genius and wisdom.

No two cities have counted more with mankind than Athens and Jerusalem. Their messages in religion, philosophy, and art have been the main guiding lights of modern faith and culture. Centuries of foreign rule and indescribable, endless oppression leave them still living, active communities and forces in the modern world, quarrelling among themselves with insatiable vivacity. Personally I have always been on the side of both, and believed in their invincible power to survive internal strife and the world tides threatening their extinction.

'THE UNNECESSARY WAR'

Churchill often reflected on the reason for the Second World War, and the failure of the nations threatened by Germany to make common cause to deter aggression. In 1948, in the first volume of his war memoirs, entitled *The Gathering Storm*, he set out his thoughts, and the need to learn the lessons of the past:

One day President Roosevelt told me that he was asking publicly for suggestions about what the war should be called. I said at once 'The Unnecessary War'. There never was a war more easy to stop than that which has just wrecked what was left of the world from the previous struggle. The human tragedy reaches its climax in the fact that after all the exertions and sacrifices of hundreds of millions of people and the victories of the Righteous Cause, we have still not found Peace and Security, and that we lie in the grip of even worse perils than those we have surmounted.

It is my earnest hope that pondering upon the past may give guidance in days to come, enable a new generation to repair some of the errors of former years and thus govern, in accordance with the needs and glory of man, the awful unfolding science of the future.

'A SCENE OF MATERIAL RUIN AND MORAL HAVOC'

Reflecting in 1948 on the differences between the First and Second World Wars, Churchill wrote in *The Gathering Storm*:

There had been fearful slaughters of soldiers in the First World War, and much of the accumulated treasure of the nations was consumed. Still, apart from the excesses of the Russian Revolution, the main fabric of European civilisation remained erect at the close of the struggle. When the storm and dust of the cannonade passed suddenly away, the nations despite their enmities could still recognise each other as historic racial personalities. The laws of war had on the whole been respected. There was a common professional meeting-ground between military men who had fought one another. Vanquished and victors alike still preserved the semblance of civilised States. A solemn Peace was made which, apart from unenforceable financial aspects, conformed to the principles which in the Nineteenth Century had increasingly regulated the relations of enlightened peoples. The reign of law was proclaimed, and a World Instrument was formed to guard us all, and especially Europe, against a renewed convulsion.

In the Second World War every bond between man and man was to perish. Crimes were committed by the Germans under the

Hitlerite domination to which they allowed themselves to be subjected, which find no equal in scale and wickedness with any that have darkened the human record. The wholesale massacre by systematised processes of six or seven millions of men, women and children in the German execution camps exceeds in horror the rough and ready butcheries of Genghis Khan, and in scale reduces them to pigmy proportions.

Deliberate extermination of whole populations was contemplated and pursued by both Germany and Russia in the Eastern war. The hideous process of bombarding open cities from the air, once started by the Germans, was repaid twenty-fold by the ever-mounting power of the Allies, and found its culmination in the use of the atomic bombs which obliterated Hiroshima and Nagasaki.

We have at length emerged from a scene of material ruin and moral havoc the like of which had never darkened the imagination of former centuries. After all that we suffered and achieved we find ourselves still confronted with problems and perils not less but far more formidable than those through which we have so narrowly made our way.

'WE CANNOT REST UPON BENEVOLENT PLATITUDES'

Following his Zurich speech in September 1946, Churchill remained a staunch supporter and leading advocate of a united Europe, playing a leading role in January 1947 in the establishment of a British United Europe Movement. Speaking on 7 May 1948 at The Hague, at the first meeting of the Congress of Europe, he set out his vision of what a united Europe could become:

President Roosevelt spoke of the Four Freedoms, but the one that matters most today is Freedom from Fear. Why should all these hard-working families be harassed, first in bygone times, by dynastic and religious quarrels, next by nationalistic ambitions, and finally by ideological fanaticism? Why should they now have to be regimented and hurled against each other by variously labelled forms of totalitarian tyranny, all fomented by wicked men, building their own predominance upon the misery and the subjugation of their fellow human beings? Why should so many millions of humble homes in Europe, aye, and much of its enlightenment and culture, sit quaking in dread of the policeman's knock?

That is the question we have to answer here. That is the question which perhaps we have the power to answer here. After all, Europe has only to arise and stand in her own majesty, faithfulness and virtue, to confront all forms of tyranny, ancient or modern, Nazi or Communist, with forces which are unconquerable, and which if asserted in good time may never be challenged again.

I take a proud view of this Congress. We cannot rest upon benevolent platitudes and generalities. Our powers may be limited but we know and we must affirm what we mean and what we want. On the other hand it would not be wise in this critical time to be drawn into laboured attempts to draw rigid structures of constitutions. That is a later stage, and it is one in which the leadership must be taken by the ruling governments in response no doubt to our impulse, and in many cases to their own conceptions.

We are here to lay the foundations upon which the statesmen of the western democracies may stand, and to create an atmosphere favourable to the decisions to which they may be led. It is not for us who do not wield the authority of Governments to confront each other or the world with sharply cut formulas or detailed arrangements. There are many different points of view which have to find their focus. We in Britain must move in harmony with our great partners in the Commonwealth, who, I do not doubt, though separated from us by the ocean spaces, share our aspirations and follow with deep attention our trend of thought. But undue precipitancy, like too much refinement, would hinder and not help the immediate mission we have to fulfil. Nevertheless we must not separate without a positive step forward.

The task before us at this Congress is not only to raise the voice of United Europe during these few days we are together. We must here and now resolve that in one form or another a European Assembly shall be constituted which will enable that voice to make itself continuously heard and we trust with ever-growing acceptance through all the free countries of this Continent.

A high and a solemn responsibility rests upon us here this afternoon in this Congress of a Europe striving to be reborn. If we allow ourselves to be rent and disordered by pettiness and small disputes, if we fail in clarity of view or courage in action, a priceless occasion may be cast away for ever. But if we all pull together and pool the luck and the comradeship – and we shall need all the comradeship and not a little luck if we are to move together in this way – and firmly grasp the larger hopes of humanity, then it may be that we shall move into a happier sunlit age, when all the little children who are now growing up in this tormented world may find themselves not the victors nor the vanquished in the fleeting triumphs of one country over another in the bloody turmoil of destructive war, but the heirs of all the treasures of the past and the masters of all the science, the abundance and the glories of the future.

'THEY GAVE ALL THEY HAD'

On 21 May 1948, Churchill spoke in Westminster Abbey at the unveiling of a memorial to the wartime British Commando forces who had been killed in action in every theatre of war between 1940 and 1945. He also spoke of the dead of the Submarine Service, and of the Airborne Forces and the Special Air Service. It was an occasion of solemnity and pride:

Today we unveil a memorial to the brave who gave their lives for what we believe future generations of the world will pronounce a righteous and a noble cause. In this ancient Abbey, so deeply wrought into the record, the life and the message of the British race and nation – here where every inch of space is devoted to the monuments of the past and to the inspiration of the future – there will remain this cloister now consecrated to those who gave their lives in what they hoped would be a final war against the grosser forms of tyranny.

These symbolic images of heroes, set up by their fellow-countrymen in honour and remembrance, will proclaim, as long as faithful testimony endures, the sacrifices of youth resolutely made at the call of duty and for the love of our island home and all it stands for among men.

[· · ·]

All were volunteers. Most were highly skilled and intensely trained. Losses were heavy and constant, but great numbers pressed forward to fill the gaps. Selection could be most strict where the task was forlorn.

No units were so easy to recruit as those over whom Death ruled with daily attention. We think of the forty British submarines, more than half our total submarine losses, sunk amid the Mediterranean minefields alone, of the heroic deaths of the submarine commanders and crews who vanished for ever in the North Sea or in the Atlantic Approaches to our nearly-strangled island. We think of the Commandos, as they came to be called – a Boer word become ever-glorious in the annals of Britain and her Empire – and of their gleaming deeds under every sky and clime. We think of the Airborne Forces and Special Air Service men who hurled themselves unflinching into the void – when we recall all this, we may feel sure that nothing of which we have any knowledge or record has ever been done by mortal men which surpasses the splendour and daring of their feats of arms.

Truly we may say of them as of the Light Brigade at Balaclava, 'When shall their glory fade?' But there were characteristics in the exploits of the Submarines, the Commandos and the Airborne Forces which, in different degrees, distinguished their work from any single episode, however famous and romantic. First there was the quality of precision and the exact discharge of delicate and complex functions which required the utmost coolness of mind and steadiness of hand and eye.

The excitement and the gallop of a cavalry charge did not demand the ice-cold efficiency in mortal peril of the submarine crews and, on many occasions, of the Airborne Force and the Commandos. Here was also that constant repetition, time after time, of desperate adventures which marked the work of the Commandos, as of the submarines, requiring not only hearts of fire but nerves of tempered steel. To say this is not to dim the lustre of the past but to enhance, by modern lights, the deeds of their successors whom we honour here today.

The solemn and beautiful service in which we are taking part uplifts our hearts and gives balm and comfort to those living people, and there are many here, who have suffered immeasurable loss. Sorrow may be assuaged even at the moment when the dearest memories are revived and brightened. Above all, we have our faith that the universe is ruled by a Supreme Being and in fulfilment of a sublime moral purpose, according to which all our actions are judged. This faith enshrines, not only in bronze but forever the impulse of these young men, when they gave all they had in order that Britain's honour might still shine forth and that justice and decency might dwell among men in this troubled world.

'THE UNDERLYING PRINCIPLES OF JUSTICE AND FREEDOM'

In the 1930s, Churchill had been the leading opponent of the British Government's plans for Indian self-rule – then called Dominion Status – fearing that it would lead inevitably to the demand for full independence. With the introduction by the Labour Government of the India Independence Bill in 1947, his opposition to full independence came to an end, and he insisted that the grant of independence was too important to be the gift of one political party; that it had to come from the whole nation. To this end, he urged his fellow Conservatives to support the Labour Government's Bill, and it was passed into law. Two independent States, India and Pakistan, came into being in August 1947. In a speech in the House of Commons on 28 October 1948, Churchill welcomed the two new nations:

Our Imperial mission in India is at an end: we must recognise that. Some day justice will be done by world opinion to our record there, but the chapter is closed.

[···]

We must look forward. It is our duty, whatever part we have taken in the past, to hope and pray for the well-being and happiness of all the peoples of India, of whatever race, religion, social condition or historic character they may be. We must wish them all well and do what we can to help them on their road. Sorrow may lie in our hearts but bitterness and malice must be purged from them, and in our future more remote relations with India we must rise above all prejudice and partiality – and not allow our vision to be clouded by memories of glories that are gone for ever. And in this temper we shall find true guidance – and, indeed, our only hope – in strict and faithful adherence to the underlying principles of justice and freedom which are embodied in the United Nations organisation, and for the maintenance of which that instrument of world government was consciously created.

It is those principles, and those principles alone, which must govern our attitude and action towards this vast branch of toiling and suffering humanity. We have long had no interest in India which counted for more with us than the well-being and peace of its peoples. So far as we may be involved in the fortunes of the Indian peoples, and of the Governments of Pakistan and Hindustan, we must judge them, not by race or religion, but impartially, by their future conduct to one another in accordance with the principles of the United Nations organisation under the Charter of human liberties which is being drawn up, and we must use our influence, such as it may be, against aggression, oppression and tyranny, from whatever quarter it comes. These principles alone must rule our actions, must enable us to steer our course in the incalculable tides on which we and our Indian fellow subjects are now embarked.

'IF WE POOL OUR LUCK AND SHARE OUR FORTUNES'

The Second World War had confirmed the power of the United States, both as the determining factor in the defeat of Germany and Japan, and as the world's economic giant. Churchill, speaking in the House of Commons on 25 March 1949, welcomed this:

Gentlemen – many nations have arrived at the summit of the world but none, before the United States, on this occasion, has chosen that moment of triumph, not for aggrandizement, but for further self-sacrifice – sacrifice for the causes by which the life and strength of mankind is refreshed. The United States has shown itself more worthy of trust and honour than any government of men or association of nations that has ever reached pre-eminence, by their action on the morrow of the common victory won by all. I wish to express the thanks of my own dear island and of its Empire, Commonwealth and also of the many countries in Western Europe who are drawing together on the broad ideals of Anglo-Saxon, British–American, call it what you will, unity, which alone gives an opportunity for the further advance of the human race.

Gentlemen, some time ago, you may possibly remember, I made a speech in Missouri at Fulton – I got into great trouble for that. But now not so much. Now it is thought better of. And I was very glad to see that General Marshall, that great statesman and soldier – I do not know whether you put soldier or statesman first in regard to so eminent a man – General Marshall has created this policy of the Marshall Aid, which shall ever bear his name – not because of what happens in the three or four years of the Aid but because of its effect as a turning point in the history of the world. General Marshall played his part, and then, we have now come to the Atlantic Pact, which when Mr. Attlee kindly showed it to me before it became public – but after it was settled – I thought it was one of the most important documents ever signed by large communities of human beings and certainly indicates a very considerable advance in opinion as far as the United States of America are concerned.

Well, there you are – you're in it now, because there's no way out, but still if we pool our luck and share our fortunes I think you will have no reason to regret it.

'PEOPLES IN BONDAGE NEED NEVER DESPAIR'

The control of the Soviet Union over Eastern Europe, and the tyrannical nature of Communism, caused Churchill to reflect on the changes that he had seen in his lifetime, and on what the future might bring. On 31 March 1949, during his second post-war visit to the United States, he spoke on this theme at the Massachusetts Institute of Technology:

In 1900 a sense of moving hopefully forward to brighter, broader, easier days predominated. Little did we guess that what has been called the Century of the Common Man would witness as its outstanding feature more common men killing each other with greater facilities than any other five centuries put together in the history of the world. But we entered this terrible twentieth century with confidence.

We thought that with improving transportation nations would get to know each other better. We believed that as they got to know each other better they would like each other more, and that national rivalries would fade in a growing international consciousness. We took it almost for granted that science would confer continual boons and blessings upon us, would give us better meals, better garments and better dwellings for less trouble, and thus steadily shorten the hours of labour and leave more time for play and culture. In the name of ordered but unceasing progress, we saluted the age of democracy expressing itself ever more widely through parliaments freely and fairly elected on a broad or universal franchise. We saw no reason then why men and women should not shape their own home life and careers without being cramped by the growing complexity of the State, which was to be their servant and the protector of their rights.

[· · ·]

In the first half of the twentieth century, fanned by the crimson wings of war, the conquest of the air affected profoundly human affairs. It made the globe seem much bigger to the mind and much smaller to the body. The human biped was able to travel about far more quickly. This greatly reduced the size of his estate, while at the same time creating an even keener sense of its exploitable value.

In the nineteenth century Jules Verne wrote *Round the World in Eighty Days*. It seemed a prodigy. Now you can get around it in four; but you do not see much of it on the way. The whole prospect and outlook of mankind grew immeasurably larger, and the multiplication of ideas also proceeded at an incredible rate.

This vast expansion was unhappily not accompanied by any noticeable advance in the stature of man, either in his mental faculties, or his moral character. His brain got no better, but it buzzed the more. The scale of events around him assumed gigantic proportions while he remained about the same size. By comparison therefore he actually became much smaller.

We no longer had great men directing manageable affairs. Our need was to discipline an array of gigantic and turbulent facts.

To this task we have certainly so far proved unequal. Science bestowed immense new powers on man, and, at the same time, created conditions which were largely beyond his comprehension and still more beyond his control. While he nursed the illusion of growing mastery and exulted in his new trappings, he became the sport and presently the victim of tides, and currents, of whirlpools and tornadoes amid which he was far more helpless than he had been for a long time.

[· · ·]

Laws just or unjust may govern men's actions. Tyrannies may restrain or regulate their words. The machinery of propaganda may pack their minds with falsehood and deny them truth for many generations of time. But the soul of man thus held in trance or frozen in a long night can be awakened by a spark coming from God knows where and in a moment the whole structure of lies and oppression is on trial for its life.

Peoples in bondage need never despair. Let them hope and trust in the genius of mankind. Science no doubt could if sufficiently perverted exterminate us all, but it is not in the power of material forces in any period which the youngest here tonight need take into practical account, to alter the main elements in human nature or restrict the infinite variety of forms in which the soul and genius of the human race can and will express itself.

'APPEASEMENT FROM STRENGTH IS MAGNANIMOUS AND NOBLE'

On 14 December 1950, while Leader of the Opposition, Churchill spoke to the House of Commons, commenting on Clement Attlee's recent visit to Washington, and on Anglo-American relations. His remarks were made against the background of the Korean War, which had broken out on 25 June 1950, and in which American and British forces were being killed in action, with the forces of twenty other nations, including South Korea, fighting under the banner of the United Nations against the aggression of Communist North Korea, whose military effort was being aided by Communist China:

We are all very glad to see that the military situation for the time being in Korea has somewhat improved. I hope also that there is truth in the reports that a measure of censorship is being established over the despatches from the front or from Tokyo by the war correspondents of all the United Nations. I should think most of us agree with General Robertson's protest upon this point. When one sees set forth day after day the exact position, numbers, condition and intentions of the United Nations troops, very often unit by unit, one cannot but feel that it is hardly fair to the soldiers who are fighting that the enemy should be presented with such complete intelligence, whereas so little seems to be known by us about the other side, and such a large measure of ignorance prevails, among the general public at least, about the enemy's disposition, strength and movements.

Indeed, the wildest estimates are given on high authority only to be contradicted and reversed a few days later.

One instance, a small one, but not without significance, particularly struck me. A Centurion tank was damaged and left behind. This was immediately published and its importance emphasised. All the secrets were published of the latest British tank. Thus this vehicle, left behind among great numbers of no doubt other broken down vehicles, and in all the litter of retreat amid the snow, acquired instantly, in the enemy's eyes, an exceptional significance. I was very glad to read – I hope it is true – that it had been successfully destroyed from the air. That would have been a very good tale to tell if true, after it had happened, but why was it necessary to attract the enemy's attention to this vehicle beforehand? That seems to me a particular illustration.

We really must have tighter control over what is published. We all seek to prevent and limit aggression, and one of the additional deterrents which we might impose upon the enemy's aggression would be to tell them that if it goes on much longer we shall cut them off from these invaluable supplies of information.

The Prime Minister's visit to Washington has done nothing but good. The question we all have to consider this afternoon in the House of Commons is, how much good? The Prime Minister spoke of the importance of renewing the series of meetings between the President and the Prime Minister which had taken place during the war and since the war. We all agree with that. We all agree with the advantages of direct discussion to which the Prime Minister has just referred.

I must say it seems to me that five years is rather a long interval, and the decision when it came, was very suddenly taken. My right hon. Friend the Member for Warwick and Leamington (Mr. Eden) spoke on 29th November and urged that we should have stronger representation at Washington at the highest level. I endorsed this when I spoke the next day. I did not wish to appear to reflect any more than he did, in the slightest degree, upon our excellent Ambassador in Washington, and I used the particular phrase, 'Ministerial representation'. That very evening we were told that the Prime Minister was going. During the afternoon there was some excitement caused in the House by the accounts of Mr. Truman's interview with the Press which appeared on the tape. But I understand that this was not the reason that led to the Prime Minister's decision to go and that this was taken earlier in the day. Certainly the decision was very hastily arrived at, after an interval of five years.

Many will think that earlier meetings might have been held. Several recent occasions occur to one. When the Soviet-inspired aggression by the North Korean Government across the 38th Parallel took place, and when the United States intervened vigorously and actively with the approval of the United Nations Assembly and we joined with them at the end of June, that was certainly an occasion which the Prime Minister might have considered for talking matters over with our great Ally and friend.

Again, after General MacArthur's brilliant counter-stroke, which gave us back Seoul and changed the whole aspect of the fighting up to that point in Korea, would have been, it seems to me, a good moment to talk over the next steps. At that moment many issues were open, which would have gained by having that direct discussion face to face between the heads of Government assisted by their military advisers. It is always easy to be wise after the event, but there were many people in this country who were wise before the event. I am by no means sure that His Majesty's Government and their expert advisers are excluded from that large number.

Those who had this view felt that it would be wiser to fortify a line, if not at the 38th Parallel, at the waist or at the best military position in advance of it, thus leaving a broad no-man's-land in which we could reconnoitre and into which we could go with mobile columns and, of course, with the all-powerful air forces available while building up all the time a strong fortified line which we could hold while, perhaps, conversations went on.

There is much to be said for strong fortified lines. If properly organised in depth, if protected in front by ever-expanding mine-fields and wire entanglements, and if developed week after week by concreted structures and excavations and firmly held with modern fire power, they would prove a terrific obstacle to the advance of infantry. All this becomes greater when both flanks rest upon the sea and the sea is in Allied command and when we have unquestioned mastery of the air. Such a position, once established, as it would have been possible to do, about 100 miles long, presents a very different obstacle to the advance and infiltration of masses of enemy infantry, from a moving front in hilly, rocky, scrub-covered country, then broadened to about 300 miles.

I am speaking only of what has happened in the past. I do not attempt to say anything about what may happen in the future. [HON. MEMBERS: 'Why not?'] It would be very unwise and unnecessary to do so in military operations. To pierce a properly fortified line not only would masses of artillery have to be accumulated, but there would also have to be very heavy concentrations of armour. These would present admirable targets to overwhelming air power. It certainly seems that the Chinese armies, if they had attacked such a line, might well have renewed on an even larger scale the painful experiences which we ourselves so often suffered on the Somme and at Passchendaele and in other bloody battlefields of the First World War.

I cannot help feeling that it would have been well if all these matters had been talked over at the right moment and in good time in Washington by the highest authorities in both our countries.

We immediately approved the Prime Minister's decision to go when he did, and I feel sure that no one regrets it now. We welcome and wholeheartedly support the Prime Minister's statement about British and American unity and how their two flags will fly together however the winds may blow. That is, indeed, the foundation, as he said in his closing words, of our safety and the best hope for the peace of the world and for the survival of free civilisation.

It is a great comfort in the darkening scene to feel that there are no party differences, or very limited party differences, in this country on this supreme issue, and that the task of trying to drive a wedge between us and the United States is left to the Communists and their fellow-travellers, aided perhaps, no doubt through folly rather than malice, by the usual Ministerial indiscretions.

Another advantage which has come from the Prime Minister's journey has been the renewed explicit declarations by the United States emphasising the priority of the defence of Europe. We are glad indeed that General Eisenhower is to be appointed to the Supreme

Command of the army – however it may be denominated – which is being constituted there. We were led to believe that this appointment would be made many weeks ago.

Progress in European defence, which was tardily begun, continues to be lamentably slow. It is more than nine months since I pointed out that no effective defence of Europe was possible without the armed strength of Germany. The movement of opinion in that direction has been continual, but nothing has been done. No agreement has been reached, and meanwhile Germany lies even more undefended than do other European countries under the menace of Communist and Russian aggression.

The months slip quickly away all the time. Several years have already been wasted, frittered away. The overwhelming Russian military power towers up against us, committees are multiplied, papers are written, words are outpoured and one declaration succeeds another, but nothing in the slightest degree in proportion to the scale of events or to their urgency has been done.

[···]

It was with the danger of Europe in my mind that I said some weeks ago that I hoped that we should not get entangled in China. In order to protect myself from the charge of being wise after the event, I venture to remind the House that on 16th November, before these recent reverses in Korea had taken place, I asked the Minister of Defence a supplementary question, which I do not think he resented in any way: '. . . whether he and the Foreign Secretary will constantly bear in mind the great importance of our not becoming, and of our Allies so far as we can influence their actions not becoming, too much pinned down in China or in the approaches to China at a time when the danger in Europe is . . . occupying all our minds?' I need scarcely say that I hold to that conviction still.

In view, however, of what has happened since then in Korea and in the United Nations Assembly, I feel it requires to be stated with more precision and refinement. We must not at any time be drawn into urging a policy which would inflict dishonour or humiliation upon the United States or upon the United Nations. Such a course would be at least as full of danger as any other now open to us. We learn from the newspapers that the proposals for a truce or cease fire which were proposed by the thirteen Asiatic and Arab states, have been opposed by the Soviet delegation. They certainly seemed to be very far-reaching proposals from our point of view.

I will not say more about them, but, while the fullest priority should be given to the defence of Western Europe, it would be a great mistake to lose our sense of proportion and cast everything to the winds elsewhere. The only prudent course open to the United States and ourselves is to stabilise the local military position and, if the opportunity then occurs, to negotiate with the aggressors and at least make sure that we negotiate from strength and not from weakness.

We shall no doubt hear from the Foreign Secretary tonight how the question of further conversations with Soviet Russia stands. There was, I think, fairly complete agreement in the House that no abrupt negative or merely dilatory action would be appropriate to the Russian request, and from what we have read in the newspapers, it does not seem likely that there will be any serious disagreement between us upon the procedure eventually to be adopted.

I am strongly in favour of every effort being made by every means, to secure a fair and reasonable settlement with Russia. I should, however, be failing in frankness to the House, and to some of those who agree with me upon this matter, to whom I am much opposed in many ways, if I did not make it clear at this stage that we must not place undue hopes upon the success of any negotiations which may be undertaken.

It is our duty – and a duty which we owe to the cause of peace and to our own consciences – to leave no effort unmade that wisdom and fair play can suggest, and that patience can bring forward. But on this side of the House we have never contemplated that if negotiations failed, we should abandon any of the great causes for which we have stood in the past, and for which the United Nations organisation stands today.

The declaration of the Prime Minister that there will be no appeasement also commands almost universal support. It is a good slogan for the country. It seems to me, however, that in this House it requires to be more precisely defined. What we really mean, I think, is no appeasement through weakness or fear. Appeasement in itself may be good or bad according to the circumstances. Appeasement from weakness and fear is alike futile and fatal. Appeasement from strength is magnanimous and noble and might be the surest and perhaps the only path to world peace.

When nations or individuals get strong they are often truculent and bullying, but when they are weak they become better mannered. But this is the reverse of what is healthy and wise. I have always been astonished, having seen the end of these two wars, how difficult it is to make people understand the Roman wisdom, 'Spare the conquered and confront the proud.' I think I will go so far as to say it in the original: 'Parcere subjectis, et debellare superbos.' The modern practice has too often been: 'Punish the defeated and grovel to the strong.'

Unhappily, except as regards the atomic bomb – about which I shall have a word to say before I sit down – we are in a very weak position and likely to remain so for several years. As I have repeatedly said, it is only the vast superiority of the United States in this awful weapon that gives us any chance of survival.

The argument is now put forward that we must never use the atomic bomb until, or unless, it has been used against us first. In other words, you must never fire until you have been shot dead. That seems to me undoubtedly a silly thing to say and a still more imprudent position to adopt.

Moreover, such a resolve would certainly bring war nearer. The deterrent effect of the atomic bomb is at the present time almost our sole defence. Its potential use is the only lever by which we can hope to obtain reasonable consideration in an attempt to make a peaceful settlement with Soviet Russia. If they had superiority, or even something like equality in this weapon with the United States, I cannot feel any assurance that they would be restrained by the con-scientious scruples or moral inhibitions which are often so vocal in this country. It would certainly be a poor service to the cause of peace to free them from all cause of apprehension until they were in every respect ready to strike.

The Soviet power could not be confronted, or even placated, with any hope of success if we were in these years of tension through which we are passing to deprive ourselves of the atomic bomb, or to prevent its use by announcing gratuitously self-imposed restrictions.

'THE MAIN FOUNDATION OF PEACE'

On 25 October 1951 the Conservative Party was returned to power at the General Election, and Churchill became Prime Minister for the second time. On 9 November 1951, three weeks before his seventy-seventh birthday, he gave his first speech as peacetime Prime Minister, at the Lord Mayor's Banquet at London's Guildhall, which had been massively damaged during the wartime Blitz, and whose historic statues of Gog and Magog – the mythical warring giants who are guardians of the City of London – had been destroyed. Churchill told the gathering:

> Though I have very often in the last forty years or so been present at your famous Guildhall banquets to salute the new Lord Mayor, this is the first occasion when I have addressed this assembly here as Prime Minister. The explanation is convincing. When I should have come here as Prime Minister the Guildhall was blown up and before it was repaired I was blown out!
>
> I thought at the time they were both disasters. But now we are all here together in a union which I hope will bring good luck. I am sure we all wish the Lord Mayor a successful year of his arduous office. I share his regrets that we have no Member for the City of London in the House of Commons. It is an error to believe that the world began when any particular Party or statesman got into office. It has all been going on quite a long time, and many movements and Parties will rise and decline, and I trust many politicians will catch the fleeting glint of popular acclaim before the continuity of our island life is cut asunder or fades away.
>
> It is only by studying the past that we can foresee, however dimly, the future. I cannot help feeling the impact of these thoughts in this war-scarred Hall. Its battered monuments remind us of other struggles against the Continental tyrants of the past, in generations before the supreme ordeal of 1940 which we all endured and won together.
>
> I am so glad, my Lord Mayor, that you have decided to replace the effigies of Gog and Magog. It was to me a painful blow when they were burnt to ashes by Hitler's bombs. They will look fine in the

gallery up there. Indeed I think they are not only ancient but up-to-date. It seems to me that they represent none too badly the present state of world politics.

World politics, like the history of Gog and Magog, are very confused and much disputed. Still I think there is room for both of them. On the one side is Gog and on the other Magog. But be careful, my Lord Mayor, when you put them back, to keep them from colliding with each other, for if that happens both Gog and Magog would be smashed to pieces and we should all have to begin all over again, and begin from the bottom of the pit.

Whatever are the differences between Gog and Magog, at any rate they are made out of the same materials. Let me tell you what the materials are: vast masses of warm-hearted, hard-working human beings wanting to do their best for their country and their neighbours, and longing to build their homes and bring up their children in peace, freedom and the hope of better times for the young when they grow up. That is all they ask of their rulers and governors and guides. That is the dear wish in the hearts of all the peoples of mankind.

How easy it ought to be with modern science standing tiptoe ready to open the doors of a Golden Age, to grant them this humble modest desire. But then there come along all these tribes of nationalists, ideologues, revolutionaries, class warfare experts, and imperialists with their nasty regimentation of academic doctrinaires, striving night and day to work them all up against one another so that the homes instead of being built are bombed and the breadwinner is killed and the broken housewife left to pick the surviving children out of the ashes. There is the structure: that is the composition which Gog and Magog have in common and there is the fate which both will suffer if you, my Lord Mayor, and others concerned in our City affairs or those who deal with world affairs do not act with ordinary common sense and keep Gog and Magog from falling upon one another.

[· · ·]

What is the world scene as presented to us today? Mighty forces armed with fearful weapons are baying at each other across a gulf which I have the feeling tonight neither wishes, and both fear, to cross, but into which they may tumble or drag each other to their common ruin. On the one side stand all the armies and air forces of Soviet Russia and all their Communist satellites, agents and devotees in so many countries. On the other are what are called 'the Western Democracies' with their far superior resources, at present only partly organized, gathering themselves together around the United States with its mastery of the atomic bomb.

Now there is no doubt on which side we stand. Britain and the Commonwealth and Empire, still centring upon our island, are woven by ever-growing ties of strength and comprehension of common need and self-preservation to the great Republic across the Atlantic Ocean.

The sacrifices and exertions which the United States are making to deter, and if possible prevent, Communist aggression from making further inroads upon the free world are the main foundation of peace. A tithe of the efforts now being made by America would have prevented the Second World War and would have probably led to the downfall of Hitler with scarcely any blood being shed except perhaps his own.

I feel a deep gratitude towards our great American Ally. They have risen to the leadership of the world without any other ambition but to serve its highest causes faithfully.

I am anxious that Britain should also play her full part, and I hope to see a revival of her former influence and initiative among the Allied Powers, and indeed with all Powers.

'BRITAIN AND THE UNITED STATES ARE WORKING TOGETHER'

On the last day of 1951, Churchill left England on board the *Queen Mary* for New York. On 17 January 1952 he was in Washington, where he addressed both Houses of Congress. The Korean War was at its height. Churchill spoke of his confidence that a third world war could be averted, if the United States were of firm and united purpose:

The vast process of American rearmament in which the British Commonwealth and Empire and the growing power of United Europe will play their part to the utmost of their strength, this vast process has already altered the balance of the world and may well, if we all persevere steadfastly and loyally together, avert the danger of a Third World War, or the horror of defeat and subjugation should one come upon us.

Mr President and Mr Speaker, I hope the mourning families throughout the great Republic will find some comfort and some pride in these thoughts.

[···]

If I may say this, Members of Congress, be careful above all things, therefore, not to let go of the atomic weapon until you are sure, and more than sure, that other means of preserving peace are in your hands. It is my belief that by accumulating deterrents of all kinds against aggression we shall, in fact, ward off the fearful catastrophe, the fears of which darken the life and mar the progress of all the peoples of the globe.

We must persevere steadfastly and faithfully in the task to which, under United States leadership, we have solemnly bound ourselves. Any weakening of our purpose, any disruption of our organization would bring about the very evils which we all dread, and from which we should all suffer, and from which many of us would perish.

We must not lose patience, and we must not lose hope. It may be that presently a new mood will reign behind the Iron Curtain. If so it will be easy for them to show it, but the democracies must be on their guard against being deceived by a false dawn.

We seek or covet no one's territory; we plan no forestalling war; we trust and pray that all will come right. Even during these years of what is called the 'cold war', material production in every land is continually improving through the use of new machinery and better organization and the advance of peaceful science. But the great bound forward in progress and prosperity for which mankind is longing cannot come till the shadow of war has passed away.

There are, however, historic compensations for the stresses which we suffer in the 'cold war'. Under the pressure and menace of

Communist aggression the fraternal association of the United States with Britain and the British Commonwealth, and the new unity growing up in Europe, nowhere more hopeful than between France and Germany – all these harmonies are being brought forward, perhaps by several generations in the destiny of the world.

If this proves true – and it has certainly proved true up to date – the architects in the Kremlin may be found to have built a different and a far better world structure than what they planned.

[···]

Members of the Congress, I have dwelt today repeatedly upon many of the changes that have happened throughout the world since you last invited me to address you here and I am sure you will agree that it is hardly possible to recognize the scene or believe it can truly have come to pass. But there is one thing which is exactly the same as when I was here last. Britain and the United States are working together and working for the same high cause.

Bismarck once said that the supreme fact of the Nineteenth Century was that Britain and the United States spoke the same language. Let us make sure that the supreme fact of the Twentieth Century is that they tread the same path.

'WE IN THIS SMALL ISLAND'

Churchill made every effort to be at Harrow School for the annual school songs. He always tried to encourage the boys to see the parts they would need to play in later years, as he did when he spoke to them on 7 November 1952:

You must not suppose that the troubles of Britain are over because in the two last terrible wars which have shaken the world in the Twentieth Century we have emerged victorious, without shame of any kind on our escutcheon, either in the making or the fighting of those struggles.

On the contrary, we may feel that in the world which has grown so much vaster all round us and towers up about us, we in this small island have to make a supreme effort to keep our place and station – a place and station to which our tradition and undying genius entitle us.

A great effort is required, and you to whom much of the future belongs will play your part in this proud, equal, democratic England.

'I WELCOME GERMANY BACK'

Churchill's attempts, after Stalin's death in March 1953, to persuade the recently elected President Eisenhower to go with him to Moscow to meet the new Soviet leaders and to seek a basis for agreement with the Soviet Union, were rebuffed. Churchill persevered in his search for détente, and also in his vision of West Germany as a world power. On 25 June 1953, he suffered a serious stroke, but he was determined to recover, and to speak that autumn at the Conservative Party conference in Margate. This he was able to do: in his speech on 10 October 1953 he answered critics of his reference the previous May to the importance, in reconciling France and Germany, of following the 'master thought' of the Locarno Treaties of 1925, of which he had been an active supporter in Cabinet at the time. These critics had argued that Locarno was an absurd precedent, having failed so conspicuously to prevent war. Churchill had no doubt as to the relevance of Locarno, or the reason for its failure. He also defended his search for talks with the new Soviet leaders:

> I asked for very little. I held out no glittering or exciting hopes about Russia. I thought that friendly, informal, personal talks between the leading figures in the countries mainly involved might do good and could not easily do much harm, and that one good thing might lead to another as I have just said.
>
> This humble, modest plan announced as the policy of Her Majesty's Government raised a considerable stir all over the place and though we have not yet been able to persuade our trusted allies to adopt it in the form I suggested no one can say that it is dead.

[. . .]

The interest of Britain and of Europe and of the NATO alliance is not to play Russia against Germany or Germany against Russia, but to make them both feel they can live in safety with each other in spite of their grievous problems and differences. For us who have a very definite part in all this, our duty is to use what I believe is our growing influence both with Germany and with Russia to relieve them of any anxiety they may feel about each other.

Personally I welcome Germany back among the great Powers of the world. If there were one message I could give to the German people as one, a large part of whose life has been spent in conducting war against them or preparing to do so, I would urge them to remember the famous maxim: 'The price of freedom is eternal vigilance'. We mustn't forget that either.

[···]

When I spoke about the master thought of Locarno, I meant of course the plan of everybody going against the aggressor, whoever he may be, and helping the victim large or small. That is no more than the United Nations was set up to do. We are told the Locarno Treaty failed and did not prevent the war. There was a very good reason for that. The United States was not in it. Had the United States taken before the First World War or between the wars the same interest and made the same exertions and sacrifices and run the same risks to preserve peace and uphold freedom which I thank God she is doing now, there might never have been a First War and there would certainly never have been a Second. With her mighty aid I have a sure hope there will not be a third.

'THE MOST MEMORABLE PUBLIC OCCASION OF MY LIFE'

On 30 November 1954, Churchill's eightieth birthday, Members of both Houses of Parliament gathered in Westminster Hall to honour him. No other British Prime Minister since Gladstone had been in office at the age of eighty. As part of the ceremony, he was presented with his portrait, painted by Graham Sutherland, and with an illuminated book signed by the Members of Parliament. In his speech of welcome, Clement Attlee, Churchill's wartime Deputy Prime Minister and his post-war successor, called him 'Caesar indeed – for you have not only carried on the war but have written your own commentary'. As for the Dardanelles, where Attlee himself had served, Attlee told Churchill and those gathered to honour him that it was 'the only imaginative strategic idea of the war. I only wish you had had full power to carry it to success.' Churchill then responded:

This is to me the most memorable public occasion of my life. No one has ever received a similar mark of honour before. There has not been anything like it in British history, and indeed I doubt whether any of the modern democracies has shown such a degree of kindness and generosity to a party politician who has not yet retired and may at any time be involved in controversy. It is indeed the most striking example I have ever known of that characteristic British Parliamentary principle cherished in both Lords and Commons: 'Don't bring politics into private life.' It is certainly a mark of the underlying unity of our national life which survives and even grows in spite of vehement party warfare and many grave differences of conviction and sentiment. This unity is, I believe, the child of freedom and fair play fostered in the cradle of our ancient island institutions, and nursed by tradition and custom.

I am most grateful to Mr. Attlee for the agreeable words he has used about me this morning, and for the magnanimous appraisal he has given of my variegated career. I must confess, however, that this ceremony and all its charm and splendour may well be found to have seriously affected my controversial value as a party politician. However, perhaps with suitable assistance I shall get over this reaction and come round after a bit.

The Leader of the Opposition and I have been the only two Prime Ministers of this country in the last fourteen years. There are no other Prime Ministers alive. Mr. Attlee was also Deputy Prime Minister with me in those decisive years of war. During our alternating tenure, tremendous events have happened abroad, and far-reaching changes have taken place at home. There have been three general elections on universal suffrage and the activity of our Parliamentary and party machinery has been absolutely free.

Mr. Attlee's and my monopoly of the most powerful and disputatious office under the Crown all this time is surely the fact which the world outside may recognize as a symbol of the inherent stability of our British way of life. It is not, however, intended to make it a permanent feature of the Constitution.

I am sure this is the finest greeting any Member of the House of Commons has yet received and I express my heartfelt thanks to the representatives of both Houses for the gifts which you have bestowed in their name. The portrait is a remarkable example of modern art. It certainly combines force and candour. These are qualities which no active Member of either House can do without or should fear to meet. The book with which the Father of the House of Commons [Mr. David Grenfell] has presented me is a token of the goodwill and chivalrous regard of members of all parties.

I have lived my life in the House of Commons, having served there for fifty-two of the fifty-four years of this tumultuous and convulsive century. I have indeed seen all the ups and downs of fate and fortune, but I have never ceased to love and honour the Mother of Parliaments, the model to the legislative assemblies of so many lands.

The care and thought which has been devoted to this beautiful volume and the fact that it bears the signatures of nearly all my fellow-Members deeply touches my heart. And may I say that I thoroughly understand the position of those who have felt it their duty to abstain. The value of such a tribute is that it should be free and spontaneous. I shall treasure it as long as I live and my family and descendants will regard it as a most precious possession.

When I read the eulogy so gracefully and artistically inscribed on the title page, with its famous quotation from John Bunyan, I must confess to you that I was overpowered by two emotions – pride and humility. I have always hitherto regarded them as opposed and also corrective of one another; but on this occasion I am not able to tell you which is dominant in my mind. Indeed both seem to dwell together hand in hand. Who would not feel proud to have this happen to him and yet at the same time I never was more sure of how far it goes beyond what I deserve.

I was very glad that Mr. Attlee described my speeches in the war as expressing the will not only of Parliament but of the whole nation. Their will was resolute and remorseless and, as it proved, unconquerable. It fell to me to express it, and if I found the right words you must remember that I have always earned my living by my pen and by my tongue. It was a nation and race dwelling all round the globe that had the lion heart. I had the luck to be called upon to give the roar. I also hope that I sometimes suggested to the lion the right places to use his claws.

I am now nearing the end of my journey. I hope I still have some services to render. However that may be and whatever may befall I am sure I shall never forget the emotions of this day or be able to express my gratitude to those colleagues and companions with whom I have lived my life for this superb honour they have done me.

'SAFETY WILL BE THE STURDY CHILD OF TERROR'

On 1 March 1955, Churchill made his last major speech in the House of Commons, where he had first spoken fifty-four years earlier. The packed Chamber listened to him, according to the newspaper reports, with deep respect and in almost total silence, as he reflected on the nuclear age and its implications:

We live in a period, happily unique in human history, when the whole world is divided intellectually and to a large extent geographically between the creeds of Communist discipline and individual freedom, and when, at the same time, this mental and psychological division is accompanied by the possession by both sides of the obliterating weapons of the nuclear age.

We have antagonisms now as deep as those of the Reformation and its reactions which led to the Thirty Years' War. But now they are spread over the whole world instead of only over a small part of

Europe. We have, to some extent, the geographical division of the Mongol invasion in the thirteenth century, only more ruthless and more thorough. We have force and science, hitherto the servants of man, now threatening to become his master.

I am not pretending to have a solution for a permanent peace between the nations which could be unfolded this afternoon. We pray for it. Nor shall I try to discuss the cold war which we all detest, but have to endure. I shall only venture to offer to the House some observations mainly of a general character on which I have pondered long and which, I hope, may be tolerantly received, as they are intended by me.

And here may I venture to make a personal digression? I do not pretend to be an expert or to have technical knowledge of this prodigious sphere of science. But in my long friendship with Lord Cherwell I have tried to follow and even predict the evolution of events. I hope that the House will not reprove me for vanity or conceit if I repeat what I wrote a quarter of a century ago:

> We know enough to be sure that the scientific achievements of the next fifty years will be far greater, more rapid and more surprising than those we have already experienced. High authorities tell us that new sources of power, vastly more important than any we yet know, will surely be discovered. Nuclear energy is incomparably greater than the molecular energy which we use today. The coal a man can get in a day can easily do 500 times as much work as the man himself. Nuclear energy is at least one million times more powerful still. If the hydrogen atoms in a pound of water could be prevailed upon to combine together and form helium, they would suffice to drive a 1,000 horse-power engine for a whole year. If the electrons – those tiny planets of the atomic system – were induced to combine with the nuclei in the hydrogen, the horse-power liberated would be 120 times greater still. There is no question among scientists that this gigantic source of energy exists. What is lacking is the match to set the bonfire alight, or it may be the detonator to cause the dynamite to explode.

This is no doubt not quite an accurate description of what has been discovered, but as it was published in the *Strand* magazine of

December, 1931 – twenty-four years ago – I hope that my plea to have long taken an interest in the subject may be indulgently accepted by the House.

What is the present position? Only three countries possess, in varying degrees, the knowledge and the power to make nuclear weapons. Of these, the United States is overwhelmingly the chief. Owing to the breakdown in the exchange of information between us and the United States since 1946 we have had to start again independently on our own. Fortunately, executive action was taken promptly by the right hon. Gentleman the Leader of the Opposition to reduce as far as possible the delay in our nuclear development and production. By his initiative we have made our own atomic bombs.

Confronted with the hydrogen bomb, I have tried to live up to the right hon. Gentleman's standard. We have started to make that one, too. It is this grave decision which forms the core of the Defence Paper which we are discussing this afternoon. Although the Soviet stockpile of atomic bombs may be greater than that of Britain, British discoveries may well place us above them in fundamental science.

[···]

There is an immense gulf between the atomic and the hydrogen bomb. The atomic bomb, with all its terrors, did not carry us outside the scope of human control or manageable events in thought or action, in peace or war. But when Mr. Sterling Cole, the Chairman of the United States Congressional Committee, gave out a year ago – 17 February 1954 – the first comprehensive review of the hydrogen bomb, the entire foundation of human affairs was revolutionized, and mankind placed in a situation both measureless and laden with doom.

It is now the fact that a quantity of plutonium, probably less than would fill the Box on the Table – it is quite a safe thing to store – would suffice to produce weapons which would give indisputable world domination to any great Power which was the only one to have it. There is no absolute defence against the hydrogen bomb, nor is any method in sight by which any nation, or any country, can be completely guaranteed against the devastating injury which even a score of them might inflict on wide regions.

What ought we to do? Which way shall we turn to save our lives and the future of the world? It does not matter so much to old people; they are going soon anyway; but I find it poignant to look at youth in all its activity and ardour and, most of all, to watch little children playing their merry games, and wonder what would lie before them if God wearied of mankind.

The best defence would of course be bona fide disarmament all round. This is in all our hearts. But sentiment must not cloud our vision. It is often said that 'facts are stubborn things'. A renewed session of a sub-committee of the Disarmament Commission is now sitting in London and is rightly attempting to conduct its debates in private. We must not conceal from ourselves the gulf between the Soviet Government and the NATO Powers, which has hitherto, for so long, prevented an agreement. The long history and tradition of Russia makes it repugnant to the Soviet Government to accept any practical system of international inspection.

A second difficulty lies in the circumstance that, just as the United States, on the one hand, has, we believe, the overwhelming mastery in nuclear weapons, so the Soviets and their Communist satellites have immense superiority in what are called 'conventional' forces – the sort of arms and forces with which we fought the last war, but much improved. The problem is, therefore, to devise a balanced and phased system of disarmament which at no period enables any one of the participants to enjoy an advantage which might endanger the security of the others.

[···]

If the Soviet Government have not at any time since the war shown much nervousness about the American possession of nuclear superiority, that is because they are quite sure that it will not be used against them aggressively, even in spite of many forms of provocation. On the other hand, the NATO Powers have been combined together by the continued aggression and advance of Communism in Asia and in Europe. That this should have eclipsed in a few years, and largely effaced, the fearful antagonism and memories that Hitlerism created for the German people is an event without parallel. But it has, to a large extent, happened. There is widespread belief throughout the free world that, but for American nuclear superiority, Europe would already have been reduced to satellite status and the Iron Curtain would have reached the Atlantic and the Channel.

Unless a trustworthy and universal agreement upon disarmament, conventional and nuclear alike, can be reached and an effective system of inspection is established and is actually working, there is only one sane policy for the free world in the next few years. That is what we call defence through deterrents. This we have already adopted and proclaimed.

These deterrents may at any time become the parents of disarmament, provided that they deter. To make our contribution to the deterrent we must ourselves possess the most up-to-date nuclear weapons, and the means of delivering them.

That is the position which the Government occupy. We are to discuss this not only as a matter of principle; there are many practical reasons which should be given. Should war come, which God forbid, there are a large number of targets that we and the Americans must be able to strike at once. There are scores of airfields from which the Soviets could launch attacks with hydrogen bombs as soon as they have the bombers to carry them. It is essential to our deterrent policy and to our survival to have, with our American allies, the strength and numbers to be able to paralyse these potential Communist assaults in the first few hours of the war, should it come.

The House will perhaps note that I avoid using the word 'Russia' as much as possible in this discussion. I have a strong admiration for the Russian people – for their bravery, their many gifts, and their kindly nature. It is the Communist dictatorship and the declared ambition of the Communist Party and their proselytizing activities that we are bound to resist, and that is what makes this great world cleavage which I mentioned when I opened my remarks.

[···]

Our moral and military support of the United States and our possession of nuclear weapons of the highest quality and on an appreciable scale, together with their means of delivery, will greatly reinforce the deterrent power of the free world, and will strength our influence within the free world. That, at any rate, is the policy we have decided to pursue. That is what we are now doing, and I am thankful that it is endorsed by a mass of responsible opinion on both sides of the House, and, I believe, by the great majority of the nation.

A vast quantity of information, some true, some exaggerated much out of proportion, has been published about the hydrogen bomb. The truth has inevitably been mingled with fiction, and I am glad to say that panic has not occurred. Panic would not necessarily make for peace. That is one reason why I have been most anxious that responsible discussions on this matter should not take place on the BBC or upon the television, and I thought that I was justified in submitting that view of Her Majesty's Government to the authorities, which they at once accepted – very willingly accepted.

Panic would not necessarily make for peace even in this country. There are many countries where a certain wave of opinion may arise and swing so furiously into action that decisive steps may be taken from which there is no recall. As it is, the world population goes on its daily journey despite its sombre impression and earnest longing for relief. That is the way we are going on now.

I shall content myself with saying about the power of this weapon, the hydrogen bomb, that apart from all the statements about blast and heat effects over increasingly wide areas there are now to be considered the consequences of 'fall out', as it is called, of wind-borne radio-active particles. There is both an immediate direct effect on human beings who are in the path of such a cloud and an indirect effect through animals, grass, and vegetables, which pass on these contagions to human beings through food.

This would confront many who escaped the direct effects of the explosion with poisoning, or starvation, or both. Imagination stands appalled. There are, of course, the palliatives and precautions of a courageous Civil Defence, and about that the Home Secretary will be speaking later on tonight. But our best protection lies, as I am sure the House will be convinced, in successful deterrents operating from a foundation of sober, calm, and tireless vigilance.

Moreover, a curious paradox has emerged. Let me put it simply. After a certain point has been passed it may be said: 'The worse things get, the better.' The broad effect of the latest developments is to spread almost indefinitely and at least to a vast extent the area of mortal danger. This should certainly increase the deterrent upon Soviet Russia by putting her enormous spaces and scattered population on an equality or near-equality of vulnerability with our small densely populated island and with Western Europe.

I cannot regard this development as adding to our dangers. We have reached the maximum already. On the contrary, to this form of attack continents are vulnerable as well as islands. Hitherto, crowded countries, as I have said, like the United Kingdom and Western Europe, have had this outstanding vulnerability to carry. But the hydrogen bomb, with its vast range of destruction and the even wider area of contamination, would be effective also against nations whose population, hitherto, has been so widely dispersed over large land areas as to make them feel that they were not in any danger at all. They, too, become highly vulnerable: not yet equally perhaps, but still, highly and increasingly vulnerable.

Here again we see the value of deterrents, immune against surprise and well understood by all persons on both sides – I repeat 'on both sides' – who have the power to control events. That is why I have hoped for a long time for a top-level conference where these matters could be put plainly and bluntly from one friendly visitor to the conference to another.

Then it may well be that we shall by a process of sublime irony have reached a stage in this story where safety will be the sturdy child of terror, and survival the twin brother of annihilation.

'THE NATION CLOSED ITS RANKS'

On 28 March 1955, Churchill addressed the House of Commons for the last time. He spoke to propose a motion that 'a Monument be erected at the public charge' to the memory of David Lloyd George – Earl Lloyd George of Dwyfor, OM – 'with an inscription expressive of the high sense entertained by this House of the eminent services rendered by him to the Country and to the Commonwealth and Empire in Parliament, and in great Offices of State'. The motion was agreed. The statue of Lloyd George that was subsequently decided on now stands on one side of the Churchill Arch – the entrance to the Chamber of the House of Commons. On the other stands a statue of Churchill himself. Churchill told his listeners in the Commons that day:

> There is, I believe, general agreement that the House made a wise rule when it prohibited the introduction of a Motion of this character for ten years after the death of the statesman concerned. This rule is comparatively new, and has been used only once, in 1938, in the case of that honoured figure Lord Oxford and Asquith.
>
> Ten years is long enough to allow partisan passions, whether of hatred or of enthusiasm, to cool, and not too long to quench the testimony of contemporary witnesses. We combine by this method the memories and feelings of men who knew David Lloyd George long and well with that sense of sober proportion and perspective which ever-changing time alone can give and keep on giving.
>
> [· · ·]
>
> David Lloyd George was a House of Commons man. He sat here for one constituency for fifty-five years. He gave sparkle to our debates. He guided the House through some of its most critical years, and without the fame and authority of the Mother of Parliaments he could never have rendered his services to the nation.
>
> [· · ·]
>
> The duty that falls to me this afternoon strikes a curious coincidence. It is exactly ten years ago to the day, 28 March, since I stood at this Box, in my present office, and, at the first opportunity after Lloyd George's death, addressed the House on his career. The discussion that followed is well worth re-reading. There will be seen the unanimity and the fervour of the testimony given to his work from all parts of the House.
>
> I was perplexed, I admit, when I was thinking of how to commend this Motion to you, Mr. Speaker, to find, on looking back, that I had already said much that I now wish to say. My friendship for this remarkable man covered more than forty years of House of Commons life, including long periods during which I served with

and under him as his Cabinet colleague. Whether in or out of office, our intimate and agreeable companionship was never darkened, so far as I can recall, by any serious spell of even political hostility.

As a first-hand witness, as I may claim to be, I wish to reaffirm the tribute I paid to his memory on his death.

Churchill then repeated his tribute of 28 March 1945, before continuing:

There is one further episode which I will mention. It fell to the lot of most of us who are here today to have to face a Second World War. Lloyd George had long been out of office. Nearly a generation had passed since he ceased to be Prime Minister, but upon 3 September, in the solemn debate which marked our entry into the struggle, he spoke words which gave confidence to many and comfort to all. I will read them to the House:

'I have been through this before, and there is only one word I want to say about that. We had very bad moments, moments when brave men were rather quailing and doubting, but the nation was firm right through, from beginning to end. One thing that struck me then was that it was in moments of disaster, and in some of the worst disasters with which we were confronted in the war, that I found the greatest union among all classes, the greatest disappearance of discontent and disaffection, and of the grabbing for rights and privileges. The nation closed its ranks then. By that means we went through right to the end, and after four and a half years, terrible years, we won a victory for Right. We will do it again.'

That is what he said of this occasion, and I am glad to read it to the House again. In supporting the Motion which is on the Order Paper the House will, I believe, be acting in harmony with its tradition, and it will strengthen the national faith in the wisdom and propriety of its judgment and the guidance which it gives. When the history of Britain for the first quarter of the twentieth century is written, it will be seen how great a part of our fortunes in peace and in war was shaped by this one man.

'THE ANXIOUS AND DARKLING AGE'

On 5 April 1955, Churchill, after suffering a series of strokes, resigned as Prime Minister. He was eighty years old. On the previous evening Churchill and his wife gave their farewell dinner at 10 Downing Street for the Queen and the Duke of Edinburgh. Among the guests was Anne Chamberlain, Neville Chamberlain's widow. Churchill's after-dinner speech was his last as Prime Minister. The notes from which he spoke have survived, set out for him by his secretary, as were so many of his speeches, in the 'speech form' or 'psalm form', as his secretariat called it, which he had used for more than half a century (the abbreviations included hv = have, tt = that, wh = which):

> Your Majesty,
> Your Royal Highness,
> Your Grace,
> My Lords, Ladies and Gentlemen.
>
> I have the honour
>   of proposing a Toast
>   wh I used to enjoy drinking
>   during the years
>   when I was a Cavalry
>   Subaltern
>
> in the Reign
>   of Your Majesty's
>   Great-great-Grandmother,
> Queen Victoria.
>
> Having served in office or in Parlt
>   under the four Sovereigns
>   who hv reigned since those days,
>
> I felt,
>
> with these credentials,

tt in asking
    Your Majesty's gracious permission,

I should not be leading
    to the creation of a precedent
        wh wd often cause inconvenience.

Madam,

    I should like to express
        the deep and lively sense
          of gratitude
            which we

and all your peoples

feel to you
    and to His Royal Highness
        the Duke of Edinburgh

for all the help and inspiration
    we receive
        in our daily lives

and which spreads
    with ever-growing strength
        throughout the British Realm
          and the Commonwealth
            and Empire.

Never have we needed it more
    than in the anxious
        and darkling age
          through wh we are passing

and which we hope
    to help the world to pass.

Never have the august duties
    wh fall upon the British Monarchy
       been discharged
         with more devotion

than in the brilliant opening
    of Your Majesty's reign.

We thank God
    for the gifts he has bestowed upon us

and vow ourselves anew
    to the sacred causes

and wise and kindly way of life
    of wh Your Majesty
       is the young, gleaming champion.

'UNITED FORCES AND COMMON PRINCIPLES'

In the summer of 1958, in Lebanon, Pan-Arab groups backed by Egyptian President Nasser, with support in Lebanon's Muslim community, attempted to overthrow the government of President Camille Chamoun, leader of Lebanon's Maronite Christians. Chamoun appealed to the United States for help. On 15 July 1958, fourteen thousand American troops landed in Beirut, and the revolt was crushed. A day earlier, on July 14, during a rebellion in Iraq, the King and many members of his family were murdered, as was the Prime Minister on July 15. That day, Churchill told the Prime Minister, Harold Macmillan, of his intention to speak on Lebanon and Iraq, but then wrote to him: 'I spent an hour or two thinking over what I would say and came to the conclusion that I had nothing worth saying. I will turn up to support you in the Lobby. Forgive my change of plan.' The introductory remarks that Churchill had prepared read:

> I have not troubled the House with any remarks since I left Office three and a half years ago. Nor should I do so now if circumstances did not warrant it. I have a feeling that the events which have recently taken place in the Middle East are of a different order from anything which has occurred, and that they confront us with the need of scanning the whole field with a gravity not unworthy of the moral and material issues which they naturally excite.

There followed four pages of Churchill's handwritten notes, with his underlinings:

> Outrage Embassy Bagdad.
>> What are we going to do?
> America & Britain must work together,
>> reach Unity of purpose.
>
> The complications which the problem presents
>> can be cured if, & only if,
>>> they are dealt with by united forces
>> & common principles
>>> not merely increase of strength.
> When we divide we lose.
>> It is not primarily a question of material force.
> Anthony Eden & Suez
>> He was right.
> These recent events prove him so.
>> It may be that his action was premature.
>
> It wd be too easy to mock USA
> We should refrain
> The Lebanon is part of the ME
>
> Comparisons are often dangerous
>> & still more often futile.

This is no time for our
    trying to balance a long account.

The accounts are balancing themselves.

I do not want to take points off the US
    & point the finger of scorn at them

How easy to say
    Look at the US & compare them with us at Suez.

<u>We were right.</u>

Chamoun – a good friend to this country.
What is really foolish is for two nations like
    England & USA
to search for points of difference

No case for picking a quarrel with USA
A clear conscience –
    We have no need for self-reproach.

[···]

The Middle East is all <u>one</u>
    One problem
The US have entered the Lebanon.
They are in every way justified.
They do not need our material or military help
If they did, I am assured they wd receive it.

'THE PAST SHOULD GIVE US HOPE'

During the two years following his resignation as Prime Minister in April 1955, Churchill worked to finish the fourth and final volume of his last book, *A History of the English-Speaking Peoples*. It was published in 1958 and took the story up to 1914. In his final paragraph Churchill wrote:

> Here is set out a long story of the English-Speaking Peoples. They are now to become Allies in terrible but victorious wars. And that is not the end. Another phase looms before us, in which alliance will once more be tested and in which its formidable virtues may be to preserve Peace and Freedom. The future is unknowable, but the past should give us hope. Nor should we now seek to define precisely the exact terms of ultimate union.

'THE ONLY SOLUTION IS DISARMAMENT'

On 29 September 1959, Churchill presented the last election address of his career, to the electors of Woodford, whom he had represented for thirty-five years. It was sixty years since his first – narrowly defeated – attempt to enter Parliament. In his speech that day he urged his electors to help return the Conservatives to power:

> I carry my mind back to the time, now fifteen years ago, when the war was nearing its end and victory was in sight. Two issues were then uppermost in our thought. How could the people of this country earn their living in the modern world? And how could we reach an understanding between the nations which would prevent the catastrophe of another war? These two great questions have not changed. To deal with them will be the prime task of the Government you elect next month.
>
> Our country faced a difficult task on the morrow of our victory. We had liquidated most of our overseas investments, and we had devoted ourselves to the production of munitions of war to the neglect of investment in our productive resources. We had mortgaged our future in the cause of freedom.
>
> Seldom in history has there been a country in circumstances such

as ours. We have grown accustomed to high living standards. Yet we produce barely half the food we need to keep ourselves alive, and, apart from coal, we are largely bereft of the raw materials on which industry feeds. We can meet our needs only by what we import. Any failure to pay for those imports would cut our lifeline as surely, even if not so quickly, as the mine and submarine threatened to do.

Yet the Socialist Government in those six years after the war pursued policies which at their best were irrelevant, and at their worst were positively detrimental, to the revival of our economic life. They followed their doctrinaire plans of nationalization and control in a vain pursuit of equality. And this equality was to be that of a levelling down.

The Conservative Party, which I led at that time, warned the country that there was no way through to prosperity along that road. I offered the Socialists a simple theme, 'Set the people free'. They rejected it. But after six painful years the country was willing to give it a trial. Today we are prosperous, balancing our accounts, meeting our liabilities, the most respected and trusted of all the great trading nations in the world. It is those things which are the basis of all prosperity so widely shared today among all classes. I would urge the country not to lose sight of that. Let nobody suppose that a continuance of our present prosperity is certain and assured. It is not. It is the result of prudent policies. Change to foolish policies, and it could vanish like snows before the sun.

Socialist victory would be a fearful and perhaps fatal handicap to the free enterprise system which keeps us all alive and on the whole very comfortable. Among our Socialist opponents there is great confusion. Some of them regard private enterprise as a predatory tiger to be shot. Others look on it as a cow they can milk. Only a handful see it for what it really is – the strong and willing horse that pulls the whole cart along.

[···]

Science offers us with one hand a chance of material progress and prosperity far exceeding anything of which we have even dreamed. It offers us the hope that after long centuries in which famine and flood, poverty and disease, cost far more lives than war itself, we might now enter a golden age. But science does not stop there. With the other hand it offers the darkness of nuclear death. The search for peace is not the special preserve of any one political party. We are all agreed on the end. It is on how we can best secure peace that we differ.

We must be on our guard lest the attention focused on the H-bomb may lead people to forget the appalling destruction which can also be wrought by what are called conventional arms – weapons which have grown immensely more powerful than those we found so devastating not so long ago.

The Soviet bloc confronts the West with an overwhelming superiority in guns, tanks, aircraft, submarines and sheer weight of manpower. These standing forces are constantly being re-equipped with the most modern arms. Against all this, Western defence has been based on the deterrent power of the nuclear bomb. The Russians for some time now have had their own nuclear bombs, but the deterrent still exists. Since no complete defence against the bomb has yet been found, any aggressor knows he would have to reckon on retribution – swift, certain and annihilating.

From out of this deadlock there are no short cuts. The only solution is disarmament applied to all kinds of weapons, freely accepted by all nations, and guaranteed by effective international control. In recent months I have seen signs of hope. The proposals which Mr Khrushchev put forward recently in New York are no different in essential purposes from the plans which Mr Macmillan and his colleagues tabled to be examined by the new United Nations Committee to which Russia has assented. That is a step forward. But much remains to be done. We must above all resist any temptation to rush into agreements which do not provide a workable system of inspection and control. Not to be firm on this principle would be a fatal error.

And we must look still further into the future. Is the reduction of armament among the great powers, and even its total abolition if this most desirable goal can be achieved, to be accompanied by the creation of an international force to keep order in the world? I would only touch on this theme, but it and many others of equal magnitude and complexity suggest themselves if both the West and Russia and her allies are ready at last to find common ground in the pursuit of peace.

I have watched with sorrow the long years of the cold war, and the withering of so many of the hopes we entertained in the spring of 1945. I played a part in awakening free Europe to the need to join together with the United States and the British Commonwealth to protect their freedom: but the cold war was none of my seeking, and I have never sought to perpetuate or prolong it. In April, 1945, as the victorious Western and Russian Forces were joining hands in victory, I wrote to Stalin:

> Do not, I beg you, my friend Stalin, underrate the divergences which are opening up. There is not much comfort in looking into a future where you and the countries you dominate, plus the Communist Parties in many other States, are all drawn up on one side, and those who rally to the English-speaking nations and their associates or Dominions are on the other. It is quite obvious that their quarrel would tear the world to pieces and that all of us leading men on either side who had anything to do with that, would be shamed before history. Even embarking on a long period of suspicions, of abuse and counter-abuse, and of opposing policies, would be a disaster hampering the great developments of world prosperity for the masses which are attainable only by our trinity.

Stalin did not listen. We all know only too well the tragic course of events which followed. However, this year we have seen at any rate some signs that the long period of suspicion and abuse may be ending.

My fervent hope is that the new Parliament may see the world moving forward into brighter days in which peace with justice is more firmly based.

'OUR FUTURE IS ONE OF HIGH HOPE'

On 9 October 1959, the Conservatives were returned to power. Churchill retained his seat and was once more a Member of the Parliament to which he had first been elected fifty-nine years earlier. He never spoke in Parliament again; but on October 31, a month before his eighty-fifth birthday, and despite an attack nine days earlier of dizziness that left him briefly unconscious, he spoke in his constituency at Woodford, at the unveiling of his statue, thirty-five years after he had first spoken there. It was the last public speech on which he was able to work himself:

Thirty-five years. That is more than half my adult life. It is certainly a period of history in which much has been built up and much torn down in this troubled world.

The question we may ask ourselves is how the balance lies between progress and ruin. When we contemplate the squalid and brutal destruction of the last war, man's ingenuity in perfecting the means of his own annihilation, and the jealousy, anxiety and hatred that consume a large part of the globe, it is easy to give a melancholy answer. Certainly it is far from reassuring to consider the position of much of Asia and Africa.

The Middle East flickers with barely repressed violence and enmity. In East Asia vast and ever expanding populations are reaching a critical stage in their development. They are on the move, and none knows whither. In many undeveloped areas of the world former systems of government are being thrown aside, and new nations are rising. We wish them well. We may watch them, anxiously, and take a justifiable pride in true progress there.

Many of these countries owe their very existence to Great Britain. In war we have defended them at great cost. In peace we have assisted them financially, technically, and with our advisers in every sphere. Above all, we have endeavoured to confer on them the benefits of justice and freedom which we have so long enjoyed ourselves in these islands. Yet amidst this sombre and perplexing scene there is much that is bright.

With all our political differences we in this country are, I think, more united than we have ever been in time of peace. Certainly we may disagree, but I see no hatred. The way ahead is a broad and clear one.

In Western Europe many of the age-old enmities are at last dispersing and the outlook for a closer unity of those who share the common fruit of Western civilization, both here and overseas, is full of promise. There is no reason why these developments should conflict with our ever-closer association with the countries of the Commonwealth and the United States. Nor, I believe, should the problems that confront the West in their relations with Soviet Russia and her allies be insuperable. Some progress has already been made, and the tensions that caused us anxiety have been slackened by meetings between the leaders. I trust that this initiative will be vigorously maintained.

It is not only in the realm of war that science is advancing with giant strides. In the formidable manifestations of the new technology, both in the East and the West, the prospect of man's adventure into the mysteries of the universe in which he lives stirs the imagination.

In all this we in Britain have a great part to play, a leading part. By our courage, our endurance, and our brains we have made our way in the world to the lasting benefit of mankind. Let us not lose heart. Our future is one of high hope.

MAPS

1   *The United Kingdom and the Irish Free State*

2 South-East England

South-East England map showing Thames, North Sea, Enfield, Epping, Chingford, Walthamstow, Woodford, Harrow, Ilford, Eton, London, Sheerness, Margate, Ascot, Croydon, Godalming, CHARTWELL, Dover. Scale: 0 kilometres 50, 0 miles 30. © Martin Gilbert 2012

3 British India

British India map showing RUSSIA, CHINA, IRAN, AFGHANISTAN, NORTH-WEST FRONTIER, Peshawar, TIBET, Amritsar, Brahmaputra, NEPAL, Mount Everest, Indus, Ganges, BRITISH INDIA, Calcutta, BURMA, Arabian Sea, Bombay, Bay of Bengal, Bangalore. Scale: 0 kilometres 1000, 0 miles 500. © Martin Gilbert 2012

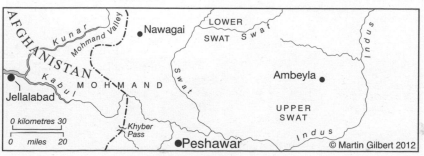

4 The North-West Frontier

The North-West Frontier map showing AFGHANISTAN, Kunar, Mohmand Valley, Nawagai, LOWER SWAT, Swat, Indus, Kabul, MOHMAND, Jellalabad, Swat, Ambeyla, Khyber Pass, UPPER SWAT, Indus, Peshawar. Scale: 0 kilometres 30, 0 miles 20. © Martin Gilbert 2012

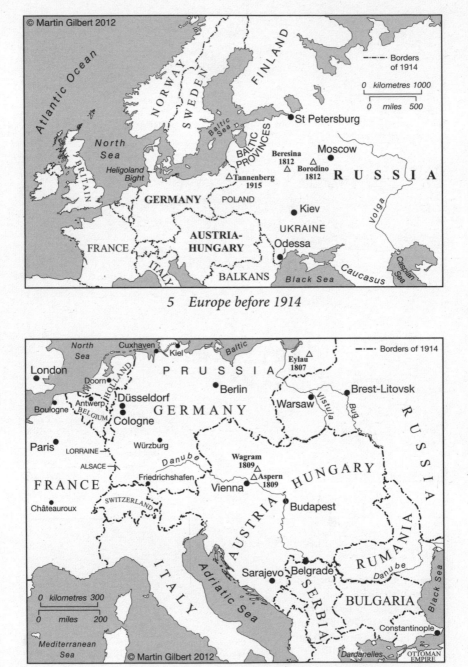

5   *Europe before 1914*

6   *Central Europe before 1914*

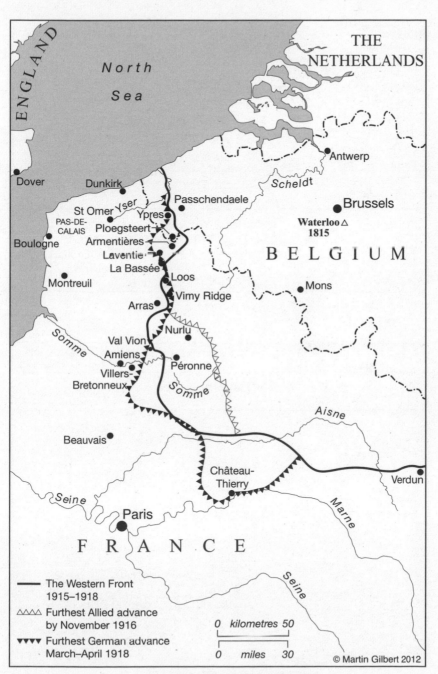

7   *The Western Front, 1914–18*

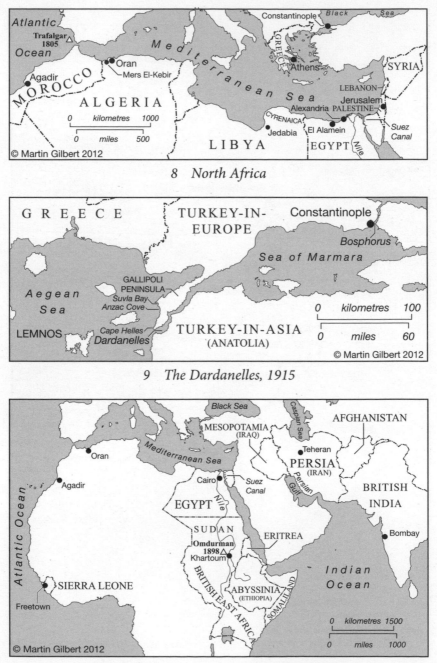

8 North Africa

9 The Dardanelles, 1915

10 From the Atlantic to the Indian Ocean

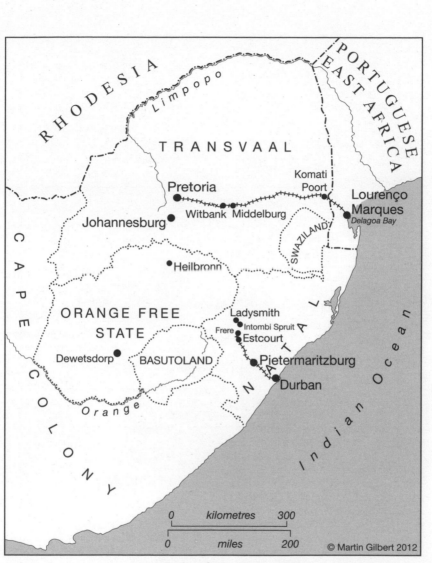

11   *South Africa, 1899–1900*

12   *Churchill's British lecture tours, 25 October to 30 November 1900*
and 5 March to 8 May 1901

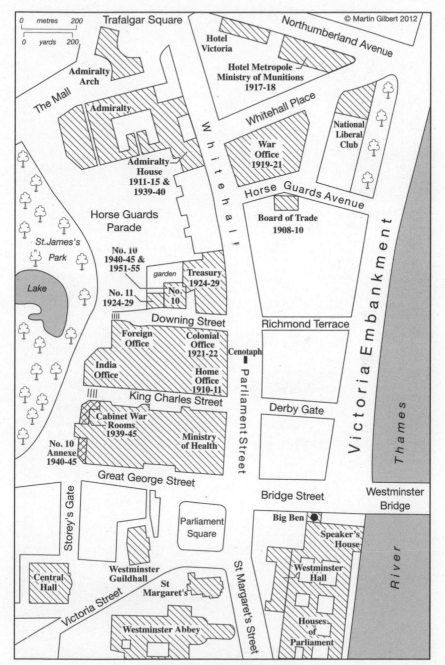

© Martin Gilbert 2012

0 metres 200
0 yards 200

Trafalgar Square

Hotel
Victoria

Hotel Metropole
Ministry of Munitions
1917-18

Northumberland Avenue

Admiralty
Arch

The Mall

Admiralty

Whitehall Place

Whitehall

War
Office
1919-21

National
Liberal
Club

Admiralty
House
1911-15 &
1939-40

Horse Guards
Parade

Horse Guards Avenue

Board of Trade
1908-10

St.James's
Park

Lake

No. 10
1940-45 &
1951-55

No. 11
1924-29

garden   Treasury
1924-29

No.
10

Downing Street

Foreign
Office

Colonial
Office
1921-22

India
Office

Home
Office
1910-11

Cenotaph

Richmond Terrace

King Charles Street

Cabinet War
Rooms
1939-45

Ministry
of Health

Derby Gate

Parliament Street

Victoria Embankment

Thames

No. 10
Annexe
1940-45

Great George Street

Bridge Street

Westminster
Bridge

Storey's Gate

Parliament
Square

Big Ben

Speaker's
House

River

Central
Hall

Westminster
Guildhall

St
Margaret's

Westminster
Hall

St Margaret's Street

Victoria Street

Westminster Abbey

Houses
of
Parliament

13   Churchill's Whitehall

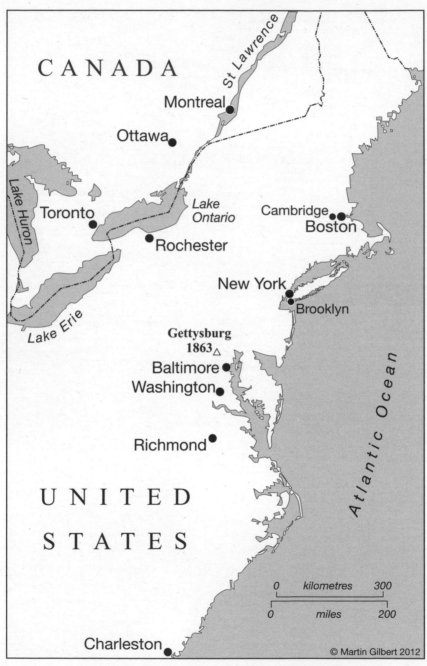

14   *The Eastern United States and Canada*

15   *Churchill's first American and Canadian lecture tour, 1900–1*

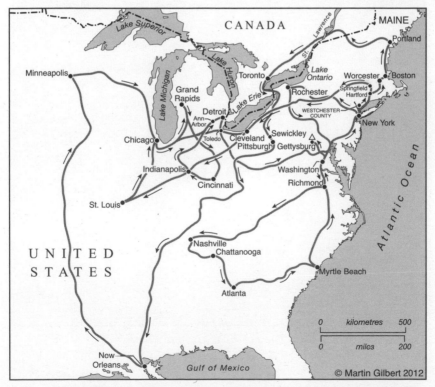

16   *Churchill's second American and Canadian lecture tour, 1930–1*

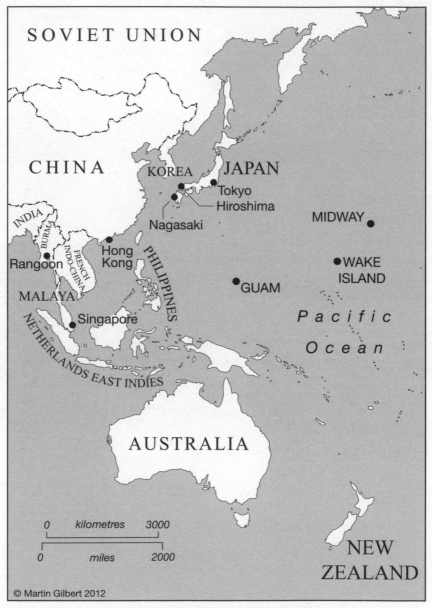

17   *The Far East and the Pacific*

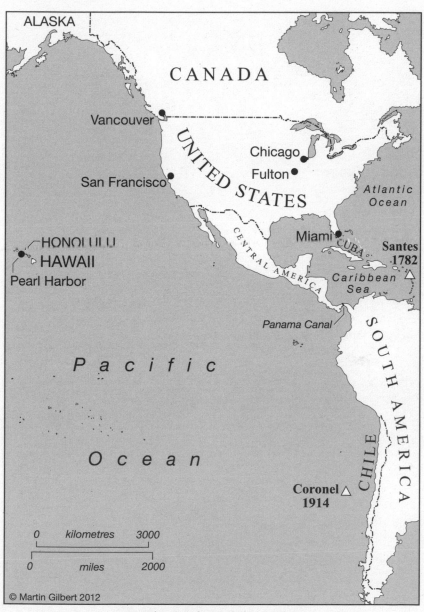

18   *The Pacific and the Americas*

19   *Western Europe and the Iron Curtain*

SWEDEN

FINLAND

Leningrad

Baltic Sea

SOVIET UNION

Moscow

BALTIC STATES

Danzig

Stettin

Warsaw

Brest Litovsk

Berlin

POLAND

GERMANY

Lublin

Kiev

Dnieper

Leipzig

Breslau

UKRAINE

SUDETENLAND

Cracow

Lvov

Prague

SUDETENLAND

CZECHOSLOVAKIA

Vienna

Budapest

AUSTRIA

HUNGARY

TRANSYLVANIA

Trieste

RUMANIA

YUGOSLAVIA

Bucharest

Black Sea

Belgrade

Danube

Adriatic Sea

BULGARIA

Sofia

ITALY

ALBANIA

Istanbul

GREECE

Aegean Sea

TURKEY

| 0 | kilometres | 300 |
| 0 | miles | 200 |

Mediterranean Sea   © Martin Gilbert 2012

— · — · — Borders of 1937
———— The Iron Curtain, 1945
- - - - Partition of Poland: Nazi-Soviet
partition line, October 1939–June 1941

20   *Eastern Europe and the Iron Curtain*

SOURCES FOR EACH OF THE READINGS

'The love of a foster-mother', late 1870s
Winston S. Churchill, *Savrola: A Tale of the Revolution in Laurania*, London, Longmans, Green, 1900, pages 43–4

'This hateful servitude', 1882
Winston S. Churchill, *My Early Life: A Roving Commission*, London, Thornton Butterworth, 1930, pages 26–7

'An element of kindness', 1883
Winston S. Churchill, *My Early Life: A Roving Commission*, London, Thornton Butterworth, 1930, page 27

'I was startled to see a furious face emerge', 1888
Winston S. Churchill, *My Early Life: A Roving Commission*, London, Thornton Butterworth, 1930, pages 31–2

'I shall save London and England from disaster', 1891
Recollection of Sir Murland de Grasse Evans, in Martin Gilbert, *In Search of Churchill: A Historian's Journey*, London, HarperCollins, 1994, pages 214–15

'To plunge or not to plunge, that was the question', 1893
Winston S. Churchill, *My Early Life: A Roving Commission*, London, Thornton Butterworth, 1930, pages 43–4

'Now I saw Death as near as I believe I have ever seen him', 1894
Winston S. Churchill, *My Early Life: A Roving Commission*, London, Thornton Butterworth, 1930, pages 51–2

'A ragged volley rang out from the edge of the forest', 2 December 1895
Winston S. Churchill, 'The Cuban Insurrection', Letter Four, dated 4 December 1895, *Daily Graphic*, 27 December 1895

'A sharp and peculiar wrench', 1 October 1896
Winston S. Churchill, *My Early Life: A Roving Commission*, London, Thornton Butterworth, 1930, pages 115–16

'I resolved to read history, philosophy, economics', 1896–7
   Winston S. Churchill, *My Early Life: A Roving Commission*, London,
   Thornton Butterworth, 1930, pages 124–6

'The rising tide of Tory Democracy', 26 July 1897
   Bath Daily Chronicle, 27 July 1897

'Delighted to get safe home again', 1897
   Winston S. Churchill, *The Story of the Malakand Field Force: An
   Episode of Frontier War*, London, Longmans, Green, 1898, pages 174–5

'The collision was prodigious', 2 September 1898
   Winston S. Churchill, *The River War: An Historical Account of the
   Reconquest of the Soudan*, volume II, London, Longmans, Green, 1899,
   pages 135–9

'At such sights the triumph of victory faded on the mind', 5 September 1898
   Winston S. Churchill, *The River War: An Historical Account of the
   Reconquest of the Soudan*, volume II, London, Longmans, Green, 1899,
   pages 220–2, 224–7

'Odd and bizarre potentates', 1898
   Winston S. Churchill, *The River War: An Historical Account of the
   Reconquest of the Soudan*, volume II, London, Longmans, Green, 1899,
   pages 217–19

'No stronger retrograde force exists in the world', 1898
   Winston S. Churchill, *The River War: An Historical Account of the
   Reconquest of the Soudan*, volume II, London, Longmans, Green, 1899,
   pages 248–50

'Death stood before me, grim sullen Death', 15 November 1899
   Winston S. Churchill, *London to Ladysmith via Pretoria*, London,
   Longmans, Green, 1900, pages 95–7

'I therefore resolved to escape', 21 December 1899
   Winston S. Churchill, *Pearson's Illustrated War News*, 30 December 1899

'I had better tell you the truth', December 1899
   Winston S. Churchill, *My Early Life: A Roving Commission*, London,
   Thornton Butterworth, 1930, pages 294–9

'I became for the time quite famous', December 1899
   Winston S. Churchill, *My Early Life: A Roving Commission*, London,
   Thornton Butterworth, 1930, page 313

'Ah, horrible war', 22 January 1900
    Winston S. Churchill, *London to Ladysmith via Pretoria*, London,
    Longmans, Green, 1900, pages 290–2

'We were nearly through the dangerous ground', 28 February 1900
    Winston S. Churchill, *London to Ladysmith via Pretoria*, London,
    Longmans, Green, 1900, pages 463–5

'Revenge may be sweet, but it is also most expensive', 29 March 1900
    Natal Witness, 29 March 1900

'Barren spoils', 31 March 1900
    Morning Post, 31 March 1900

'I have zealously tried to avoid all danger', 22 April 1900
    'Two days with Brabazon', 22 April 1900, published in the *Morning Post*,
    28 May 1900; reprinted in Winston S. Churchill, *Ian Hamilton's March*,
    London, Longmans, Green, 1900, pages 58–9

'The results were substantial', 1900–1
    Winston S. Churchill, *My Early Life: A Roving Commission*, London,
    Thornton Butterworth, 1930, pages 374–6

'We have no cause to be ashamed', 18 February 1901
    Hansard, House of Commons, 18 February 1901, columns 407–15

'The wars of peoples will be more terrible than those of kings', 13 May 1901
    Hansard, House of Commons, 13 May 1901, columns 1572–5

'Never to let the war pass out of your minds for a day', 4 October 1901
    Randolph S. Churchill, *Winston S. Churchill*, companion volume II,
    Part 1: *1901–1907*, London, Heinemann, 1969, pages 83–90

'An England of wise men', 1906
    Winston S. Churchill, *Lord Randolph Churchill*, London, Macmillan,
    1906, pages 488–9

'The cause of the poor and the weak all over the world', 17 December 1906
    Hansard, House of Commons, columns 1063–1078

'Time to see their homes by daylight', 6 July 1908
    Hansard, House of Commons, 6 July 1908, columns 1330–1

'Humanity will not be cast down', 10 October 1908
    The Right Honourable Winston Spencer Churchill, MP, *Liberalism and*

the Social Problem, London, Hodder & Stoughton, 1909, pages 189–210

'The dark waters of a friendless world', 23 May 1909
    The Right Honourable Winston Spencer Churchill, MP, *Liberalism and the Social Problem*, London, Hodder & Stoughton, 1909, pages 297–317

'The unnatural gap between rich and poor', 5 September 1909
    The Right Honourable Winston Spencer Churchill, MP, *Liberalism and the Social Problem*, London, Hodder & Stoughton, 1909, pages 357–83

'The dark angel', 15 September 1909
    Nash's – Pall Mall, October 1924; reprinted in Winston S. Churchill, *Thoughts and Adventures*, London, Odhams, 1932, page 82

'We propose to tax not wages but wealth', 8 January 1910
    Robert Rhodes James (editor), *Winston S. Churchill: His Complete Speeches, 1897–1963*, London, Chelsea House, 1974, volume II, p. 1449

'The noble status of citizenship', 30 May 1910
    Hansard, House of Commons, 30 May 1910, columns 1823–28

'A constant heart-searching', 20 July 1910
    Hansard, House of Commons, 20 July 1910, column 1354

'A catastrophe in our national life', 17 February 1911
    Hansard, House of Commons, 17 February 1911, columns 239–40

'An island well-guarded hitherto, at last defenceless', July 1911
    Winston, S. Churchill, *The World Crisis, 1911–1914*, London, Thornton Butterworth, 1923, page 45

'The enormous number of hazards', 1913
    'In the Air', *Nash's – Pall Mall*; reprinted in Winston S. Churchill, *Thoughts and Adventures*, London, Odhams, 1932, pages 183–4

'An ultimatum such as had never been penned in modern times', July 1914
    Winston S. Churchill, *The World Crisis, 1911–1914*, London, Thornton Butterworth, 1923, pages 192–3

'The war will be long and sombre', 11 September 1914
    The Times, 12 September 1914

'No reason to despair', 27 November 1914
    Hansard, House of Commons, 27 November 1914, columns 1601–2, 1607–9

'Anxiety will make its abode in our brain', 15 February 1915
    Hansard, House of Commons, 15 February 1915, columns 922, 923–4,
    924, 925, 927–8, 933, 936, 938–9

'An event shocking and unnatural in its character', 18 March 1915
    Winston S. Churchill, *The World Crisis, 1915*, London, Thornton
    Butterworth, 1923, page 244

'The sorrow of youth about to die', 26 April 1915
    The Times, 26 April 1915

'Rugged kindness and warm-hearted courtesy', 22 May 1915
    Winston S. Churchill, *The World Crisis, 1915*, London, Thornton
    Butterworth, 1923, pages 374–5

'Trust the people', 5 June 1915
    Dundee Courier, 7 June 1915

'I seized the largest brush and fell upon my victim', 2 July 1915
    The Right Honourable Winston S. Churchill, OM, CH, MP, *Painting as
    a Pastime*, London, Odhams, 1948, pages 16–17

'This unhappy but not inglorious generation', 18 September 1915
    Robert Rhodes James (editor), *Winston S. Churchill: His Complete
    Speeches, 1897–1963*, London, Chelsea House, 1974, volume III, pages
    2387–91

'I have a clear conscience', 11 November 1915
    The Times, 13 November 1915

'We are passing through a bad time now', 15 November 1915
    Hansard, House of Commons, 15 November 1915, columns 2391–403

'It was a comfort to be with these fine troops', November 1915
    Winston S. Churchill, *The World Crisis, 1915*, London, Thornton
    Butterworth, 1923, pages 500–1

'Sending the wounded soldiers back three or four times', January 1916
    Winston S. Churchill, *The World Crisis, 1915*, London, Thornton
    Butterworth, 1923, page 515

'If you can't grin keep out of the way till you can', 26 January 1916
    Churchill's letter to his wife, 27 January 1916, in Martin Gilbert,
    Winston S. Churchill, volume III, *The Challenge of War, 1914–1916*,
    London, Heinemann, 1988, page 651

'A definite and practical proposal to make', 7 March 1916
    Hansard, House of Commons, 7 March 1916, columns 1423, 1423–6,
    1429, 1429–30

'There can be no excuse', 17 May 1916
    Hansard, House of Commons, 17 May 1916, columns 1582–3, 1589

'Whatever is done must be done in the cold light of science', 23 May 1916
    Hansard, House of Commons, 23 May 1916, columns 2012–27

'Martyrs not less than soldiers', November 1916
    Winston S. Churchill, *The World Crisis, 1916–1918*, part 1, London,
    Thornton Butterworth, 1927, pages 195–6

'The trials of our latter-day generals', 1917–18
    The Right Honourable Winston S. Churchill, *Marlborough: His Life and
    Times*, volume II, London, George G. Harrap, 1933, pages 93, 93–5

'I, who saw him on twenty occasions', 1917–18
    Nash's – Pall Mall, November 1928; reprinted in The Rt. Hon. Winston
    S. Churchill, CH, MP, *Great Contemporaries*, London, Thornton
    Butterworth, 1937, page 228

'The toils, perils, sufferings and passions of millions of men', 1917–18
    Winston S. Churchill, *The World Crisis: The Unknown War – The
    Eastern Front*, London, Thornton Butterworth, 1931, pages 17–18

'The meaning of war with the American Union', 6 April 1917
    Winston S. Churchill, *The World Crisis, 1916–1918*, part 1, London,
    Thornton Butterworth, 1927, pages 225–7

'The country is in danger', 11 December 1917
    Hansard, House of Commons, 11 December 1917, columns 2023–7

'The most tremendous cannonade I shall ever hear', 21 March 1918
    Winston S. Churchill, *The World Crisis, 1916–1918*, part 2, London,
    Thornton Butterworth, 1927, pages 411–12

'An utter absence of excitement or bustle', 28 March 1918
    Collier's, 12 July 1930; reprinted in Winston S. Churchill, *Thoughts and
    Adventures*, London, Odhams, 1932, page 166

'Such a tyrant and such a champion', 28 March 1918
    'Tiger of France', *Collier's*, 29 November 1930; reprinted in The Rt Hon.
    Winston S. Churchill, *Great Contemporaries*, London, Thornton

Butterworth, 1937, page 312

'A great actor on the stage', 30 March 1918
'Tiger of France', *Collier's*, 29 November 1930; reprinted in Winston S. Churchill, *Thoughts and Adventures*, London, Odhams, 1932, pages 170–1

'There was no rigmarole or formalism', 1918
Winston S. Churchill, *The World Crisis,1916–1918*, part 2, London, Thornton Butterworth, 1927, pages 471–3

'Victory had come after all the hazards', 11 November 1918
Winston S. Churchill, *The World Crisis, 1916–1918*, part 2, London, Thornton Butterworth, 1927, pages 541–3

'The ache for those who would never come home', 11 November 1918
Winston S. Churchill, *The World Crisis: The Aftermath*, London, Thornton Butterworth, 1929, page 19

'The dauntless and devoted people', 1914–18
Foreword by the Rt Hon. Winston S. Churchill, PC, CH, MP, in Marthe McKenna, *I Was a Spy!*, London, Jarrolds, 1932, page 5

'Rebuild the ruins. Heal the wounds', 26 November 1918
Dundee Courier, 27 November 1918

'The heart of the Russian people', 19 February 1919
The Times, 20 February 1919

'The future was heavy with foreboding', 1919
Winston S. Churchill, *The Second World War*, volume I, *The Gathering Storm*, London, Cassell, 1948, pages 4–7

'A frightful and overwhelming force', 18 July 1919
Nash's – Pall Mall, June 1924; reprinted in Winston S. Churchill, *Thoughts and Adventures*, London, Odhams, 1932, pages 183–4

'The agony of Russia', 20 January 1920
Hull Daily Mail, 21 January 1920

'The clemency of the conqueror', 8 July 1920
Hansard, House of Commons, 8 July 1920, columns 1727–31

'Thoroughly tired of war', 28 July 1920
Evening News, 28 July 1920

'A measureless array of toils and perils', 4 August 1920
Winston S. Churchill, *The World Crisis: The Aftermath*, London,
Thornton Butterworth, 1929, page 268

'From the confusion of tyranny to a reign of law', 16 February 1922
Hansard, House of Commons, 16 February 1922, columns 1266–71

'Destructive tendencies have not yet run their course', 11 November 1922
Speech notes, in Churchill Papers, The Sir Winston Churchill Archive
Trust, Churchill College, Cambridge, CHAR 9/66 B

'I am not going to be muzzled', 13 November 1922
Dundee Courier, 14 November 1922

'I have always stuck to the middle road', 27 November 1923
Robert Rhodes James (editor), *Winston S. Churchill: His Complete Speeches,
1897–1963*, London, Chelsea House, 1974, volume IV, pages 3417–19

'I am too old a campaigner to be disheartened', 19 March 1924
Robert Rhodes James (editor), *Winston S. Churchill: His Complete
Speeches, 1897–1963*, London, Chelsea House, 1974, volume IV, pages
3448–9

'The powers now in the hands of man', September 1924
Nash's – Pall Mall, September 1924; reprinted in Winston S. Churchill,
Thoughts and Adventures, London, Odhams, 1932, pages 247–51

'The ambulances of State aid', 28 April 1925
Hansard, House of Commons, 28 April 1925, columns 34–110

'What shall I do with all my books?' December 1925
Nash's – Pall Mall, December 1925; reprinted in Winston S. Churchill,
Thoughts and Adventures, London, Odhams, 1932, pages 300–1

'Will our children bleed and gasp again?', 1927
Winston S. Churchill, *The World Crisis, 1916–1918*, part 2, London,
Thornton Butterworth, 1927, page 544

'It is equally vain to prophesy or boast', 15 April 1929
Hansard, House of Commons, 15 April 1929, columns 27–8, 36, 45–6,
63–4, 67–8

'An unlimited capacity of adaptiveness', 1930
Winston S. Churchill, *Parliamentary Government and the Economic
Problem*, Oxford, Clarendon Press, 1930

'Alarming and also nauseating', 23 February 1931
     Winston S. Churchill, *India: Speeches*, London, Thornton Butterworth,
     1931, pages 87–97

'I certainly suffered every pang', 12 December 1931
     Winston S. Churchill, 'My New York Misadventure', *Daily Mail*,
     4 January 1932

'We of the English-speaking lands', 1932
     American lecture tour, speech notes, in Churchill Papers, The Sir
     Winston Churchill Archive Trust, Churchill College, Cambridge, CHAR
     9/99

'These bands of sturdy Teutonic youths', 23 November 1932
     Hansard, House of Commons, 23 November 1932, column 81

'When we read about Germany', 23 March 1933
     Hansard, House of Commons, 23 March 1933, columns 538–52

'The monstrosity of the Totalitarian State', June 1934
     'Are Parliaments Obsolete?', *Pearson's Magazine*, June 1934

'I was under his spell', May 1935
     A. W. Lawrence (editor), *T. E. Lawrence by his Friends*, London,
     Jonathan Cape, 1937, pages 201–2

'Haunting fears and suspicions', 7 June 1935
     Hansard, House of Commons, 7 June 1935, columns 2251–2

'Do you not tremble for your children?' September 1935
     Vincent Sheean, *Between the Thunder and the Sun*, London, 1943,
     quoted in Martin Gilbert, *Winston S. Churchill*, volume V, *1922–1939*,
     London, Heinemann, 1976, page 666

'Somebody has to state the truth', 26 September 1935
     Quoted in Martin Gilbert, *Winston S. Churchill*, volume V, *1922–1939*,
     London, Heinemann, 1976, page 669

'Every kind of persecution', November 1935
     'The Truth about Hitler', *Strand*, November 1935

'Decided only to be undecided', 12 November 1936
     Hansard, House of Commons, 12 November 1936, column 1107

'We are with Europe but not of it', 29 May 1938

Winston S. Churchill, 'Why Not "The United States of Europe"?', *News of the World*, 29 May 1938

'The abandonment and ruin of Czechoslovakia', 5 October 1938
  Hansard, House of Commons, 5 October 1938, columns 364–74

'One healthy growl', 17 November 1938
  Hansard, House of Commons, 17 November 1938, columns 1128–9

'Where I failed, for all my brilliant gifts', 9 December 1938
  Robert Rhodes James (editor), *Winston S. Churchill: His Complete Speeches, 1897–1963*, London, Chelsea House, 1974, volume V, pages 6067–69

'Another confrontation and trial of strength', 9 February 1939
  The Rt Hon. Winston S. Churchill, *Step by Step, 1936–1939*, London, Thornton Butterworth, 1939, pages 329–30

'A scale immensely greater', 21 February 1939
  Hansard, House of Commons, 21 February 1939, column 256

'A devoted vanguard of the British nation', 24 April 1939
  The Times, 25 April 1939

'The Ambassador should not have spoken so', 14 June 1939
  Harold Nicolson Papers, and Walter Lippmann Papers; quoted in Martin Gilbert, *Winston S. Churchill*, document volume V, *The Coming of War, 1936–1939*, London, Heinemann, 1976, pages 1519–20

'A most formidable expression of the British national will', 2 August 1939
  Hansard, House of Commons, 2 August 1939, columns 2438–44

'The resurgence of the one-man power', 8 August 1939
  Randolph S. Churchill (editor), *Into Battle: Speeches by the Right Hon. Winston S. Churchill, PC, MP*, London, Cassell, 1941, pages 197–9

'A war to establish and revive the stature of man', 3 September 1939
  Hansard, 3 September 1939, columns 295–6

'We must expect further losses', 26 September 1939
  Hansard, 26 September 1939, columns 1239–47

'Rough times lie ahead', 1 October 1939
  Randolph S. Churchill (editor), *Into Battle: Speeches by the Right Hon. Winston S. Churchill, PC, MP*, London, Cassell, 1941, pages 131, 134–5

'The storm will not pass. It will rage and it will roar', 20 January 1940
  Randolph S. Churchill (editor), *Into Battle: Speeches by the Right
  Hon. Winston S. Churchill, PC, MP*, London, Cassell, 1941, pages
  159–62

'Ceaseless trial and vigilance on cold, dark, stormy seas', 23 February 1940
  Randolph S. Churchill (editor), *Into Battle: Speeches by the Right Hon.
  Winston S. Churchill, PC, MP*, London, Cassell, 1941, pages 170–2

'I felt as if I were walking with destiny', 10 May 1940
  Winston S. Churchill, *The Second World War*, volume I, *The Gathering
  Storm*, London, Cassell, 1948, pages 526–7

'Number one', from 10 May 1940
  Winston S. Churchill, *The Second World War*, volume II, *Their Finest
  Hour*, London, Cassell, 1949, pages 14–15

'Blood, toil, tears and sweat', 13 May 1940
  Randolph S. Churchill (editor), *Into Battle: Speeches by the Right Hon.
  Winston S. Churchill, PC, MP*, London, Cassell, 1941, pages 207–8

'I sang my usual song', 31 May 1940
  Winston S. Churchill, *The Second World War*, volume II, *Their Finest
  Hour*, London, Cassell, 1949, pages 96–100

'We shall not flag or fail. We shall go on to the end,' 4 June 1940
  Randolph S. Churchill (editor), *Into Battle: Speeches by the Right Hon.
  Winston S. Churchill, PC, MP*, London, Cassell, 1941, pages 215–23

'We shall fight on unconquerable', 17 June 1940
  Randolph S. Churchill (editor), *Into Battle: Speeches by the Right Hon.
  Winston S. Churchill, PC, MP*, London, Cassell, 1941, page 224

'We have to think of the future and not of the past', 18 June 1940
  Randolph S. Churchill (editor), *Into Battle: Speeches by the Right Hon.
  Winston S. Churchill, PC, MP*, London, Cassell, 1941, pages 225–34

'If Hitler fails to invade', 20 June 1940
  Charles Eade (editor), *Secret Session Speeches by the Right Hon. Winston
  S. Churchill, CH, MP*, London, Cassell, 1946, facsimile page 14

'The supreme hour', 4 July 1940
  Randolph S. Churchill (editor), *Into Battle, Speeches by the Right Hon.
  Winston S. Churchill, PC, MP*, London, Cassell, 1941, pages 239–45

'We shall not fail in our duty, however painful', 4 July 1940
Randolph S. Churchill (editor), *Into Battle: Speeches by the Right Hon. Winston S. Churchill, PC, MP*, London, Cassell, 1941, pages 245–6

'A War of the Unknown Warriors', 14 July 1940
Randolph S. Churchill (editor), *Into Battle: Speeches by the Right Hon. Winston S. Churchill, PC, MP*, London, Cassell, 1941, pages 247–51

'Never in the field of human conflict', 20 August 1940
Randolph S. Churchill (editor), *Into Battle: Speeches by the Right Hon. Winston S. Churchill, PC, MP*, London, Cassell, 1941, pages 252–62

'Let God defend the Right', 11 September 1940
Randolph S. Churchill (editor), *Into Battle: Speeches by the Right Hon. Winston S. Churchill, PC, MP*, London, Cassell, 1941, pages 272–5

'These next few weeks are grave and anxious', 17 September 1940
Charles Eade (editor), Secret Session Speeches by the Right Hon. Winston S. Churchill, CH, MP, London, Cassell, 1946, pages 22–3

'Man's instinctive defiance of tyranny', 30 September 1940
The Times, 1 October 1940

'Sleep to gather strength for the morning', 21 October 1940
Randolph S. Churchill (editor), *Into Battle: Speeches by the Right Hon. Winston S. Churchill, PC, MP*, London, Cassell, 1941, page 297

'The only guide to a man is his conscience', 12 November 1940
Hansard, House of Commons, 12 November 1940, columns 1617–19

'Give us the tools, and we will finish the job', 9 February 1941
Charles Eade (editor), *The Unrelenting Struggle: War Speeches by the Right Hon. Winston S. Churchill, CH, MP*, London, Cassell, 1942, pages 62–3

'Wonderful exertions have been made', 27 April 1941
Charles Eade (editor), *The Unrelenting Struggle: War Speeches by the Right Hon. Winston S. Churchill, CH, MP*, London, Cassell, 1942, pages 112–13

'Our pulses throb and beat as one', 16 June 1941
Charles Eade (editor), *The Unrelenting Struggle: War Speeches by the Right Hon. Winston S. Churchill, CH, MP*, London, Cassell, 1942, pages 173–5

'We shall give whatever help we can to Russia', 22 June 1941
    Charles Eade (editor), *The Unrelenting Struggle: War Speeches by the Right Hon. Winston S. Churchill, CH, MP*, London, Cassell, 1942, pages 179–80

'Never give in', 29 October 1941
    Charles Eade (editor), *The Unrelenting Struggle: War Speeches by the Right Hon. Winston S. Churchill, CH, MP*, London, Cassell, 1942, pages 286–8

'We had won the war', 7 December 1941
    Winston S. Churchill, *The Second World War*, volume III, *The Grand Alliance*, London, Cassell, 1950, pages 539–40

'A strange Christmas Eve', 24 December 1941
    Charles Eade (editor), *The Unrelenting Struggle: War Speeches by the Right Hon. Winston S. Churchill, CH, MP*, London, Cassell, 1942, page 332

'Prodigious hammer-strokes have been needed', 26 December 1941
    Charles Eade (editor), *The Unrelenting Struggle: War Speeches by the Right Hon. Winston S. Churchill, CH, MP*, London, Cassell, 1942, pages 353–4, 360–1

'Some chicken! Some neck!' 30 December 1941
    Charles Eade (editor), *The Unrelenting Struggle: War Speeches by the Right Hon. Winston S. Churchill, CH, MP*, London, Cassell, 1942, pages 363–6, 366–7, 367–8, 368–70

'Havoc continued to reign', 1942
    Winston S. Churchill, *The Second World War*, volume IV, *The Hinge of Fate*, London, Cassell, 1951, pages 95–6, 96–7, 102, 102–3, 110–11, 114; Winston S. Churchill, *The Second World War*, volume V, *Closing the Ring*, London, Cassell, 1952, page 6

'Tonight the Japanese are triumphant', 15 February 1942
    Charles Eade (editor), *The End of the Beginning: War Speeches by the Right Hon. Winston S. Churchill, CH, MP*, London, Cassell, 1942, pages 50–6

'Testing, trying, adverse, painful times lie ahead', 23 April 1942
    Charles Eade (editor), *Secret Session Speeches by the Right Hon. Winston S. Churchill, CH, MP*, London, Cassell, 1946, pages 70–2, 73–5

'Carrying a large lump of ice to the North Pole', 12–15 August 1942
    Winston S. Churchill, *The Second World War*, volume IV, *The Hinge of Fate*, London, Cassell, 1951, pages 428, 430–3, 434, 435

'These vile crimes', 29 October 1942
    Charles Eade (editor), *The End of the Beginning: War Speeches by the Right Hon. Winston S. Churchill, CH, MP*, London, Cassell, 1942, page 203

'I cannot feel that de Gaulle is France', 10 December 1942
    Typescript of Secret Session speech, in Churchill Papers, The Sir Winston Churchill Archive Trust, Churchill College, Cambridge, CHAR 9/156

'Your feats will gleam and glow', 3 February 1943
    Charles Eade (editor), *Onwards to Victory: War Speeches by the Right Hon. Winston S. Churchill, CH, MP, 1943*, London, Cassell, 1948, pages 9–11

'The heart of Austria', 18 February 1943
    Charles Eade (editor), *The End of the Beginning: War Speeches by the Right Hon. Winston S. Churchill, CH, MP*, London, Cassell, 1942, page 62

'The enemy is still proud and powerful', 19 May 1943
    Charles Eade (editor), *Onwards to Victory: War Speeches by the Right Hon. Winston S. Churchill, CH, MP*, 1943, London, Cassell, 1948, page 102

'I have no idea what I said', 1 June 1943
    Winston S. Churchill, *The Second World War*, volume IV, *The Hinge of Fate*, London, Cassell, 1951, page 740

'Tyranny is our foe', 6 September 1943
    Charles Eade (editor), *Onwards to Victory: War Speeches by the Right Hon. Winston S. Churchill, CH, MP, 1943*, London, Cassell, 1948, pages 183–4

'I admired the Admiral's sporting spirit', 12 June 1944
    Winston S. Churchill, *The Second World War*, volume VI, *Triumph and Tragedy*, London, Cassell, 1954, pages 11, 12

'An impressive performance', 20–23 July 1944
    Winston S. Churchill, *The Second World War*, volume VI, *Triumph and Tragedy*, London, Cassell, 1954, pages 22–4

'The soul of France did not die', 2 August 1944
    Hansard, House of Commons, 2 August 1944, columns 1479–80

'Have the people the right to turn out a Government?', 28 August 1944
    Winston S. Churchill, *The Second World War*, volume VI, *Triumph and Tragedy*, London, Cassell, 1954, pages 111–12

'The foundation of all democracy', 31 October 1944
    Hansard, House of Commons, 31 October 1944, columns 662–8

'He stood, when at his zenith, without a rival', 28 March 1945
    Hansard, House of Commons, 28 March 1945, columns 1377–88

'Victory had cast its sure and steady beam upon him', 17 April 1945
    Hansard, House of Commons, 17 April 1945, columns 40–77

'The German war is therefore at an end', 8 May 1945
    Charles Eade (editor), *Victory: War Speeches by the Right Hon. Winston S. Churchill, OM, CH, MP*, London, Cassell, 1946, pages 126–8

'You never flinched or wavered', 9 May 1945
    Charles Eade (editor), *Victory: War Speeches by the Right Hon. Winston S. Churchill, OM, CH, MP*, London, Cassell, 1946, pages 129–30

'It is the victors who must search their hearts', 13 May 1945
    Charles Eade (editor), *Victory: War Speeches by the Right Hon. Winston S. Churchill, OM, CH, MP*, London, Cassell, 1946, pages 132–8

'Enormous problems lie before us', 26 May 1945
    Robert Rhodes James (editor), *Winston S. Churchill: His Complete Speeches, 1897–1963*, London, Chelsea House, 1974, volume VII, pages 7167–8

'Some form of Gestapo', 4 June 1945
    Charles Eade (editor), *Victory: War Speeches by the Right Hon. Winston S. Churchill, OM, CH, MP*, London, Cassell, 1946, pages 186–92

'Nothing is easier than to prevent free speech,' 3 July 1945
    Robert Rhodes James (editor), *Winston S. Churchill: His Complete Speeches, 1897–1963*, London, Chelsea House, 1974, volume VII, pages 7200–4

'Dear Desert Rats', 21 July 1945
    Charles Eade (editor), *Victory: War Speeches by the Right Hon. Winston S. Churchill, OM, CH, MP*, London, Cassell, 1946, pages 216–17

'My profound gratitude', 26 July 1945
   Winston S. Churchill, *The Second World War*, volume VI, *Triumph and Tragedy*, London, Cassell, 1954, page 584

'No boy or girl should ever be disheartened', 26 February 1946
   Randolph S. Churchill (editor), *The Sinews of Peace: Post-War Speeches by Winston S. Churchill*, London, Cassell, 1948, pages 89–92

'An iron curtain has descended', 5 March 1946
   Randolph S. Churchill (editor), *The Sinews of Peace: Post-War Speeches by Winston S. Churchill*, London, Cassell, 1948, pages 102–5

'Greatheart must have his sword and armour', 8 March 1946
   Randolph S. Churchill (editor), *The Sinews of Peace: Post-War Speeches by Winston S. Churchill*, London, Cassell, 1948, pages 106–10

'Let Germany live', 5 June 1946
   Hansard, House of Commons, 5 June 1946, columns 2029–33

'Our two countries have struggled along together', 14 July 1946
   Randolph S. Churchill (editor), *The Sinews of Peace: Post-War Speeches by Winston S. Churchill*, London, Cassell, 1948, pages 171–2

'The United States of Europe', 19 September 1946
   Randolph S. Churchill (editor), *The Sinews of Peace: Post-War Speeches by Winston S. Churchill*, London, Cassell, 1948, pages 201–2

'When did punishment begin?', 12 November 1946
   Hansard, House of Commons, 12 November 1946, column 20

'No two races have set such a mark upon the world', 1948
   Winston S. Churchill, *The Second World War*, volume V, *Closing the Ring*, London, Cassell, 1952, pages 470–1

'The Unnecessary War', 1948
   Winston S. Churchill, *The Second World War*, volume I, *The Gathering Storm*, London, Cassell, 1948, page viii

'A scene of material ruin and moral havoc', 1948
   Winston S. Churchill, *The Second World War*, volume I, *The Gathering Storm*, London, Cassell, 1948, pages 13–14

'We cannot rest upon benevolent platitudes', 7 May 1948
   Randolph S. Churchill (editor), *Europe Unite: Speeches 1947 and 1948 by Winston S. Churchill*, London, Cassell, 1950, pages 316–17

'They gave all they had', 21 May 1948
Randolph S. Churchill (editor), *Europe Unite: Speeches 1947 and 1948 by Winston S. Churchill*, London, Cassell, 1950, pages 336–8

'The underlying principles of justice and freedom', 28 October 1948
Hansard, House of Commons, 28 October 1948, columns 250–1

'If we pool our luck and share our fortunes', 25 March 1949
Randolph S. Churchill (editor), *In the Balance: Speeches 1949 and 1950 by Winston S. Churchill*, London, Cassell, 1950, pages 32–9

'Peoples in bondage need never despair', 31 March 1949
Randolph S. Churchill (editor), *In the Balance: Speeches 1949 and 1950 by Winston S. Churchill*, London, Cassell, 1950, pages 40–51

'Appeasement from strength is magnanimous and noble', 14 December 1950
Hansard, House of Commons, 14 December 1950, columns 1362–70

'The main foundation of peace', 9 November 1951
Randolph S. Churchill (editor), *Stemming the Tide: Speeches 1951 and 1952 by Winston S. Churchill*, London, Cassell, 1953, pages 187–90

'Britain and the United States are working together', 17 January 1952
Randolph S. Churchill (editor), *Stemming the Tide: Speeches 1951 and 1952 by Winston S. Churchill*, London, Cassell, 1953, pages 220–7

'We in this small island', 7 November 1952
Speech notes, in Churchill Papers, The Sir Winston Churchill Archive Trust, Churchill College, Cambridge, CHAR 2/336

'I welcome Germany back', 10 October 1953
Randolph S. Churchill (editor), *The Unwritten Alliance: Speeches 1953–1959 by Winston S. Churchill*, London, Cassell, 1961, pages 220–7

'The most memorable public occasion of my life', 30 November 1954
Randolph S. Churchill (editor), *The Unwritten Alliance: Speeches 1953–1959 by Winston S. Churchill*, London, Cassell, 1961, pages 57–67

'Safety will be the sturdy child of terror', 1 March 1955
Randolph S. Churchill (editor), *The Unwritten Alliance: Speeches 1953–1959 by Winston S. Churchill*, London, Cassell, 1961, pages 224–34

'The nation closed its ranks', 28 March 1955
    Randolph S. Churchill (editor), *The Unwritten Alliance: Speeches 1953–1959* by Winston S. Churchill, London, Cassell, 1961, pages 246–50

'The anxious and darkling age', 4 April 1955
    Speech notes, in Martin Gilbert, *Winston S. Churchill*, volume VIII, *Never Despair, 1945–1965*, pages 1120–1

'United forces and common principles', 15 July 1958
    Speech notes, in Martin Gilbert, *Winston S. Churchill*, volume VIII, *Never Despair, 1945–1965*, pages 1271–2

'The past should give us hope', 1958
    Winston S. Churchill, *A History of the English-Speaking Peoples*, volume IV, *The Great Democracies*, London, Cassell, 1958, page 304

'The only solution is disarmament', 29 September 1959
    Randolph S. Churchill (editor), *The Unwritten Alliance: Speeches 1953–1959 by Winston S. Churchill*, London, Cassell, 1961, pages 323–4, 326–7

'Our future is one of high hope', 31 October 1959
    Randolph S. Churchill (editor), *The Unwritten Alliance: Speeches 1953–1959 by Winston S. Churchill*, London, Cassell, 1961, pages 331–2

PICTURE ACKNOWLEDGEMENTS

The publishers have made every effort to trace copyright holders. Any who have not been acknowledged are invited to get in touch with the publishers so that appropriate acknowledgement may be made in future printings.

MG = author's collection.

First section

(1) Churchill as a schoolboy: Getty Images; (2) swimming pool at Harrow: courtesy of the Harrow School Archives.

(3) Churchill as a soldier, South Africa, 1900: Getty Images; (4) *The River War* and (5) *London to Ladysmith*: MG; (6) Churchill as prisoner, Pretoria, 18 November 1899: Time & Life Pictures/Getty Images; (7) page from *Pearson's Illustrated War* News, 30 December 1899; (8) lecture announcement, 29 November 1900: MG/© The Cardiff Naturalists' Society.

(9)–(11) Enfield speech, 18 September 1915: PA/PA Archive/Press Association Images; (12) Churchill in Dundee, 11 November 1922: Topham Picturepoint/TopFoto.co.uk; (13) on the podium, Dundee, 11 November 1922: MG/D. C. Thompson & Co. Ltd.

(14) Churchill at the Victoria Palace Theatre, 19 March 1924: MG; (15) Churchill on Budget Day, 28 April 1925: MG; (16) Churchill walking down Whitehall, 15 April 1929: Getty Images; (17) Churchill at the Mansion House, 24 April 1929: Les Putnam/AP/Press Association Images; (18)–(19) Churchill in his study at Chartwell, 25 February 1939: Time & Life Pictures/Getty Images.

(20) 'Now They Listen to Churchill', 13 August 1939: MG; (21) Churchill broadcasting, 1 October 1939: © Hulton-Deutsch Collection/Corbis.

Second section

(22) Churchill on HMS *Exeter*, 15 February 1940: Getty Images.

(23) Anglo-French Supreme War Council, Paris, 31 May 1940: MG/Keystone Press; (24) Churchill's appeal, 4 July 1940: MG; (25) Churchill inspects bomb damage, London, 10 September 1940: MG/Fox Photos; (26) Churchill at the Guildhall, 31 December 1940: Getty Images.

(27–8) Churchill addresses both Houses of Congress, 26 December 1941: (27) © Bettmann/Corbis, (28) Topham/AP/ TopFoto.co.uk; (29) Churchill addresses the Canadian Parliament, 30 December 1941: Imperial War Museum/H016429; (30) Churchill arriving in Russia, 13 August 1942: MG; (31) Churchill at the Kremlin, August 1942: © 2006 Alinari/Topfoto/TopFoto.co.uk.

(32) Churchill addresses troops, Tripoli, 3 February 1943: Imperial War Museum/E22258; (33) Churchill at Carthage, 1 June 1943: Imperial War Museum/NA3253; (34) Churchill addresses cadets at Harvard, 6 September 1943: Imperial War Museum/H32728; (35) Churchill addresses troops at Normandy, 22 July 1944: Imperial War Museum/ B7888.

(36) Churchill at Westminster Abbey, 28 March 1945: PA/PA Archive/Press Association Images; (37) Churchill broadcasts to the nation, 8 May 1945: Imperial War Museum/H41844.

Third section

(38) View from the balcony of the Ministry of Health, 9 May 1945: Getty Images; (39) Churchill on the balcony of the Ministry of Health, 9 May 1945: © Illustrated London News Ltd/Mary Evans.

(40) Churchill in Whitehall, 9 May 1945: Topham/Picturepoint/ TopFoto.co.uk; (41) Churchill electioneering, 26 May 1945: MG; (42) Churchill electioneering, 4 July 1945: Central Press/Getty Images.

(43) Churchill and Truman, 5 March 1946: US Marine Corps, courtesy of Harry S. Truman Library; (44) Churchill delivering speech at Fulton: Popperfoto/Getty Images; (45) Churchill and Eisenhower arriving in Richmond, Virginia, 8 March 1946: MG; (46) Churchill at The Hague, 7 May 1948: MG.

(47) Churchill at Harrow School, 7 November 1952: Central Press Photos/MG; (48)–(49) Churchill at Margate, 10 October 1953: Keystone/MG; (50) Churchill at Westminster Hall, 30 November 1954: Topham/Picturepoint/TopFoto.co.uk.

(51) Churchill in the South of France, January 1956: Emery Reves/MG.

INDEX

Compiled by Sir Martin Gilbert